PRAXIS AS A PERSPECTIVE ON INTERNATIONAL POLITICS

Bristol Studies in International Theory

Series Editors: **Felix Berenskötter**, SOAS, University of London, UK, **Neta C. Crawford**, Boston University, US and **Stefano Guzzini**, Uppsala University, Sweden, PUC-Rio de Janeiro, Brazil

This series provides a platform for theoretically innovative scholarship that advances our understanding of the world and formulates new visions of, and solutions for, world politics.

Guided by an open mind about what innovation entails, and against the backdrop of various intellectual turns, interrogations of established paradigms, and a world facing complex political challenges, books in the series provoke and deepen theoretical conversations in the field of International Relations.

Also available

The Civil Condition in World Politics
Beyond Tragedy and Utopianism
Edited by **Vassilios Paipais**

Snapshots from Home
Mind, Action and Strategy in an Uncertain World
By **K.M. Fierke**

What in the World?
Understanding Global Social Change
Edited by **Mathias Albert** and **Tobias Werron**

The Idea of Civilization and the Making of the Global Order
By **Andrew Linklater**

Find out more

bristoluniversitypress.co.uk/
bristol-studies-in-international-theory

Bristol Studies in International Theory

Series Editors: **Felix Berenskötter**, SOAS, University of London, UK, **Neta C. Crawford**, Boston University, US and **Stefano Guzzini**, Uppsala University, Sweden, PUC-Rio de Janeiro, Brazil

Coming soon

Broken Solidarities
How Open Global Governance Divides and Rules
By **Felix Anderl**

Care and the Pluriverse
Rethinking Global Ethics
By **Maggie FitzGerald**

Find out more
bristoluniversitypress.co.uk/
bristol-studies-in-international-theory

Bristol Studies in International Theory

Series Editors: **Felix Berenskötter**, SOAS, University of London, UK, **Neta C. Crawford**, Boston University, US and **Stefano Guzzini**, Uppsala University, Sweden, PUC-Rio de Janeiro, Brazil

---

International advisory board

Find out more
bristoluniversitypress.co.uk/
bristol-studies-in-international-theory

PRAXIS AS A PERSPECTIVE ON INTERNATIONAL POLITICS

Edited by
Gunther Hellmann and Jens Steffek

BRISTOL
UNIVERSITY
PRESS

First published in Great Britain in 2023 by

Bristol University Press
University of Bristol
1-9 Old Park Hill
Bristol
BS2 8BB
UK
t: +44 (0)117 374 6645
e: bup-info@bristol.ac.uk

Details of international sales and distribution partners are available at bristoluniversitypress.co.uk

British Library Cataloguing in Publication Data
A catalogue record for this book is available from the British Library

ISBN 978-1-5292-2046-9 hardcover
ISBN 978-1-5292-2047-6 paperback
ISBN 978-1-5292-2048-3 ePub
ISBN 978-1-5292-2049-0 ePdf

Cover design: blu inc, Bristol
Front cover image: © 2022 [The contributors]

Bristol University Press uses environmentally responsible print partners.

Printed in Great Britain by CPI Group (UK) Ltd, Croydon, CR0 4YY

Contents

Notes on Contributors

Mathias Albert is Professor of Political Science at the University of Bielefeld (Germany).

Chris Brown is Emeritus Professor of International Relations at the London School of Economics and Political Science (UK).

Christian Bueger is Professor of International Relations at the Department of Political Science, University of Copenhagen (Denmark).

James W. Davis is Professor of International Politics, University of St Gallen (Switzerland).

K.M. Fierke is Professor in the School of International Relations, University of St Andrews (UK).

Jörg Friedrichs is Associate Professor of Politics at the Oxford Department of International Development and Official Fellow of St Cross College, University of Oxford (UK).

Gunther Hellmann is Professor of Political Science in the Department of Social Sciences at Goethe University, Frankfurt am Main (Germany).

Patrick Thaddeus Jackson is Professor of International Studies in the School of International Service at American University (US).

Oliver Kessler is Professor of International Relations at the University of Erfurt (Germany).

Jan Klabbers is Professor of International Law at the University of Helsinki (Finland).

Friedrich Kratochwil is Professor Emeritus of International Relations at the European University Institute (Italy).

Anthony F. Lang, Jr. is Professor in the School of International Relations, University of St Andrews (UK).

Cecelia Lynch is Professor of Political Science at the University of California, Irvine (US).

Jens Steffek is Professor of Transnational Governance at Technical University of Darmstadt (Germany).

Antje Wiener is Professor of Political Science and Global Governance at the University of Hamburg (Germany).

Acknowledgements

This volume originated from a book-making workshop that the editors convened in the summer of 2019 at Goethe University Frankfurt. The workshop took place at the Research Centre Normative Orders and was funded by the Hessian Ministry of Higher Education, Research, Science and the Arts, whose generous support we gratefully acknowledge. For their encouragement and thoughtful comments on the book proposal we would like to thank the editorial board of the *Bristol Studies in International Theory* series, in particular Stefano Guzzini. Nick Onuf and two anonymous reviewers also provided very helpful and constructive advice on the manuscript. Steven Wenham, Caroline Astley and Lorna Blackmore from Bristol University Press and Dawn Preston from Newgen Publishing accompanied the manuscript from proposal to production stage with great enthusiasm and professionalism. Not least, we are indebted to our student assistants Jens Bartsch, Florian Hubert, Yannick Laßhof and Fenja Meinecke who greatly helped us with the organization of the workshop and the preparation of the manuscript.

Gunther Hellmann and Jens Steffek
Frankfurt am Main and Darmstadt
April 2021

1

Introduction: Praxis as a Perspective on International Politics

Gunther Hellmann and Jens Steffek

The theory of International Relations (IR) is in a state of soul-searching, if not disorientation.[1] The great 'inter-paradigm debates' that still marked the discipline in the 1990s and early 2000s have all but disappeared. Proliferation of ever new approaches and increasing fragmentation of debates dominate the disciplinary landscape today. IR theory discussions are now clustering within specific academic schools and subfields that revolve around their preferred 'ism' and hardly speak to each other, while much of the mainstream of the discipline is turning its attention to questions of methodology rather than theory. Practitioners of international politics, all the while, find it increasingly difficult to see the relevance of these academic debates for their own work and the pressing political (as well as theoretical) challenges posed by the rise of authoritarianism and populism, escalating climate change and the return of global pandemics.

There is, however, a family of theoretical approaches that hold the twin promise to alleviate the current state of parochialism and fragmentation and to reach out to those who practice international politics and not just study IR. These approaches ground their theorizing in the 'praxis', or practice, of international relations. Since much of this interaction is performed in the language of law, this turn to praxis and practice also facilitates much needed cooperation between IR and international legal scholarship.

---

[1]   For an overview informing the take by one of the two editors, see Hellmann (2020).

Situating praxis theorizing

To speak of praxis theorizing instantly raises a few terminological questions, at least from an IR theory perspective, since major segments of IR usually figure under the label 'practice theory' in the aftermath of a 'practice turn' (Neumann, 2002; Bueger and Gadinger, 2018). Accordingly, the concepts of 'practice' and 'practices' are much more prevalent than 'praxis'. The latter, however, played an important role already in an early phase of pragmatist and Wittgenstein-inspired social theory (Bernstein, 1971; Bloor, 1983), and a small segment of IR theory (Kratochwil, 1989: 210; 2018: 410–40; Onuf, 1989: 35–65), well before 'constructivism' assumed its prominent role as a new IR 'ism' in the 1990s. Following this strand and the clues that these social theorists and IR scholars, in turn, took from Aristotle, Hume, Marx, Wittgenstein and Dewey, we believe it is helpful to explore some of the different uses and meanings associated with 'praxis' in contrast to prevalent understandings of 'practice' and 'practices' in IR.

The traditions of praxis theorizing just mentioned basically conceptualize praxis as *social action here and now*. The Aristotelian and Marxian understandings both add a teleological twist in the sense of a liberating activity aimed at achieving a 'happy life' (Aristotle) or 'emancipation' (Marx). Yet in a Wittgensteinian and pragmatist tradition, such distinctly normative connotations remain in the background. Rather, in identifying with Goethe's famous line from *Faust* ('In the beginning was the *Deed*'),[2] these social philosophers emphasize not only that praxis is the basis of everything else that necessarily follows (in a temporal sense) but also that it is unique *and* rule-following at the same time; that it entails both conscious (reflective) action and unconscious (instinctive) doing; and that it is inevitably transitory. In this conceptualization of praxis, the distinction between theory and practice turns on a notion of 'theory' which is, by necessity, not only post hoc but also pattern-*seeking* for very practical cognitive needs. Theorizing relates to sense-*making* after the fact (or 'deed'), whereas praxis relates to coping here and now – or simply: our ability of 'going on' (Kratochwil, 2018: 151, 416–17). In this understanding theorizing is, of course, a form of praxis, but the same does not apply vice versa.

The English word 'practice' usually, if implicitly, also covers this dimension of the meaning of praxis as coping. Yet in the context of the so-called practice

---

[2]   Goethe (2014 [1808]: 33, emphasis in original); in contrast to the translation provided by Stuart Atkins of the German 'Tat' as 'Act' we have preferred the more forceful 'Deed'; see also Marx's 3rd thesis in his *Theses on Feuerbach* (Marx, 1969 [1888]: 15). On the primacy of praxis in pragmatism, see Putnam (1995: 52); on its priority in Wittgenstein's work, see Bloor (2001).

turn in the social sciences in general (Schatzki et al, 2001) and in IR in particular (see Cornut, 2017 for a recent overview), the focus has more often been on 'a' practice as something that needed to be placed in the context of a dualistic distinction between materiality and discursiveness, where practice was relegated more to the 'material' than the 'discursive' side of things (Neumann, 2002: 629–30; Bueger, 2017: 329). Alternatively, 'practices' have also been prominently defined as 'competent performances' or 'socially meaningful *patterns* of action' (Adler and Pouliot, 2011: 4, emphasis added).

To be sure, no serious IR practice turn theorist would claim that *all* social action is shaped by *competent* performances. For far too long too much research in the field has pointed to utter *in*competence in the practice of international politics and foreign policy (Jervis, 1976; Janis, 1982). Yet the bias towards 'competence' and 'patterned' action of significant portions of 'practice turn' research has decidedly ignored the emphasis on what the pragmatists have termed the *genuine creativity* of social action (Dewey, 1938: 101–19; Joas, 1992), as well as the fact that patterns are not 'things' out there in the world but are created by us in the process of sense-making in order to be able to 'go on'.

Conceiving of practice and practices as competent and patterned performances which express a 'logic of habit' (Hopf, 2010), therefore, significantly delimits what falls into the focus of practice turn scholarship. To be sure, practices as *typical ways of acting* – or '*Handlungsweisen*', as Wittgenstein's notion of 'practices' is usually translated from his original writing in German (Wittgenstein, 2009 [1953]) – do cover a significant part of social action in general and of the politics of international relations praxis in particular. Yet many of the most interesting subjects in IR scholarship (i.e. international politics) relate to phenomena which are either recognized for their 'uniqueness' or are rendered into objects of study for the purposes of 'scientific generalization' via 'simplification' or the ascription of 'case' status in a particular 'universe of cases' (King et al, 1994: 42–6, 125). However, when we theorize international politics in this generalizing fashion and, for instance, 'see ... durable relationships of enmity and amity between and among states, or any patterns of enduring practices between and among them' (Hopf, 2010: 547), this type of 'seeing' is as much based on attribution (due to a certain way of our conditioning as observers) as it is based on revelation. This is what Wittgenstein refers to, among others, in his 'duck–rabbit' example of 'aspect seeing' (Wittgenstein, 2009 [1953]: 203–4; Day and Krebs, 2010) and the arbitrariness of attributing 'likeness' or patterns in 'seeing' something.

Some positivists even acknowledge this. In their influential book *Designing Social Inquiry*, King, Keohane and Verba emphasize the importance of distinguishing between 'systematic' and 'non-systematic' factors in the process of 'scientific generalization'. Yet they also concede that the unambiguousness of this distinction depends on human cognition and the reliability of distinguishing between patterns and 'nonpatterns' – and that humans 'are not very good at recognizing nonpatterns. (Most of us see patterns in random ink blots!)' (King et al, 1994: 21). Therefore, relationships of enmity and amity do not reveal *themselves* to us. Rather, it is we who try to make *practical sense* of such relationships by *describing* them in such terms, and it is also we who *ascribe patterns* to them as a result of comparison.

Drawing this out is important because the notions of praxis which inform the chapters in this volume do not restrict social action in international relations to repetitive or patterned agency in the more restrictive understanding of 'practice turn' scholarship. When we theorize the praxis of international politics, we are as much interested in understanding what we have come to identify as *typical* ways of conducting relations among states (e.g. practices of negotiating, threatening or punishing) as we are in 'seeing' and describing in novel ways how individual human beings and societies make choices in 'problematic situations' under conditions of uncertainty and how they interact across borders.

Praxis theorizing in this understanding may take the form of more detached description expressed in more or less familiar vocabularies; it may focus on exploring concepts and how they are used; or it may choose a more explicitly normative form of 'redescription' (Rorty, 1989: chapters 1– 3) that entices readers to look at things differently and act differently as a result. Yet in all these cases the attitude accompanying this type of praxis theorizing downplays or outrightly rejects implicit dualistic framings of empirical social science *versus* normative political theory or the opposition of history (and uniqueness) *versus* theory (and generalization), which so often mark IR discourse. Instead, it emphasizes that habit and patterned agency *as well as* conceptual explication/innovation and creative problem-solving form a continuum in praxis – irrespective of whether this praxis relates to everyday practical life, international politics or the theorization of either.

In this understanding the contributors to this volume locate themselves in a broadly conceived tradition of theorizing international politics and international law which is – despite all the drawbacks of premature intellectual closure and a detrimental narrowing of theoretical horizons associated with typical IR 'isms' – probably still best captured by the label 'constructivism', at least if we conceive constructivism's 'original promise' in terms of 'restructuring the way of inquiry by taking on the pragmatists' criticism of orthodox theorizing seriously', as Fritz Kratochwil put it recently (Kratochwil, 2019).[3]

---

[3] See also Kratochwil (2018, chapter 1). On similar understandings of constructivism, see also Kessler and Steele (2016) (which introduces a 'special issue' of the *European Review of International Studies* on the theme of 'third generation' IR constructivism) and Nexon et al (2017).

Fritz Kratochwil and praxis theorizing

While sticking (somewhat uneasily) with the label 'constructivism', Fritz Kratochwil has in recent years elaborated his own take on praxis in one of the most ambitious, persistent and transdisciplinary attempts in IR to reconcile theory and practice. *Praxis*, the tome that Kratochwil published in 2018, builds on a line of work that has been unfolding since the 1980s and is a major provocation to mainstream theorizing in academic IR (Kratochwil, 2018). His approach rejects the popular strategy of deductive theory-building and hypothesis-testing to discover eternal laws of politics. For Kratochwil, such an endeavour is simply chimeric. In terms of method, it rejects the mathematical abstraction and formal modelling that make social science look so alluringly professional, and it also rejects 'ideal theory'. Not least, the concept of praxis defies the conventional distinction between theory and practice (Kratochwil, 2019).

With the explicit turn to praxis as a guiding concept in the 2000s, Kratochwil's scholarship transcended its earlier focus on norms, rules and principles that had gained him the reputation of being a leading IR constructivist (Kratochwil, 1989). Although it never fit in comfortably, Kratochwil's earlier work needs to be seen in the context of the inter-paradigm debates that dominated mainstream IR from the 1970s to the 1990s. In his attacks on the intellectual poverty of neo-realism and rational choice, Kratochwil underlined the 'force of prescriptions'. The point was to show that social and legal norms, and not just considerations of power or economic self-interest, have a considerable influence on international politics. That norm-centred framing of his contribution allowed Kratochwil to hook up to the ongoing debates about the causes of international conflict and the chances of cooperation.

At the same time, Kratochwil was unwilling to play the positivist game and use norms as 'variables' in research designs aimed at establishing causal mechanisms and law-like regularities. 'While it is true that rules and norms often function like causes, in many contexts they work differently', he wrote. 'Norms are used to make demands, rally support, justify action, ascribe responsibility, and assess the praiseworthy or blameworthy character of an action' (Kratochwil, 1984: 686). That definition of what norms can do defied the mainstream conceptualization of norms as triggers of action but promised to accommodate the complexity and historical situatedness of decisions. With the notion of praxis as an overarching conceptual frame, Kratochwil cast the net even wider and abandoned 'the sterile debate' about norms and ideas in mainstream IR (Kratochwil, 2000: 77). Since law and social norms inform practical judgements, they remain in the picture of *Praxis*, even though they lose pride of place when compared with Kratochwil's earlier writings.

Other dimensions of praxis have become more important, such as the broader connection between knowledge and action. For Kratochwil, knowledge as *knowing how* resides in the competent performance of an act. His praxis perspective centres on what actors, including academic observers, do when they act in making choices here and now. To act means to engage others as social actors, where 'the crucial "social" element' highlights that '*actions of agents are meaningfully oriented toward each other*' (Kratochwil, 2010: 447, emphasis in original). To act also means to *judge*, and in placing the notion of judgement at the centre of praxis (Kratochwil, 2018: 427–40), Kratochwil here joins forces with pragmatists such as Dewey (1938, Part II: 101–280) who have insisted all along, if via different intellectual routes, that judgements are always made in *specific* contexts (or 'problematic situations') and that they are made for *specific* purposes (or 'ends-in-view', as Dewey (1938: 167–80) put it). 'Inquiry' in this sense is creative problem-solving which applies in equal fashion to everyday social action (*praxis*) *here and now* as it applies to problem-solving in the social sciences – or 'social inquiry' as both Dewey (1938: 487–512) and Kratochwil (2018: 45) put it – as necessarily post hoc observation, description, explanation and rationalization. Neither 'trans-historical truths that are tested against the world "out there"' (Kratochwil, 2018: 32) nor eternal laws of politics are possible or even necessary because sound *judgement* is all we need and all we can get. Such judgements are always *made*, and in competently making them we equally need to properly grasp the context of social action here and now *in acting* (praxis), as we need to re-enact the judgements of others in *theorizing* social action post hoc when we reconstruct their perspective on and acting in the social world. As social scientists this requires us to engage with the whole spectrum of social action – culture and history, norms and ideas, values and aspirations.

Unlike newer versions of 'practice theory', Kratochwil's praxis perspective stands in the broad tradition of humanism that suggests a holistic perspective on human beings and social action. Humans judge, choose and act under the impression of their emotions, their backward-looking experience and their forward-looking expectations, with an urge to make sense of the world and attach meaning to their own role in it. Even when we observe the social world, we remain situated in it. This is why 'praxis' is at odds with the textbook ideal of a detached, disinterested and 'objective' observer. Its ideal is not the 'discovery' of objective facts about international politics but to better understand what is required in political action to arrive at competent judgement in specific historical situations.

Since Kratochwil's book *Praxis* epitomizes the necessary breadth and depth of praxis theorizing, it will serve as a major point of reference for all the chapters in this volume. However, the overarching purpose of this volume is not to celebrate Kratochwil's accomplishments but to critically engage with his ideas and proposals in the context of the broader debate about praxis, practice and practices and to pursue multiple avenues in order to explore where praxis theorizing might head in broadening its scope. The contributors to this book accept the premise that competent judgement matters in international affairs, no matter what our precise role in them is. They also accept the premise that this is easier said than done and that proper praxis theorizing needs to do justice to the complexities of practical judgement (in contrast to academic idealizations of parsimonious theorization). Hence, they are eager to explore to what extent praxis theorizing can be a viable guide to academic investigations and interventions. And interventions they are, since our words committed to paper are altering the social world they describe. As Giddens pointed out with his 'double hermeneutics', our own, social scientific vocabulary becomes part of the actions and institutions of those that we study, just as their vocabulary becomes part of our descriptions of the social world (Giddens, 1987: 30–1).

Outline of the volume

This book consists of four parts. The first section contains different explorations and illustrations of praxis theorizing in terms of what it might mean, how it is practised and how it relates to other qualitative approaches in the field of IR. In the second section, contributors focus on one essential dimension of the engagement with praxis theorizing, that is, the role of law in constituting praxis. The third section focuses on the biological 'hard-wiring' of human beings as agents, the fundamental contingency of sociality and the historicity of social and cultural transformation. The fourth section is dedicated to the relationship between praxis and academic analysis, performance and observation.

The first section kicks off with two illustrations of praxis theorizing based on backward-looking remembering and forward-looking imagination and 'prophesizing'. In Chapter 2, K.M. Fierke alerts us to how Kratochwil's notion of praxis, understood as acting here and now, relates past and future to present situations. History, she argues, is remembering, and as such is always part of a future project. What stitches together past and future are our present concerns. From this point of departure, Fierke problematizes the 'we' that constitutes David Hume's common world of 'commerce and conversation' and wonders how we can see those who have been written out of history. She takes the issue of slavery as her example, beginning with Hume's own troubling silence on the transatlantic slave trade in which his native Scotland was heavily involved. She then moves on to the 'eerie and troubling silence' surrounding Abraham Lincoln's Gettysburg Address and his inability to 'see' the real victims of slavery when constituting the 'we' of the union rejoining North and South after the American Civil War. Her chapter ends with reflections on the importance of redefining a global 'we' as the subject of conversation.

In Chapter 3, Cecelia Lynch assesses Kratochwil's conceptions of 'prophecy' and religion to highlight insights and tensions vis-à-vis time, history, community of meaning and certainty for praxis. What fascinates her in particular is the question of how one might think about 'immanence' in the theological/philosophical matrix within which Kratochwil theorizes. In putting Kratochwil in conversation on issues of praxis and prophecy with interlocutors such as Ian Shapiro and Michael Walzer, but also with selected theologians and social theorists such as Walter Brueggemann and Cornel West, or scholars in the tradition of pragmatism such as Jason Springs and Molly Cochran, Lynch hopes to probe forms of accompaniment with, rather than a complete U-turn from, Kratochwil's Humean analysis. These contrasts also put into sharper relief demands for action that might differ from Kratochwil's, especially with regard to multiple precarities that Lynch sees in the contemporary time.

Chapters 4 and 5 approach praxis theorizing from different angles. Christian Bueger examines what it implies to consider theorizing as a practice. He argues that the shift to the verb and the valuation of the actual work of theorizing has substantial consequences. Four are highlighted: the need for a reconceptualization of theorizing, which shifts from looking at it in terms of an achievement by an individual scholar to an understanding that sees theory as a collective achievement situated in a distinct milieu and locale; the need to focus on process and actions, rather than the object ('the theory'); the need to grasp the practical knowledge, various skills, material resources and objects that are assembled in the production of theory; and the need to recognize that there is a multiplicity of styles of theorizing. Against this background, different understandings of 'theory' and styles of theorizing come to the fore. Bueger illustrates these with examples he calls 'mechanism', 'meditation', 'method' and 'experimentation', each of which is said to ground theorizing differently in practice.

In Chapter 5, Gunther Hellmann reconstructs Kratochwil's understanding of theorizing in a tradition of linguistic turn-inspired critical reflection of praxis, which emphasizes the inherent contingency and radical openness of social action. He sides with what he redescribes, in a Rortyan vocabulary, as Kratochwil's anti-representationalist attack on typical practices of IR theorizing which range over a broad spectrum from Waltz, Keohane and Wendt all the way to contemporary forms of theorizing in the wake of the 'practice turn'. Instead of authorizing (presumably 'ontologically real') things in 'the world out there' to 'make' our theories true – irrespective of whether these 'really real' things come in the form of 'pictures of reality', 'empirical data' or 'quantum minds' – Hellmann argues that we should side with Wittgenstein's, Rorty's and Kratochwil's emphasis on the inherent contingency of our currently used, presumably 'final' vocabulary and rest content with translating 'theorizing' with Wittgenstein as regarding 'the facts as "proto-phenomena" – that is, simply to say: this is the language-game that is being played' (Wittgenstein, 2009 [1953]: 654).

Chris Brown opens the second section of the book on praxis and law in Chapter 6 with reflections on sanctions and punishment in international relations. He critically reviews the capacity of Kratochwil's *Praxis* to guide us in situations when international law is broken. Brown contends that praxis is not action-guiding in the direct sense of being able to help us decide what to do in particular situations, even if it is able to tell us broadly how we should go on in the world. To illustrate this tension, he discusses Russia's annexation of Crimea in 2014 and the international responses to it. Brown argues that Kratochwil's thinking can tell us why neither the International Criminal Court nor the International Court of Justice are going to be helpful in this case, but it fails to give us an alternative answer. He concludes that producing such answers simply isn't what the practice turn as elaborated in *Praxis* is all about, and that, accordingly, this approach is of limited help to those who have a commitment to engaging more directly with the world of international politics.

In Chapter 7, Anthony F. Lang, Jr. explores the role that Aristotle plays – and could be playing – in a praxis approach. He first shows that Kratochwil invokes Aristotle a number of times but critiques him for having an overly theoretical focus. Lang argues that Aristotle is more beneficial than Kratochwil makes him out to be for understanding the practical dimensions of international law and politics. In particular, Aristotle provides an alternative understanding of the rule of law and how it relates to the wider international political order, one that differs both from Kratochwil and from contemporary international law. By highlighting these aspects of Aristotle's work, Lang suggests that Kratochwil is overly focused on Aristotle's theoretical side and misses the very practical dimensions of his work. As ancient constitutionalism relied more heavily on the social and the political than the narrowly legal, Lang suggests the phrase 'practical constitutionalism' to bring this dimension of Aristotle's work to the fore.

Jan Klabbers in Chapter 8 seeks to start a conversation on the role that international rules, institutions and decisions play in achieving, channelling, promoting or facilitating particular distributive results. His inquiry is inspired by the observation that in the almost 500 pages of *Praxis*, Kratochwil pays little attention to distributive questions. Klabbers claims that getting to the distributive effect of rules, institutions and decisions requires a dual intellectual operation. It will require, firstly, relaxing the strongly state-centric approach prevailing in the study of international affairs, in combination with, secondly, a realization that law, politics and economics should not be neatly separated but rather should be treated as single decision-making moments or units. He illustrates his theoretical discussion with the case of the venerable Universal Postal Union to show how concrete (non-state) interests combine with the role of a concrete (non-state) institution.

The third section of the volume focuses on the nexus between human biology, social contingency and historical transformation on the one hand and praxis on the other. In Chapter 9, James W. Davis discusses the perspective of the first-person plural in Kratochwil's conception of praxis, examining links and tensions between Kratochwil's constructivism and current behavioural research in the fields of psychology and neuroscience. He argues that without a conception of 'we', there is no language or discourse, no possibility for authority or justice, and perhaps more controversially, no feelings or sentiments. Davis wonders how the so constructed 'we' relates to the psychological and biological agent 'I' who is engaged in praxis. He contends that the thick constructivism that underpins Kratochwil's notion of praxis at once is too radical and too conservative. It is too radical because it neglects how biology constrains what human beings in social settings can construct. Yet in ignoring how culture affects biology, it is simultaneously too conservative.

Oliver Kessler takes Kratochwil's notion of acting as vantage point to explore the problem of intersubjectivity and contingency in Chapter 10. He seeks to clarify the difference between positive and constructivist approaches in relation to expectations, common sense and 'how to go on' as central to praxis. To unpack his argument, he takes Kratochwil's discussion on game theory as vantage point to highlight the problem of intersubjectivity. He distinguishes a 'thin' version that operates in-between existing actors and a 'thick' version where intersubjectivity actually constitutes the actors in the first place. He then explores the contours of this 'thick' version of intersubjectivity by exploring the use of the concept 'society' in *Praxis*, in terms of what he calls 'triple contingency'. In the final section, he explores the different mechanisms of sense-making in dyadic and triadic constellations and argues that questions of knowledge, expertise and power are differently constituted in these two settings.

In Chapter 11, Mathias Albert prompts a conversation between Kratochwil's praxis approach and theories of social differentiation that are both concerned with the evolution of societies, domestically and internationally. He contends that Kratochwil's uses of 'theory' are rather ambivalent, lacking a distinction between 'IR theory' and other uses and concepts of 'theory'. He then enquires into Kratochwil's account of social constitution, particularly with a view to social differentiation as a defining characteristic of social systems. Albert argues that while Kratochwil's account is quite clear in this respect, it is biased towards the legal system as an integrative force under the condition of functional differentiation. While such a privileging of the legal system might not necessarily be legitimate from a view of 'pure' functional differentiation, it could be upheld as an empirical argument about social evolution. However, for that purpose Kratochwil, as well as other practice theorists, would need to twist their account of social change in the direction of a theory of social evolution.

In Chapter 12, Jörg Friedrichs explores how discursive practices in social science can sustain, subvert and transform social realities. Taking Anthony Giddens's original framework of 'double hermeneutics' as a starting point, he develops an extended framework of 'triple hermeneutics' to show how reflexive approaches can serve sustaining, subversive and transformative purposes. He argues that Max Weber's interpretive social science is inherently conservative and geared towards stabilization. Friedrichs contrasts it with critical genealogy, developed in different versions by Nietzsche and Foucault, as inherently radical and geared towards subversion. Finally, he shows how the young Nietzsche's 'history for life' and Hume's dialectics of history were inherently reformist and geared towards transformation. Overall, Friedrichs concludes, reflexive approaches turn out to be far more relevant to social order and change than conventional wisdom suggests.

Friedrichs's musings on the purposes of social science build a bridge to the fourth section, which reflects upon the role of theorists and the practice of theorizing as a type of political intervention. In Chapter 13, Antje Wiener considers Kratochwil's praxis approach to international studies as a series of academic interventions with two lasting effects. The first consists in the project of studying human action and its effect on the transformation of norms, rules and orders through redrawing disciplinary boundaries of international studies. Second, she argues that Kratochwil's work enabled subsequent generations to engage in critical questions about international studies and advance knowledge building on these interdisciplinary strands of theoretical engagement. *Praxis* is used here as a foil to discuss effects of academic intervention, taking into account the positions of privilege and responsibility. Wiener reads *Praxis* as a 'most compellingly expressed urge to act through theory'. This is done, she argues, by engaging interdisciplinary knowledge through contesting the work of others and holding their claims to account. The purpose of intervention consists in bringing knowledge to bear in order to identify transformations within the fundamentally contested Western narrative of world order.

The last two chapters discuss the tension between a 'scientific' approach to social and political life emphasizing contemplative study, and a 'political' approach that emphasizes enacting concrete courses of action. In Chapter 14 Patrick Thaddeus Jackson argues that Kratochwil is able to produce an account of the relationship between contemplating and enacting that avoids the errors of reification. He appreciates that there is neither an analysis of 'the political' nor a doctrinaire pronouncement of the (uniquely) 'scientific method' in Kratochwil's work. To elucidate these points, Jackson places

Kratochwil in dialogue first with Max Weber, whose celebrated but often misunderstood 'vocation' lectures gesture at the road that Kratochwil ultimately takes. Jackson then suggests that it is useful to read *Praxis* alongside works of the pragmatist tradition, especially John Dewey's, to properly tease out the implications of treating both scholarly knowledge production and the responsible exercise of coercive authority as practices. Kratochwil's analysis of law as a living tradition of sense-making, rather than as a formal or rationalist alternative to political contestation, serves as an exemplary account of how the relationship between contemplating and enacting might be figured.

In Chapter 15, Jens Steffek places the praxis approach in the humanist tradition of social and political thought, interpreting it as a quest for wholeness in a modern world full of reductionism and fragmentation. He finds the humanist legacy of praxis in Kratochwil's epistemological position, which suggests that we can, and should, grasp human agency in all its facets by studying complex, historically situated situations of decision-making. Having outlined this perspective on praxis, Steffek highlights the inherent tension between the desire for wholeness and the scholarly habit of distancing and detachment. The central question for him is how world-observing scholars can adequately understand a real-world praxis that they do not enact. Kratochwil deploys an Aristotelian concept of praxis, in combination with American pragmatism, to argue that there is continuity between scientific inquiry and real-world practices. Taking issue with this continuity thesis, Steffek argues that the reflexive-critical stance of the social scientist who dissects real-world practices to gain knowledge about them is hard to reconcile with the habitual conduct of actors who rely on tacit and unquestioned knowledge.

In the last chapter, Fritz Kratochwil replies to his critics. His concluding commentary is organized around some core themes that emerged in the previous chapters. The first cluster of problems pivots around the notion of 'theory' and the relation between practising theory and going on in situations, individually and collectively. Kratochwil rejects the view that theorizing – related as it is to our time and our purposes as researchers and citizens – could provide us with something like a pure and unadulterated 'view from nowhere' or produce eternal truths that end all further questioning. He explains that if we act in order to achieve something, we are not simply observers of the world. The common academic ideal of theorizing as seeing 'how things really are' just distracts us from what is really at stake when we intervene into the world and try to realize the good life through our actions in time. Theorizing, properly conceived, is a form of critical intervention. Kratochwil then addresses another group of problems that revolve around the conception of the 'we' in social, political and legal practices. How can a 'we' as an aggregate of individuals turn into a 'we' of the first-person plural?

He concedes that repeated interaction, role-taking and communication are necessary parts of both individuation and socialization but insists that for the reproduction of a society and a body politic, more needs to happen. Beyond communication and cooperation on practical tasks, the members also need to make a commitment to the 'project' of remaining a group and, importantly, accept the transgenerational nature of an ongoing concern that requires them to act together.

References

Adler, Emmanuel and Vincent Pouliot (2011) 'International practices', *International Theory* 3, 1, pp 1–36.

Bernstein, Richard (1971) *Praxis and Action: Contemporary Philosophies of Human Activity* (Philadelphia: University of Pennsylvania Press).

Bloor, David (1983) *Wittgensteinian: A Social Theory of Knowledge* (Houndmills, Basingstoke: Macmillan).

Bloor, David (2001) 'Wittgenstein and the priority of practice', in Theodore R. Schatzki, Karin Knorr-Cetina and Eike von Savigny (eds) *The Practice Turn in Contemporary Theory* (London: Routledge), pp 103–14.

Bueger, Christian (2017) 'Practice', in Xavier Guillaume and Pinar Bilgin (eds) *Handbook of International Political Sociology* (London: Routledge), pp 324–34.

Bueger, Christian and Frank Gadinger (2018) *International Practice Theory* (2nd edn) (London: Palgrave Macmillan).

Cornut, Jérémie (2017) 'The practice turn in International Relations theory', in *Oxford Research Encyclopedia of International Studies*, available at: http://internationalstudies.oxfordre.com/view/10.1093/acrefore/9780190846 626.001.0001/acrefore-9780190846626-e-113/version/0, accessed 13 June 2018.

Day, William and Victor J. Krebs, eds (2010) *Seeing Wittgenstein Anew: New Essays on Aspect-Seeing* (Cambridge: Cambridge University Press).

Dewey, John (1938) *Logic: The Theory of Inquiry* (Dewey, The Later Works, 1925–1953, Vol. 12) (Carbondale, IL: Southern Illinois University Press).

Giddens, Anthony (1987) *Social Theory and Modern Sociology* (Stanford, CA: Stanford University Press).

Goethe, Johann Wolfgang von (2014/1808) *Faust I & II* (Princeton, NJ: Princeton University Press).

Hellmann, Gunther (2020) 'International Relations theory', in Dirk Berg-Schlosser, Bertrand Badie and Leonardo Morlino (eds) *The Sage Handbook of Political Science* (London: Sage Publications), pp 1282–99.

Hopf, Ted (2010) 'The logic of habit in International Relations', *European Journal of International Relations* 16, 4, pp 539–61.

Janis, Irving (1982) *Groupthink: Psychological Studies of Policy Decisions and Fiascoes* (Boston, MA: Houghton Mifflin).

Jervis, Robert (1976) *Perception and Misperception in International Politics* (Princeton, NJ: Princeton University Press).

Joas, Hans (1992) *Die Kreativität des Handelns* (Frankfurt am Main: Suhrkamp).

Kessler, Oliver and Brent Steele (2016) 'Introduction: Constructing IR. The third generation', *European Review of International Studies* 3, 3, pp 7–13.

King, Gary, Robert O. Keohane and Sidney Verba (1994) *Designing Social Inquiry: Scientific Inference in Qualitative Research* (Princeton, NJ: Princeton University Press).

Kratochwil, Friedrich (1984) 'The force of prescriptions', *International Organization* 38, 4, pp 685–708.

Kratochwil, Friedrich (1989) *Rules, Norms, and Decisions: On the Conditions of Practical and Legal Reasoning in International Relations and Domestic Affairs* (Cambridge: Cambridge University Press).

Kratochwil, Friedrich (2000) 'Constructing a new orthodoxy? Wendt's "Social Theory of International Politics" and the constructivist challenge', *Millennium* 29, 1, pp 73–101.

Kratochwil, Friedrich (2010) 'Sociological approaches', in Christian Reus-Smit and Duncan Snidal (eds) *Oxford Handbook of International Relations* (Oxford: Oxford University Press), pp 444–61.

Kratochwil, Friedrich (2018) *Praxis: On Acting and Knowing* (Cambridge: Cambridge University Press).

Kratochwil, Friedrich (2019) 'A pragmatic view of practice in International Relations', in *Oxford Research Encyclopedia of International Studies*, DOI: 10.1093/acrefore/9780190846626.013.526.

Marx, Karl (1969 [1888]) 'Theses on Feuerbach', in *Karl Marx and Frederick Engels: Selected Works in Three Volumes*, Vol. 1 (Moscow: Progress Publishers), pp 13–15.

Neumann, Iver (2002) 'Returning practice to the linguistic turn: the case of diplomacy', *Millennium* 31, 3, pp 627–51.

Nexon, Daniel, Ted Hopf, Stacie Goddard, Alexander Montgomery, Oliver Kessler, Christian Bueger, Cecelia Lynch, Ty Solomon, Swati Srivastava and David M. McCourt (2017) 'Seizing constructivist ground? Practice and relational theories', *An International Studies Quarterly Online Symposium*, available at: https://www.dhnexon.net/wp-content/uploads/2020/05/ISQSymposiumMcCourt-1.pdf, accessed 15 June 2018.

Onuf, Nicholas (1989) *World of Our Making: Rules and Rule in Social Theory and International Relations* (Columbia, SC: University of South Carolina Press).

Putnam, Hilary (1995) *Pragmatism: An Open Question* (Oxford: Blackwell).

Rorty, Richard (1989) *Contingency, Irony, and Solidarity* (Cambridge: Cambridge University Press).

Schatzki, Theodore R., Karin Knorr-Cetina and Eike von Savigny, eds (2001) *The Practice Turn in Contemporary Theory* (London: Routledge).

Wittgenstein, Ludwig (2009 [1953]) *Philosophische Untersuchungen – Philosophical Investigations*, transl. Gertrude Elizabeth M. Anscombe, Peter M.S. Hacker and Joachim Schulte (4th revd edn) (Malden, MA: Wiley-Blackwell).

PART I

Theorizing Praxis

2

Knowing, Remembering, Showing But Still Not Seeing: Critical Praxis, Slavery and the Modern 'We'

K.M. Fierke

Introduction

A central concern of Kratochwil's book *Praxis* regards our entanglement in institutionalized interactions and discourses, and the importance of a 'thick' constructivism for beginning to understand the nature of praxis as it relates to knowing, seeing, remembering, forgetting, showing, acting and so forth. The book represents a critique not only of thin constructivism, but of practices of science that seek to universalize knowledge, which rely on a questionable metaphysics of the world as existing 'out there' and capable of being understood from 'everywhere at once'. Insofar as this conceptualization of science is a product of 'our' own conceptual structures and assumptions, originating with the Enlightenment and modernity, critical voices within are tasked with placing these structures in historical context, to begin to see the extent to which knowledge production, and its reliance on memory, is always undertaken from the perspective of present concerns and future projects.

While agreeing with Kratochwil's overall argument, this chapter reflects on the potential limits of history, conversation and critique that arise from the institutions and structures within which 'we' are embedded. To take history seriously, while crucial, does not entirely solve the problem Kratochwil identifies. History is remembering, and remembering is always part of someone's future project, by which past and future are linked through present concerns. From this point of departure, the 'we' that constitutes the common world of 'commerce and conversation' has to be problematized, in order to begin to see the unseen or those who have been written out of history.

The first section of the paper explores Kratochwil's argument about Hume's 'commerce and conversation', placing Hume in the historical context of Enlightenment Scotland and problematizing his silence on the transatlantic slave trade. Section two moves to questions of remembering, looking in particular at the 'eerie and troubling silence' surrounding Lincoln's Gettysburg Address and the inability to 'see' the real victims of slavery. Section three explores the difference between 'showing' and 'seeing', and Kratochwil's concern about the difficulties that stand in the way of a 'global public forum'. The argument ends with reflection on the subsequent importance of redefining a global 'we' as the subject of conversation and acknowledgement of the 'unseen' in history.

Knowing and Hume's silence

Kratochwil (2018) examines the need for philosophy to realize its purpose and potential as a critical voice. He starts with a concrete situation, that is, Hume's efforts to challenge Newtonian arguments about the unity of science and the rational reconstruction of the scientific project, which form the core of modernity and the Scottish Enlightenment. The unity of science argument obscures the importance of history and praxis, given that 'we are always in the midst of things'. We can't 'view the world from nowhere' (Kratochwil, 2018: 357), as it is always in the making, rather than already made. The social world is constituted on the basis of mind-dependent facts rather than natural facts.

Hume discounts attempts to determine what 'is' or 'is not' on the basis of brute facts and 'things out there'. Knowledge is, in his view, nonetheless possible (Kratochwil, 2018: 361). We can still 'go on' in the face of uncertainty because true philosophy emerges within a common world and engages with it. Beginning with a social world, based on convention and custom, and the importance of history, Hume conceived of a non-essentialist human nature, characterized by malleability and 'embeddedness in time and historical conjunctures' (Kratochwil, 2018: 362). Habit, long-usage and sentiment are, in this argument, more central to thought and action than rational choice (Kratochwil, 2018: 366). The world doesn't exist 'out there' but rather we are always within the world, which conditions our thoughts. Far from given or fixed, human nature is 'part and parcel of further articulations occurring in history' (Kratochwil, 2018: 369). There are multiple potential ways to understand 'what is', which are determined by the 'semantic grids' that are engendered by interests that emerge from 'commerce and conversation' (Kratochwil, 2018: 371).

The problem, I would like to suggest, regards the difficulty posed by the 'we' that is the subject of 'commerce and conversation', and the extent to which, from within, the critical voice is limited. While Hume pushed against the boundaries of scientific discourse, he was also constrained by it. While knowledge may be possible, the question of 'whose' commerce and conversation delineates what is and what is not, given that it defines not only the project of philosophy but the writing of history. It is not only that ideal theory doesn't reflect the world 'as it is', but any notion of history, written from the perspective of present concerns, remains trapped in a particular 'commerce and conversation' that defines the boundaries of what is permitted, allowed or required conduct. In Hume's context, these boundaries arose from racialized distinctions and commerce that involved the commodification of particular types of people.

Both the critical voices and the silences surrounding race and the slave trade are evident in Hume's context, highlighting the extent to which the 'we' of conversation excludes, justifies and elides based on a common definition of 'interesse'. In addition to being a philosopher, Hume was a merchant assistant, who travelled via Bristol (a port of the slave trade) to France, where he later became the British chargé d'affaires, writing dispatches to the British Secretary of State from Paris. In 1766, upon returning to Britain, he encouraged Lord Hertford to invest in a number of slave plantations in the Windward Islands (Waldman, 2014). In 1767 he was appointed Under Secretary of State for the Northern Department, where he was given 'all the secrets of the kingdom' (Sack, 2018: np). Given this professional lineage, he was clearly aware of Britain's role in the transatlantic slave trade. Ince (2018) argues that while Hume condemned Britain's empire of monopoly, war and conquest, the critique did not extend to transatlantic slavery. An enlightened sensibility would, in Hume's argument, judge slavery to be an uncivil institution; however, it was also a commercial institution that was central to the 18th-century global economy. Hume's response to this paradox was to ignore the relationship between slavery and commerce and confine his criticism of slavery to ancient feudal or Asian manifestations, which was part of a broader ideological programme to separate commerce from its imperial origins. Within this 'semantic grid' liberal commerce was the antithesis of empire. In this respect, the 'peace, prosperity and civilization' associated with commerce was in a complementary relationship to the violence, exploitation, slavery, conquest and occupation of the globe (Muthu, 2012). The first could be seen; the victims of the latter recessed into a background where they were largely invisible.

Philosophers of the Scottish Enlightenment, including Frances Hutcheson, Adam Smith and John Millar, are often associated with the abolition of slavery, although the relationship is arguably more ambiguous (Doris, 2021). Hume, as a key figure of the second generation of the Scottish Enlightenment, along with many of his contemporaries, viewed Blacks as inferior, in part because of circumstances that did not allow for 'innovation' and 'dexterity' (Webster, 2003), although he also suggests that the enslaved have an innate inferiority (see Popkin, 1980; Immerwahr, 1992). To take the point away from Hume as individual, the tension is embedded in the assumptions and practices of the Enlightenment. On the one hand, liberty is a natural human right and reason and scientific knowledge are understood to be responsible for human progress; on the other, this reasoning coexists with slavery, which rested on a hierarchy of race, in a global context of slave trade. As one of the architects of the US Constitution, with its construction of free and equal citizens, Thomas Jefferson believed slavery should be abolished in America yet owned 600 people over the course of his lifetime and did not succeed in extricating himself from what he referred to as the 'deplorable entanglement of slavery' (The Jefferson Monticello, 2021). Jefferson, like Hume, believed Blacks to be inferior to Whites, but he questioned whether this was due to an inherent inferiority or decades of degrading enslavement (The Jefferson Monticello, 2021). This brief sketch of Hume's Enlightenment context reinforces Kratochwil's point that to begin to understand requires attention to historical context. However, it further highlights the extent to which the common discourse of a particular time and place relies on exclusions and silences which facilitate future projects that may be a source of harm to those outside the 'we'.

Remembering and forgetting slavery

Kratochwil's chapter on remembering and forgetting is first and foremost about theoretical progress in International Relations (IR) vis-à-vis a history of the discipline, but the argument applies to the writing of history as well. He argues that in a period of radical change, historical reflection cannot arise from lessons or 'what really happened' (Kratochwil, 2018: 314). Instead, through historical reflection we become aware of the 'dialectic of choice' by which past is joined in the present with the future through recollection and by means of a political project (Kratochwil, 2018: 314). He points to the problematic nature of relying on 'brute facts' from a storehouse of data which allow us to test theories (Kratochwil, 2018: 315). In this model, practices of conceptualization are prior to any measurement or operationalization, which provide the basis of judgements of similarity and what counts as an 'instance of something' (Kratochwil, 2018: 319). He contrasts the (Newtonian) scientific notion that something only truly 'is' if it does not change, with the position of modern physics by which 'things' and 'objects' are not fixed entities but 'temporary stabilizations of various processes' (Kratochwil, 2018: 319). In this respect, Wendt's (2015) quantum argument that language use is a form of measurement, by which wave functions collapse into the physical properties of language, provides a way to think about the process of temporary stabilization. To return to Hume or Jefferson, their use of language represents a measurement that contributes to a temporary stabilization of a world within which ideas of liberty and human progress coexist with the barbaric practices of the transatlantic slave trade. Their conceptualizations, even in the form of critique, are part of a vocabulary that is deeply imbricated with the larger political project of the Enlightenment. The conceptual apparatus draws lines that depend on a judgement regarding the 'humanity' of certain types, in the light of a set of values rather than things 'out there'. But this moral sentiment also requires 'not seeing' and thus forgetting. Kratochwil's further point is that although 'history' is past and seems to be objective, fixed and a secure source of knowledge, it is malleable because remembered from a certain situation in the present for which things past now have relevance. History is an encounter with the individual and collective self rather than data or lessons (Kratochwil, 2018: 326). Who 'we' are is shaped by where we think we came from, which relates to identities and collective memories that allow us to be a person and a group that moulds 'society' as an ongoing and transgenerational concern among its members (Kratochwil, 2018: 328).

In theoretical or scientific discourse, what constitutes a thing is dependent on the categories of the scientist. The problem doesn't go away in the narration of history, however. In this case, we necessarily shift to the categories of the historical actors themselves, and how they draw boundaries between what is seen and unseen. Hume 'knows' through his embeddedness in commerce and conversation, but this constitution of knowing through a 'we' comes with blinders. It is not a complete view but partial, by which the status of the enslaved as human is contestable (in the US context, the enslaved were a mere three fifths human).[1] The central point of contestation was whether inferiority arises from human nature, based on a White–Black distinction, or historical circumstances, that is, the practice of slavery itself.

The human/human-'lite'/non-human categorizations further impact on how recollection takes place, including how victims are constructed, and the types of societal obligations that flow from this. Drawing on the funeral oration of Pericles in Thucydides' *Peloponnesian Wars*, Kratochwil highlights the transition from tribal societies, in which obligations were located in the family or clan, to the more modern honouring of the dead that reinforced loyalty to the polis. In demonstrating the notion of an 'encumbered self', collective memory can no longer be considered the aggregate of individual memory but becomes a phenomenon in its own right (Kratochwil, 2018: 331). Various forms of ritual and ceremony provide

---

[1]   Federal Convention (1787: 29).

a powerful venue for mobilizing memory. In the light of our concern here with the inability to 'see' slavery, his elaboration of Lincoln's Gettysburg Address is of particular interest.

Lincoln's funeral address is a narrative about a 'new beginning' following large-scale violence which, in order to establish the future project of a 'United' States, has to be based on a notion of reconciliation. Like Pericles' funeral oration, it becomes a statement of 'mission' that connects past to future. The statement relies on several conceptual moves. It refers to the exemplary nature of the original founding. The Civil War is a 'test' of the viability of the project, and a common trial through which the 'union' frees itself from the stigma of slavery and resolves to rededicate itself to its original task. As Kratochwil (2018: 348) notes, the 'union is depicted as a victim that succumbed to the sin of slavery and now seeks redemption'. He further states that the speech contains an 'eerie and troubling silence' in regard to the 'sufferings of the actual victims, the slaves' (Kratochwil, 2018: 348). Lincoln's address, as Meister (1999: 141) notes, provides a moral framework by which the defeated South could avoid the perception of humiliating punishment for slavery and secession and accept a Northern victory.

The main subject of 'we' in this case is a union. The union rejoins North and South, and particularly the 'White' South which has experienced not only humiliating defeat but the loss of a system of human chattel slavery upon which their commerce depended. In Lincoln's address, the emancipation of the latter from their Southern owners is implied and assumed, but the humanity of the enslaved and the continuing violation of their humanity remains largely unseen as a subject of reconciliation. As Lepore (2018: 296) notes, Lincoln did not mention slavery in the address, although during his earlier election campaign he bemoaned the silence surrounding it:

> You must not say anything about it in the free states *because it is not here*. You must not say anything about it in the slave states *because it is there*. You must not say anything about it in the pulpit, because that is religion and has nothing to do with it. You must not say anything about it in politics *because that will disturb the security of 'my place'*. There is no place to talk about it as being a wrong, although you say yourself it *is* a wrong. (As quoted in Lepore, 2018: 279; emphasis in original)

Slavery is surrounded by silence on all sides, as if it is not there. Much as in the case of the transatlantic slave trade of Hume's Scotland, Lincoln's words of 'emancipation' display an ambivalence regarding the humanity of those whose freedom is a by-product of the Civil War. As Lepore (2018: 296) notes, the reconciliation of North and South required a new consensus that the war was fought not about slavery but rather states' rights or the preservation of the union, which, much like Lincoln's Gettysburg Address, sought to bring White southerners on board and avoid strengthening their sense of loss. Even in the time just prior to the Emancipation Proclamation in 1862, Lincoln continued to insist that the purpose of the war was to save the Union,[2] although he did change his mind by 1864, at which point he excluded the option of victory without the abolition of slavery.

The claim that history is written by the victors is commonplace in discussions of contemporary conflicts, for instance, war crime tribunals or the International Criminal Court (see, e.g., Peskin, 2005), but the problem goes much deeper. The historical practice of displacing and enslaving African populations continued for over 400 years, leading to the deaths of some 12 million people. It was not only that the victors' interpretation dominated, but the fact that the enslavers or traders controlled the archives, the diaries, the ledgers, and often destroyed even these. Within these sources, the victim often appears as only a name, as the property of someone, with nothing that would constitute their humanity.[3] Not unlike Lincoln's address, history records the commerce of the slave trade in a form that often obscures the perpetration. The perpetration cannot be separated from a relationship to those who suffered the terror of having their autonomy, their language and their customs stripped away, as they were unwillingly transported to locations where they would be in the hands of strangers, who treated them as property or otherwise intended to do them harm.

Showing and seeing

How would it be possible to write a 'better' history which incorporates the voices of the voiceless, thereby shining a light on the tragic consequences of Enlightenment 'progress'? Kratochwil's chapter on 'showing' opens with reference to a scene from Aeschylus (Kratochwil, 2018: 104), *The Liberation Bearers,* to illustrate the importance of 'showing' rather than hiding a bloody deed. He connects the verb 'to show', from which the word for 'justice' is derived, to entreat the chorus to become a witness. Justice begins with 'showing' what is the case, which is important for moving towards a more inclusive conception of law. In this respect, making the unseen seen brings things out into the open, which is a prerequisite not only for justice but for increased security and stability. Kratochwil argues, among others, that the issue is not first and foremost one of defining what transparency 'really

---

[2] In a letter to Horace Greeley (Basler, 1953), he wrote: 'If I could save the Union without freeing any slave, I would do it, and if I could save it by freeing all the slaves I would do it, and if I could save it by freeing some and leaving others alone, I would also do it.'

[3] Even these records did not begin to appear until abolition was on the agenda, and only to ensure the compensation of the enslavers when the initiative finally materialized.

is', but rather to examine the web of neighbouring concepts and practices in which it is enmeshed and to highlight that greater transparency is not merely a matter of casting light on the facts but one of witness, which speaks to issues of responsibility that the 'global public' *cannot make good* (Kratochwil, 2018: 110, italics added). Why they 'cannot make good' is not entirely clear.

That showing is supposed to lead to 'knowing' presupposes some kind of norm-infused common knowledge. The need for institutionalized dialogue arises from unobservable intentions, which may be connected to observed behaviour, the understanding of which requires more than interpretation or data checks (Kratochwil, 2018: 113). Because we are not entirely 'transparent', even to ourselves, we become what we are through interaction with others – our plans and projects influence what we want to know and what we can expect from others, that is, through conversation, even while we also need protected spaces from which something remains out of view. 'Getting it right', he suggests, involves more than just 'seeing something', as suggested by the term transparency. It means that any data have to be seen within a whole gestalt.

Transparency suggests a straightforward relationship between showing and seeing – an object is visible and can thus be seen. Kratochwil, by contrast, is talking about, on the one hand, unobservables, and on the other, intersubjective norms, and the role of some kind of institutional dialogue in weaving these together into something more, and this more links to the importance of local knowledge. The problem he identifies is the tendency of international institutions to develop 'one size fits all' approaches, based on purely theoretical or textbook knowledge, which don't deal with problems of radical uncertainty.

Arguably, the failure to incorporate local knowledge points towards another dimension of 'seeing', or more specifically 'not seeing', that goes beyond transparency to a blindness within the norms that constitute the possibility of seeing. Understanding the normative problem is crucial to the construction of a more global conversation. If 'commerce and conversation' has constructed blinders by which 'we' fail to see barbarous practices of harm, which go hand in hand with a universalizing notion of cultural and scientific progress, the inability to take into account local knowledge is constitutive of the absences.

'Scientific' discourse, along with forms of commerce such as the slave trade, facilitated the silencing of local knowledge. As such, the problem is not merely one of multiple voices being written out of the dominant narrative of 'Western civilization', but a multiplicity of practices as well. The process of colonization, no less than a physical dislocation to slavery, involved what Ngũgĩ wa Thiong'o (2009: 70) refers to as 'dis-memberment', by which indigenous knowledge was supplanted and replaced by European memory.

The point is graphically and symbolically expressed by the European colonial practice of cutting off the heads of African kings, as carriers of knowledge and memory from the body. The heads were then buried facing the earth, in opposition to indigenous burial practice (Ndlovu-Gatsheni, 2018: 11). The symbolic practice was bound up in the epistemicide of a continent, which involved not only forceful physical dislocation, but that of culture, tradition and knowledge systems as well.

While Hume and his contemporaries attempted to distance 'civilized' Europe from the brutal practices of empire in its name, the laws and norms arising from 'commerce and conversation' obscured the racial distinctions embedded within them, thereby contributing to an inability to engage with either the local knowledge of the victims or its representatives. In this respect, universalizing theory, as a product of Western conversation, constructed an absence of racial distinction but one that is not equivalent to being colour blind. In her powerful argument regarding the erasure of race in Kant's thought, Jasmine Gani (2017) argues, similar to Kratochwil, that universalizing theory and notions of progress have been at the expense of historical analysis. Gani places Kant's universalizing theory in its historical context, arguing that it is the very universalism of his law of hospitality that erases the historical and racist context in which it was conceived. Further, this erasure persists in more contemporary interpretations of Kantian cosmopolitanism, as evident in the erasure of race in academic and European practices towards refugees and immigrants (Gani, 2017: 429).

While there is not space here to recount her complex argument in detail, the problem arises from the historical context in which Kant was writing, the kinds of legal distinctions he draws on, in which 'communication' is expressed via residence and appropriation and the establishment of civil laws, justified by 'common will'. On the one hand, the law was written not with the poor and needy seeking refuge in mind, but rather European preoccupations with appropriating riches in other parts of the world. On the other hand, while trying to rein in practices of imperialism, Kant makes a separation between colonialism and race, which was a preceding facilitating condition of the former. Questions of race are absent from the discourse, even while it rests on foundational assumptions that his laws applied only to those capable of reason, which combined with a prevailing view, reinforced by Kant himself, that non-White people were lacking in reason. Gani's argument adds further insight into why the 'one size fits all' model of international institutions, and universalizing theory, make it difficult to take local knowledge into account. While presumably colour blind – that is, it does not refer specifically to race – it imposes normative constraints arising from a context where 'commerce and conversation' historically and in the present do not 'see' beyond the needs and interests of a geographically constrained 'we'.

Reconstituting the conversation

The previous section highlighted the extent to which the boundaries that constitute what is seen and unseen are embedded in the very norms and legal structures of international society as it emerged against a backdrop of the slave trade, slavery and imperialism. While no longer legal,[4] residues of this 'commerce and conversation' remain with us, enshrined in universalizing structures that are purportedly colour blind. This reflection on Kratochwil's rich and insightful book has attempted to bring out the problem of what it means to critically engage with a history of commerce and conversation that has defined the 'we' of conversation in geographically limited terms, thereby delegitimizing other forms of local knowledge and subjectivity. While problematizing the limits of 'conversation', and the boundaries of the 'we' from which it historically arose, I want to end by raising a question of what 'conversation' at this historical juncture might mean. The problem is not merely one of Enlightenment Scotland or America but persists in the present. As Kratochwil (2018: 392) notes, 'what one sorely misses in the contemporary debate is precisely the critical examination of the silent and not so silent presuppositions of thought'. The question is how to push at the boundaries of these presuppositions when 'we' and 'our' norms, legal structures or theories are permeated with them, such that a global public *might* begin to make good on issues of responsibility. What would it mean to reconstitute the conversation on more global terms in order to 'get it right'?

Kratochwil's concluding chapter provides significant insight into the requirements of such a conversation. As distinct from notions of an unchanging and universal truth, assumed by universalizing theories, 'conversation' requires meaningful communication that involves give and take among different positions, as well as an ability to listen and reflect and draw one's own assumptions and prejudices into question (Kratochwil, 2018: 457). It involves a notion of interest that allows for correcting one's original position in the attempt to tackle genuine problems. Insofar as this intention is embedded in Hume's concept of commerce and conversation, the problem lies not in his theory of praxis but rather in historical praxis in practice, and the difficulty of going beyond a human preference for talking to those who share our convictions (Kratochwil, 2018: 451) to engage with a wider world, including those with whom we disagree. As Kratochwil (2018: 411) argues, the key function of praxis must be a 'critical' one, rather

---

[4] Having said this, a recent Netflix documentary on the 13th Amendment to the US Constitution (DuVernay, 2016), which explores the intersection between race, justice and mass incarceration in the US, makes the point that slavery is illegal, except as punishment for conviction of a crime. DuVernay argues that slavery has been perpetuated since the end of the Civil War through the mass incarceration of people of colour.

than foundational or axiomatic; its insights are more akin to a dialectic or therapeutic 'working through' of problems. But the question is how we get there, particularly in the light of a history which, as he rightly points out, is irreversible, and one that has been heavily influenced by a praxis of not seeing, not hearing and thus not involving large portions of the world's population in a conversation that has deeply impacted on them.

Those engaged with decolonizing the academy, and more specifically IR theory, have, over the past decades, and more recently with the emergence of Global IR, questioned the articulation of IR theory from one corner of the world (e.g. Chan et al, 2001; Tickner and Wæver, 2009; Ling, 2013; Acharya, 2014; Wiener, 2018) and have sought to provincialize Europe (Chakrabarty, 2000). In a recent intervention, Vivienne Jabri and I (Fierke and Jabri, 2019) raise a question about what a more global 'conversation' might look like, while exploring the emotional obstacles that stand in the way.[5] One such obstacle, embedded in the 'silent presuppositions', also on the part of critical scholars, is the deeply engrained assumption that the scholarly practices of the West are superior, arising as they do from institutions that have a history of scientific rigour and funding (often due to the legacy of the slave trade) that has made them so. Such an assumption comes into play in a consideration of who can 'count' as a participant in conversation (Kratochwil, 2018: 452). It raises questions about how emotions and cognition interact in 'decoding' messages or making information meaningful (Kratochwil, 2018: 454) in a larger global context shaped through a history of bullying entire populations and discounting local knowledges through processes of 'orientalization' (Said, 2003). The internalization of this history and collective memory only adds to the difficulty of common deliberation or the creation of a practical politics that allows us to 'go on' through 'conversation'. The scientific practice is emulated across the globe to the neglect of more local knowledge.[6] Calls for greater inclusiveness of 'gender' and 'diversity', while increasingly emphasized within universities, have simultaneously contributed to a backlash (sometimes referred to as a 'whitelash') reflected not least in political outcomes such as Brexit and the election of Donald Trump in the US.[7] We are in the process of losing the capacity for 'conversation', at

---

[5]   As the article was already in press at the time when I read *Praxis*, I try here to engage Kratochwil's argument with some of the concerns raised in the article.

[6]   A survey of how IR is studied around the world revealed that the differences are far less stark than one might expect (Tickner and Wæver, 2009), not least because the main categories of the discipline have percolated out from the US core to the periphery.

[7]   See Shilliam (2018) for an argument regarding the role of a racialized distinction between the 'deserving' and 'undeserving' poor arising from the post-colonial settlement over the last 200 years, which is assumed in arguments of the 'White working class' that have been so central to these developments.

a time when it is needed more than ever given the threat to deliberative democracy – or the global environment – posed by the increasing toxicity of politics. Arguably this breakdown arises from an unwillingness to broaden the conversation, instead clinging to memories of greatness and empire and a conversation and commerce that has historically been limited to the few, with a mode of governance and hospitality defined by the drawing of sovereign boundaries.

Here the transgenerational dimensions of knowledge production, as well as memory and knowing, are key. 'We' cannot reverse time or reconstitute the voices or practice of those who have been destroyed in the context of, and arguably as a result of, the universalizing impulses of modernity. As Kratochwil (2018: 419) notes, time is irreversible. While we 'know' about slavery, and any number of other historical atrocities, we still do not 'see' it in the sense of witnessing to and acknowledging the damage it has done across generations.[8] Acknowledging one's own complicity or responsibility for a system that has been evil for some, even while good for 'us', is perhaps one of the most challenging terrains of memory and politics. While, as Kratochwil notes, Hume provided a framework for transcending the accepted wisdom of the day, the question is what it might mean to reapproach knowledge of the world as the subject of a more open-ended 'conversation' in which a 'global' 'we' might redefine the boundaries of 'our' engagement and 'our' future project.

References

Acharya, Amitav (2014) 'Global International Relations (IR) and regional worlds: a new agenda for International Studies', *International Studies Quarterly* 58, 4, pp 647–59.

Basler, Roy B., ed (1953) 'Lincoln to Horace Greeley, August 1862', in *The Collected Works of Abraham Lincoln* (5th edn) (New Brunswick, NJ: Rutgers University Press), pp 388–9.

Chakrabarty, Dipesh (2000) *Provincialising Europe: Postcolonial Thought and Historical Difference* (Princeton, NJ: Princeton University Press).

Chan, Stephen, Peter Mandaville and Roland Bleiker, eds (2001) *The Zen of International Relations* (London: Palgrave Macmillan).

Doris, Glen (2021) 'Hume's thoughts on personal liberty', unpublished manuscript, available at: https://www.academia.edu/890401/Making_excuses_for_Hume_slavery_racism_and_a_reassessment_of_David_Hume_s_thoughts_on_personal_liberty, accessed 26 February 2021.

DuVernay, Ava (2016) '*13th*', Netflix documentary, released on 7 October 2016.

---

[8] Germany is perhaps unique in the extent to which it has acknowledged the Holocaust, even while some still wish to deny its occurrence.

Federal Convention of 1787, The Records of (1787) 3–5th, pp 2–57.

Fierke, Karin M. and Vivenne Jabri (2019) 'Global conversations: relationality, embodiment and power in the move towards global IR', *Global Constitutionalism* 8, 3, pp 506–35.

Gani, Jasmine K. (2017) 'The erasure of race: cosmopolitanism and the illusion of Kantian hospitality', *Millennium* 43, 3, pp 425–46.

Immerwahr, John (1992) 'Hume's revised racism', *Journal of the History of Ideas* 3, pp 481–6.

Ince, Onur Ulas (2018) 'Between commerce and empire: David Hume on slavery, political economy, and commercial incivility', *History of Political Thought* 39, 1, pp 107–34.

Kratochwil, Friedrich (2018) *Praxis: On Acting and Knowing* (Cambridge: Cambridge University Press).

Lepore, Jill (2018) *These Truths: A History of the United States* (London: W.W. Norton & Co.).

Ling, Lily H.M. (2013) *The Dao of World Politics: Towards a Post-Westphalian Worldist International Relations* (London: Routledge).

Meister, Robert (1999) 'Forgiving and forgetting: Lincoln and the politics of national recovery', in Carla A. Hesse and Robert Post (eds), *Human Rights in Political Transitions: Gettysburg to Bosnia* (New York: Zone Books), pp 135–76.

Muthu, Sankar, ed (2012) *Empire and Modern Political Thought* (Cambridge: Cambridge University Press).

Ndlova-Gatsheni, Sabelo J. (2018) *Epistemic Freedom in Africa* (London: Routledge).

Ngũgĩ wa Thiong'o (2009) *Something Torn and New: An African Renaissance* (New York: BasicCivitas).

Peskin, Victor (2005) 'Beyond victor's justice: the challenge of prosecuting the winners at the International Criminal Tribunals for the former Yugoslavia and Rwanda', *Journal of Human Rights* 4, 213–31.

Popkin, Richard H. (1980) 'Hume's racism', in Richard A. Watson and James E. Force (eds) *The High Road to Pyrrhonism* (San Diego, CA: Austin Hill Press), pp 251–66.

Sack, Harald (2018) 'You don't exist – says David Hume', *SciHi Blog*, available at: http://scihi.org/david-hume-philosophy-enlightenment/, accessed 21 June 2019.

Said, Edward (2003) *Orientalism* (25th anniversary edn) (London: Penguin Books).

Shilliam, Robbie (2018) *Race and the Undeserving Poor* (Newcastle: Agenda Publishing).

Smithsonian National Museum of African American History and Culture (2019) 'This deplorable entanglement', in *Slavery at Jefferson's Monticello: Paradox of Liberty*, available at: https://www.monticello.org/slavery-at-monticello/liberty-slavery/%E2%80%9C-deplorable-entanglement%E2%80%9D, accessed 20 June 2019.

Tickner, Arlene B. and Ole Wæver, eds (2009) *International Relations Scholarship Around the World* (London and New York: Routledge).

Waldman, Felix (2014) *Further Letters of David Hume* (Edinburgh: Edinburgh Bibliographical Society), pp 65–9.

Webster, Alison (2003) 'The contribution of the Scottish Enlightenment to the abandonment of the institution of slavery', *The European Legacy* 8, 4, 481–9.

Wendt, Alexander (2015) *Quantum Mind and Social Science* (Cambridge: Cambridge University Press).

Wiener, Antje (2018) *Contestation and Constitution of Norms in Global International Relations* (Cambridge: Cambridge University Press).

3

Friedrich Kratochwil:
Prophet of Doubt?

Cecelia Lynch

Introduction

Praxis fittingly brings together Friedrich Kratochwil's lifelong work and passion (! – I use the word passion despite Kratochwil's reliance on Hume, and later Arendt, to call for 'sober and cool' [Kratochwil, 2018: 475] analysis) for anti-theory, or more accurately, a 'meta-theoretical stance characterized by certain "ontological" assumptions concerning human actions – or praxis' (Kratochwil, 2018: 18). In this chapter, I call Kratochwil's stance a 'theology of action', and I refer to Kratochwil himself as a 'prophet of doubt'. Thus, the question mark in the title is not a reflection of my own argument but is instead directed to what Fritz himself might prefer, as he is unlikely ever to refer to himself as a prophet of anything.

I argue, nevertheless, that Kratochwil's elucidations – throughout his career and culminating in this volume – of the ills of social science theorizing, in particular their philosophical problems and historical inconsistencies, is very like the role of the prophet in Jewish, Christian and Islamic theologies.[1] Of course, it is necessary to state how I see that role and what validity I can claim for my stance. My own ongoing work on religion/secularism, tensions in Christian ethics, Muslim and Christian ethics in humanitarianism (vis-à-vis neoliberal and security pressures), and interpretation vis-à-vis post-colonial

---

[1]   In this chapter I address scholars of prophecy from Christian and Jewish traditions. Unfortunately, at this time I am not well enough versed in Islamic scholarship on prophecy, although Islam certainly venerates prophets, including Jesus but especially, of course, the Prophet Muhammad.

and racialized assumptions in the field of International Relations (IR) have required that I delve more into theology, decoloniality and particular social theory articulations of the ethical vis-à-vis the existence of precarity.[2] In addition, my work has taken me to religious studies and theology, which are two different disciplines that sometimes overlap in their debates but frequently deploy a critical stance towards each other. Both critical social theory and critical theology lead to an appreciation of the prophetic that moves away from the usual, 'secularized' understanding of the term. As a result, this chapter on Kratochwil's opus reflects issues that have arisen in my own investigations on practice over a period of time. It seems to me, moreover, that the task of examining the kinds of embeddedness and potential ruptures that the prophetic represents is all the more important given our contemporary pandemics: namely, ever accelerating climate change, the global disruptions of movement and social interaction due to COVID-19, and the troubling of historical and philosophical foundations and claims embodied in the growing recognition of anti-Black and anti-Indigenous racism.

Time, meaning and history

First, however, it is necessary to see how Kratochwil's work has continually troubled the grounds of 'grand theorizing' in the social sciences and especially in international relations. For Kratochwil (and many scholars of practice), one of the most significant problems resulting from the attempt to build grand theory concerns the insistence on taking concepts out of time and history. Such theorizing becomes delinked from contextualized meanings and therefore has no insightful meaning itself. It becomes one size fits all, leading to bad prognosis and bad predictions. Early on in *Praxis*, for example, Kratochwil expresses his shock at 'the lack of interest in "the messy details"' of political analysis. One contemporary example is how 'we are appalled by the [Russian] seizure of the Crimean Peninsula, although there had been large-scale military exercises the year before that provided a dry run' for the subsequent invasion (Kratochwil, 2018: 15). This is but one of numerous instances in which Kratochwil, insisting on the connection between praxis and immanence, emphasizes the importance of 'substantive problems in interdisciplinary work' (Kratochwil, 2018: 18) that are situated in time and place. Kratochwil rightly rejects 'the view from nowhere', also known as 'the end of history', or the possibility of a transcendent good outside of time and history.

---

[2] See Lynch (2020).

Exploring time and meaning requires an exploration of approaches to history. Kratochwil states that we need to understand the differences between 'a genuine historical understanding and prophetic understandings' of history. While both are inadequate – the former often presupposes a 'correct' interpretation of the past, without acknowledging the problems inherent in memory as well as interpretation itself – the latter, in this reading, results in a false belief in the ability to predict, based on the reading of dubious 'signs' (Kratochwil, 2018: 408). Pursuing the investigation of the problems of historical interpretation and the belief in the ability to predict, in turn, leads to an investigation of how we interpret and how norms and sociality develop; and such an examination leads especially to David Hume. I assert that each of these aspects of Kratochwil's investigations are critical for the field of IR. I also assert that his critique of prophecy applies not to the term itself or the traditions of which it forms a part in theological debate, but rather to the notion of 'false prophecy', which in Kratochwil's terms can be interpreted as the various teleologies of 'grand theorizing' in the field. This argument will be expanded later.

Kratochwil's Humean theology of action

Using Hume as his foil, Kratochwil develops the core of genuine (if we can use that term) constructivism. This is because Hume directs us to language and in particular to conventions, conjunctions and conversation. In other words, Hume directs us to look carefully at the bones as well as the meat of 'praxis', of what people do, what people expect from what they do and, hence, why what they do is meaningful. Hume also dismantles arguments in favour of Cartesian certainty as well as the ability to predict the future.[3] Kratochwil, in addition, uses Hume to move beyond formally discrete kinds of perspectivism, or what many call 'relativism':

> In a way, the merit of Hume's work is not only the realization that certainty and warranted knowledge cannot be grounded in the 'things' out there, or in the subject's reason, but also that even if such foundations are faulty, this does not mean that the skeptics are right and that *no knowledge* is possible. Here the notions of intersubjectivity and of participation in a common life-world attain their importance. Although we cannot reach the certainty we seek there either, *we*

---

[3] For a different take on the difficulties of prediction, including the tendency in the social sciences to engage in 'self-fulfilling prophecies', see Hellmann (2020). Hellmann discusses these difficulties by using Wittgenstein and the American pragmatist tradition, including James and Dewey, rather than Hume.

become aware that we no longer need such absolute foundations for our knowledge-warrants, because we can 'go on' and pursue our individual and collective projects in the face of an uncertainty we can live with. (Kratochwil, 2018: 361)

Instead, Kratochwil discusses criteria for judgement between competing norms and values and competing narratives of the past. Here he defers indefinitely any 'strong' criteria, that is, any enumeration of 'rights' or 'goods' to be attained, because establishing such criteria would itself violate his caution to understand the particularities of participation in any given historical time. This consistent deferral occasioned a great deal of discussion, perhaps some miscomprehension, and also pushback in the workshop that set this volume in motion. But from time to time, Kratochwil offers glimpses into what he sees as a better life; a better world; and even a more moral or ethical approach to politics. Part of what would constitute such a better world, of course, would be a wider recognition of the partiality of our knowledge, and the necessity of respecting pluralism. In addition, he suggests that such pluralism cannot be confined to Western modes of philosophizing. As he states in the book's first chapter, one of the most significant flaws in the interdisciplinary search for seductive visions of grand theorizing is taking 'for granted that the Western conceptual baggage is appropriate for providing orientation, even though it clearly prevents us from even seeing, or "naming," some of the fundamental ruptures that are occurring before our eyes' (Kratochwil, 2018: 15). A question that I return to in the conclusion, therefore, concerns *how far* to exit from the Western conceptual baggage, and whether Aristotle and Hume provide sufficient openings to do so or whether instead we need to move farther afield, outside Western-situated traditions of thought altogether.

Prophecy and doubt

When all (476 pages of text alone) is said and done, *Praxis* accords a fairly minor role to prophecy and prophets. When the terms do appear, however, Kratochwil deploys them to underscore the problems of static conceptions of time and a certainty in something called 'false religion', which includes the unthinking following of 'tradition' that easily becomes dangerous. Such an understanding is apparent, for example, in Kratochwil's references to these terms as well as his quotes from Hume's texts. The modern construction of the basis of political authority in contracts, for example, entailed the emancipation of politics and law 'from the sacred, or from a moral order that is based on tradition and its unproblematically accepted customs' (Kratochwil, 2018: 43). On page 357, tradition becomes 'a dead weight' that often engenders 'complacency'. Both 'false religion' and contemporary social science theorizing rely on 'seductive but highly problematic metaphors of a telos promising emancipation and redemption, rather than on actual analysis' (Kratochwil, 2018: 15). In each of these references, then, religion, prophecy and tradition equal unwarranted certainty, false confidence in unconditional prediction and static notions of ethics and morality; in contemporary modernity, they have become secularized into the ahistorical development of 'theory'. Later in the book (Kratochwil, 2018: 407–10), Kratochwil refines his critique by zeroing in on the temporal problems of prophecy vis-à-vis both the historian and the philosopher of history: all employ plots, but their functions differ. Philosophers of history, and especially prophets (unlike historians), interpret things and events as 'signs' to predict an inevitable (if still vague in terms of details) future. Here, Kratochwil calls into question both the assumption of an ability to see into the future (a problem of temporality) and what can flow from it – universalizing the audience of the prophet.

These are important refinements. Still, I assert that Kratochwil's understanding of prophecy, tradition and the role of the prophet in time and history is too thin, and I ask what difference that makes. While Kratochwil's usage reflects conventional 'secularized' understandings of religion and prophecy, these very understandings too often reduce 'religious' phenomena, actors and traditions to static caricatures. It would take me too far afield in this chapter to discuss all the literature that takes issue with such constructions, but suffice it to say that even Charles Taylor, whom Kratochwil cites more than once in *Praxis,* reads religious tradition to be an extremely dynamic enterprise (Taylor, 2007). Increasingly, students of religion (including myself), drawing on Taylor and others, think of religious traditions as 'living' and dynamic, not static repositories of past statements of dogma.[4] Talal Asad, from a different but partially complementary vantage point, argues in favour of centring the present in discussions of tradition: 'Questions about the internal temporal structure of tradition are obscured if we represent it as the inheritance of an unchanging cultural substance from the past' (Asad, 2003: 222). Cornel West, following Hans-Georg Gadamer and Edward Shils, goes even further, explicating tradition as an essential component of practice itself:

> Tradition per se is never a problem, but [the problem is] rather those traditions that have been and are hegemonic over other traditions. All that human beings basically have are traditions – those institutions and practices, values and sensibilities, stories and symbols, ideas and metaphors that shape human identities, attitudes, outlooks, and dispositions. These traditions are dynamic, malleable, and revisable,

---

[4] See, for example, Lynch (2009).

yet all changes in a tradition are done in light of some old or newly emerging tradition. (West, 1989: 230)

Thus, practice only happens in the midst of tradition(s), which can, in any particular case, be multiple and overlapping. An additional problem with Kratochwil's secularist view of tradition, in my reading, is related to his equally thin explanation of 'segmentation' and hierarchy in 'primitive societies' (Kratochwil, 2018: 62–9). I assert – again referring to Western philosophy's linear view of history and progress – that including such an exposition is unnecessary and actually detrimental to Kratochwil's overall argument, primarily because it assumes a problematic form of developmentalism (of societies) that goes against the grain of his search for pluralism and his position against grand theory. As it stands, such an explanation also connects to the ahistorical critique of the prophet and tradition, as well as of 'false' religion. Kratochwil's corpus rejects ahistoricity, a stance which he should, I assert, hold consistently, and which would, I believe, ultimately reject such a conceptually heavy but historically thin treatment of social worlds.

My concern with prophecy and its implications stems from an interest, which I share with Kratochwil, in critiquing ahistorical theory-building and ahistorical assumptions about politics that deny (unequal) relations of power. I am also interested in the limitations of what Kratochwil refers to as 'Western conceptual baggage'. Prophecy in this reading, of course, has little to do with the kinds of readings of signs or pay for play that often stand in for it. These kinds of readings are better represented in theological terms by the notion of 'false prophecy'. Instead, I draw here from the prolific theologian Walter Brueggemann's work on the 'prophetic imagination'. I then compare it with Michael Walzer's use of prophecy, Ian Shapiro's appreciation and critique of Walzer,[5] and Cornel West's notion of 'pragmatic prophecy', to inquire whether, and if so how, Kratochwil's commitment to pragmatism and my interest in the boundary-breaking potential of prophecy intersect and speak to ongoing debates in IR. I conclude with an assessment of Jason Springs's discussion of criteria for determining 'false prophecy', and Molly Cochran's early and more recent deployment of pragmatism to address puzzles in IR, in order to pose several questions for the ongoing assessment of practice.

For Brueggemann, who draws alternately on Flannery O'Connor and scholars of ancient Israel, prophecy is about cutting through the assumptions of ahistorical readings of the political that are perpetuated by established, dominant powers. These assumptions include, first and foremost, the idea

---

[5] I thank Fritz for noting the impact of the Walzer/Shapiro treatment of prophecy on his own thinking.

that such configurations of power, with the current kingdom in which the prophet finds herself enjoying a position of dominance, will last throughout historical time; that is, putting an end to history and suppressing any dissent. For example, in discussing the laments of Jeremiah, Brueggemann describes the context as one in which Solomon has established a royal regime of constant 'satiation', where 'all promises are reduced to tradable commodities' (Brueggemann, 2001: 33), and which 'is fed by a management mentality in which there are no mysteries to honor, only problems to be solved' (Brueggemann, 2001: 37). This royal satiation numbs the senses as well as the ability to develop a clear analysis of the arc of time and movement of history, finally prompting Jeremiah to cry out: 'Is there no balm in Gilead? Is there no physician there?' (Brueggemann, 2001: 50).

Brueggemann contrasts Solomon's leadership to that of Moses, who engaged in the 'praxis' of 'prophetic imagination': 'Prophetic imagination as it may be derived from Moses is concerned with matters political and social, but it is as intensely concerned with matters linguistic (how we say things) and epistemological (how we know what we know)' (Brueggemann, 2001: 1). Prophecy, then, concerns empirical observation, language and epistemological stance, all intimately connected to society and politics. Jeremiah's laments, while certainly poetic, are most of all grounded in participation in a particular historical time and place, as are the actions of Moses. Still, it is critical to understand the differences in situation in order to assess what kinds of action might respond to the prophet's trenchant analysis. 'Prophecy' entails reconfiguring the problem to meet extant conditions, while still recognizing a degree of indeterminacy in praxis, as Kratochwil's discussion of Rorty demonstrates (Kratochwil, 2018: 158–9).

Readers can at this point very likely see where this is going in relation to Kratochwil. Note, for example, Kratochwil's challenge to Waltz's assertions regarding the permanence of the bipolar configuration of power during the Cold War, or Keohane's frequent attempts to 'reign in' (pun intended) any methodology or ontology that does not square with his epistemological 'best practices'. Note also, of course, Kratochwil's constant unmasking of the empirical as well as epistemological and ontological problems inherent in both Waltz's and Keohane's ahistorical claims. Kratochwil's career took off (perhaps miraculously, given the constraints of the time) in the midst of the Waltzian satiation of IR theory, which, in combination with emergent neoliberal institutionalism, put to rest any philosophical 'mysteries' in favour of assessing the world purely as 'problems to be solved'. Kratochwil in *Praxis*, then, can be read as reaching the pinnacle of his own powers in taking on these certainties, representing an effective prophet of doubt for the field of IR and its static notions of social scientific and philosophical inquiry, just as Brueggemann reads Isaiah, Jeremiah and Micah as effective prophets who unsettled the politics and therefore praxis of their times.

From a more intellectual (or non-essentialized) theological stance, then, the role of the prophet is to name and cut through the false ontological and epistemological assumptions that undergird 'kings' and 'kingdoms', which portray themselves as invincible and outside history. I realize that Kratochwil's project is not that of the revolutionary activist who attempts to overthrow power in the interests of the oppressed. Brueggemann does not claim revolution as a goal in his discussion of Hebrew prophets, either. Nevertheless, Kratochwil's work in this volume as well as others across his career has opened spaces for many in the field of IR to do work that would otherwise not be possible. (I return to this point later in discussing the question of the prophet's audience.)

Kratochwil's prophecy of doubt vis-à-vis claims of epistemological certainty in IR has much in common with Michael Walzer's discussion of prophets as challengers to hegemonic power.[6] But there are also important differences, as Ian Shapiro (1990) and Jeffrey Stout (2001) show. Shapiro's discussion of Walzer's political theory points out that Walzer (like Brueggemann) focuses on the function of prophets in conducting 'immanent criticism of dominant ideologies' (Shapiro, 1990: 58). The prophet challenges dominance and especially hegemony (in this reading, 'based on various social characteristics: physical strength, familial reputation, religious or political office, landed wealth, capital, and technical knowledge', Shapiro, 1990: 58). Prophets, along with sages, storytellers, poets and other writers, are not inherently subversive characters in this reading. But the fact of dominance or hegemony itself, and the fact that such people are themselves carriers of 'the common culture' (Walzer, 1987: 40; quoted in Shapiro, 1990: 58), makes social criticism both possible and necessary.

Walzer's understanding of dominance is informed by Gramsci's notion of hegemony, but Walzer moves beyond Gramsci in emphasizing the communal requirements of immanent critique. Such critique takes place in the 'moral world', which for Walzer is not reducible to the social world (Walzer, 1987: 43, 46). Walzer's favourite prophet, Amos (considered one of the 12 'minor' prophets in terms of the brevity of the book in his name, addressing the period 760–755 BCE), lived under the rule of Kings Jeroboam II and Uzziah and was a contemporary of the better-known Isaiah. Amos, like many of the Hebrew prophets, condemned the hypocrisy of these elites, especially concerning the growing disparities of wealth

---

6   I focus in this section on Walzer's (1987) work, and especially Shapiro's (1990) detailed treatment of it in his *Political Criticism*, because they elucidate issues of particular concern to this chapter and to Kratochwil himself, who suggested them. However, Walzer also published *In God's Shadow: Politics and the Hebrew Bible,* in 2012, which includes his more expansive assessment of the authors and figures in the Hebrew Bible for the development of his political theory.

increasingly characteristic of ancient Israeli society. Amos demonstrates for Walzer that '[m]orality is always potentially subversive of class and power' (Shapiro,1990: 69). But this is only true if the prophet is ensconced in her community, which enables her to speak authoritatively of and from its traditions and values. The prophet can, therefore, deploy terms that make sense to the community to warn against immoral practices and advocate in favour of moral ones:

> Amos ... expressed his injunctions in terms the Israelites themselves embraced, so although we may be able to extract a minimal injunction from his teaching – such as 'do not oppress the poor' – his power and authority 'derives from his ability to say what oppression means, how it is experienced, in this time and place, and to explain how it is connected with other features of a shared social life'. (Walzer, 1987: 45, 89–91; also quoted in Shapiro, 1990: 69)

Similarly, Kratochwil's prophecy of doubt has affinities and differences with Cornel West's 'prophetic pragmatism', a concept which at first glance has the potential to unite the pragmatism that Kratochwil advances in his understanding of practice and the prophetic voice that the critic of hegemony exercises in articulating extant problems and conditions. West moves in a similar direction to Kratochwil, especially in their respective discussions of Richard Rorty. West also, however, grounds his perspective in the American pragmatist move away from conventional philosophy, from Ralph Waldo Emerson through John Dewey and W.E.B. DuBois. His characterization of this move is similar to what Kratochwil draws from Hume: 'The claim is that once one gives up on the search for foundations and the quest for certainty, human inquiry into truth and knowledge shifts to the social and communal circumstances under which persons can communicate and cooperate in the process of acquiring knowledge' (West, 1989: 213).

West, like Kratochwil, is concerned with moving democratic thought away from foundational systems of knowledge and ethics, but he genuflects much more strongly to Marx and, like Walzer, Gramsci, especially in his desire also to engage praxis in the service of economic justice. Prophetic pragmatism understands pragmatism (like Dewey)

> as a political form of cultural criticism and locates politics in the everyday experiences of ordinary people. Unlike Dewey, prophetic pragmatism promotes a more direct encounter with the Marxist tradition of social analysis. The emancipatory social experimentalism that sits at the center of prophetic pragmatic politics closely resembles the radical democratic elements of Marxist theory, yet its flexibility

shuns any dogmatic, a priori, or monistic pronouncements. (West, 1989: 213–14)

In addition, West wants to reformulate praxis by drawing on the rhetoric and creative ruptures represented by both W.E.B. DuBois and prophetic religious traditions in the service of racial justice. West thus agrees with Richard Rorty on the anti-foundational part of his endeavour but departs from him on the kinds of action needed for redressing injustices.

From West's perspective, prophecy has the potential to serve a stronger and more particular, if always dynamic, vision of justice and morality than it does for many other prophetic observers, one informed especially by the analysis of class, race and also gender. Indeed, West's understanding of both modernity and especially contemporary politics compels such an analysis: '[t]o write a masterful text of social theory and politics that does not so much as mention – God forbid, grapple with – forms of racial and gender subjugation in our time is inexcusable on political and theoretical grounds. To do so is to remain captive to a grand though flawed Eurocentric and patriarchal heritage' (West, 1989: 223). I return to this call in the conclusion.

False prophecy

Here, though, it is important to discuss how to distinguish between 'false' and 'genuine' prophecy. I argued previously that Kratochwil's dismissal of the term actually refers to what religious studies scholars and theologians call 'false prophecy'. It is not difficult to find examples of the hypocrisy of such false prophets: the public 'fall from grace' of Jerry Falwell, Jr (see Butler, 2020), or the unhinged rantings of QAnon, are only recent examples. But is it possible to determine criteria for such false prophecy? To think this through, I draw on Jason Springs's prescient discussion of prophetic pragmatism vis-à-vis false prophecy in articulating the critical role of 'moral imagination' in fostering 'healthy conflict', that is, productive debate about seemingly unresolvable contemporary issues (Springs, 2018). Springs systematically assesses the criteria developed by Abraham Joshua Heschel (2001; see Brandom, 2021), which is crucial for making the dual argument that Kratochwil's conception of prophecy rests on its 'false' (if frequently very public) variants, even as he acts as a prophet of doubt for the field of IR.

Springs, like Walzer, Brueggemann and West, sees the prophet as expressing justifiable 'moral outrage' at injustices perpetrated by hegemonic interests. But he also points out that anyone can express moral indignation, and that such expression is dangerous when coupled with claims of 'unassailable authority'. Building on the classic work of Heschel (also an important source for Brueggemann; Heschel was a friend and contemporary of Martin Luther King, Jr.), Springs lays out criteria by which we might judge false prophecy from the genuine article. First, the prophet/prophecy must be embedded in a particular problematic and historical context:

> On a prophetic pragmatist account, genuine rhetoric of prophetic indictment will always be caught up in what King, Heschel, and West demonstrate to be a broader and extended prophetic dialectic. The process of push and pull, resisting and succumbing, entails moral judgment, deliberative considerations, and self-correcting reflection. (Springs, 2018: 140–1)

Second, 'the prophet's experience, story, and personal development', particularly in connection with and response to the historical and contextual problems at stake, are key. Finally, and perhaps most importantly, the prophet holds herself accountable – she is not 'above the law', and she must provide persuasive reasons rooted in a thorough immersion in social norms and rules and the moral obligations they entail.[7]

The upshot here is that Kratochwil displays many of the characteristics of the prophet according to these contributions to religious studies and theological analysis. Kratochwil has consistently indicted the attempt to create 'grand theory' on the basis of a 'view from nowhere' that can never be attained. His own formation in philosophy, law and social theory provides the basis of his trenchant critiques, which he has developed and refined over time in response to critics as well as contextual political changes. Yet, as I argued before, he deploys the term prophecy inaccurately, although conventionally in a secularist sense, in the service of his otherwise prescient arguments regarding the philosophical and historical problems of the field of IR, as well as his warnings against the kinds of 'bad science' and bad scholarship that result from them. In doing so, he actually reads much more like the historical prophets and their functions than he realizes.

One might then ask whether it really matters that we understand prophecy in its theological sense, if Kratochwil's arguments about IR stand? There are two reasons to bring 'Kratochwil as the prophet of doubt' into play in this analysis. The first simply concerns disciplinary accuracy, which Kratochwil himself deploys so effectively vis-à-vis law and sociology in addition to 'international studies'. It is important, I assert, to accord disciplinary accuracy

---

[7] Springs (2018: 154) provides a careful exposition of how to move towards 'healthy conflict' on seemingly intractable issues, which is an enterprise to which I cannot unfortunately do full justice here (although his insights and model would clearly be apt for debates in IR and the social sciences!). For example, according to his discussion, it is arguable whether West at times has engaged in intemperate rhetoric that can 'be used to feed the invidiousness of political discourse more generally'; reasons and accountability can take a back seat to discourse that fuels negative forms of conflict.

to studies of religion and religious ethics as well as those of law and the social sciences. The second, however, allows an exploration into areas in which a theological exploration of prophecy versus praxis might illuminate important points about praxis and the possibility of ethics, for both Kratochwil in particular and IR in general.

Kratochwil, as is well known, draws on Hume in arguing for the necessity of grounding action/ praxis in the analysis of and participation in extant socio-historical conditions. Kratochwil's deployment of Hume also emphasizes the importance of 'imagination'. He explains that Hume 'sets against this project of certainty his philosophy of human nature and of the mind (rather than reason), in which "imagination" and "experience" are the most important elements' (Kratochwil, 2018: 352).

> This new perspective dramatically changed the role of philosophy, which no longer can pretend to stand outside of a common life, claiming an authority independent of all beliefs, customs, and even 'prejudices.' Instead, philosophy had to recognize its responsibility by not reflecting from the outside, taking social life as an object, but by realizing its purpose and potential as a critical voice *within* the institutionalized interactions and the discourses of a society on problems of common concern. Rather than looking for incontrovertible foundations, Hume suggests that since we always begin 'in the midst' of a concrete situation, we should systematically examine how we got here, what alternatives offer themselves, and how they are furthering or hindering the realization of our individual or collective projects. (Kratochwil, 2018: 352–3)

For Brueggemann, this 'critical voice within institutionalized interactions and the discourses of a society' is also the role of the prophet. It also returns us to the importance of seeing 'tradition' as related to custom in this sense, as a source of dynamic interpretation instead of unthought foundationalism. This relationship also calls into question the developmentalist ideas behind notions of 'primitive' societies that, too often, rely on early 20th-century anthropologizing constructions that have made numerous problematic and historically unsupportable assertions about 'difference'.

The prophet's 'universe'/to whom does the prophet speak?

Thus far, all of our students of prophecy agree that (a) the prophet's situation *within* institutional norms and practices enables her to speak creatively about their hypocritical deployment by hegemonic elites; (b) while prophets engage in creative ruptures of the status quo, they also draw back from pure utopianism, that is, prophets must deploy arguments that arise from and make sense in their contexts; and (c) prophets point to visions of the future while understanding the instability of the path. As Shapiro says of Walzer, '[n]o social good ever achieves perfect dominance, ... and herein lies the basis of social criticism' (Shapiro, 1990: 69).

One question, however, is whether there is room for manoeuvre in the prophet's audience. In other words, to whom does the prophet speak, and to whom should she speak? The basis of Shapiro's criticism of Walzer's notion of prophecy (and his political theory in general) is his strong linkage to community. Shapiro goes as far as to ask whether, in the end, the power of Walzer's prophets rests on 'autobiography':

Walzer conflates the distinction between universality and particularity in moral argument with the unrelated distinction between the emotional connectedness or disconnectedness of the social critic. It is possible to be a particularist with respect to the first of these distinctions, to believe that general moral and social theories should be eschewed because they invariably fail and are pernicious in a variety of ways, but to hold at the same time that the feelings and motivations of the social critic are irrelevant to the moral content of her social criticism. I will argue that this latter is the superior view. (Shapiro, 1990: 88)

Shapiro uses Walzer's discussion of French resisters Jean-Paul Sartre and Simone de Beauvoir versus Albert Camus to illustrate his point. Camus, for Walzer, remained tied to the *pied noir* French-Algerian community (he supported Algerians' civil rights but opposed separation from France) and therefore represents a more credible form of critique (and prophecy). Sartre and de Beauvoir, in contrast, condemned from afar in Paris, denouncing the French and, in the case of de Beauvoir, stating (after the 1958 referendum) that her links with her country were severed. Shapiro takes issue with Walzer here, pointing out that we have multiple affective ties, and that 'it seems pointless' to say that de Beauvoir's sentiments should rest with France instead of with Left revolutionary thought (Shapiro, 1990: 87), if the latter represents who she is and how she feels and judges the counter-revolutionary violence.

Kratochwil himself has an interesting discussion that connects to the question of the prophet's target audience (inter alia, he particularly notes the biblical problem of prophesying 'the future of all mankind' as a turning point in Isaiah, on page 408), but he also reformulates the problem, drawing on Abraham and Abraham's distinction between 'outward-looking' and 'inward-looking' approaches to practices. Kratochwil agrees with Abraham and Abraham that the 'inward-looking' approach, which takes the philosophical contributions of pragmatists more seriously by accepting that ' *"theorizing" is itself a practice*', represents 'a more serious engagement' with the pragmatist tradition. Kratochwil also points out, however, that this approach tends to 'recover in a Deweyan fashion the "vocation" of pragmatism, which "demands that we recognize our scholarship as political tools ... [which] are integral to the constitution of a global public"', and he questions whether this vocational aspect, as well as the turn to a 'global public', are necessary (Kratochwil, 2018: 426). Instead, for Kratochwil, it is 'at best an open question – in need of further vetting – whether the notion of a "global public" conceived analogously to the democratic public' is either 'a viable political goal' or a viable philosophical one.

For Brueggemann, 'the prophetic imagination', while definitely situated, still has the potential to carry beyond temporal and communal boundaries. Stout shows in detail how this can be so, providing a more robust and sophisticated analysis of four types of critical distance that prophecy/ social criticism may take while still avoiding the 'God's-eye view' or 'escape from history' (Stout, 2001: 325). For West, 'prophetic pragmatism' draws considerably on the American pragmatist tradition which, as Molly Cochran's work argues, provides a means to negotiate and move beyond the particularist/universalist divide (Cochran, 2000). This is done through a conceptual grounding that is 'as thoroughly antifoundationalist as possible' while blending (through a synthesis of Dewey, Rorty and feminist theory) a larger vision for pragmatic critique and moral action (Cochran, 2000: xix and *passim*).

Such an appeal to moral imagination is characteristic of American pragmatism as well as religious ideas of prophecy. It also begs the question, once again, of what kinds of action the prophet sees as warranted and necessary. As Cochran points out, '[t]he rub is in the doing' (Cochran, 2019: 10). In particular, does the prophet deploy imaginative critique to connect 'the messy details' of politics to concrete forms of action? Kratochwil frequently demurs, although West uses Gramsci as an example of 'concrete and detailed investigations' that 'are grounded in and reflections upon local struggles, yet [are] theoretically sensitive to structural dynamics and international phenomena' (West, 1989: 231). West and Cochran move in different ways towards notions of experimentation, both individual and institutional, always with the proviso that because human agency is fallible and inevitably produces unintended consequences, 'further inquiry', reflection and revision are constantly required. The question for practice is how much room for manoeuvre exists in Kratochwil's Humean notion of practice, i.e., between 'going on' through 'imagination and experience' and 'improvisation and doing things differently' to find 'alternatives' that 'further our individual and collective projects' (see previous quotes from *Praxis* as well as page 425).

As West argues, such imperfect and contingent action means that his notion of prophetic pragmatism relates to tragic thought (as well as romanticism): 'it confronts candidly individual and collective experiences of evil in individuals and institutions – with little expectation of ridding the world of *all* evil'. Such evils, moreover, are 'neither inevitable nor necessary but rather the results of human agency, i.e., choices and actions' (West, 1989: 288). Perhaps it is fitting, then, that Kratochwil turns to Homer in the final chapter of his tome on practice.

> Homer's story is not one with a single theme, or a record of how of one reaches one's goal via its sub-goals, in fulfilling a prophecy, or being able to chart a clear course. Rather it is an epic in which the various threads are woven together in order to show how the tapestry of a meaningful life emerges from the existential choices of a protagonist facing the existential problems presented to him. Therefore, it is far removed from providing instructions via codified 'best practices' but shows how one can rise to the occasion through judgment, imagination, and the experience gained by endurance and suffering, mastering thereby the challenges by one's wits, rather than by brute strength, or dumb luck. (Kratochwil, 2018: 470)

This passage not only accords in many ways with the kinds of situations in which Brueggemann's prophets find themselves but also enables us to see anew how it differs from the criteria for 'false' prophecy articulated by Heschel and Springs. It also returns us to the question of what kinds of practice/praxis are warranted in Kratochwil's prophecy of doubt. Kratochwil is clear that the social sciences have been (and, one can infer, will be in the future!) inhibited by their philosophical blinders (if they do not recognize them as such), and he speaks from what we all know to be one of the most in-depth stores of knowledge of political and legal philosophical traditions extant today. The question that many have put to Kratochwil in the past and continue to put in the present, however, is how to judge action in particular cases in the present – or, indeed, how to act at all. Kratochwil's moving final remarks, as well as indications throughout the book, illuminate flashes of 'hope' in a future that is less compromised by certainty and dubious commitments to ahistorical foundationalism, although his reference to Homer ties in primarily to his understanding of *eudaimia* via the creation of a meaningful life. Yet I also know from personal recollections that Kratochwil has acted in the face of academic injustices against both faculty and staff, on more than one occasion, which connects the meaningful life to broader, even political, action. In these ways, Kratochwil's work can be said to mirror the prophetic task of speaking from and for his community of social scientists. In general, Kratochwil's work and oeuvre cast doubt on the epistemological certainties of the present and its relations of power while offering glimpses, but not a full road map, into a 'politics of freedom' and a rediscovery of our humanity in the world.

Conclusion: Action and meaning in our common life

Such a recovery of our – and others' – humanity returns us to the necessity of exiting from 'Western conceptual baggage'. What might this mean for praxis, and for action in our world? Debates about religion and the 'non-West' raise such issues of time and history and also connect humanity in creative ways to the non-human. Is more of an exit from Western conceptual baggage – including not only epistemological errors but also the linear developmentalism regarding a purported move from 'the primitive' to the modern – critical and necessary to cope with *our* existential problems, both of theory and of maintaining the world we live in vis-à-vis climate disasters, racist brutalities (from chattel slavery to the present) and invisible but rampant and globalized disease? For West, as we have seen, taking issues such as gender and race seriously is critical for our examination of 'the concrete', even though he qualifies such inclusion as 'far from a guarantee for a credible progressive politics' (West, 1989: 233). Can, or should, Kratochwil's understanding of praxis ultimately lead us in these directions, too?

Kratochwil's prophecy of doubt, which aims 'to advocate a non-ideal analysis, based on the criticism of certain identifiable ills with which we become familiar through our participation in common life instead of a view from nowhere or imperative fiat' (Kratochwil, 2018: 428), is perhaps most similar to Brueggemann's characterization of Moses, both in terms of intent and implication. As Brueggemann states:

> I believe that Moses did not engage in anything like what we identify as social action. He was not engaged in a struggle to transform a regime, rather, his concern was with the consciousness that undergirded and made such a regime possible. ... I stress the point for two reasons: first because the prophetic purpose is much more radical than social change; and second because the issues that concern the Mosaic tradition are much more profound than the matters we usually regard as social action. (Brueggemann, 2001: 21)

Examining Kratochwil's oeuvre vis-à-vis the concept of prophecy raises critical questions for the ongoing exploration of praxis: the purpose and audience of the prophet, the conceptual versus material forms of action prescribed and the extent of 'Western' traditions for coping with the problems of our times. Kratochwil's position on these issues is, like that of the 'genuine' prophet, open to evaluation and assessment, and he has provided persuasive reasons for his indictment of much extant social theory without claiming 'unassailable authority'.

In the end, the overarching concern of Kratochwil's prophecy of doubt is 'with the consciousness that made' the regime of social theory possible, similar to Robert Brandom's assessment of Rorty as '*inter alia*, the prophet of a particular kind of emancipatory reflective reason' (Brandom, 2021: xxvi).[8] Perhaps it is then up to each of us to engage in the additional forms of individual and institutional experimentation and innovation – praxis – that might also be required of our times.

Acknowledgements

I especially want to thank Gunther Hellmann and Jason Springs, in addition to Fritz himself, for careful readings of this chapter.

References

Asad, Talal (2003) *Formations of the Secular: Christianity, Islam, Modernity* (Stanford, CA: Stanford University Press).

Brandom, R. (2021) 'Foreword', in Richard Rorty, *Pragmatism as Anti-Authoritarianism*, ed. by Eduardo Mendieta (Cambridge, MA: Harvard University Press), pp vii–xxvi.

Brueggemann, Walter (2001) *The Prophetic Imagination* (2nd edn) (Minneapolis, MN: Fortress Press).

Butler, Anthea (2020) 'Jerry Falwell, Jr.'s fall, Liberty University and the myth of the Moral Majority', *Religion News Service/RNS*, available at: https://religionnews.com/2020/08/27/jerry-falwell-jr-s-fall-liberty-university-and-the-myth-of-the-moral-majority/, accessed 26 February 2021.

Cochran, Molly (2000) *Normative Theory in International Relations: A Pragmatic Approach* (Cambridge: Cambridge University Press).

Cochran, Molly (2019) 'Keynote Address on Pragmatism and Nicholas Rengger's Anti-Pelagianism', St. Andrew's University, Scotland.

Hellmann, Gunther (2020) 'How to know the future – and the past (and how not): a pragmatist perspective on foresight and hindsight', in Ulrike Jasper, Myriam Dunn Cavelty and Andreas Wenger (eds), *The Politics and Science of Prevision* (New York: Routledge), pp 45–62.

Heschel. Abraham J. (2001) *The Prophets* (New York: Harper Perennial Modern Classics).

Kratochwil, Friedrich (2018) *Praxis: On Acting and Knowing* (Cambridge: Cambridge University Press).

Lynch, Cecelia (2009) 'A neo-Weberian approach to religion in international politics', *International Theory* 1, 3, pp 381–408.

---

[8] This is from the foreword to the English translation of Rorty's final book, *Pragmatism as Anti-Authoritarianism*, previously published only in Catalan and Spanish, which articulates Rorty's pragmatist project for a new Enlightenment. I thank Gunther Hellmann for this source.

Lynch, Cecelia (2020) *Wrestling with God: Ethical Precarity in Christianity and International Relations* (Cambridge: Cambridge University Press).

Shapiro, Ian (1990) *Political Criticism* (Berkeley and Los Angeles: University of California Press).

Springs, Jason A. (2018) *Healthy Conflict in Contemporary American Society: From Enemy to Adversary* (Cambridge: Cambridge University Press).

Stout, Jeffrey (2001) 'Walzer on exodus and prophecy', in Ted M. Vial and Mark A. Hadley (eds), *Ethical Monotheism, Past and Present: Essays in Honor of Wendell S. Dietrich* (Providence, RI: Brown Judaic Studies), pp 307–38.

Taylor, Charles. (2007) *A Secular Age* (Cambridge, MA: Harvard University Press).

Walzer, Michael (1987) *Interpretation and Social Criticism* (Cambridge, MA: Harvard University Press).

Walzer, Michael (2012) *In God's Shadow: Politics and the Hebrew Bible* (New Haven, CT: Yale University Press).

West, Cornel (1989) *The American Evasion of Philosophy: A Genealogy of Pragmatism* (London: Macmillan).

4

Styles of Theorizing International Practice

Christian Bueger

Introduction

What do we mean by theory and how is it related to practice? The question has been one of the recurrent themes for negotiating the identity of the discipline of International Relations (IR). Debates concern what kind of knowledge scholars should produce and value, what should count as 'theory' and 'empirics', but also what status is granted to those that 'make' theory and those that focus on 'practice'. While these debates run through the history of the discipline, three recent developments have given them impetus.

A landmark debate in the *European Journal of International Relations* in 2013 explored whether the age of theory in IR had ended. Scholars asked whether they had witnessed a 'retreat from theory' (Dunne et al, 2013: 406), mourned the end of unifying grand theory that would order the discipline (Mearsheimer and Walt, 2013), and were worried about the proliferation of theories and naive hypothesis testing (Guzzini, 2013; Jackson and Nexon, 2013). The discovery of non-Western IR and theory from the Global South brought another source of discomfort to the discipline. The potential of post-colonial forms of knowledge cast new doubt on the extent and limitations of Western epistemology and its concepts of theory (see Acharya and Buzan, 2010; Shilliam, 2010; Seth, 2011). Yet the emergence of a movement of scholars associated with 'international practice theory' also called for new thinking on theory and for grounding it in practice (Adler and Pouliot, 2011; Bueger and Gadinger, 2018). In declaring 'practice' as the foundational unit of theoretical thought, they re-raised the tension between theory and practice in new ways.

The triple uncertainty over theory opens a new moment to rethink the making of theory in IR. Taking insights from these three debates into account, this chapter asks whether and how practice theories lead to new, innovative thoughts on 'theory' and the relation to practice. The mere label of 'practice theory' is interesting: it brings together two terms which are often seen as dichotomous or at least are keenly kept apart. How does practice theory open the space for rethinking the relation? As I seek to show, various innovative 'styles' of theorizing have become formulated that merge theory and practice in interesting new ways. In discussing these, my objective is to add to the more general debates on how to reconceptualize theory in IR. But I also intend to offer some insights for those primarily concerned about practice theory, considering that more has been written on the concept of 'practice' than about 'theory'. While ontological vocabularies are now well advanced, as is the methodological discourse, too little attention has been placed on how one theorizes with practice theory.

The argument proceeds as follows. I first review the new moment of theoretical uncertainty across disciplines and discuss the positions that practice theorists take in regard to theory. I argue that some of them promise innovation as they transform our understanding of theory substantially by shifting emphasis to process and activities. They foreground the creative acts of *making* theory and the 'practice of theorizing' gains centre stage. Such a move might be productive since it collapses or dissolves the dichotomy of theory and practice. It also opens up new discussions of the relation between theory making and other scholarly and non-scholarly practices.

I then continue to interrogate the contemporary practice theory debate to identify different 'styles of theorizing'. By a style of theorizing, I refer to a particular way of merging theory and practice. I detect four styles of theorizing practice distinguished by two axes: firstly, the site in which theorizing is situated (library vs field), and secondly, whether order or messiness is prioritized (generalization vs singularization). This leads to four styles: 'mechanism', 'meditation', 'method' and 'experimentation'. I discuss paradigmatic exemplars of each style. Thinking with and through such styles in the conduct of research allows for more reflexivity on what our research practices add up to. They also provide new points of orientation for newcomers to the practice of theorizing.

The new theoretical uncertainty

Given that 'theory' is one of the core concepts of social science, it was always under debate. Yet discussions significantly intensified in the past decade. Across the social sciences there is a visible new uncertainty over the meaning and status of the concept. Uncertainty prevails not only in IR but also in its neighbouring disciplines. Paying attention to the debates in sociology and anthropology is insightful, as these have articulated many of the new uncertainties and opportunities much more forcefully. Scholars increasingly question what is meant by theory, if it should be the core objective and ultimately the gold standard of academic work, but also how it relates to 'empirics' and 'practice' more broadly.

Gradually scholars began to recognize that the concept of theory is much more contested than is often assumed. Usage of the concept differs substantially and, hence, it has a high level of ambiguity and polysemy. Dunne et al (2013: 406) cite Robert Merton (1967), who was already noting the problematic diversity of understandings of theory. In sociology, Gabriel Abend (2008: 174) has shown perhaps most forcefully the polysemy of theory, or what he calls the 'semantic confusion' around the term. Martin (2015) and Swedberg (2017) make similar observations and stress the multiplicity of meaning of theory. In IR, for instance, Dunne et al (2013: 407–12) have documented such plurality and suggested five different 'types' of theories: explanatory, critical, normative, constitutive theory and theory as a 'lens'.

Within sociological debates there have been strong calls to disassociate theory from the work of classical theorists. We should not equate theory with the work of a mastermind, they argue. Not only classic 'theorists' have theory. Equating theory with masters, whether that is Max Weber, Talcott Parsons and Niklas Luhmann in sociology, or Kenneth Waltz and Alexander Wendt in IR, is problematic; it distracts from how theory is actually made and done (Lizardo, 2014; Martin, 2015; Swedberg, 2017). Furthermore, the status attribution that comes along with the label of theorist is a concern. As Omar Lizardo (2014: 3) phrases it, 'one of the grave dangers ... today is the continuing survival of an approach to theory that conceives of the theory field as an "aristocracy of theorists" ruling over mere empirical under-laborers. From this perspective, theory is something that is done by a select few who have a special vision; they are only discovered, never made.'

Yet the counter-tendency appears equally troublesome, that is, when proliferation occurs. Scholars increasingly tend towards making their own theories, rather than relying on a range of classic grand theories. In IR, Dunne et al (2013) see the proliferation of theories and the resulting plurality as highly problematic and call for an integrated pluralism that can avoid too much fragmentation and enables cross-theory conversations. Martin (2015) criticizes pluralism for its tendency that in order to make a career, a scholar is supposed to have her own theory. This may lead to the proliferation of verification, rather than falsification, as scholars need to prove that their theory got it right.

One origin for inappropriate theory building might be found in the increasing tendency of the social sciences to turn to method; while method sophistication is growing, theory literacy seems to be in decline. As Richard

Swedberg (2014: 1) notes, 'sociologists and other social scientists are today very methodologically competent, but considerably less skilful in the way they handle theory'. Mearsheimer and Walt (2013: 428) diagnose similar trends for IR when they suggest that the number of scholars that pay serious attention to theory is in decline, while the focus on quantitative methods and 'simplistic hypothesis testing' is on the rise. Yet it is not only the turn to methods, but also new ideas that scholars should prioritize (mathematical) models over theory (Clarke and Primo, 2012), should 'return to the empirical' (Adkins and Lury, 2009: 5) or focus on descriptivism enabled by the age of big data (Savage, 2009; Burrows and Savage, 2014), that lead to concerns over the status of theory.

In anthropology, likewise, there is a new debate on theory that adds the crucial importance of place (Harrison, 2016, 2017). Scholars such as Arturo Escobar (2008: 285), for instance, speak of a new 'theoretical moment'. As Harrison (2017: 28) summarizes this argument, 'there is an expansion of the space and, thereby, a multiplication of the sites (along with the networks in between them), where various modes and forms of theorizing take place and are being claimed and acknowledged as such.' This leads to the 'creation of more decentralized and decolonized conditions' of making theory and forms of knowledge beyond northern epistemologies (Harrison, 2017: 28). 'Ex-centric' sites of theory and knowledge production come to the fore (Harrison, 2016). Southern scholarship leaves the periphery and moves to the centre. Similar movement and moments have emerged in IR. Received notions of theory and epistemologies have become challenged by debates on non-Western IR, Worlding Beyond the West and post-colonialism (see Acharya and Buzan, 2010; Shilliam, 2010; Seth, 2011). Together they highlight the geospatial dimension of theory production, question that theory is only produced in the West and argue for incorporating other forms into the canon of IR.

In the following, I discuss the responses of 'practice theory' to the new uncertainty. This is to show what new avenues practice theorizers provide and hence to provoke some mental stimulation for those interested or planning to engage in practice theorizing. Much discussion on 'practice' and adjunct concepts has taken place, but less on the meaning of theory.[1]

The practice turn's 'theory debate'

'Theories of practice' and the broader 'practice turn' are widely recognized as one of the core recent innovations in social science. The 'turn' was triggered

---

[1] For other discussions of theory in IR's practice turn, see Grimmel and Hellmann (2019) and Hofius (2020).

by the critique that too much of cultural theorizing had abandoned action and overemphasized linguistic structure or belief, while not adequately considering the 'mundane' and 'everyday' or the importance of material objects and infrastructures (Drieschova and Bueger, 2021). Hardly any of the social sciences have been left untouched by this call for centring in 'practice'. Advocates for turning to practice, however, did not claim to introduce a new grand theory. Built on pluralist grounds, they agree that there is no unified or consistent 'practice theory', but rather a collective of theories and approaches with family resemblance that share a range of commitments (see Reckwitz, 2002; Adler and Pouliot, 2011; Bueger and Gadinger, 2018). Such diversity is seen as the strength of practice theories, as it makes them adaptable and sensitive.

The mere label of 'practice theory' combines two terms often seen as opposites. Friedrich Kratochwil (2011), for instance, has pointed out that the label is an oxymoron: there cannot be a theory *of* practice, since practice is contingent and varied across context, while theory stands for the generic and context-independent. While this argument is a bit more complex, as will be shown later in the chapter, Kratochwil's warning stresses the considerable tension built into the practice theoretical debate. Indeed, practice theories have not escaped the new theoretical uncertainty. While this is a gross simplification, and not everyone will agree with this, practice theorists advance the following three positions.

A first position is concerned with rescuing received notions of (grand) theory: scholars continue to work out comprehensive theories and then apply them. Practice theorists such as Pierre Bourdieu, Andreas Reckwitz or Theodore Schatzki arguably pursue a project of developing a logically consistent general vocabulary of practice, and a substantial number of researchers intend to apply their insights. A second position indicates the opposite route. Embracing romantic ideas of authenticity and distinctiveness, 'abandoners' suggest that, insofar as there is no 'general' and 'universal', the notion of theory is unproductive and energy is better invested in describing and analysing the particularity of practice. They call for giving up any substantial notion of theory and argue that if scholarship is interested in the more general at all, then it is the descriptivist search for patterns. This position can be associated with those naively drawing on the dictum 'to just follow the actors', advocating for 'grounded theory' or other forms of empiricism.

The third position, which I shall discuss in more detail, aims at redefining what we mean by theory. Appreciating many ideas developed by the abandoners, 'transformers' nonetheless suggest continuing to operate with and claim a concept of theory. They argue for a re-evaluation of what kind of mental tools and what kind of epistemic work we associate with the term. Scholars such as Isabel Stengers or Bruno Latour return to foundational moments of Western science, while others rely on American pragmatism or non-Western epistemologies, or they base their reasoning in the observation of scholarly practices, taking a more inductive stance that investigates what scholars do when they make theory. Overall, the tenet is to fundamentally challenge the theory–empirics distinction. Scholars entangle themselves in practice not only in aiming at developing theory from within practice, but in understanding theorizing equally as a practice.

My interest in the following is to further elaborate on the position of the transformers. These invite us to understand theorizing as activity. In the next section I lay out some basic considerations on understanding theorizing as a practice.

Theorizing: some basic considerations and themes

What unites the transformers is the idea of shifting from theory to the practice of 'theorizing'. Scholars across the social sciences have made significant efforts to argue for such a move. 'To focus mainly on theory, which is typically done today, means that the ways in which a theory is actually produced are often neglected', argues Swedberg (2014: 1). According to Lizardo (2014: 3), 'we should begin to move away from our obsession with theory as a finished product or as canon of works and towards a conception of theorizing as a creative activity'. In IR, Guzzini (2013) has perhaps made this point most profoundly in arguing that we should shift to discussing 'modes of theorizing' and how they establish different relations to the world. As the anthropologist Harrison sums up the move,

> contrary to traditional thinking, theory has a symbiotic and dialectical rather than a dichotomous relationship to practice. Theory and practice are inextricably interrelated and mutually reinforcing modes of social practice. This approach propels a shift from a focus on a valorization of theory as textualized product to 'theorizing' as a form of creative work performed in diverse dialogic contexts. (Harrison, 2016: 172)

The shift to the verb and the valuation of the actual 'work' required to produce theory has substantial consequences: it suggests the need to de-centre the individual mind and understand theory as a collective achievement situated in a distinct milieu and locale; to focus on process and actions, rather than the object ('the theory'); to grasp the practical knowledge, various skills, material resources and artefacts that are assembled in the production of theory; and to recognize the multiplicity of forms or styles of theorizing.

It shifts focus away from epistemology, towards a richer understanding of science as practice. For Isabel Stengers (2000: 107), for instance, we need 'to refer the question of theory, not to a question of its epistemological status, but to the sciences as collective practices, and to avoid any epistemological opposition between a "true theory", a legitimate theory, and an "ideological" theoretical claim.' As Stengers highlights, theorizing is a collective process and cannot be appropriately grasped from an individualist perspective. Any theorizer – a subject engaged in the practice of theorizing – works always in relation to and with others, even if those relations are only made within reading and referencing practices or by using preconceived concepts and tools (Knorr-Cetina, 2014: 43; Reed and Zaid, 2014).

The move to practices is also liberating as it shifts emphasis away from a concept of theorizing as following standardized general rules (of abstraction or generalization) towards a non-technical, more open, productive, creative, intuitionist or even affective understanding. Theorizing becomes a generative activity of revealing, making perceptible, and of nurturing and caring for particular phenomena, collectives or objects. As argued, for instance, by Annemarie Mol,

> a 'theory' is something that helps scholars to attune to the world, to see and hear and feel and taste it. Indeed, to appreciate it. ... A theory helps to tell cases, draw contrasts, articulate silent layers, turn questions upside down, focus on the unexpected, add to one's sensitivities, propose new terms, and shift stories from one context to an-other. (Mol, 2010: 262)

Making such moves also opens up the possibility of drawing on practice theory to understand theorizing. This clarifies that even under the new openness, rules will still matter, yet tacit knowledge and forms of recognizing the practice of theorizing equally do. Drawing on Schatzki's (1996: 89) definition of practice, theorizing involves doing and saying, such as the articulation of statements recognized as 'theoretical'. But it also involves practical understandings, such as those standards of competence through which a practice is evaluated and by which acts are recognized as good theorizing.

Finally, theorizing also implies skills and tacit knowledge. Knorr-Cetina (2014), for instance, refers to intuitions and the use of tools and concepts a researcher learns via exposure to the state of the art of a discipline. Swedberg (2017: 191) likewise refers to theorizing as a craft and suggests that 'to theorize well, sociologists need to have practical knowledge of how to handle theory'. Yet more formal rules also matter for practices, such as the explicit standards formulated in philosophical trainings, textbooks or the more practical standards that Klein (2014), Weick (2014) or Swedberg (2017) call for.

Interrogating theorizing as a practice provides us with new concepts and categories of what is involved and at stake in performing theorizing. It clarifies that theory includes various actions and that tacit knowledge and practical understandings matter, as do explicit rules.

Relationalist theories of practice provide an important addition. Following actor-network theory advocates, such as Bruno Latour, Annemarie Mol or John Law, theorizing can be understood as an attempt to produce universals out of particulars. For Law (2004) this implies that theorizing is an act of arranging mess so that a particular order (universal) emerges. A universal, in turn, should not be understood as transcendental, but rather as an epistemic object that is able to travel. In Latour's (1987) words, theory can be understood as an 'immutable mobile', that is, an object that has the capacity to maintain a degree of stability across different contexts and places. It is immutable in the sense that it has achieved a certain degree of stability and coherence, so it can become mobile, that is, transferable to other situations. The immutable mobile is both particular in that it only becomes stable by having formed relations in particular situations, and general in that it becomes transferable across contexts. As Latour argues, producing such an immutable mobile requires considerable work and different actors and objects to act concertedly.

For Latour and others, acts of theorizing are flows, circulations and movements through which objects, activities and statements become related to each other and relations become more and more stable and coherent. Theorizing is then building relations that last. It is the fabricating of universals and immutable mobiles that can traverse context. Theorizing is dependent on various other practices, and it requires one to produce a collective which becomes inscribed in the theory and is interested in maintaining and nurturing it. In summary, to think of theorizing as a practice, we need to consider it as an activity, that is, creative, collective, situated, organized by tacit knowledge, emotions and normative understandings, and concerned about the production of immutable mobiles. While analytically it can be isolated from others, theorizing is always embedded in particular situations and related to other practices and collectives.

Styles of theorizing practice

Drawing on the previous sketch of theorizing as a creative, intuitive attempt to build relations that last, the goal of this section is to derive ideal types in conversation with a number of theorizers of practice. This is to appreciate that within the transformer movement quite different ideas of how to theorize have emerged. I shall call such ideal types 'styles of theorizing', borrowing from Ian Hacking (1992) and Chunglin Kwa (2011).

Two basic categories are particularly apt for grasping different styles of theorizing practice: 'locale' and 'purpose'. By locale I refer to the sites, places and arrangements from within which theorizing takes place. While in one way or the other all practice theorizers seem to claim that they initiate theorizing in the 'midst of practices' or from a 'problematic situation', how the theorizing subject is actually situated differs substantially. As the major differentiation we can take the degree to which a theorizer relies on mediated experiences and received textual representations of practices or draws on immediate experience gained through proximity to practice in the form of bodily exposure, direct observations, unmediated learning and training and other forms of participating in a practice.[2]

The first subcategory we can label *library research* (Abbott, 2014). Theorizing relies here on 'found data', whether in physical or digital form, and the main sites of theorizing are the archive, the library or the desk. Many of the data that theorizers rely on will not have been created with the purpose of practice research or even research in mind. The majority of such data will come in some well-ordered form. Whether these are bureaucratic records, letters, a diplomatic cable or scholarly works, these texts are structured and written according to organizing principles. The second subcategory is *field research*. Although the term 'field', and some of the associated assumptions, have increasingly evoked criticism in anthropology and political science (Bueger, 2021), it is a useful denomination to describe those theorizers which rely on 'lived data' produced in proximity to practice. Such data might be fabricated through interviews and conversations, *in situ* observations or attempts to acquire and participate in a practice, for instance by conducting 'auto-ethnography'.[3] Library research hence implies interpreting found data for practice theoretical purposes, while field research faces the challenge of how to produce such data by translating practice theoretical concepts. Library research, in contrast to field research, allows for and often implies making claims on grander temporal and spatial scales, since texts are often already aggregated data. Historical and broad comparative research across scale is hardly possible from a field research position.

The second category is 'purpose', and here I refer to the ambition of theorizing to produce 'order'. While some theorizers have the motivation to work out and (re)produce the orderliness of practice through generalization, others argue that given the messiness of practice, any attempt to produce order through scholarly analysis increases messiness rather than reducing it.[4] By *generalization* I refer to the more or less ambitious attempts to produce concepts and statements which are seen as transferable independently from context and scale. They aim at producing figurations that can act as immutable mobiles and traverse context, time and space. By *singularization* I refer to those forms of theorizing that have the ambition to work out the specificities of a situation and represent its messiness. This might be

---

[2]   'Textual' representations might include visual documents, paintings, recordings or videos.

[3]   See, for instance, Merit Müller's (2018) auto-ethnography of ballet practices.

[4]   As discussed, for instance, by Law (2004).

Table 4.1: Styles of theorizing practice

		Purpose	
		Order and generalization	*Mess and singularization*
Locale	*Library*	'Mechanism'	'Meditation'
	Field	'Method'	'Experiment'

by studying the effect of a singular 'event', such as the invention of a new concept or technology, or an analysis of a particular action context, problematic situation or practical figuration and the requirements they spur. For the generalizers the purpose of theorizing lies much more in producing order, while the singularizer will often aim at disrupting and destabilizing taken-for-granted orders by showing how things could be otherwise, or by introducing and adding new concepts and elements to a context. In consequence, the scholarly arguments presented by the singularizer often will be about the mode of theorizing, rather than the form, in the sense that the objects produced and 'added' will not necessarily have any meaning outside the context or figuration that is studied.

These categories and subcategories provide us with four ideal types that form a useful heuristic to work out different styles of theorizing. They can be brought together in a graph, which is presented in Table 4.1. As with any other ideal typification, this has obvious limits. For instance, it would be hard to put a particular theorizer, such as Michel Foucault,[5] in any of the four boxes, as throughout his career he has moved between those boxes a great deal. My goal here is not to provide neat boxes so we can sort out and in scholarly work, but to provide orientation and a tool to trigger reflection for students of practice to consider how they have been practising or want to practice theorizing. In the following section I further flesh out each of the styles in conversation with selected practice theorizers. As Table 4.1 shows, each of the four styles congregates around a particular concept, that of mechanisms, meditation, method or experiment.

Exploring some exemplars

The following thoughts draw on a selective reading of recent practice theoretical works and how these deal with the problem of theory and practice. They present interesting instances of the categories discussed earlier.

---

[5]   Assuming that he can indeed be read as a practice theorizer; see Bueger and Gadinger (2018).

As my discussion reveals, there is also an indication that we might have not paid adequate attention to the fourth type, that is, the experimental style. I shall start with a discussion of library researchers and then address those theorizing in the field.

Two recent practice theoretical books can be read as two exponents of theorizing in the library. Emanuel Adler's (2019) *World Ordering: A Social Theory of Cognitive Evolution* already carries the concepts of order and theory in the title and will be read here as an example of a style of theorizing that I shall call 'mechanism'. Friedrich Kratochwil's (2018) *Praxis: On Acting and Knowing* is, as the back cover states, 'devoted to theory building'. It serves as an example of a style that I describe as 'meditation'. Both books rely exclusively on found data.

Mechanism

While there are many varieties in what is meant by 'mechanism' (Levy, 2013), contemporary philosophers of science have described it as particular arrangements of parts. As Glennan and Illari (2018: 92) define it, 'a mechanism for a phenomenon consists of entities (or parts) whose activities and interactions are organized so as to be responsible for the phenomenon'. According to this understanding, known as the 'new mechanics', mechanisms have a number of features. They produce, underlie or maintain a particular phenomenon, that is, they do things; they have a certain kind of regularity, yet they are not necessarily deterministic, as parts of the mechanism might interfere or break down (Glennan and Illari, 2018; Craver and Tabery, 2019). Mechanisms are processes and may be incomplete. While an understanding of theorizing as designing mechanisms brings us closer to projects that aim to rescue general theory and might be misunderstood as such, mechanisms are always tied to the particular phenomena that they produce.

The mechanisms that Adler's *World Ordering* is interested in are those that produce the phenomenon of change in orders. He describes such changes as cognitive evolution, suggesting that such a viewpoint can bring both change and stability simultaneously into focus. He gives a concise outline of the parts he arranges that produce the phenomenon of evolution when he writes that 'social orders originate, derive from, and are constituted constantly by practices, the background knowledge bound with them, and the communities of practice that serve as their vehicles' (Adler, 2019: 2). In a second statement, his ambition to outline mechanism comes even stronger to the fore.

Cognitive evolution theory claims that practices and the background knowledge bound with them are the structural 'stuff' that is passed on in replication in the sociocultural world, that communities of practice are their vehicle, and that practices account for both the consecutive and simultaneous change and metastability of social orders in general, and of international social orders in particular. (Adler, 2019: 3)

In the book Adler first puts in considerable work to capture this 'stuff', that is, the key components of 'practice', 'background knowledge' and 'community of practice'. He then sets out to describe how they hang together in mechanisms, alluding to evolution selection, meaning fixation and what he coins a 'master mechanism': epistemic practical authority (Adler, 2019: 3). Altogether he outlines seven mechanisms of how the parts hang together (Adler, 2019: 4).

As these quotes indicate, Adler is interested in generalizing, and he does so by working out mechanisms that explain a particular phenomenon, that is, the evolution of orders. How do data on practices feature in this process of theorizing? While primarily conducting conceptual work, in reconstructing mechanisms Adler continually draws reconstructions of practices into the discussion, such as those that order the European Union or cyberspace.

Meditation

Kratochwil's *Praxis*, in contrast, is less concerned about generalization and order; instead of laying out mechanisms and parts, his style is more concerned about process and tinkering. Meditation is a suitable description of such a style. Paul Rabinow (2003) provides a useful reconstruction of what is at stake when he lays out how Foucault conceived of meditation as one of the essential modes of knowing and caring (contrasted with memory and method). As Rabinow (2003: 8) suggests, 'in the late antique world, meditation differed profoundly ... from today'. If today's understanding 'carries the connotation of either an attention to inward states or of attempts to empty the mind', meditation in the antique was an exercise of thought that 'prepared one for the lifelong battle against external events' (2003: 8, 9). These exercises, Rabinow (2003: 10) argues, required the elaboration of a 'tool chest' which would aid one in accomplishing the 'complex task of facing the future'. For Rabinow (2003: 10) meditation hence implies the elaboration of tools in order 'to have them ready when needed'.

In *Praxis*, Kratochwil continues a style of theorizing – or 'mode of thinking', as he calls it (Kratochwil, 2019) – that he described in his previous book as meditation (Kratochwil, 2014). Similar to Rabinow, his quest is to elaborate tools for the 'battles' of the future, which he describes as situations of action, or as 'praxis'. Praxis is the conceptual workhorse in these meditations. In situations of praxis, theorizing and other practices come together (see Hellmann, Chapter 5, this volume). Contrary to Rabinow, Kratochwil situates his meditations in particular disputes that have revolved around problems of praxis. He spends considerable energy in his meditations to question and disrupt prevailing and received tools, above all concepts of (ideal) theory. His goal is to disorder in order to forge new but loose connections responsive to situations of praxis (see Wiener, Chapter 13, this volume). To do so he establishes particular relationships to the reader. Following along the lines of Francis Bacon's aphoristic writing style, he forces one to think with him and leaves many of the consequences of his meditations to the reader's own interpretation. The reader has to actively participate, allowing her to add interpretation and meaning. *Praxis* is not only *about* praxis. Reading Kratochwil is itself a situation of praxis and a singular event.

As Mathias Albert (Chapter 11, this volume) remarks, in taking this course, and aiming at examining the 'silent and not so silent pre-suppositions of thought' (Kratochwil, 2018: 392), Kratochwil develops an understanding of theory that can illuminate praxis. It is an approach that does not provide answers but widens our understanding of topics (Brown, Chapter 6, this volume).

Method

In contrast to library workers, field workers situate themselves in a field of practice. They rely on data that they gain through observation and participation. The majority of current practice researchers in IR seek proximity in such a way and intend to theorize from the field. This has led to two styles: one in which method translates between theorizing and the practices studied, and another that is more creative and experimentalist and implies not only participation, but also intervention in a practice.

The methods style looks to anthropology and the ethnographic spectrum of methods. It sprang directly from the methods debate in the practice turn.[6] The core argument here is that theory and methods form tight packages, as most profoundly expressed by Davide Nicolini (2017). For him, practice theory provides 'a set of concepts (a theoretical vocabulary) and a conceptual grammar (how to link these concepts in a meaningful way) that allows us to generate descriptions' (Nicolini, 2017: 24). It provides a way to allow 'the world to speak through it' (Nicolini, 2017: 25). For the methods style, 'practice theory is not a theoretical project (in the traditional sense), but a methodological orientation supported by a new vocabulary' (Nicolini, 2017: 25).

In IR, spearheaded by Iver Neumann's work on diplomatic practice, participant observation emerged as the gold standard for practice researchers.

---

[6] See Pouliot (2013, 2014), Bueger (2014) and the contributions in Jonas et al (2017).

The argument here is that practices need to be studied as they are performed in real time. Participant observation allows for the recording of bodily movements and the capturing of activities that do not entail speech (Bueger, 2014: 399). Only this would allow one to reconstruct practices and their organization, and hence in turn to theorize them. Yet, in reality, the majority of IR researchers admit that participant observation is too demanding and difficult (Pouliot, 2013). In consequence, the discourse turned towards what kind of reconstructions are possible from qualitative interviews, or the study of texts and other artefacts (Pouliot, 2013; Bueger and Gadinger, 2018: chapter 6).

In a recent study paradigmatic of the methods style, Adler-Nissen and Drieschova (2019a) set out to study how technology affects the practice of diplomacy. Claiming to rely on an 'inductive methodology', they blend participant observation, the analysis of textual artefacts (draft diplomatic agreements) and interviews with diplomats (Adler-Nissen and Drieschova, 2019a: 536). The study describes in detail how European Union diplomats in Brussels use the 'track change' function to negotiate documents. They claim that 'more general patterns' are identifiable (Adler-Nissen and Drieschova, 2019a: 536). This allows them to scale up their argument not only to the level of contemporary diplomacy, but also to that of world politics more generally. It also provides a basis for positing new conceptual tools of general value – the concepts of affordance, shareability, visualization and immediacy. The article is noteworthy for its sophisticated use of methods as the core translation mechanism that allows the authors to transcend scale and theorize in such a way. The article itself includes not only a lengthy discussion of methods, but also a 20-page supplementary data file that describes research design, details of observations and interviews and how the interpretation and theorization processes unfolded. It details the work that was necessary to combine 'insights and empirical material from observations of negotiations ... to develop a deeper and more complete understanding of the fascinating, but understudied phenomenon' (Adler-Nissen and Drieschova, 2019b: 1).

The article illustrates how to theorize with methods, but also the gaze of generalization that often goes along with the style. It aims to tell stories of broader and general scholarly significance, and often to address macro phenomena, such as neoliberalism or diplomacy. It is 'method' that fills the gap between theorizing and the practices studied and that translates between the two.

Experimentation

The fourth and final style emerged gradually out of dissatisfaction with the methods orientation. This concerned firstly the growing recognition of the performativity of methods (Law, 2004). Understanding methods as acts of practical world making implies that whatever methods one chooses, one finds oneself always entangled in the practice under study. A researcher will always leave traces. Couldn't that recognition be turned from an ethical problem into a virtue in its own right? The other observation was that the growing range of studies based on participant observation or proxies continued to rely on an outsider and spectator position (Eikeland and Nicolini, 2011: 167). Instead of relying on external standards, would it make more sense to rely on the demands, rules or standards of the practice itself as guidelines? Would it be possible to immerse oneself fully into a practice without requiring a recourse to mechanisms, meditation or methods to control the fear of becoming natives? It is here where the distinction between theory and practice fully collapses under practice as the sole concept. Theorizing becomes an activity that is always already inscribed in any practice.

There is considerable variety in how such a style is practised. Some researchers advocate for action research (Eikeland and Nicolini, 2011) or have turned to design thinking and composition (Escobar, 2017; Austin, 2019), while others experiment with forms of engaging with and writing about practice (Bueger, 2015; Bogusz, 2017). For lack of a better term, I call this style of theorizing experimentation. Not every researcher adopting this style will agree with this label. Yet it adequately captures two important aspects. Theorizing is experimental in the sense that it tries out new ways of engaging with practitioners, of being a scholar, and of writing and presenting academic work. Experimenting is, moreover, a practice that aims at producing; scholars share a concern with making, creating, producing when they intervene in the practice. They want to add theory to the practice within which they immerse themselves. This can involve the making of designs, concepts, models or other tools to be injected in the practice.

To provide an example from my own implementation of the experimental style, in a research project on the global governance of piracy, an invited 'lessons learned' project provided the opportunity for developing new conceptualizations for what practitioners were doing (Bueger, 2015, 2020). It was an effort at 'helping practitioners to articulate what they already do, and therefore somehow know', as Eikeland and Nicolini (2011: 169) phrase it. Working with and for the practitioners allowed for understanding and articulating practices such as communique writing and institutional work and how they structure counter-piracy governance. This intervention was hence designed to capture basic international governance practices, as much as it was an attempt to assist practitioners 'to see beyond the current horizon of their own practice and expand the existing practice in new and groundbreaking directions' (Eikeland and Nicolini, 2011: 170).

Theorizing creatively

A recent article on the relation between theory and practices argues that 'theory must not go on holiday' (Grimmel and Hellmann, 2019). But where should it go instead? The authors' answer is that it should return to philosophy and seek counselling by pragmatists and Wittgensteinians. Is more philosophy the route to better theorizing? This chapter has argued for taking a different course. Perhaps theorizers in IR and elsewhere do need some holidays. This would provide the space to get away from an understanding of theory as rule following or as administering data, and to recover theorizing as a playful, intuitive, emotional and creative practice of sensibilities and care.

The turn away from worshipping grand theorists and the new uncertainty over the status and meaning of theory creates that opportunity. Practice theorizing provides a new opening. As argued, not all the scholars that can be clustered around the term 'practice turn', however, subscribe to the idea of reformulating and reworking received understandings of theory. Some aim at rescuing them by turning to the elaboration of grand vocabularies, or by applying such. Others argue that we should abandon the term and turn our attention to descriptivism and other tools, such as concepts and models. Yet a significant movement across the social sciences strives for transforming understandings of theory by turning attention to how it is made, and what kind of 'work' it implies.

This chapter has synthesized core themes developed by scholars making such a move and thinking through theory as practice. Drawing in views from sociology, anthropology and sciences studies has given us an idea of how our understanding of theorizing shifts and what is at stake. We leave the realm of epistemology and the idea of theorizing as following philosophical rules and enter sociological and historical understandings of the practice. It aims to re-centre from the isolated theorizing mind to the collective. Tacit knowledge, emotions and intuition matter, as do skills received through training in theorizing. To theorize is to form stable relations to a host of things, actors and statements. It is to make relations that last and that can travel across situations. It is to merge theory and practice and to translate the concept and the concrete into each other. The new multiplicity of styles of theorizing that appears requires our attention.

To provide a point of orientation how the diversity of new styles might be organized and how one can travel in different directions, I have provided a typology organized around two axes: whether theorizing is based in the library or the field, and whether it aims at generalizing and reducing mess, or singularization and leaving mess to mess. Four styles of theorizing come to the fore. Organized around mechanism, mediation, method and experimentation, they imply different kinds of work and forms of merging and intervening into theory and practice. It is the last, the experimenting style, which has so far received the least attention in IR, yet it holds particular promise. Let's experiment!

Acknowledgements

For comments and suggestions, I am grateful to Emanuel Adler, Philippe Beaulieu-Brossard, Alena Drieschova, Kristin Eggeling, Frank Gadinger, Max Lesch, Antje Wiener, the participants at the 2019 book workshop in Frankfurt, as well as the editors. Research for this chapter has benefitted from a grant by the Economic and Social Research Council (ES/S008810/1) and the Danish Ministry of Foreign Affairs administered by the DANIDA Fellowship Center.

References

Abend, Gabriel (2008) 'The meaning of "theory"', *Sociological Theory* 26, 2, pp 173–99.

Abbott, Andrew (2014) *Digital Paper: A Manual for Research and Writing with Library and Internet Materials* (Chicago, IL: University of Chicago Press).

Acharya, Amitav and Barry Buzan, eds (2010) *Non-Western International Relations Theory* (London: Routledge).

Adkins, Lisa and Celia Lury (2009) 'Introduction: What is the empirical?', *European Journal of Social Theory* 12, 1, pp 5–20.

Adler, Emanuel (2019) *World Ordering: A Social Theory of Cognitive Evolution* (Cambridge: Cambridge University Press).

Adler, Emanuel and Vincent Pouliot (2011) 'International practices', *International Theory* 3, 1, pp 1–36.

Adler-Nissen, Rebecca and Alena Drieschova (2019a) 'Track-change diplomacy: technology, affordances, and the practice', *International Studies Quarterly* 63, pp 531–45.

Adler-Nissen, Rebecca and Alena Drieschova (2019b) 'Supplementary data file', available at: https://oup.silverchair-cdn.com/oup/backfile/Content_public/Journal/isq/63/3/10.1093_isq_sqz030/1/sqz030_supplemental_file.docx?Expires=1619290022&Signature=1R4ijHTSFZZ87wpxAjtGLIQ4Gm2R240qNWphF3QlZosepdiivs6COLIFvD0yatE7~ao-8oW20REJ~I~wEG3~CGBv6pX1ltEKgJEA6gG7OsHJSxlNKKgmnyX1hKF~DZCnjd9A~mHYiDmOltzsL6i3533Aag3TAHiKeDkYUMwOwQtfSxR-99GiZEX67-VZEg4AGqpN0F1MFfZ8mWXPdj5zw-IvhK4fSJZ0GC14acWUQubrcnh4qfuEdMfj4N6UrY1Q~xQaQRQTnZZsAuyiKk9qQ9XBLn2sePUypxP4Sjd~atFg6jhCelCd9VDt3879oiC016nnan0hbILREiLWnSCnTQ_&Key-Pair-Id=APKAIE5G5CRDK6RD3PGA, accessed 26 March 2021.

Austin, Jonathan Luke (2019) 'Security compositions,' *European Journal of International Security* 4, 3, pp 249–73.

Bogusz, Tanja (2017) 'From crisis to experiment: Bourdieu and Dewey on research practice and cooperation', in Anders Buch and Theodore R. Schatzki (eds), *Questions of Practice in Philosophy and Social Theory* (London: Routledge), pp 156–75.

Bueger, Christian (2014) 'Pathways to practice: praxiography and international politics', *European Political Science Review* 6, 3, pp 383–406.

Bueger, Christian (2015) 'Experimenting in global governance: learning lessons with the Contact Group on Piracy', in Richard Freeman and Jan-Peter Voß (eds), *Knowing Governance: The Epistemic Construction of Political Order* (London: Palgrave Macmillan), pp 87–104.

Bueger, Christian (2021) 'Conducting field research when there is no 'field': a note on the praxiographic challenge', in Sarah Biecker and Klaus Schlichte (eds), *The Political Anthropology of Internationalized Politics* (Lanham, MD: Rowman and Littlefield), pp 29–45.

Bueger, Christian and Frank Gadinger (2018) *International Practice Theory* (2nd edn) (London: Palgrave Macmillan).

Burrows, Rogers and Mike Savage (2014) 'After the crisis? Big data and the methodological challenges of empirical sociology', *Big Data and Society* 1, 1, pp 1–6.

Clarke, Kevin A. and David M. Primo (2012) *A Model Discipline: Political Science and the Logic of Representation* (Oxford: Oxford University Press).

Craver, Carl and James Tabery (2019) 'Mechanisms in science', in Edward N. Zalta (ed), *The Stanford Encyclopedia of Philosophy* (Summer 2019 edn), available at: https://plato.stanford.edu/archives/sum2019/entries/science-mechanisms/, accessed 26 February 2021.

Drieschova, Alena and Christian Bueger (2021) 'Conceptualizing international practices: establishing a research agenda in conversations', in Alena Drieschova, Christian Bueger and Ted Hopf (eds), *Conceptualizing International Practices* (Cambridge: Cambridge University Press), pp 1–24.

Dunne, Tim, Lene Hansen and Colin Wight (2013) 'The end of International Relations theory?', *European Journal of International Relations* 19, 3, pp 405–25.

Eikeland, Olav and Davide Nicolini (2011) 'Turning practically: broadening the horizon', *Journal of Organizational Change Management* 24, 2, pp 164–74.

Escobar, Arturo (2008) *Territories of Difference: Place, Movements, Life, Redes* (Durham, NC: Duke University Press).

Escobar, Arturo (2017) *Designs for the Pluriverse: Radical Interdependence, Autonomy, and the Making of Worlds* (Durham, NC and London: Duke University Press).

Glennan, Stuart and Phyllis Illari (2018) 'Varieties of mechanisms', in Stuart Glennan and Phyllis Illari (eds), *The Routledge Handbook of Mechanisms and Mechanical Philosophy* (London and New York: Routledge), pp 91–104.

Grimmel, Andreas and Gunther Hellmann (2019) 'Theory must not go on holiday: Wittgenstein, the Pragmatists, and the idea of social science', *International Political Sociology* 13, 2, pp 198–214.

Guzzini, Stefano (2013) 'The ends of International Relations theory: stages of reflexivity and modes of theorizing', *European Journal of International Relations* 19, 3, 521–41.

Hacking, Ian (1992) '"Style" for historians and philosophers', *Studies in the History and Philosophy of Science* 23, 1, pp 1–20.

Harrison, Faye V. (2016) 'Theorizing in ex-centric sites', *Anthropological Theory* 16, 2–3, pp 160–76.

Harrison, Faye V. (2017) 'Engaging theory in the new millennium', in Simon Coleman, Susan B. Hyatt, and Ann Kingsolver (eds), *The Routledge Companion to Contemporary Anthropology* (London and New York: Routledge), pp 27–56.

Hofius, Maren (2020) 'Towards a "theory of the gap": addressing the relationship between practice and theory', *Global Constitutionalism* 9, 1, 169–82.

Jackson, Patrick Thaddeus and Daniel H. Nexon (2013) 'International theory in a post-paradigmatic era: from substantive wagers to scientific ontologies', *European Journal of International Relations* 19, 3, pp 543–65.

Jonas, Michael, Beate Littig and Angela Wroblewski, eds (2017) *Methodological Reflections on Practice Oriented Theories* (Berlin and Heidelberg: Springer).

Klein, Daniel B. (2014) 'Three frank questions to discipline your theorizing', in Richard Swedberg (ed), *Theorizing in Social Science: The Context of Discovery* (Stanford, CA: Stanford University Press), pp 106–30.

Knorr-Cetina, Karin (2014) 'Intuitionist theorizing', in Richard Swedberg (ed), *Theorizing in Social Science: The Context of Discovery* (Stanford, CA: Stanford University Press), pp 29–60.

Kratochwil, Friedrich (2011) 'Making sense of "international practices"', in Emanuel Adler and Vincent Pouliot (eds), *International Practices* (Cambridge: Cambridge University Press), pp 36–60.

Kratochwil, Friedrich (2014) *The Status of Law in World Society: Meditations on the Role and Rule of Law* (Cambridge: Cambridge University Press).

Kratochwil, Friedrich (2018) *Praxis: On Acting and Knowing* (Cambridge: Cambridge University Press).

Kratochwil, Friedrich (2019) 'Response to Christian Reus-Smit's review of "Praxis: On Acting and Knowing"', *Perspectives on Politics* 17, 3, pp 830–1.

Kwa, Chunglin (2011) *Styles of Knowing: A New History of Science from Ancient Times to the Present* (Pittsburgh, PA: University of Pittsburgh Press).

Latour, Bruno (1987) *Science in Action: How to Follow Scientists and Engineers through Society* (Cambridge, MA: Harvard University Press).

Law, John (2004) *After Method: Mess in Social Science Research* (London: Routledge).

Levy, Arnon (2013) 'Three kinds of "new mechanism"', *Biology and Philosophy* 28, pp 99–114.

Lizardo, Omar (2014) 'The end of theorists: the relevance, opportunities, and pitfalls of theorizing in sociology today', text based on the Lewis Coser Memorial Lecture, delivered 17 August 2014 in San Francisco, available at: http://akgerber.com/OpenBook010.pdf, accessed 26 March 2021.

Martin, John Levi (2015) *Thinking Through Theory* (New York: W.W. Norton).

Mearsheimer, John J. and Stephen M. Walt (2013) 'Leaving theory behind: why simplistic hypothesis testing is bad for International Relations', *European Journal of International Relations* 19, 3, pp 427–57.

Mol, Annemarie (2010) 'Actor-network theory: sensitive terms and enduring tensions', *Kölner Zeitschrift für Soziologie und Sozialpsychologie* 50, 1, pp 253–69.

Müller, Sophie Merit (2018) 'Distributed corporeality: anatomy, knowledge and the technological reconfiguration of bodies in ballet', *Social Studies of Science* 48, 6, pp 869–90.

Nicolini, Davide (2017) 'Practice theory as a package of theory, method and vocabulary: affordances and limitations', in Michael Jonas, Beate Littig and Angela Wroblewski (eds), *Methodological Reflections on Practice Oriented Theories* (Berlin and Heidelberg: Springer), pp 19–34.

Pouliot, Vincent (2013) 'Methodology', in Rebecca Adler-Nissen (ed), *Bourdieu in International Relations: Rethinking Key Concepts in IR* (London: Routledge), pp 45–58.

Pouliot, Vincent (2014) 'Practice tracing', in Andrew Bennett and Jeffrey T. Checkel (eds), *Process Tracing: From Metaphor to Analytic Tool* (Cambridge and New York: Cambridge University Press), pp 237–59.

Rabinow, Paul (2003) *Anthropos Today: Reflections on Modern Equipment* (Princeton, NJ and Oxford: Princeton University Press).

Reckwitz, Andreas (2002) 'Toward a theory of social practices: a development in culturalist theorizing', *European Journal of Social Theory* 5, 2, pp 243–63.

Reed, Isaac Ariail and Mayer N. Zald (2014) 'The unsettlement of communities of inquiry', in Richard Swedberg (ed), *Theorizing in Social Science: The Context of Discovery* (Stanford, CA: Stanford University Press), pp 85–105.

Savage, Mike (2009) 'Contemporary sociology and the challenge of descriptive assemblage', *European Journal of Social Theory* 12, 1, pp 155–74.

Schatzki, Theodore R. (1996) *Social Practices: A Wittgensteinian Approach to Human Activity and the Social* (Cambridge: Cambridge University Press).

Seth, Sanjay (2011) 'Postcolonial theory and the critique of International Relations', *Millennium* 40, 1, pp 167–83.

Shilliam, Robbie, ed (2010) *International Relations and Non-Western Thought: Imperialism, Colonialism and Investigations of Global Modernity* (London: Routledge).

Stengers, Isabelle (2000) *The Invention of Modern Sciences* (Minneapolis, MI: University of Minnesota Press).

Swedberg, Richard (2014) *The Art of Social Theory* (Princeton, NJ: Princeton University Press).

Swedberg, Richard (2017) 'Theorizing in sociological research: a new perspective, a new departure?', *Annual Review of Sociology* 43, pp 189–206.

Weick, Karl E. (2014) 'The work of theorizing', in Richard Swedberg (ed), *Theorizing in Social Science: The Context of Discovery* (Stanford, CA: Stanford University Press), pp 177–94.

5

Practising Theorizing in Theorizing Praxis: Friedrich Kratochwil and Social Inquiry

Gunther Hellmann

[N]o one can pretend to be practically versed in a science and yet scorn theory without declaring that he is an ignoramus in his field, inasmuch as he believes that by groping about in experiments and experiences, without putting together certain principles (which really constitute what is called theory) and without having thought out some whole relevant to his business (which, if one proceeds methodically in it, is called a system), he can get further than theory could take him.

(Kant 1999 [1793], p 279)

After theory had once arisen life does not go on just the same.
(Dewey 2015 [1919], p 2; emphasis in original)

Concepts are, as Wittgenstein taught us, uses of words. Philosophers have long wanted to understand concepts, but the point is to change them so as to make them serve our purposes better.

(Rorty 2000, p 25)

Introduction

The concepts of 'theory' and 'practice' may not figure as centrally in everyday life as they figure in academic life. Yet, as the title of Kant's essay from which the introductory quote has been taken indicates, 'common sayings' such as that something 'may be true in theory, but is of no use in practice' also reveal that the duality of theory *versus* practice shapes our most fundamental ways of sense-making in everyday life. It also goes without saying that the practice of theorizing is nothing that practitioners beyond the 'sciences' worry too much about because their praxis is usually defined in terms of some practical choices which do not, at least in the first instance, relate to thinking about thinking. Academics, however, have to come to terms with 'theory' one way or another – or risk being spurned as an 'ignoramus' if they don't. This is especially true for International Relations (IR), which, 'even in the West ... did not become a predominantly academic, formally theoretical discipline until after 1945' (Buzan, 2018: 393) and has defined itself in 'theoretical' terms ever since (Wæver, 2013).

Since practising theory is at the heart of any academic practice, one should not be surprised that one can observe a very broad spectrum of practices in doing theory. The key impulse for writing this chapter was that Fritz Kratochwil's *Praxis* (Kratochwil, 2018) provides more than one reason to reflect anew about what it means to do or practise theory, that is, to *theorize*. His important book serves as a backdrop because it is a fascinating and exemplary exercise in practising theory while leaving most students initiated into the classical rituals of doing 'IR theory' perplexed. These students are told right at the start that problems of praxis cannot be 'subjected to "theoretical treatment"' or 'theory building' (Kratochwil, 2018: prelims). After completing the book and its many illuminating and learned excursions across disciplinary boundaries and back into 'the origins' of society, law and (international) politics, these students will wonder what else, if not a thoroughly *theoretical treatise*, they have been reading. It may not be what is typically called 'theory' in IR, but it is certainly not its opposite – whatever that may be. As a matter of fact, one way to read the book is as a 'practical guide' to *practising theorizing* differently – to *change* our practice of theorizing in Rorty's sense rather than to merely *understand* 'theory' better.

This is what I will argue in this chapter. I will indeed claim that Kratochwil is providing a model to emulate of what it means to theorize. As so often with his scholarly writings, he is not providing us with 'easy reading'. As a matter of fact, he is making it fairly difficult for readers to figure out what his core messages are. My own puzzlement was initially stirred in particular by – what seemed at least to me to be – a strange, even awkward way of using the words 'theory' or 'theoretical'. The very fact that chapter 1 of *Praxis* breaks with the aesthetic strategy of all remaining chapter titles by dodging the obvious title 'Theorizing' made me wonder what was gained by prominently associating the Kratochwilian approach to theorizing *praxis* with Hume and 'constructivism' instead of calling it simply 'Theorizing'. Using the gerund as the fitting grammatical form for what English grammar books call 'action verbs' made impressive sense throughout the book in getting a new 'interdisciplinary' grip on the origins and histories of society, law and (international) politics in terms of 'constituting', 'changing', 'sanctioning' and so forth. The same seemed obvious to me as far as 'theorizing' is concerned – precisely because it emphasized some *doing* in contrast to a *thing*, 'theory', that we might 'treat', 'build' or 'test'. Moreover, Kratochwil himself explicitly (if rather late) states that we have to accept 'that *"theorizing" is itself a practice*' (Kratochwil, 2018: 426, emphasis in original).

Re-reading *Praxis* as a 'practical guide' to practising theorizing differently would, therefore, be my suggestion as to how one might resolve the tensions between Kratochwil's advocacy of a constructivist 'meta-theoretical stance' (Kratochwil, 2018: 18) on the one hand and his harsh criticism of social science scholarship on the other. The chapter is organized in three cuts of 'theorizing' – 'cuts' because the perspective on theorizing changes only slightly if one highlights different angles. The ordinary uses and combinations of the verbs *to practise* and *to theorize* with the noun or gerund of *theory* and *practice* already provide some important openings and delimitations. Four combinations are possible in principle, but only three make sense: to say that one theorizes practice, practises theorizing or theorizes theorizing all make sense because these combinations refer to doings which we do observe in one way or another in IR. To say that one practises practice is 'senseless' in Wittgenstein's understanding of a combination of words which has been 'excluded from the language, withdrawn from circulation' (Wittgenstein, 2009 [1953]: PI §500) because the sense of combining verb and noun in this fashion does not refer in any meaningful sense to an observable praxis.

Theorizing praxis

To theorize the subject matter of international politics properly starts with clarifying what praxis is all about, because an adequate understanding of praxis – in terms of 'individual and collective choices' – has significant consequences for practices of theorizing. Importantly, Kratochwil here joins Aristotle, Marx, Wittgenstein and the pragmatists in arguing that *praxis* must not be reduced to the mere 'practices' which are at the centre of the 'practice turn' (Kratochwil, 2018: 425–6). As Jens Steffek and I have argued in the 'Introduction', the much broader notion of praxis ought to be understood in terms of social action as interaction here and now, individually and collectively. Praxis happens or unfolds as interaction in time. It is unique and rule-following at the same time; it entails conscious (reflective) acting – what Dewey calls 'intelligent action' in solving complex 'problematic situations' – as well as subconscious, more instinctive or 'habitual' doing (Dewey, 1938). As *social* action it is significantly linguistic practice which, in turn, implies that the inherent rule-following of competent language users also entails that 'practitioners'[1] constantly form novel sentences and, thus, also novel aims. Chomsky's theory that the 'finite grammars' of all natural languages 'can generate an infinite number of sentences' (Chomsky, 2002 [1957]: 24) and the 'empirical proof' of his theory which in the meantime has been furnished from different angles might even convince sceptics. This is another way of saying that complexity and contingency are *constitutive* of praxis (see also Kessler, Chapter 10, this volume).

I am reading Kratochwil as saying that we ought to conceive of international political praxis as creative social practice and that we, therefore, also ought to trace it to human choices. Here we are already entering the 'theorizing' stage of praxis. In Kratochwil's account these human choices manifest themselves in a very broad range of different forms: the formation or 'constituting' of society and law, the evolution or transformational change of sovereignty, the function and impact of norms in shaping social action and practical choices, rulings of international courts, the justification and critique of foreign policy decisions and so on. *Theorizing* this praxis (as a form of *making sense* of it) is necessarily post hoc and usually distanced in space and time from the actual interaction. To speak of praxis as 'manifesting itself' in particular forms is an indirect acknowledgement that *naming* what *constitutes* praxis and how these constitutive things hang together conceptually, sequentially or causally is already a form of theorizing. Praxis does not 'speak', only practitioners do – and their ways of 'speaking' or making sense of what has been done takes place *after* (inter)acting (with 'speech acts' being a special case).

This is one of the crucial differences, but at the same time also one of the important connections, between theory and praxis, illustrating why they belong to the same semantic field. The process of understanding and explaining praxis (here collectively summarized under the heading of 'theorizing') ought to be separated from the actual doing and (inter)acting. Of course, this is *not* to say that actors don't 'know' what they are doing when acting. However, it does mean that what Wittgenstein calls 'rule-following' *in* acting refers to something that we do 'blindly'.[2] In a strict sense, therefore,

---

[1] In this chapter I use the word 'practitioner' to refer to any individual or collective agent engaged in some praxis, be it politics or IR theorizing.

[2] Wittgenstein (2009 [1953]: PI §§ 201–19) (the 4th edition of Wittgenstein's 'Investigations' separates what has long been regarded as two parts as 'Philosophical Investigations' (PI) and 'Philosophy of Psychology' (PP); I will signal the distinction accordingly). Importantly, in the German original Wittgenstein's claim (§ 202) that ' "following a rule" is a practice' translates as 'Darum ist "der Regel folgen" *eine Praxis*' (emphasis added). The English 'a practice' can be translated as both 'Praxis' and '*Handlungsweise*', where '*Handlungsweise*' allows for *patterned action* whereas 'Praxis' accentuates the *uniqueness of acting here and now*. I am reading Wittgenstein here as *intending* to emphasize the difference between 'Praxis' and 'practice(s)' or '*Handlungsweise(n)*'.

theorizing praxis necessarily takes place after 'praxis' has 'happened'. This is one reason why we, as human beings, have come to distinguish between theory and practice in our ordinary linguistic practice after sapience complemented mere sentience in the evolution of the human species. But the very fact that 'thinking' and 'acting' are inextricably connected *in* praxis via language also means that theory and praxis are also mutually constitutive and thus form 'a unity' (Gadamer, 1983: 49) as well.

In preparing the ground for the next section, a final distinction needs to be highlighted. There is an important difference between what might be called the 'internal theoretical' perspective of the political practitioner as far as her praxis is concerned and the 'external theoretical' perspective of an outside observer, say, an academic theoretician. If theorizing praxis refers to making sense of how the things we do and observe hang together conceptually, sequentially or causally, practitioners of politics are likely to content themselves in using a vocabulary in describing and explaining their praxis *and* practices which meets their practical needs in a double sense. They must, in contrast to the academic theoretician, come to an end of merely *thinking* about what they have been doing and will, therefore, choose vocabularies which meet the practical needs of sufficiently explaining their practice(s) vis-à-vis an imagined community of practitioners. Moreover, since they are responsible for what has been done, their theorizing will most likely also draw on reasons which help to *justify* their praxis. In doing so, however, they cannot avoid drawing on the collective conceptual reservoir developed by theoreticians and practitioners alike in constituting their very practices which had to be acquired by them in becoming competent performers of political praxis in the first place.

The external theoretical perspective, in addition, depends on, and actually only gains the aspired academic premium for, descriptions of praxis which meet William James's 'simple test of tracing a concrete consequence', that is, that they '*make* a difference' (James, 1922: 49–50, emphasis in original) in our ways of making sense of praxis in contrast to the perspective of political practitioners. In making that difference the external perspective has to succeed in walking a tightrope which Giddens and Adorno described from two different angles: on the one hand, it has to recognize the 'double hermeneutics' (Giddens, 1984: xxxii–xxxv) of the subject matter of the social sciences in contrast to the natural sciences, that is, that their descriptions are merely re-marking an already 'marked state', to paraphrase George Spencer-Brown (1972: 4; see also Friedrichs, chapter 12, this volume). On the other hand, 'external' theorizing must not be reduced to the mere 'affirmation and mental doubling of that which exists anyhow', a criticism which Adorno raised likewise vis-à-vis 'positivism' and what he called 'half-education' (Adorno, 1959: 186, my translation). To the extent that social science theorizing is, therefore, part and parcel of the constitution of society, it is, inevitably, also a form of 'critique' – in the sense of an obligation, 'not an *option*' (Giddens, 1984: xxxv, emphasis in original). Taking the 'internal perspective' of the political practitioners seriously does not imply 'that somebody's *own* vocabulary is always the best vocabulary for understanding what he is doing'. Rather than according it an epistemically privileged position, it merely means that we owe it to him or her *morally* to take the respective view into account when we theorize it from the outside (Rorty, 1982: 200–3, quote at 202, emphasis in original).

Hans-Georg Gadamer is making a similar point about engaging with praxis when he argues that 'the root of what we can call theory' is

> seeing what is. This does not mean the triviality of determining factual presence. Even in the sciences, a 'fact' is not defined as the merely present which one fixes by measuring, weighing, and counting; 'fact' is rather a hermeneutic concept, which always refers to *a context of conjecture and expectation*, to *a complicated context of inquiry*. What is not quite so complicated, but all the more difficult to perform, is *for any individual in her or his practical life to see what is*, instead of what she or he would like to be. The *general elimination of prejudices* that methodized science requires of its researchers may well be a laborious process – yet it is still easier than overcoming the illusions that constantly arise from one's own ego. (Gadamer, 1983: 43–4; my translation, emphasis added)

This is not the way Kratochwil would put it – even though he shares a common appreciation of Aristotle with Gadamer. However, if I am not reading too much between the lines of *Praxis*, his *inherently normative* understanding of the complexity and contingency of power-infused political praxis similarly leads him to infer a moral obligation on us as theorizing external observers that our theorizing has to *do justice to* these complexities.

Practising theorizing

Theories as reified things, things we 'build' in order to 'test' them 'against the world "out there"' (Kratochwil, 2018: 32) or with which we 'treat' social practice via 'application', is Kratochwil's horror image of theorizing. Whereas his reading of Wittgenstein had taught him that the meaning of a concept *is* its use, and whereas this realization could have made it easier for him to simply follow Feyerabend's shrugging acknowledgement that academic theorizing actually *is* 'an essentially anarchic enterprise' (in the sense that the history of science shows that 'anything' does indeed 'go' [Feyerabend, 1993 (1975): 9]), Kratochwil has always found it hard to just stand by. His Wittgenstein-inspired appreciation of the 'linguistic turn' and his classical education, which had taught him 'above all ... the respect for the "word"' (Kratochwil, 2011b: 4), combined to yield a radically different understanding of (academic) theorizing to what was overwhelmingly taught in IR departments as 'theory'.

A rough summary of his alternative understanding might go as follows: theorizing comprises all the creative things we do with words – things which help us in making sense of and doing justice to what we conceive to be our subject matter, here international politics. This is a rough summary only because the 'we' and the limits of what we should *properly* do with words need to be more cautiously circumscribed in Kratochwil's understanding. Even if the notion of 'one right answer' is a self-destructive illusion in Kratochwil's view, he does believe that we – that is, those of us who consider theorizing international politics as our profession and are recognized as professionals – at a minimum *wrestle* with the 'virtually impossible' Herculean task of 'getting it right' (Kratochwil, 2018: 121, 156–65, 350–3). This disposition finds one expression in his view that we need to 'establish "criteria" for the "right" or problematic use of concepts and their embeddedness in the semantic field informing the practices of the actors' (Kratochwil, 2018: 7). Yet when it comes to the concept of 'theory' he rightly hesitates to engage in what the sociologist Gabriel Abend recommends as 'semantic therapy in order to clarify ... conceptual confusions' regarding the *proper* 'meaning of "theory"' (Abend, 2008: 192; see also Bueger, Chapter 4, this volume). Here I take Kratochwil to join Rorty's Wittgenstein in simply resting 'content to let a thousand language-games be played without suggesting the need for philosophical supervision' (Rorty, 2020: 230) of what 'theory' 'really' means. Better than explicating 'criteria' for the 'right' use of 'theory' is to actually show how *practising* theorizing differently makes a practical difference.

For instance, Kratochwil's 'genealogy', 'conceptual history' or 'archeology' of sovereignty (Kratochwil, 2018: 75–103) is one illustration of theorizing which traces a constitutive practice of inter-state interaction in a grand historical narrative of transformative change. It is much less interested in 'defining' the 'nature' of sovereignty than exploring its origins and historical transformation. Another example of his preferred theorizing practices is the use of analogies and analogous reasoning in the emergence of a global public sphere. Analogous reasoning here helps in highlighting similarities and differences while at the same time leaving space for unique shapes and understandings of 'public sphere' in different historical periods (Kratochwil, 2018: 134–48). Similarly, 'cases' (Kratochwil, 2018: 24–32) or thought experiments (Kratochwil, 2018: 258–9) are as useful in Kratochwil's view as are 'histories' as 'proto-theories' (Kratochwil, 2018: 336 and 338–48 for illustrations). In applying all these tools, he is not only shedding light on political practice from different angles, he is also exemplifying *via use*, that is, pragmatically, what genealogies, archaeologies, metaphors, analogies and histories actually 'are'. He is not trying to clear up 'semantic confusions' about 'genealogy', 'analogy' or 'history' via definitions, he is working pragmatically by giving examples – or, to paraphrase Wittgenstein: Kratochwil is 'teaching' us theorizing 'by means of *examples* and by *exercises*' in how we might work with these words (Wittgenstein 2009 [1953], § 208, emphasis in original; see also Savickey, 2012).

The important Wittgensteinian point about 'giving examples' is a double one here. Examples are immensely useful theorizing tools because they are meant to *open up* thinking space, not close it down as in *necessarily determinate* causal 'explanations' which connect 'some definite thing taken as cause and some definite thing taken as effect' (Kuhn, 1990: 309). In the same way, *closing* thinking space is the very aim of the type of 'theories' in IR which rely on if–then generalizations based on *ceteris paribus* conditioning or 'causal mechanisms'. In contrast, giving examples in a Wittgensteinian and Kratochwilian sense expresses an attitude vis-à-vis theorizing which respects that social action always unfolds against a horizon of possibilities which we know we *cannot* 'know' in full. This is why examples have a tremendously important 'heuristic' function: they '*point beyond*' themselves, as Wittgenstein emphasizes, at least if we take care in our 'teaching' of not 'getting stuck with' the examples we actually choose (Wittgenstein, 2009 [1953]: PI § 208, emphasis in original, my translation based on the German original on p 89). Examples *are* a form theorizing praxis and they have theoretical significance precisely because they point beyond themselves into an open horizon of creative human possibility.

Since aiming for 'completeness' (Wittgenstein 2009 [1953]: PP § 202) cannot and must not be our aim, examples are a useful and cautionary theorizing tool in understanding praxis. They are even *necessary* because 'rules' do 'not suffice for establishing a practice'. Since rules leave 'back-doors open, praxis has to speak for itself' (Wittgenstein, 1997: § 139, my translation) – and it does so via examples. In this sense examples enable us to 'go on' – a phrase which both Wittgenstein and Kratochwil often use – because they provide the 'know how' to 'go on'. Both Wittgenstein and Kratochwil are critical of limiting forms of knowledge about social action (or praxis) to what Gilbert Ryle captured under the heading of 'knowing-that' (in contrast to 'knowing-how', Ryle [1945]) – knowledge that is framed in 'factual' or in causally 'explanatory' (and related generalizing 'predictive') terms. Yet knowing-that can *never exhaust* the possibilities of human agency (Hawthorn, 1991). Therefore, to the extent that theorizing praxis reflects the 'knowing-how' to 'go on' it does so in terms of what Charles Sanders Peirce called the necessarily *transitory* stage of 'thought at rest' *after* the 'irritation of doubt' has come to an end in the course of 'inquiry' – knowing full well that doubt will reassert itself and become 'a new starting point for thought' (Peirce, 1878 [1997]: 33).

At first glance, looking at 'examples' does not look too different compared with the widespread appreciation of 'case study' methodology in the social sciences. Yet the typical 'realist' or 'nominalist' take on what a 'case' is usually boils down to using them in either 'single' or 'comparative' case studies in order to '*overwhelm* the uniqueness inherent in the objects and events in the social world' and realize 'the goal of generalization' (Ragin, 1992: 2–8; emphasis in quote on p 2 added). Thus, the underlying 'ontology' here is of a *closed* universe of social action which is decipherable via studying cases which, in turn, are amenable, at least in principle, to generalization in an 'if–then' pattern of *ceteris paribus* conditioning.

This is fundamentally at odds with the Wittgensteinian view shared by Kratochwil, which stresses contingency and novelty and, therefore, also indeterminacy as inherent in social action. Precisely because political practice and linguistic practice are two sides of one coin and precisely because we constantly come up with novel sentences, words and political aims, our creative theorizing habits are as much oriented backward (as in Kratochwil's 'histories' or 'genealogies') as they are oriented forward (as in Kratochwil's sympathy with Hume's appreciation of 'imagination'). Who we are and where we find ourselves at any point in time involves ever changing backward-looking *and* forward-looking processes of sense-making (Hellmann, 2020). If these theorizing habits were to merely correctly 'represent' some 'givens' in the past or present, we would neither have constantly rewritten histories and reproduced historical controversies, nor would we continuously get rid of outmoded words and concepts (such as 'race') or invent new ones (such as 'Anthropocene') to get a better grip on international politics and humanity's future. Just imagine what an 'IR' dictionary of key concepts would have looked like 30 or 100 years ago compared with today. Rorty's introductory plea to switch from too heavy a focus on semantics to pragmatics, that is, from (merely) trying to better 'understand' our concepts to actually 'changing' them so that they serve our practical purposes better, is another way of emphasizing the creative and practical potential of theorizing.

In staking out his 'metatheoretical stance' along these lines, it is fairly obvious why alternative theorizing practices cannot 'get it right' in Kratochwil's view. Although he is not putting it this way, I take him to believe (and would myself argue) that most of the prevailing theorizing habits in IR commit a similar and fundamental mistake: they basically believe (a) that *describing* 'the world' of international politics *accurately* is fairly straightforward and also sufficiently determinate in terms of coming to an agreement on what is the case, (b) that theories are things which can and ought to be 'developed' in order to be 'applied' to this 'world' and (c) that language can at a minimum be relegated to the status of a residual category in the process of theorizing if it cannot be ignored altogether. I take Kratochwil to think that these defects are similarly visible in a fairly diverse set of typical IR scholarship. Let's take a quick look at some of them.

It shows, for instance, in Kenneth Waltz's plea to move beyond 'mere description' by 'constructing' theories which, above all, yield 'explanatory power'. In Waltz's understanding, the construction process entails theorizing steps such as 'arrang(ing) phenomena so that they are seen as mutually dependent' or 'envisioning a pattern where none is visible to the naked eye'. Yet, interestingly, when Waltz writes that 'explanation through simplification' has to replace 'accurate reproduction through exhaustive description' (Waltz, 1979: 1–10), he, at a minimum, sounds as if the latter is possible in principle even though it is 'merely' descriptive rather than 'explanatory'.

Two other realists, John Mearsheimer and Stephen Walt, who recently also joined the camp of 'scientific realism' officially, largely agree with Waltz that 'developing' and 'employing' theories is key. In their view, prevailing theorizing habits in IR have degenerated into 'simplistic hypothesis testing' due to the deleterious impact of books such as King et al's (1994) *Designing Social Inquiry* (Mearsheimer and Walt, 2013: 445–6). Like Waltz, they define theories as 'simplified pictures of reality' which 'explain how the world works in particular domains'. They also rely on a strong distinction between 'theory' and 'empirics' and emphasize 'explanatory power'. Yet unlike Waltz, who stresses the difficulties of stating a theory with 'enough precision and plausibility' (Waltz, 1979: 14), Mearsheimer and Walt do not see insurmountable problems in 'clearly' defining key assumptions and concepts and how they relate to each other, in assuring 'falsifiability' or in coming up with 'unambiguous predictions'. Whereas all three place a premium on 'developing' theories, Waltz is much less concerned about 'entities and processes that exist in the real world'. Moreover, he does not place as much emphasis as Mearsheimer and Walt do on 'accurately reflect(ing) how the world operates' (all quotes Mearsheimer and Walt 2013: 433).

'Accuracy' and the orientation along 'scientific' methods are critical categories for other 'scientific realists'. Wendt, for instance, deploys this vocabulary in a similar fashion in his early 'constructivist' work as he does in his subsequent 'quantum' work (e.g. Wendt, 1999: 56; 2015: 50, 290). In his view, accuracy is important because representing the world correctly is key to 'scientific' validity or fruitfulness. Since things in the world, such as 'the states system', are taken to be 'real' in a 'deep', 'ontological' sense and since they are 'found in international life' or 'given' in the form of 'self-organizing, mind–independent structures', 'interaction with that *reality* should *regulate* [our] theorizing about it' (Wendt 1999: 5, 36, 63–4, emphasis in passage at p 63 added). In this understanding, 'states' are as 'real' as agents as individual human beings are, and sentences such as 'states are people too' are explicitly meant to be *non*-metaphorical since they are referring to things like 'states' – and the meanings of such things are, at least in part, '*also regulated* by a mind-independent, extra-linguistic world' (Wendt, 1999: 215–24, 53; emphasis added). This is the strange idea that 'the causal arrows run ... from "the world" to our understanding' (Kratochwil, 2018: 325), the strange idea that 'the world' *co-causes* language. Yet 'the world does not speak. Only we do. The world can, once we have programmed ourselves with a language, cause us to hold certain beliefs. But it cannot propose a language for us to speak' (Rorty, 1989: 6).

A differently grounded, if equally representationalist, approach to theorizing politics comes in the form of King et al's 'logic of scientific inference', which Mearsheimer and Walt are critical of, even though all of them share a representationalist view (King et al, 1994). The vocabulary of simplification, precision, accuracy and 'scientific generalization' about 'reality' is equally present here, although the burden lies less with 'depth ontology' or 'theory building' than with proper 'data', 'methods', 'models' and 'inferences'. While King et al would never put it the way Wendt's fellow 'scientific realist', Colin Wight, does – that 'the world does in a very real and important sense talk to us' and that 'language-independent reality ... resists' our way of interacting with it (Wight, 2007: 45, 48) – they would and do insist that 'accurate description' is an important and achievable, if insufficient, prerequisite of proper theorizing (King et al, 1994: 18). Getting 'it' right is not too difficult. 'Good historical writing' and 'good models' here are key in accomplishing adequate 'descriptive inference', in their take. 'Good historians understand which events were crucial', especially as far as the critical distinction between 'systematic' and 'nonsystematic' factors in history are concerned. They do so by constructing 'accounts that emphasize essentials rather than digressions' (King et al, 1994: 53). Similarly, even though it is granted that models simplify by necessity and only 'approximate' some aspect of the world, creating 'good models' seems to be not too difficult since the good ones 'abstract only the "right" features of the reality they represent' (King et al, 1994: 49) – a pretty vague specification for an understanding of 'scientific research' which normally prefers the rhetoric of 'precision'.

A final example closer to 'home' comes in the form of an alternative 'practice theory'. In a broad-ranging survey of a broad variety of 'practice-theoretical approaches', Christian Bueger and Frank Gadinger (2018) spell out commonalities and differences among them as far as intellectual sources, theoretical grounding and methodological applications are concerned. Since 'practices' are at the centre and since some intellectual reference points are unsurprisingly identical to Kratochwil's, there is more common ground than with the representationalist theorizing practices discussed previously. Yet some critical differences remain due to foundational choices in this variant of 'practice theory', such as the emphasis on repetition, routinization and 'materiality' and the marginal role 'linguistic practice' plays (see also Kratochwil, 2011a). While some 'approaches' explicitly draw on Wittgenstein and the inherent normativity of practice(s), Bueger and Gadinger's identification of the 'main weaknesses' of some of the practice approaches they highlight signal where their own preferences in 'practice theory' lie. Foucault's weakness is said to be that he 'tends towards linguistic and discursive practices', a weakness that is also associated with 'narrative approaches' as far as the 'linguistic dimension' is concerned; 'Bourdieusian praxeology', in contrast, is charged with 'downplaying materiality', while Schatzki's Wittgensteinian take is said to be 'difficult (to translate) into empirical research' (Bueger and Gadinger, 2018: 31–2). In other words, in stressing that practice theory 'is an empirical project rather than a theoretical one' and in calling for a corresponding 'readjustment of the relation between theory and practice' (Bueger and Gadinger, 2018: 165, 29), the basic approach to theorizing sounds not too dissimilar from the representationalist approaches discussed previously. To be sure, there are repeated warnings to 'overcome the dualism of theory and empirics' or to 'destabilize' the separation of theory and empirical research, yet the praxeographical vocabulary which calls for 'generat(ing) empirical data about practices' or recommends 'generalizing' about 'how practices achieve overarching regularity across time and space' (all quotes Bueger and Gadinger, 2018: 135–7) leaves a lot of ambiguity as to how theorizing actually ought to be practised. What seems clear, though, is that Bueger and Gadinger would hesitate to subscribe to the view shared by Goethe, Wittgenstein, Gadamer, Rorty and Kratochwil that theorizing *is* observing and that it does not *depend* on 'empirics' or 'data'. They would most likely have a hard time saying with Goethe (see initial quote) that we do not 'seek for something behind the phenomena' because 'they themselves are the theory' or to follow Wittgenstein when he writes that 'our mistake is to look for an explanation where we ought to regard the facts as "proto-phenomena". That is, where we ought to say: *this is the language-game that is being played*' (Wittgenstein 2009 [1953]: PI § 654, emphasis added). I take Kratochwil to make a similar point when he says that 'the causal arrows run from "understanding" to the world, and not from "the world" to our understanding or to our theory' (Kratochwil, 2018: 325) – that is, that our understandings constitute 'the empirical' as much as they constitute 'the theoretical'.

These diverse examples of IR theorizing highlight a few common problematic features which I think Kratochwil would rightly criticize as manifestations of 'both classical and modern (Cartesian) epistemology' which continues to rely 'on the mirror quality of language … . As soon as meaning was, however, no longer determined merely through representation, but was seen as part of the constitutive function of language itself, a new paradigm emerges' (Kratochwil, 2018: 46). Kratochwil calls this 'constructivism', Rorty 'anti-representationalism' (Rorty, 1999).

Theorizing theorizing

Practitioners of IR theory usually provide reasons why they practise theorizing in a certain fashion. All of the aforementioned scholars do so in one form or another – and they at least implicitly agree that theorizing theory (doing 'meta-theory') unfolds less in the realm of 'the empirical' than 'the normative' – to use this problematic distinction for once. Kratochwil's formula for theorizing theory boils down to the 'critical' and 'systematic reflection on the observations' of other theorizing observers from various academic disciplines, a form of 'translation' based on 'certain "ontological" assumptions concerning human action – or *praxis*'. Moreover, I read Kratochwil as saying that 'the linguistic turn' provides all the necessary 'ontological' assumptions to elaborate how his 'thick constructivism' will be put to work (all quotes in this paragraph Kratochwil, 2018: 18–19, emphasis in original). In this final section I will offer a third cut at 'theorizing' in meta-theoretical terms which draws in particular on Wittgenstein and Rorty, two praxis theoreticians of the 20th century who stand for 'the linguistic turn' like few others. I will offer what Rorty calls a 'redescription' of theorizing theorizing in the light of 'the linguistic turn' which I think Kratochwil might be able to subscribe to.

Theorizing theorizing thoroughly in the light of the linguistic turn starts with marking what 'representationalist' forms of theorizing get wrong by relegating linguistic practice to residual category status (in the best of cases) and by treating mind or language 'as containing representations of reality' (Rorty, 1991: 2). In the previous section I have argued that the chosen samples of alternative theorizing practices in IR build in various ways and with different degrees of rigidity on such a representational understanding where 'the world out there', 'reality' or 'data' function as non-linguistic items which 'make' theory x 'true' – that is, 'that the world splits itself up, on its own initiative, into sentence-shaped chunks called "facts"' (Rorty, 1989: 5), which then serve as authoritative and truth-making 'representeds' in our 'representings'. As Rorty suggested already around 1970, this highly problematic view was a legacy of Descartes's key invention, the 'mind–body problem', which 'called ontology into being' in the first place, leaving us afterwards with 'three hundred years of ontologizing' (Rorty, 2014 [1970]: 213, 5). In Robert Brandom's words, 'cogito, ergo sum' functioned as a 'regress-stopper' in the following way:

> If the reality I know is known by being represented by my representings of it, then I must know my representings themselves in some other way

than just by representing them in turn. For the alternative would launch a semantic regress, of representings of representings of representings ... in which no terminal knowledge is ever finally achieved. (Brandom, 2021: xv)

Immediate knowledge of this type, therefore, simply had to be 'immune to error' or 'incorrigible' (Rorty, 1970; Brandom, 2021). In Rorty's telling (Rorty, 1979: 165–212), the resulting Cartesian-cum-'neo-Kantian' idea of incorrigible 'privileged representations' had already been debunked by analytical philosophy in the 1950s and 1960s. In Brandom's reconstruction of Rorty's intellectual trajectory, it took a few more decades for him to develop the 'vocabulary vocabulary' into a full-fledged 'anti-authoritarian' (Rorty, 1999) replacement for Cartesian 'semantic representationalism' (Brandom, 2019, 2020, 2021).[3]

As so often when IR wanted to get on top of 'philosophy of science' theorizing, full-blown 'Cartesian mindedness' (Brandom, 2019: 16–18) infected the discipline rather late. In a sense Wendt was to IR what Descartes was to modern-day philosophy. Waltz could still write his *Theory of International Politics* (Waltz, 1979) without ever once mentioning the words ontology or epistemology. Yet a few years later Wendt in particular had succeeded in gradually convincing an astounding number of IR theoreticians that one could not choose a serious 'scientific approach to social inquiry' without actually conceiving of 'international *theory*' in terms of 'the *ontology* of the states system' (Wendt, 1999: 1, 6; emphasis in original).[4] Accordingly, 'social theory' was rightly conducted in Wendt's view as 'Cartesian science' (Wendt, 2006).[5] Patrick Jackson's recovery of the 'largely unnoticed

---

[3] See also Brandom's 2020 online seminar 'Two Forms of Contemporary Antirepresentationalism: Pragmatism and Expressivism', available at: http://www.pitt.edu/~rbrandom/Courses/Antirepresentationalism%20(2020)/AR%202020%20a.html, accessed 26 November 2020.

[4] It should be acknowledged that Kratochwil had also prominently applied the 'ontology versus epistemology' vocabulary in the 1980s (see Kratochwil and Ruggie, 1986). Yet in terms of popularizing ontology talk, Wendt unquestionably deserves the first prize.

[5] For Kratochwil's critique, see Kratochwil (2000). Rorty formulated a much broader critique of what Brandom later termed 'Cartesian mindedness' from the late 1960s onwards (Rorty, 1970, 2014 [1970]; see also Brandom, 2011: 107–15). From his first articles in the 1980s onwards Wendt affirmatively accepted 'Cartesian dualism' (Wendt, 2006: 185–6), if, in his most recent work, 'only epistemic(ally)' (Wendt, 2015: 93). Yet in doing so he has provided proof for Rorty's central anti-representationalist charge that the 'things' themselves somehow 'authorize' how they ought to be described or explained. 'Quantum theory' is Wendt's most recent 'proof' that humans are able to 'adequately represent the deep structure of reality' and, what is more, that we can for the first time 'test scientifically' what he calls the ill-conceived 'classical worldview'. Quantum theory

and largely uncriticized' Cartesian 'mind–world dualism' came in here subsequently in a supporting role – despite Jackson's fundamental critique of 'Cartesian science'. Yet by explicitly 'foreground(ing) ontological concerns' (Jackson, 2011: 31, 38), Jackson at least indirectly joined forces with Wendt by underlining the purported need to face up to 'an ideal-typical choice between *mind–world dualism* and its opposite, which I will call *mind–world monism*' (Jackson, 2011: 35, emphasis in original).

I read Kratochwil's work for the last decades as saying that we would be better off today had we stopped 'the game of ontology' (Rorty, 2014 [1970]: 214) long ago by *dissolving* it, rather than by trying to 'solve' it. 'Dissolving' here does not mean, as Jackson puts it, 'to make the problem simply go away ... by demonstrating that it is, in some sense, a false problem' (Jackson, 2011: 116). Rather, to dissolve here means to simply recognize it in passing as a 'problem' we shouldn't even have started to think to *have* in the first place (Rorty, 1991: 93–110). In this sense I also read Kratochwil to say that practising theorizing as he does in chapters 2–11 of *Praxis* is more useful than wasting time on theorizing theorizing. He agrees that we cannot do without completely, which is why he at least sketches his own 'metatheoretical stance' in a 'constructivist' vein and largely in terms of a *fully* taken 'linguistic turn'. Yet, compared with Jackson, I see him more on Rorty's side. Rather than wanting to entice IR theorizers to place themselves in an ideal-typical two-by-two matrix which locates four possible solutions on an axis 'mind' versus 'world' and an axis 'knowledge' versus 'observation' (Jackson, 2011: 37), Kratochwil emphasizes that we should simply rest satisfied in having 'debunked the idea of the primacy of the epistemological project' some time ago, that we should similarly abandon ontological anxiety and that we should focus instead on 'the importance (of the power) of judgment ... that provides the validation of "reflective" choices' which should, in turn, be buttressed by 'persuasive reasons' (Kratochwil, 2018: 10). Moreover, he explicitly embraces 'Rorty's method' of 'therapeutic re-description' because he takes it to provide us 'with the possibility of seeing the old in a new way and creating new opportunities for practices and experiences that sidestep the old vocabulary which is getting in the way' (Kratochwil, 2018: 159).

The latter is complementary to the theorizing virtues discussed previously about opening horizons of possibility rather than closing them. To the extent that Rorty's 'ironist' is not carried away by 'the final vocabulary she

---

fills in that function of authorization since it is 'giving us access to that deep structure for the first time' (Wendt, 2015: 58). In this reading Rorty's anti-authoritarian critique of representationalists submitting to 'God' or 'Nature' would simply be extended to 'Quantum'. See also Der Derian and Wendt (2020).

currently uses' and accepts that 'the choice between vocabularies' is 'made neither within a neutral and universal metavocabulary nor by an attempt to fight one's way past appearances to the real, but simply by playing the new off against the old' (Rorty, 1989: 73), she will not spend too much time on getting this or that author 'right' but rather think about what it might take to persuade others to learn her preferred new vocabulary. The combination of both moves – the attitude of being open to reprogramming ourselves with new vocabularies in the light of novel ('internal' as well as 'external') theorizing about political praxis *and* the attitude of being committed to giving (and asking for) reasons why (and whether) the proposed new vocabulary might be an improvement over the previous one – is a sensible redescription of meta-theorizing in terms of a *discursive practice* because it clarifies what it takes *pragmatically* 'to go on' with theorizing while justifying the particular theorizing move not in terms of a closing argument but in the form of an invitation for a continuing conversation.

This is how I would translate Brandom's more elaborate summary of Rorty's major achievements. Since Brandom has been Rorty's most prominent PhD student and since he is by now globally recognized as a highly sophisticated philosopher in his own right, it might be best to quote him here at some length. His target here is, among others, the charge levelled at Rorty that he had abandoned 'reason': Brandom, in contrast, thinks that,

> far from rejecting the notion of *reason*, Rorty seeks a broader, deeper conception of it. To that end, his pragmatism follows ... Dewey in thematizing the radical transformation wrought by engaging in specifically *discursive* social practices: practices of giving, seeking, and assessing reasons. Rather than jettisoning reason, Rorty argues that the Enlightenment needs to be brought to completion by rejecting the semantic representationalism at the core of its epistemology precisely because that strand of its thought is not compatible with the critical, anti-authoritarian conception of reason and the role of reasoning in the normative life of human beings that he takes to be the principal glory of that movement of thought. Indeed, like his hero Hegel before him, Rorty is, inter alia, the prophet of a particular kind of emancipatory reflective reason. For he practices, preaches, and theorizes about the sort of self-consciousness that consists in redescription: in deploying new vocabularies that alter what we take to be a reason for what, and so what we can mean and think. (Brandom, 2021: xxvi; emphasis in original)

If my reading of Kratochwil's 'meta-theoretical stance' is correct, he should be able to fully endorse this understanding of theorizing.

Conclusion

Theorizing *praxis* starts with respect for what our fellow human beings did, do and will (or might) do *and* what 'we all' – as practical or academic theoreticians – said, say and will (or might) say, among others, about such doings and sayings. It means to practise theorizing based on the regulative idea that we engage in never ending processes of giving and asking for reasons why our current descriptions of how things hang together *should* be 'acknowledged' as 'knowledge' in Wittgenstein's sense (Wittgenstein, 1997: § 378). These are descriptions of 'how *things* in the broadest possible sense of the term *hang together* in the broadest possible sense of the term' (Sellars, 1963 [1962]: 1, emphasis in original) – that is, how they hang together *conceptually* (how we name, distinguish and relate things semantically), *sequentially* or *systematically* (how we order things in narration or 'mere description') or *causally* (how we hang things together in terms of cause and effect).

Theorizing in this sense is an ongoing discursive process of exchanging arguments about these hangings together where we never know which 'truth' will obtain eventually. It would certainly be normatively preferable that the Habermasian 'better argument' will have its way. However, I see Kratochwil here siding again with Wittgenstein and Rorty – against Habermas (Kratochwil, 2018: 428). Habermas wants to stick with a strong notion of 'context-independent truth' of 'justified belief' because we might, in his view, otherwise lose 'the conceptual means for doing justice to the intuitive distinctions between convincing and persuading, between motivation through reasons and causal exertion of influence, between learning and indoctrination', thereby losing 'the critical standards operating in everyday life' (Habermas, 1998: 371, 377; 1996: 18–19). With Wittgenstein,[6] Rorty argues against the view 'that there is a non-context-dependent distinction between real and apparent justification, or that the *überzeugen–überreden* distinction is not just in the ear of the audience'. In Rorty's (and what I take similarly to be Kratochwil's) view, Habermas's argument of the force of the 'better argument' cannot rescue the distinction between '*Überreden*' and '*Überzeugen*' because

> all reasons are reasons for particular people, restrained (as people always are) by spatial, temporal, and social conditions. To think otherwise is to presuppose the existence of a natural order of reasons to which

---

6 'At the end of reasons comes persuasion ['*Überredung*' in the German original, my translation]. (Think what happens when missionaries convert natives.)' (Wittgenstein, 1997: § 612).

our arguments will, with luck, better and better approximate. The idea of such an order is one more relic of the idea that truth consists in correspondence to the intrinsic nature of things, a nature which somehow precedes and underlies all descriptive vocabularies. The natural order of reasons is for arguments what the intrinsic nature of reality is for sentences. But if beliefs are habits of action the one regulative ideal is as unnecessary as the other. (All quotes Rorty, 2000: 60; emphasis in original)

In Kratochwil's reading, 'winning the argument' in Habermas's view boils down to 'factually achieved assent, which silences opposition. Thus oddly enough the ideal speech situation has again a suspiciously Hobbesian ring in that a unique solution is postulated' (Kratochwil, 2018: 428). This is certainly not how theorizing as discursive practice *ought* to be organized – and, unfortunately, it is also not how Wittgensteinian 'knowledge' as 'acknowledgement' *is* achieved in political practice and theorizing. Just look at Donald Trump's claim about the election results in Georgia in 2020 that 'the real truth is' that he 'won by 400,000 votes' (Gardner and Firozi, 2021) – certainly a far cry from an *ideal* speech situation, yet one cannot ignore that the claim uttered in the *real* speech situation was soon forcefully *acknowledged* by Trump's supporters. In theorizing political praxis, we should therefore acknowledge Peirce's early observation that 'the sole object of inquiry' – where 'inquiry' relates to *any* type of problem-solving inquiry – 'is the settlement of opinion. We may fancy that this is not enough for us, and what we seek, not merely an opinion, but a true opinion. But put this fancy to the test, and it proves groundless; for as soon as a firm belief is reached we are entirely satisfied, whether the belief be true or false' (Peirce, 1997[1877]: 13–14).

Gadamerian 'seeing what is' will not always be pleasant and, if anything, Kratochwil has always been ready to deliver unpleasant truths while setting the benchmark for demanding theorizing higher than most. At the same time he has always been ready to live up to the Weberian ideal of 'scientific "fulfilment"' in this context, that is that science '*wants* to be "surpassed" and become obsolete' (Weber, 1973: 316; my translation, emphasis in original). The sociology of science tells us that this ideal is hard to live up to under the realities of academic competition and practical social theorizing. Still, actually achieving it here and there in individual cases should be easier than realizing the Cartesian 'quest for certainty'. While the sometimes harsh anti-theoreticist rhetoric of Kratochwil's *Praxis* may irritate some readers, reading the book closely and empathetically shows that it is certainly one of few candidates in IR theorizing which are eligible for Weber's prize.

Acknowledgements

I am grateful to the contributors of this book, especially Jens Steffek as co-editor, for comments on earlier versions during the book-making workshop in Frankfurt and afterwards. I also thank Jens Bartsch and Florian Hubert for research support and technical assistance.

References

Abend, Gabriel (2008) 'The meaning of "theory"', *Sociological Theory* 26, 2, pp 173–99.

Adorno, Theodore W. (1959) 'Theorie der Halbbildung', in Alexander Busch (ed), *Soziologie und moderne Gesellschaft: Verhandlungen des 14. Deutschen Soziologentages vom 20. bis 24. Mai 1959 in Berlin*, pp 169–91.

Brandom, Robert B. (2011) *Perspectives on Pragmatism: Classical, Recent and Contemporary* (Cambridge, MA: Harvard University Press).

Brandom, Robert B. (2019) 'Fetishism, anti-authoritarianism, and the second Enlightenment: Rorty and Hegel on representation and reality', Keynote Lecture at the Second Meeting of the Richard Rorty Society, 22–24 November 2019, available at: https://www.pitt.edu/~rbrandom/Cour ses/Antirepresentationalism%20(2020)/Texts/Brandom%20FAASE%20 19-11-23%20c.docx, accessed 10 December 2020.

Brandom, Robert B. (2020) 'Rorty on vocabularies', in Pedro Góis Moreira (ed), *Revisiting Richard Rorty* (Wilmington, DE: Vernon Press), pp 1–23.

Brandom, Robert B. (2021) 'Foreword: Achieving the Enlightenment', in Eduardo Mendieta (ed), *Richard Rorty. Pragmatism, A Version: Anti-Authoritarianism in Epistemology and Ethics* (Cambridge, MA: Harvard University Press), pp vii–xxvi.

Bueger, Christian and Frank Gadinger (2018) *International Practice Theory* (2nd edn) (London: Palgrave Macmillan).

Buzan, Barry (2018) 'How and how not to develop IR theory: lessons from core and periphery', *The Chinese Journal of International Politics* 11, 4, pp 391–414.

Chomsky, Noam (2002 [1957]) *Syntactic Structures* (New York: Mouton de Gruyter).

Der Derian, James and Alexander Wendt (2020) '"Quantizing international relations": the case for quantum approaches to international theory and security practice', *Security Dialogue*, 51, 5, pp 399–413, available at: https:// doi.org/10.1177%2F0967010620901905, accessed 8 February 2021.

Dewey, John (1938) *Logic: The Theory of Inquiry* (New York: Henry Holt and Company).

Dewey, John (2015 [1919]) 'Lectures in social and political philosophy', *European Journal of Pragmatism and American Philosophy* 7, 2, pp 1–39.

Feyerabend, Paul (1993 [1975]) *Against Method: Outline of an Anarchistic Theory of Knowledge* (London: Verso).

Gadamer, H.G. (1983) *Lob der Theorie. Reden und Aufsätze* (Frankfurt am Main: Suhrkamp).

Gardner, Ami and Paulina Firozi (2021) 'Transcript and audio of the call between Trump and Raffensperger', *Washington Post,* 5 January, available at: https://www.washingtonpost.com/politics/trump-raffensperger-call-tra nscript-georgia-vote/2021/01/03/2768e0cc-4ddd-11eb-83e3-322644d 82356_story.html, accessed 5 January 2021.

Giddens, Anthony (1984) *The Constitution of Society: Outline of the Theory of Structuration* (Berkeley: University of California Press).

Goethe, Johann Wolfgang von (1988 [1833]) 'Selections from "Maxims and Reflections"', in D. Miller (ed), *Goethe, Scientific Studies* (New York: Suhrkamp Publishers), pp 303–12.

Habermas, Jürgen (1996) 'Coping with contingencies: the return of historicism', in Józef Niznik and John T. Sanders (eds), *Debating the State of Philosophy: Habermas, Rorty and Kolakowsky* (London: Praeger), pp 1–24.

Habermas, Jürgen (1998) 'Richard Rorty's pragmatic turn', in Jürgen Habermas, *On the Pragmatics of Communication* (Cambridge, MA: MIT Press), pp 343–82.

Hawthorn, Geoffrey (1991) *Plausible Worlds: Possibility and Understanding in History and the Social Sciences* (Cambridge: Cambridge University Press).

Hellmann, Gunther (2020) 'How to know the future – and the past (and how not): a pragmatist perspective on foresight and hindsight', in Andreas Wenger, Ulrike Jasper, and Myriam Dunn Cavelty (eds), *The Politics and Science of Prevision: Governing and Probing the Future* (London: Routledge), pp 45–62.

Jackson, Patrick T. (2011) *The Conduct of Inquiry in International Relations: Philosophy of Science and Its Implications for the Study of World Politics* (London: Routledge).

James, William (1922 [1907]) *Pragmatism: A New Name for Some Old Ways of Thinking* (New York: Longmans, Green).

Kant, Immanuel (2012 [1793]) 'On the common saying: that may be correct in theory, but it is of no use in practice', in Immanuel Kant, *Practical Philosophy* (The Cambridge Edition of the Works of Immanuel Kant in Translation), trans. G. Mary (Cambridge: Cambridge University Press), pp 273–310.

King, Gary, Robert O. Keohane and Sidney Verba (1994) *Designing Social Inquiry: Scientific Inference in Qualitative Research* (Princeton, NJ: Princeton University Press).

Kratochwil, Friedrich (2000) 'Constructing a new orthodoxy? Wendt's "Social Theory of International Politics" and the constructivist challenge', *Millennium* 29, 1, pp 73–101.

Kratochwil, Friedrich (2011a) 'Making sense of "international practices"', in Emanuel Adler and Vincent Pouliot (eds), *International Practices* (Cambridge: Cambridge University Press), pp 36–60.

Kratochwil, Friedrich (2011b) 'A wanderer between two worlds: an Attempt at an intellectual biography', in Friedrich Kratochwil, *The Puzzles of Politics: Inquiries into the Genesis and Transformation of International Relations* (London: Routledge), pp 1–11.

Kratochwil, Friedrich (2018) *Praxis: On Acting and Knowing* (Cambridge: Cambridge University Press).

Kratochwil, Friedrich and John G. Ruggie (1986) 'A state of the art on an art of the state', *International Organization* 40, 4, pp 753–75.

Kuhn, Thomas S. (1990) 'Dubbing and redubbing: the vulnerability of rigid designation', in C. Wade Savage (ed), *Scientific Theories* (Minneapolis: University of Minnesota Press), pp 198–218.

Mearsheimer, John J. and Stephen M. Walt (2013) 'Leaving theory behind: why simplistic hypothesis testing is bad for International Relations', *European Journal of International Relations* 19, 3, pp 427–57.

Peirce, Charles Sanders (1997 [1877]) 'The fixation of belief', in Louis Menand (ed), *Pragmatism: A Reader* (New York: Vintage Books), pp 4–6.

Peirce, Charles Sanders (1997 [1878]) 'How to make our ideas clear', in Louis Menand (ed), *Pragmatism: A Reader* (New York: Vintage Books), pp 26–48.

Ragin, Charles C. (1992) 'Introduction: Cases of "what is a case?"', in Charles C. Ragin and Howard S. Becker (eds), *What Is a Case: Exploring the Foundations of Social Inquiry* (Cambridge: Cambridge University Press), pp 1–17.

Rorty, Richard (1970) 'Incorrigibility as the mark of the mental', *Journal of Philosophy* 67, 3, pp 399–429.

Rorty, Richard (1979) *Philosophy and the Mirror of Nature* (Princeton, NJ: Princeton University Press).

Rorty, Richard (1982) *Consequences of Pragmatism (Essays 1972–1980)* (Minneapolis: University of Minnesota Press).

Rorty, Richard (1989) *Contingency, Irony, and Solidarity* (Cambridge and New York: Cambridge University Press).

Rorty, Richard (1991) *Objectivity, Relativism, and Truth* (Cambridge and New York: Cambridge University Press).

Rorty, Richard (1999) 'Pragmatism as anti-authoritarianism', *Revue Internationale de Philosophie* 207, pp 7–20.

Rorty, Richard (2000) 'Universality and truth', in Robert B. Brandom (ed), *Rorty and His Critics* (Malden, MA: Blackwell), pp 1–30.

Rorty, Richard (2014 [1970]) 'Cartesian epistemology and changes in ontology', in Stephen Leach and James Tartaglia (eds), *Mind, Language, and Metaphilosophy: Early Philosophical Papers* (Cambridge: Cambridge University Press), pp 208–26.

Rorty, Richard (2020) *On Philosophy and Philosophers: Unpublished Papers, 1960–2000*, ed. Wojciech P. Malecki and Chris Voparil (Cambridge: Cambridge University Press).

Ryle, Gilbert (1945) 'Knowing how and knowing that', *Proceedings of the Aristotelian Society* 46, pp 1–16.

Savickey, Beth (2012) 'Wittgenstein's use of examples', in Marie McGinn and Oskari Kuusela (eds), *The Oxford Handbook of Wittgenstein* (Oxford: Oxford University Press), pp 667–96.

Sellars, Wilfrid (1963 [1962]) 'Philosophy and the scientific image of man', in Wilfrid Sellars, *Science, Perception and Reality* (Atascadero, CA: Ridgeview Publishing Company), pp 35–78.

Spencer-Brown, George (1972) *Laws of Form* (New York: Julian Press).

Waever, Ole (2013) 'Still a discipline after all these debates?', in Tim Dunne, Milja Kurki, and Steve Smith (eds), *International Relations Theories: Discipline and Diversity* (Oxford: Oxford University Press), pp 306–27.

Waltz, Kenneth N. (1979) *Theory of International Politics* (Reading, MA: Addison-Wesley).

Weber, Max (1973) 'Vom inneren Beruf zur Wissenschaft', in Max Weber, *Soziologie, universalgeschichtliche Analysen, Politik*, ed. Johannes Winckelmann (Stuttgart: Alfred Kröner), pp 311–39.

Wendt, Alexander (1999) *Social Theory of International Politics* (Cambridge: Cambridge University Press).

Wendt, Alexander (2006) 'Social theory as Cartesian science: an auto-critique from a quantum perspective', in Stefano Guzzini and Anna Leander (eds), *Constructivism in International Relations: Alexander Wendt and His Critics* (London: Routledge), pp 181–219.

Wendt, Alexander (2015) *Quantum Mind and Social Science* (Cambridge: Cambridge University Press).

Wight, Colin (2007) 'Inside the epistemological cave all bets are off', *Journal of International Relations and Development* 10, pp 40–56.

Wittgenstein, Ludwig (1997) *Über Gewissheit* (8th edn) (Frankfurt am Main: Suhrkamp).

Wittgenstein, Ludwig (2009 [1953]) *Philosophische Untersuchungen - Philosophical Investigations*, translated by Elizabeth Anscombe, Peter M.S. Hacker, and Joachim Schulte (4th edn) (Malden, MA: Wiley-Blackwell).

PART II

Praxis and the Law

If Not Rome or The Hague, Where? Reflections on Sanctioning and Punishing

Chris Brown

Introduction

Praxis is a big book in every sense of the term (Kratochwil, 2018). It offers profundity on a wide range of topics over an equally wide range of disciplines – International Relations and Law are central but Political Philosophy and Social Theory are also addressed. But what, centrally, is *Praxis* about? Mathias Albert was faced with this question when writing his *International Affairs* review and, wisely, ducked it by describing the book as a collage, a judgement Friedrich Kratochwil invited by choosing Altdorfer's 'Die Alexanderschlacht' as its cover illustration, a painting which is ostensibly about the Battle of Issus but actually offers a pictorial comment on more or less everything, up to and including the Day of Judgement (Albert, 2019). Such a collage makes for an exciting, challenging and often entertaining read, but it also means that any attempt to describe the main arguments of the book is in danger of falling into Borges's trap of trying to create a map of the empire on a scale of 1:1 – in order really to do justice to this book of 500 pages it would be necessary to write another book of 500 pages (Borges, 1975).

To avoid falling into this trap I intend to focus on one set of arguments relating to sanctioning and punishment, chapters 6 and 7 of *Praxis*. The argument I want to develop is that Kratochwil's answer to the issues raised by these topics is, in effect, a non-answer – he explains why current approaches to sanctioning and punishment are misconceived without providing an alternative. Perhaps of greater significance is the fact that he does not himself see this as problematic – he sees it as no part of his self-chosen brief to provide answers that are policy-relevant. Thereby hangs a more important tale: is the lack of interest in policy-relevant answers to the questions raised here indicative of a wider problem with the approach Kratochwil takes to politics and law?

Kratochwil on sanctions

As noted previously, *Praxis* is a book that defies summary, but it is at least clear that Kratochwil sees the practice of law as an important source of ideas and methods of reasoning for the study of international relations. On his account law – and, interestingly, I think in particular the common law tradition of England and (most of) the US – offers a take on politics, international and domestic, that avoids the sterility and logical errors of neo-positivist thought and provides the foundation for a practice theory that is potentially more fruitful than the Bourdieuian version espoused by, inter alia, Vincent Pouliot and Emanuel Adler (Adler and Pouliot, 2011). This is a strong claim which is well defended throughout the volume, but the chapters of *Praxis* where it needs to be cashed out are, I think, those on 'Sanctioning' and 'Punishing' – interestingly, these are the two longest chapters in the book, which in itself indicates their importance. This, as it were, is where the rubber hits the road, where legal reasoning and political practice unavoidably come together, so what Kratochwil has to say on these matters is interesting not just in terms of how the question posed in the previous section could be answered but also, arguably, in terms of his project taken as a whole.

Chapter 6, 'Sanctioning,' opens with an extended introduction which attempts to situate the practice of sanctioning, to

> [place] sanctions within the proper semantic field and show how sanctions connect with notions of legitimacy, authority, harm punishment and responsibility. Furthermore, this semantic field has then to be related to the practice of securing social order by deterring transgressions and inducing compliance, which in turn makes the examination of the efficacy of sanctions necessary. (Kratochwil, 2018: 193)

This immediately establishes an important point. It is clear that although an instrumental approach to sanctions is sometimes required, this cannot be the whole of the story. This is important because a great deal of the literature on sanctions focuses on effectiveness to the exclusion of other factors, as Kratochwil demonstrates in the rest of the introduction. His point is that states often impose sanctions without much concern for their instrumental effectiveness, for symbolic reasons, to assuage domestic concerns or to express deep disapproval of particular actions. For example, in a reference to the annexation of Crimea in 2014, Kratochwil remarks, surely correctly, that nobody expects the sanctions against the Russian Federation to actually get us back to the status quo ante (Kratochwil, 2018: 194). These sanctions are imposed to send a signal that Russia's conduct was unacceptable (but what does that mean? Unacceptable to whom?) and perhaps to persuade domestic opinion in Europe and the US that something was being done. An analysis of the effectiveness of sanctions is still required in this case as in others where sanctions have been applied, and much of the rest of this chapter concerns such an analysis, but instrumentality is not necessarily the most important dimension of sanctioning.

The introduction to Kratochwil's chapter is important and will be returned to again, but it is worthwhile here to rehearse briefly the rest of the content of this chapter. Reflecting the various dimensions of sanctioning, Kratochwil discusses positive sanctioning, approving, then, at greater length, sanctions and self-help, the latter being an important dimension of sanctioning in an allegedly anarchic world. His intention here is to contest the notion that self-help

> [is] just another way of retaliation when the law has run out, i.e., that in the absence of central enforcement 'taking the law into your own hands' need not be intersubjectively justified. But this view obscures the fact that self-help is a recognisable legal institution that plays an important role in international life as well as in domestic society. (Kratochwil, 2018: 206)

This position is developed at length, with the general discussion of the issue being followed by specific concentration on the idea of the feud as a form of self-help, on notions of self-defence and, interestingly, on counter-measures. The chapter ends with a discussion of sanctions and multilateralism – a critical analysis of some aspects of UN peacekeeping – and, finally, a return to cases, and specifically to the difficulties involved in comparing cases. This final discussion is particularly important because by discussing particular cases Kratochwil demonstrates that a simple cause-and-effect approach to efficacy does not work, and that accounts that focus exclusively on the intentions of actors are equally misleading. The important thing to realize is that action is always embedded in a strategic context of interdependent decision-making, and this strategic context applies to intentional approaches as well as to cause-and-effect approaches. The takeaway message here is that the decision to sanction might actually be the product of a range of pressures that produce an outcome that is the best 'all things considered' but which does not fully meet any of the various objectives involved.

Returning to the example mentioned previously, this latter proposition seems on the face of it a good way of describing the decision to impose sanctions on the Russian Federation after the annexation of Crimea and the incursion into the Donbas. The major European and NATO countries clearly felt the need to 'do something' about what they saw as Russia crossing a red line, but they disagreed among themselves about what the 'something' in question should be and what kind of relations with the Russian Federation should be aimed at. The resulting package of measures represented all kinds of cross-cutting pressures, were the product of inter-state bargaining and were imposed without the belief that they would achieve their ostensible object – as already noted, no one expected that they would reverse the annexation of Crimea. This, though, leads immediately to another question – given that the sanctions are not going to 'work' in the sense that they will force Russia to disgorge Crimea, at some point presumably they will have to be abandoned and relations with Russia regularized; what kinds of political manoeuvrings will be necessary to bring this about? I will return to this later.

By drawing attention away from a purely instrumental approach to sanctioning, Kratochwil makes it easier to see the underlying mechanisms that have led to the decision to impose sanctions in this case – easier to see that this was never a decision about how to get the Russians out of Crimea but rather a decision about how Western powers should respond to this patently illegal act, without any sense that the response would be instrumentally effective. Kratochwil's survey of the sanctioning literature may have brought us to this point – but perhaps there are other dimensions to this problem that haven't been explored. Here it is useful, as promised, to go back to the introduction to Kratochwil's chapter and identify a road not taken.

In the introduction Kratochwil notes that it is

> [rather] surprising that the big sanctioning debates over the last few decades have mainly focused on economic sanctions while the discussions of sanctions implying the use of force was either left to advocates of humanitarian intervention or to proponents of criminal prosecutions for human rights violations. Notions of a *guerre d'exécution* or some modern version of this have practically vanished from the ongoing debates. Even realists apparently have accepted the notion that forceful action requires some form of consent to the operation by the Security Council. (Kratochwil, 2018: 193)

This is, it seems to me, more or less right, but it opens up other questions. Such a *guerre d'exécution* took place in 1990/91 in response to Iraq's invasion of Kuwait, with UN sanction (Freedman, 1993). Iraq's act was clearly one of aggression against a fellow member of the UN, and the violent response was legally sanctioned as a result; whether it was wise is another question – in the event, it didn't turn out too badly but could have led to catastrophe. But the Crimea case was also pretty clearly an act of aggression by one state against another. The pretence that the troops that supported separatists in the Ukraine were locally raised, or volunteers, was just that, a pretence, and Russian President Vladimir Putin has effectively admitted that this was so (Putin, 2014). This was an act of aggression; the use of force in response was not directly considered, for obvious reasons – compelling Russia to withdraw could have, almost certainly would have, led to a disastrous war – but the failure to respond in the way the international community did in 1990 also has consequences which may still not have played out. To put the point I'm making differently, to explore the politics of sanctioning on the assumption that only economic sanctions are available skews the discussion in ways that may not be entirely helpful. Fortunately, the next chapter of *Praxis*, 'Punishing', takes us into the area I want to explore, offering insight on the 'crime of aggression', which is perhaps the angle we ought to bring to bear on the events of 2014 – although, of course, there is no guarantee that the end result will be any more satisfactory.

Kratochwil on punishment

Conventionally, international law is seen as more or less analogous to civil rather than criminal law. States are the major subjects of international law, along with inter-state bodies; individuals are not, with minor exceptions. States may attempt to resolve their disputes by legal means, but, even when they do so, in the absence of enforcement mechanisms they may ultimately resort to self-help measures, *in extremis* to war, more usually to the kind of positive and negative sanctions discussed earlier. The post-1945 world, however, has seen the emergence of international criminal law, initially via ad hoc tribunals and more recently via the establishment of an International Criminal Court (ICC) alongside the analogously civil International Court of Justice, and by the development of notions such as universal jurisdiction. In this new legal order individual heads of government, previously protected by the concept of sovereign immunity, are now potentially subject to the criminal law and liable to punishment. Kratochwil's chapter 7, 'Punishing', addresses this new development.

It would be fair to say that he is not well disposed towards this conception of how the law should work as between states. The key point he makes comes early on: criminal law assumes that there must be a source of authority such that punishment is legitimate – a monarch, God or 'we the people'. 'But' he asks, 'if this "we" is a precondition for the legitimacy of punishment how do we arrive in the international arena at such a "we"?' (Kratochwil, 2018: 250). He rightly suggests both that this is a question that is not asked often enough, and that it is difficult to answer because developing the necessary sense that criminality is a problem for a 'we' rather than for individual settlement is usually a long drawn-out process. The history of the emergence of the King's

Courts in England makes the point. It took the work of a number of strong rulers – Henry II, Henry III and Edward I – to establish that the act of murder was an offence not against the individual victim or his or her family, or against the village or manor, but rather an offence against the King's peace, something to be acted upon in the King's Courts – today's criminal trials maintain the terminology here; whereas civil trials in the UK are of the form Brown vs Smith, criminal trials are the Queen (Regina) vs Brown (or, e.g., the Commonwealth of Massachusetts vs Brown in those jurisdictions where the fiction that the Queen stands in for the actual 'we' that is the people no longer holds). The 'we' that in the British criminal process is represented by 'Regina' but now has a wider popular legitimacy did not simply emerge by some kind of natural process of evolution but by the exercise of brute force on the part of ruthless rulers; in many parts of the world, it remains the case that the feud and the payment of blood money are as important as, or more important than, the impersonal notion of criminal law.

The point is that an international 'we' does not currently exist and cannot be simply willed into existence. World society, the international community – these are terms that do have some meaning but not enough that the universal aspirations they convey can do real work. Kratochwil highlights the problems involved in determining the authority necessary for punishments to be legitimate, especially insofar as the punishments take the form of interventions, whether UN Security Council authorized or not. What he finds disturbing is that the 'criminals' identified in this way are no longer seen as 'enemies' in the Schmittian sense of a *justus hostis* but are seen as the servants of evil, an identification which is made with particular force precisely because the legitimacy of the original judgement that a crime has been committed is so hazy (Schmitt, 2007). In the process, the UN Charter's role as a limiter of force is subverted; instead, it legitimizes force in response to supposed crimes. As N.J. Rengger has noted at length, doctrines such as the Responsibility to Protect make international law and the ethics of force focus on the promotion of justice or the elimination of injustice rather than their original role of restraining force (Rengger, 2013).

This is all very well, but it does present a somewhat one-sided view of the world by focusing on the reactions to the 'crimes' rather than on the 'crimes' themselves. Consider as an analogy the politics of the anti-war movement in the UK as crystallized in the 'Stop the War Coalition', which was formed in 2001 in response to the war in Afghanistan and has been an opponent of all use of military force by the West ever since. The point is that the Coalition rarely criticizes the non-Western use of force that is often (admittedly not always) the stated reason for the Western use of force; thus, the use of NATO air power in Syria is condemned but the bombing of Syrian rebels by the Syrian regime and Russia is ignored or excused. And, returning to the earlier example, when Russia invaded Ukraine and annexed

Crimea, the response of the Stop the War Coalition was dominated by a very vocal (and unnecessary) demand that there be no military action by the West. I am pretty confident Kratochwil shares very little ideologically with the Coalition, but the logic of his position is similar. His focus throughout is on the illegitimacy of the self-proclaimed international policemen rather than on the actions of the putative international criminals.

Kratochwil discusses international criminal law in the context of two narratives, law as management and law as deliverance. The short discussion of law as management presents a quick overview of the claims made on behalf of allegedly post-sovereign, universal jurisdiction, human rights-based laws and the way in which the narrative that backs up these claims actually falls apart on close inspection.[1] Law as deliverance explores a more complex story and leads into a discussion of the crime of aggression and its fate from the Nuremburg and Tokyo tribunals through to the definition of aggression which came into force at the ICC in 2017.

There have been two bursts of creativity on this subject in the last century, the first at the time of the international tribunals held at Nuremberg and Tokyo after 1945, and the second linked to the establishment of the ICC, the Rome Statute of which did not include aggression as a justiciable crime, but which promised that it would at a later date, a promise now met. In these debates the concept of aggression has had two facets which are in principle separable but are difficult to keep apart, as Page Wilson has clarified (Wilson, 2012). On the one hand, the determination that aggression has taken place can be seen as triggering measures of collective enforcement among states in line with the concept of collective security; on the other hand, aggression can be seen as an international crime giving rise to individual responsibility. That these two aspects of aggression cannot be kept apart is identified as an issue by Kratochwil in his discussion of the Tokyo Tribunal which he, correctly I think, identifies as of more interest than Nuremberg on this topic. He describes some 'pretty strange' conclusions that followed from the preoccupation with crimes against peace and the planning of an aggressive war, quoting Chief Justice Webb as reported by Gerry Simpson as arguing: '[the] logical conclusion of the aggressive war doctrine was that a soldier or civilian who was opposed to the war but after it began decided it should be carried out … was guilty of waging aggressive war' (Wilson, 2012: 275).

---

[1]   There is a small mistake in the examples given of this narrative disintegrating: the British Law Lords did not send Pinochet home (Kratochwil, 2018: 267). The final judgment of the Law Lords was that Pinochet could be extradited to Spain albeit only on the basis of those incidents of torture that took place in the short period after Britain incorporated the Torture Convention into British law and before Pinochet left office. It was the Home Secretary who, as a political decision, sent Pinochet home, ostensibly on health grounds.

Kratochwil points out that: '[such] an argument would have altered the whole conceptual apparatus that traditionally distinguished between the *ius ad bellum* and the *ius in bello* – the former not being determinative of the latter' (Kratochwil, 2018: 276). This is indeed the case; regarding aggression as a crime for which individuals at the command level and below are potentially to be held responsible does change the game in a dramatic way – but Kratochwil's obvious belief that this is a 'pretty strange' proposal does not take into account the changes that have taken place in recent thinking on the ethics of war and on international practice.

Opposition to the proposition that the *ius ad bellum* is not determinative of the *ius in bello* is central to the recent attempt to rethink the just war tradition by analytical philosophers such as Jeff McMahan (2009) and David Rodin (2002). The argument of these so-called revisionists is that the conventional account of the Law of Armed Conflict which argues that all combatants possess essentially the same set of rights and duties whether taking part in an aggressive war or not, a position summarized by one of its defenders, Michael Walzer, as the 'moral equivalence' of combatants, is morally wrong (Walzer, 2015: 34ff) – for the revisionists there is no moral equivalence between combatants fighting a just war and combatants in an unjust war. Combatants in an unjust cause are not entitled to act aggressively or to defend themselves, and the fact that they were conscripted into the army and may not share the beliefs of their leaders is irrelevant in the context of their moral responsibility, precisely the 'pretty strange' conclusion noted by Kratochwil.

My point is not that this approach to the ethics of force is the right one to take – I have argued elsewhere that it is not (Brown, 2017) – but that it is more influential and less eccentric than Kratochwil assumes in his discussion of Tokyo and of the recent ICC-related debates around defining aggression. It is right to point to the problems of political justice as he does in the final section of the chapter, and it is right to argue that many of the debates around the definition of aggression are misconceived, but it is a mistake to underestimate their significance. To illustrate this point, consider the British debates over the legality of the 2003 Iraq War occasioned by the publication of the so-called Chilcot Report (Iraq Inquiry, 2017). A great deal of effort has gone into examining the way in which the final opinion of the Attorney General, which declared the war to be legal, was produced, and how it differed from earlier opinions – this has become a cause célèbre in the UK, at times taking attention away from the political issues generated by the war. The point is that it was the insistence of the British military that they be assured that this was a legal action and not an act of aggression that pushed the Attorney General to produce the opinion he did. Here is a clear case where the often abstruse and insecurely based debates about the crime of aggression had a real impact. The US military, hypersensitive to the legal aspects of the *conduct* of war – as witnessed by the important role of Judge

Advocates General when drone strikes are under consideration – seem not to have been anywhere near as concerned by the legality of the war as such; the United States' non-membership of the ICC or the European Convention on Human Rights (ECHR) meant that they did not feel this to be a pressing issue in the way their British colleagues did. Interestingly, aggression was not, at the time, covered by the Rome Statute, nor was the ECHR directly relevant; what influenced the UK military seems to have been the general sense that these matters were now, and ought to be, covered by law, rather than concern over any particular statute.

Although these debates about the crime of aggression have been rather more significant than one might have gathered from Kratochwil's account, his critique of some of the reasoning involved is justified, and, as his accounts of the French post-war show trials of Petain and Laval and of the various travails that have befallen the Justices of the ICC demonstrate, preserving the most basic principles of justice in this kind of trial is nearly impossible. The presumption of innocence can only be a barely maintained fiction; ad hoc tribunals almost by definition assume the guilt of those being tried, and the more formal procedures of the ICC do very little to correct this bias. Kratochwil's critique of the naivete of some of the advocates of international criminal law is also well founded – the absurdity of the apparent belief of one of its most distinguished advocates that Hitler's genocidal policies were carried out because he had noted the lack of effective reaction to the Armenian genocide is rightly identified (Kratochwil, 2018: 310). Still, at the end of the chapter, although a lot of poor reasoning has been exposed, one gets very little sense that anything positive has been established. Certainly, it is difficult to see how anything has been established that could provide useful policy advice on what we can or should do in response to, for example, the Russian actions of 2014, which clearly constituted an act of aggression against a UN member and a breach of recently signed treaties. Following the argument of chapter 6, we have seen that the sanctions that were actually imposed were extremely unlikely to reverse this act of aggression, and we have seen in chapter 7 that attempts to understand acts of aggression as either triggering a collective security response or leading to a justiciable crime of aggression are equally unlikely. In effect, after over 100 pages of tightly packed analysis – much of it, of course, very valuable in its own terms – Kratochwil's conclusion is not to have a conclusion, at least not one that is likely to be of use to a policy maker.

Theory and practice: a short digression

Before attempting to assess the implications of this lack of a conclusion for Kratochwil's project, a short digression may be helpful – a digression on the general question, what is International Relations (IR) theory for (Brown,

2016)? One answer might be that it isn't 'for' anything, it just 'is'; it is simply there to be contemplated and admired in all its complexity. Alternatively, I would suggest that IR *theory* is about improving (in some non-trivial sense of the term) the actual *practice* of international relations (defined very widely) – but that doesn't take us very far because of the multiple ways in which theory and practice are actually related when the bracketed terms are allowed to expand. Some IR theorists, mostly of a neo-positivist slant, understand this relationship as encapsulated by the idea of providing advice to the modern Prince or the latter's electorate, or, more ambitiously, aiming to speak truth to power. Realists such as John Mearsheimer and Stephen Walt tell us how to handle the rise of China, or, usually, why we are getting our response to issues such as the rise of China wrong. Liberals such as G. John Ikenberry explain the virtues of multilateral institutions. As I will suggest later in this chapter, there is something to be said in favour of this approach to the relationship between theory and practice, but it is clearly not the approach that Kratochwil adopts in *Praxis*.

Instead, Kratochwil is clearly contributing to a different kind of IR theory, conventionally labelled post-positivist or critical IR theory. What is this kind of theory for? Stephen K. White in his *Political Theory and Postmodernism* offers an interesting distinction. Contrasting the driving force – moral, political and aesthetic – behind the critical theory of the Frankfurt School with that which animates post-structuralists and post-modernists, he distinguishes between '[a] sense of "responsibility to act" and a sense of "responsibility to otherness". Corresponding to this distinction is one relating to language; its "action-coordinating" function and its "world-disclosing" function' (White, 1991: x). This is, I think, helpful. Although Kratochwil's work on critical legal theory does not map neatly onto any of White's starting points, in the end result the language he uses clearly is oriented towards 'world disclosure' rather than 'action coordination'. When we read Kratochwil on sanctions and punishment we see these topics in different ways to the way we saw them before engaging with his arguments, and this widening of our understanding is clearly part of a valuable exercise of world disclosure. Still, is it not reasonable to expect that a book entitled *Praxis* might also offer some contribution to the task of action coordination?

Praxis and policy

Returning to the main subject of this chapter, it may be helpful to begin to address the relationship between *Praxis* and policy by looking again to the events involving Russia and Crimea in 2014 and asking how the problem posed by Russian action might be resolved, given that it is clear that sanctions will not bring about a reversal of this deed. In practical terms the answer here is, I think, clear. It is more or less inevitable that eventually the Western powers will want to put the events of 2014 behind them and strike a deal with President Putin, a deal which will almost certainly involve Western recognition that Crimea is now part of the Russian Federation; there is more flexibility possible in the Donbas region, here one could anticipate some kind of local autonomy guaranteed on the understanding that the region remains at least nominally part of Ukraine. This would be very unsatisfactory from the point of view of the Ukrainian government, but it is unlikely that anything better will be on offer.

If – I think it is actually when rather than if – such a deal is made, it will be regarded by many as an act of appeasement; all the old tropes about Munich 1938 will be wheeled out, and they will be justified. There is a prima facie case that in 2014 President Putin committed the crime of aggression, and the deal set out previously would indeed allow him to hang on to most of the proceeds of his crime. And yet it is equally clear that there is no other course of action that makes any sense. Neither the Russian Federation nor President Putin himself can be forced into the dock to answer the charge of aggression, and the maintenance of sanctions which, however much harm they are doing to the Russian economy, have no chance of reversing the Russian annexation, cannot be sustained in the long term. The practical solution here is clear – a deal has to be struck, and sooner would be better than later.

This would be a practical solution, but would it be an ethically satisfactory solution? Would it be a solution that was consistent with the kind of arguments set out in *Praxis*? Having challenged the reasoning behind sanctioning and demolished the case for punishment, it is difficult to see how Kratochwil could object to the ending of sanctions in this case, but neither could he make a principled case in its favour, given his refusal to provide an alternative to the ideas he dismisses. In some respects, the attitude of realists seems more to the point. Figures such as Walt and Mearsheimer have in terms suggested that the deal outlined should be endorsed as a reasonable outcome given the power relations involved (Mearsheimer, 2014; Walt, 2015). Critics will say that this is in the tradition of E.H. Carr's support for the policy of appeasement in the first edition of *Twenty Years Crisis*, and which disappeared in later editions (Fox, 1985). But in that case there was actually the opportunity to resist the aggressor by military means, which with a nuclear armed power such as Russia is no longer possible, and Hitler's ambitions were unappeasable, whereas there is at least some reason to believe that President Putin's ambitions, though directed against the West, can be frustrated without a disastrous world war (Belton, 2020). But if realism has an answer in this case, and if the kind of constructivism espoused by Kratochwil does not, is this not an indication that there are rather serious limits to the value of this kind of work? Our eyes have been opened, a world has been disclosed to us, but, if we want some help with arriving at an acceptable solution to an intractable problem, we had better look elsewhere.

Perhaps, though, the relevant dimension of *Praxis* is indeed to be found elsewhere, other than in the two chapters that on the face of it look most obviously relevant to my subject matter. It is later in the book, when Kratochwil turns to 'Acting' (chapter 10) and 'Judging and Communicating' (chapter 11), that we get to the practice turn in IR theory and get some better sense of what Kratochwil understands as the practical dimension of *Praxis*. To me rather surprisingly, much of his argument here is directed against ideal theorists of a post-Rawlsian disposition in their approaches to global justice, or more recently, to the ethics of force internationally. He recognizes that the philosophical underpinnings of these post-Rawlsian theories are very similar to those of the so-called neo-positivists who fail to realize that intersubjective social relations cannot be treated in the same way as the reference objects of the natural scientists. The result is that ideal theory produces solutions which, by ignoring the realities of a world where compliance cannot be assumed, can have little contact with practice and thus cannot be action-guiding. For Kratochwil this is unacceptable; his own approach, set out in *Praxis*, is designed to avoid this sterility. *Praxis* is, necessarily, about practice.

But what does *Praxis* actually have to say about practice? It is clearly not in any straightforward way about 'action coordination'. As we have seen in the Crimea 2014 case, *Praxis* is effective at showing us the limits of the concepts we might employ to approach this case, but it does not offer alternatives, leaving us to look elsewhere for policy relevance. So, what does practice mean for *Praxis*? The answer, I think, for Kratochwil lies in a cashing out of the Aristotelian idea of *phronesis*. His understanding of *phronesis* is set out most explicitly in the final pages of the book, which he describes as 'in lieu of a conclusion' – here we find approval for conceptions of politics derived from a number of sources: from the classics, in particular, interestingly, from the *Odyssey*;[2] from Hannah Arendt's thoughts on politics and the good life; and, most important I think, an account of politics as a conversation and not as an approach to problem-solving. This latter position is referenced to David Hume (Kratochwil, 2018: 475) but it could equally be seen as reflecting Michael Oakeshott's rejection of a 'teleocratic' conception of politics. Oakeshott contrasts his own understanding of politics as a conversation about the common arrangements of a society with that of the teleocrats, who see politics as directed towards particular enterprises, in the modern age usually involving measures to increase GDP or reduce inequality – his

---

[2] Interesting because Odysseus isn't usually seen as 'prudent' but rather as 'wily' or 'crafty'; Emily Wilson's excellent recent translation begins: 'Tell me about a complicated man', which seems right but isn't what we normally think of as a description of a *phronimos* (Homer, 2018: 105).

commitment to the former is based on the belief that the latter requires a unity of purpose that does not, in fact, exist (Oakeshott, 1991a, b).

This notion of practice is action-guiding in the rather limited sense that it tells us broadly what our orientation should be towards the political questions of the day – namely sceptical towards those offering easy solutions – but it is not action-guiding in the more obvious sense of being able to help us to decide what to do in particular situations. Given this understanding of the nature of politics, the focus on events in 2014 that has been a feature of this discussion is seriously misconceived. Kratochwil's critique can tell us why the models of appropriate conduct summarized by the metonyms of Rome and The Hague are not going to be helpful, but he cannot give us an alternative answer. To do so would be to concede ground to the teleocratic understanding of politics as a problem-solving activity. This simply isn't what the practice turn as elaborated in *Praxis* is all about.

Conclusion

To put the same point in another way, the problem with the strategy employed in this chapter, namely, to ask what *Praxis* has to offer in the matter of finding a response to a specific example of an action which would seem to merit sanctioning and punishment, is that it misunderstands the scope and intention of Kratochwil's book. *Praxis* is not a work of social science, but rather a work of philosophy – it is concerned with 'practice' but only in a very broad sense and as the basis for a critique of philosophically naive approaches to social action. As a social scientist I might be unhappy with this, as I see it, very limited ambition, but that is my problem, not Kratochwil's – he is under no obligation to meet my expectations as to what a book on *Praxis* might be expected to deliver.

This is clearly true, and as a general rule one should never criticize an author for writing the book that he or she wanted to write rather than the book that the reviewer would have preferred him or her to have written. Obviously not all works of scholarship have or should have directly practical applications. As noted previously, one answer to the question 'what is IR theory for?' is that it isn't *for* anything, it just *is*. If we are civilized human beings we do not ask what, say, the study of medieval poetry is for, nor, for that matter, do we ask why so many physicists have spent so much of their time and our money constructing the Large Hadron Collider under the Swiss-French border at Geneva. The pursuit of knowledge for its own sake, with no practical application in mind, is one of the glories of human civilization and needs no further justification. Still, I find it difficult to avoid a feeling of discontent as I come to the end of the book. To have worked through a study that offers so much food for thought, that offers such a sophisticated account of the world of praxis and then to find that all this wisdom actually cannot offer us any way through the real problems that we, as citizens or as practitioners, must face, is, I think, a little depressing. But, to reiterate, that is my problem, not Kratochwil's.

References

Adler, Emanuel and Vincent Pouliot, eds (2011) *International Practices* (Cambridge: Cambridge University Press).

Albert, Mathias (2019) 'Review of F. Kratochwil *Praxis* and S. Lechner and M. Frost's *Practice Theory and International Relations*', *International Affairs* 95, 2, pp 469–70.

Belton, Catherine (2020) *Putin's People: How the KGB Took Back Russia and then Took on the West* (London: Collins).

Borges, Jorge Luis (1998) 'On exactitude in science', in Jorge Luis Borges, *Collected Fictions* (London: Penguin Books), p 325.

Brown, Chris (2016) 'Theory and practice in International Relations', in Ken Booth and Toni Erskine (eds), *International Relations Theory Today* (2nd edn) (Cambridge: Polity Press), pp 39–52.

Brown, Chris (2017) 'Revisionist just war theory and the impossibility of a moral victory', in Andrew R. Hom et al (eds), *Moral Victories* (Oxford: Oxford University Press), pp 85–100.

Fox, William Thornton Rickert (1985) 'E.H. Carr and political realism: vision and revision', *Review of International Studies* 11, 1, pp 1–16.

Freedman, Lawrence (1993) *The Gulf Conflict 1990 – 1991* (Princeton, NJ: Princeton University Press).

Homer (2018) *The Odyssey*, trans. Emily Wilson (New York: W.W. Norton).

Iraq Inquiry, The (2017) The Report: Executive Summary, available at: https://webarchive.nationalarchives.gov.uk/20171123122743/http://www.iraqinquiry.org.uk/the-report/, accessed 23 December 2020.

Kratochwil, Friedrich (2018) *Praxis: On Acting and Knowing* (Cambridge: Cambridge University Press).

McMahan, Jeff (2009) *Killing in War* (Oxford: Oxford University Press).

Mearsheimer, John (2014) 'Why the Ukraine crisis is the West's fault', *Foreign Affairs* 93, 5, pp 85–9.

Oakeshott, Michael (1991a) *On Human Conduct* (revd edn) (Oxford: Clarendon Press).

Oakeshott, Michael (1991b) *Rationalism in Politics and Other Essays* (2nd edn) (Indianapolis, IN: Liberty Fund).

Putin, Vladimir Vladimirowitsch (2014) Address by President of the Russian Federation to the State Duma, 18 March, available at: http://en.kremlin.ru/events/president/news/20603, accessed 23 December 2020.

Rengger, Nicholas J. (2013) *Just War and International Order* (Cambridge: Cambridge University Press).

Rodin, David (2002) *War and Self Defence* (Oxford: Oxford University Press).

Schmitt, Carl (2007) *The Concept of the Political: Expanded Edition* (Chicago, IL: University of Chicago Press).

Walt, Stephen M. (2015) 'Why arming Kiev is a really, really bad idea', *Foreign Policy*, 9 February, available at: https://foreignpolicy.com/2015/02/09/how-not-to-save-ukraine-arming-kiev-is-a-bad-idea/, accessed 23 December 2020.

Walzer, Michael (2015) *Just and Unjust Wars* (5th edn) (New York: Basic Books).

White, Stephen K. (1991) *Political Theory and Postmodernism* (Cambridge: Cambridge University Press).

Wilson, Page (2012) *Aggression, Crime and International Security* (London: Routledge).

7

Practical Constitutionalism

Anthony F. Lang, Jr.

Introduction

In his recently published book *Praxis*, Friedrich Kratochwil argues that action should be at the centre of our investigations in International Relations (IR). In making that claim, he positions himself against two theoretical starting points: (1) the agent is simply a vessel for structural factors, so 'causes' matter more than 'reasons'; and (2) there is no real agency because of the instability of the subject. One might argue that he is locating a middle ground between positivism (position 1) and post-structuralism (position 2). He does this through an overview of a wide range of themes at the intersection of international politics and international law.

In any work that seeks to recover a praxis-based approach, Aristotle is an obvious figure; indeed, Kratochwil's subtitle to the book (*On Acting and Knowing*) comes directly from Aristotle's two categories of virtues, the practical and the theoretical (Aristotle, 1941: 952). Aristotle has long been in the background and sometimes foreground of Kratochwil's work. In *Praxis*, Kratochwil invokes Aristotle a number of times. At the same time, he critiques Aristotle for what Kratochwil argues is the former's overly theoretical focus at the expense of practical politics. Instead, in *Praxis*, Kratochwil finds more benefit in the work of David Hume, about whom he has written previously (Kratochwil, 2011a [1981]).

In this chapter, I argue that Aristotle is more beneficial than Kratochwil makes him out to be for understanding the practical dimensions of international law and politics. In particular, I argue that Aristotle provides an alternative understanding of the rule of law and how it relates to the wider international political order, one that differs both from Kratochwil and from contemporary international law. As Kratochwil notes, Aristotle became a reference point for many in the early modern and modern periods in support of a law-governed polity. In recent years, this invocation of the rule of law has become a mantra for advocates of global governance, one that has lost any connection to the political context within which the rule of law might function. Aristotle provides important insights into the rule of law, which is not a simple universalizing device but functions differently in accordance with the constitutional framework within which it sits. In addition, for the rule of law to function, there needs to be a citizen body that is economically equal and well educated. Equality and education help to create citizens who are willing to rule and be ruled, the political virtues that Aristotle argues are central to a well-governed polity.

Does this insight of Aristotle's help us to understand international affairs? International political economists have long argued for the centrality of economics for understanding international affairs, but rarely do theorists sitting at the intersection of law and politics address this dimension.[1] Aristotle's second point about the importance of education for understanding and acting in politics is more difficult to identify at the global level. There exist global institutions, such as UNESCO, which are focused on education. To identify these, however, is a challenge, and yet, if Aristotle is correct, it is one that requires more effort and attention than has thus far been the case in the scholarship on international politics and law.

The chapter proceeds as follows: the first section sets out Kratochwil's use of Aristotle throughout his work. The second part of the chapter explores in some depth Aristotle's idea of the rule of law, highlighting the importance of equality and education in how the rule of law functions. Highlighting these two dimensions of Aristotle's work suggests that Kratochwil's focus on Aristotle's theoretical side misses these very practical dimensions of his work. This also highlights the fact that ancient constitutionalism relied more heavily on the social and the political rather than the narrowly legal. The phrase 'practical constitutionalism' highlights this element of Aristotle's work. The concluding section turns briefly to the international level to see if there are any contextual backgrounds that mirror Aristotle's concerns with economics and education. The chapter proposes practical global constitutionalism as a way to bring in such contextual factors in our understanding of the global legal and political order.

Kratochwil's Aristotle

One cannot possibly claim to cover all of Kratochwil's works; with such a prolific writer, there are too many texts to try to address the 'real Fritz

---

[1] For one approach that does, see the work on 'new constitutionalism' as in Gill and Cutler (2014).

Kratochwil' or even 'how Fritz Kratochwil understands Aristotle'. The aim here is to focus on a few key texts and to bring out the central aims of his engagement with Aristotle and, following upon that, his understanding of constitutional theory.

In *Rules, Norms, and Decisions* (Kratochwil, 1989), Aristotle figures prominently in the argument. The focus of this book, however, is on forms of legal argument and the ways in which those forms are misunderstood by IR scholars and, to a lesser extent, international legal theorists. Aristotle provides Kratochwil a means, however, to address this problem through the former's conception of *topoi*, or 'commonplaces' for 'practical reasoning' (Kratochwil, 1989: 38). Kratochwil deploys this rhetorical concept to help us understand not only how speakers make arguments but how listeners assent to those arguments. This point is important, for the modern-day English understanding of rhetoric implies a superficial focus on language, in the sense of 'that's just rhetoric, it doesn't mean anything'. In the ancient world, especially in thinkers such as Aristotle and Cicero, rhetoric was a sophisticated science that sought to understand how speakers shape and influence their audience. This relates directly to Kratochwil's project in which he is trying to understand how rules and norms lead to decisions and how those decisions then shape the international legal and political order. For Kratochwil, classical rhetoric leads to a constructivist focus on language, which he and Nicholas Onuf created in their two different but parallel 1989 books (Kratochwil, 1989; Onuf, 1989).

Kratochwil's understanding of rhetoric also points to the idea of praxis. As he argues, '[r]hetoric is concerned with the problem of praxis, i.e., with gaining adherence to an alternative in a situation in which no logically compelling solution is possible but a choice cannot be avoided' (Kratochwil, 1989: 210). So, while the book is about legal argumentation, it is also about political practices and how legal arguments shape what practices are possible.[2] Kratochwil points out that Aristotle's focus on rhetoric is not simply one of psychological persuasion; rather, at the core of Aristotle's understanding of rhetoric is the enthymeme, a type of logical reasoning that draws on examples and shared assumptions of a society. That is, rather than an airtight logical proof which relies on a closed sphere of definitions, enthymemes are 'rhetorical proofs' which enable a speaker to convince an audience of a point as a result of connecting examples and assumptions.

---

[2] This differentiates Kratochwil's approach from that of Martii Koskenniemi, whose 1989 book *From Apology to Utopia* reads very much as the work of an international legal theorist, more interested in the formal nature of legal argument than in the ways it leads to different forms of political action (Koskenniemi, 2006 [1989]).

In Kratochwil's 2014 book *The Status of Law in World Society*, Aristotle appears again, now in a slightly different role. Rather than being a theorist of rhetoric and the function of *topoi* in argumentation, one of Aristotle's own *topoi* is referenced. This is the famous discussion of the rule of law in the *Politics*, which has long influenced both legal and political theory. The following is the quote from the *Politics*, a slightly longer version than what Kratochwil cites in his text:

> That is why it is thought to be just that among equals everyone be ruled as well as rule, and therefore that all should have their turn. We thus arrive at law; for an order of succession implies law. And the rule of the law, it is argued, is preferable to that of any individual. On the same principle, even if it be better for certain individuals to govern, they should be made only guardians and ministers of the law. For magistrates there must be – this is admitted; but then men say that to give authority to any one man when all are equal is unjust. There may indeed be cases which the law seems unable to determine, but such cases a man could not determine either. But the law trains officers for this express purpose, and appoints them to determine matters which are left undecided by it, to the best of their judgment. Further, it permits them to make any amendment of the existing laws which experience suggests. Therefore, he who bids the law rule may be deemed to bid God and Reason alone rule, but he who bids man rule adds an element of the beast; for desire is a wild beast, and passion perverts the minds of rulers, even when they are the best of men. The law is reason unaffected by desire. (Aristotle, 1996: 88)[3]

Kratochwil first refers to this passage as the 'traditional *topos* of *nomos basileus* (the law is king) which in republican thought became the "rule of law" trope, invoked in *Marbury vs. Madison*' (Kratochwil, 2014: 5). Later in the text, he undertakes a more extended discussion of this *topos*. In his 'Meditation 3: On Constitutions and Fragmented Orders', Kratochwil begins with a discussion of ancient constitutionalism, with a focus on the Greeks. In it, he argues that Aristotle's *topos* was part of his argument that constitutions and legal orders could be 'made' rather than result from customs and social norms (Kratochwil, 2014: 75–6). This approach to constitutionalism reached its apogee in the written constitutions of the French and American revolutions, conscious efforts to recreate a society anew, a more radical effort in the

---

[3]   The traditional way of referring to texts in the Aristotelian corpus is via book, chapter and line number. I have decided not to use this method for this chapter for ease of reference.

French case than in the American (Arendt, 1968).[4] Aristotle appears in the 2014 book a few more times, mainly in support of Kratochwil's references to practical wisdom and judgement.

In *Praxis*, Aristotle appears in two key moments of the argument. First, in setting out his understanding of constructivism, Kratochwil introduces Aristotle's naturalist account of communication. Noting, as does Aristotle, that many species live in semi-organized communities, Kratochwil draws on Aristotle's famous quote from Book I of the *Politics* in which the ability to speak makes human society radically different – 'there is no dispute that an entirely new world emerges with such speech' (Kratochwil, 2018: 24). This fundamental point makes the 'Aristotelian heritage' crucial for constructivist theorizing, especially if there is to be any link between this theoretical agenda and natural or scientific accounts of the world in which we live. While Aristotle's science is certainly problematic in a number of ways, the importance of communication for differentiating the human condition from the rest of the natural world remains a central feature of many contemporary accounts of human nature.

Having located his constructivism in relation to Aristotle, Kratochwil turns to Aristotle later in the text when he explores the nature of meaningful action. In a book entitled *Praxis*, a chapter 'On Acting' will certainly be at the core of the argument, and Aristotle helps Kratochwil advance his conception of what it means to act in a meaningful way. He argues that Aristotle introduces a number of ways of knowing. Aristotle helps us to see that 'an agent is neither served by logic alone, nor is s/he helped by the knowledge of what is true in general' (Kratochwil, 2018: 397). Rather, because action takes place in time, it becomes more particular and practical in orientation, rendering some forms of knowing less helpful than others. Experience and judgement are the practical virtues that Aristotle brings forth. Kratochwil finds this an important step, but critiques Aristotle for concluding that theoretical knowledge is the most important, suggesting that this conclusion results from the influence of his teacher, Plato, who had even less time for practical knowledge than Aristotle did. Kratochwil reminds us that Aristotle believed the 'highest form of knowledge has to do with the transcendent unchanging being and he suggested that someone engaging with the contemplation of these ideas becomes similar even to God' (Kratochwil, 2018: 399). Indeed, in the quote on the rule of law

---

4   Kratochwil's reading of Aristotle here is somewhat unique, especially if compared with Charles McIlwain's famous *Constitutionalism: Ancient and Modern*, in which he argues that the ancient constitution was largely based on custom and it was not until the revolutions of the 18th century that the consciously designed constitution emerges (McIlwain, 2008 [1948]).

cited earlier, Aristotle defends law because of its generality and lack of emotion, equating it to God or Reason, which normal political action cannot attain. Because of this privileging of theoretical knowledge over the practical, Kratochwil leaves Aristotle behind and turns to the other figure who has oriented many of his philosophical underpinnings, David Hume, who helps him to round out his understanding of praxis and its relationship to politics.

Kratochwil's Aristotle, then, begins in logic, moves to nature and ends in different forms of knowledge. Aristotle clearly informs and structures much of the way in which Kratochwil has approached constructivism, law and politics. As noted previously, it is no accident that the subtitle of *Praxis* reflects the two Aristotelian virtues, the practical and the theoretical. In the end, Kratochwil wishes to bring the practical to the fore in ways that he does not find Aristotle capable of doing. Aristotle puts the theoretical virtues before the practical ones, and Kratochwil is correct in that this is undoubtedly a heritage of his teacher Plato. Aristotle's naturalism and desire to find universally true understandings of the human condition also move him away from the contingent toward the general.[5] The next section of this chapter argues that there is in Aristotle's work more resources for understanding the practical than Kratochwil allows. It explores in more detail the *topos* of the rule of law and connects it to Aristotle's practical concerns with how to structure a political order through economics and education. Admittedly, Aristotle's concerns here are linked to his desire for a universal truth, that is, how to create a political order that will not fall to revolution. But to achieve this universally good goal, Aristotle's method is a practical one which relies upon contingent, particular policies and which creates a particular understanding of constitutionalism, or practical constitutionalism.

Aristotle's practical constitutionalism

Aristotle's political thought has long been a source of constitutional theory, not only in his reference to the rule of law, but perhaps more importantly in the way in which he is invoked as the first 'political scientist' through his compilation of constitutions from the ancient Greek world. This attempt at comparative politics provides an early example of how one might gather data and test them against a set of hypotheses. Aristotle's goal, though, differs importantly from contemporary political science in that he sought not only to establish causal relations but a much more important goal: what is the best regime and how can it be made to last.

---

[5]   For one account of how Aristotle's naturalism remains at the core of the modern scientific method, see Leroi (2014).

This chapter is not the place to summarize Aristotle's insights into politics. Instead, the chapter highlights the relationship of his ideas about law to a constitutional context and suggests how they are more practical than Kratochwil indicates in his use of him. This is not really a critique of Kratochwil's account of Aristotle, which, frankly, is more fully grounded in the broad Aristotelian corpus. Instead, this section draws out some of the practical dimensions of Aristotle's work in order to develop this idea of practical constitutionalism and how it might help us to see the rule of law in a way that goes beyond its status as a *topos* for liberal or republican ideas of law.

As noted previously, Aristotle's famous statement on the rule of law comes in Book III of the *Politics*, after he has set out the different forms of government. These forms, which have both good and bad versions, result from how many rule, that is, one, few or many. The fullest discussion of the rule of law comes within Aristotle's analysis of the rule by one, which in the positive form is monarchy and in the negative form is tyranny. Aristotle raises the question of whether rule by one or rule by many is better; his conclusion, as many scholars have pointed out, is not entirely clear. He concludes Book III by noting that the best form of government is 'that which is administered the best, and in which there is one man, or a whole family, or many persons, excelling all the others together in excellence, and both the rulers and subjects are fitted, the one to rule, the others to be ruled, in such a manner as to attain the most desirable life' (Aristotle, 1996: 91). This suggests that Aristotle may not have been seeking to determine the absolute best form of government but was seeking to establish how to make different forms of government function well.

Following from this point, he differentiates between the good and bad of each of the three forms, and respect for the law and the goodness of the laws appears to be a critical component in determining whether those forms are positive or negative. As he states in chapter 11 of Book III:

> that laws, when good, should be supreme; and that the magistrate or magistrates should regulate those matters only on which the laws are unable to speak with precision owing to the difficulty of any general principle embracing all particulars. But what are good laws has not yet been clearly explained; the old difficulty remains. The goodness or badness, justice or injustice, of laws varies of necessity with the constitutions of states. This, however, is clear, that the laws must be adapted to the constitutions. But, if so, true forms of government will of necessity have just laws, and perverted forms of government will have unjust laws. (Aristotle, 1996: 78)

Aristotle makes two other important points about law. The first concerns equality. After setting out his position that laws function differently in different states, he turns to a discussion of equality. He points out that 'we see that legislation is necessarily concerned with only those who are equal in birth and capacity; and that for men of pre-eminent excellence there is no law – they are themselves a law. Anyone would be ridiculous who attempt to make laws for them' (Aristotle, 1996: 82). This leads him into a discussion of ostracism and why it is sometimes necessary to remove the wealthy and successful from a polity. The importance of equality returns in Book V, where he has a much longer discussion of how to prevent a revolution. While he notes that revolutions arise from a range of different sources, perhaps the most important is the demand for equality among citizens. When unequal conditions become more prominent in a social and political order, dissatisfaction with that order surges. This explanation for revolution is not just relevant for the ancient world but has become one of the most prominent findings of modern-day political science (Gurr, 1970).

A second point about law comes soon after the discussion of equality. In Book IV, Aristotle goes on to argue that it is not simply the existence of law, but that two subsidiary criteria exist for law to serve as a means to distinguish good from bad government: 'Hence, there are two parts to good government; one is the actual obedience of citizens to the laws, the other part is the goodness of the laws which they obey' (Aristotle, 1996: 103). The importance of citizens who will obey laws relies on Aristotle's assumption about the virtues of the good citizen. A good citizen is one who can rule and be ruled, and being ruled means being able to obey the law. This requires the cultivation of a particular type of person, not a slavish rule follower but a citizen who can both engage in the making of rules and be willing to follow those rules.

Thus, the rule of law within Aristotle has some nuance. Laws will function differently in different political systems, and law will only function if the laws are followed by citizens who feel themselves to be equal and who are able to play some role in governing themselves. Aristotle's understanding of law, then, is not a universal rule applied across all cases in the same way but provides an ethos that should govern how we understand our role as citizens in a political order. But to achieve that good order, no matter what our form of government, a political order needs to institute certain practices to ensure that the law functions effectively. What are those practices?

First, as explored at some length in Book V of the *Politics*, a good political system is one that does not fall victim to a revolution. Aristotle, in many ways, seems to have written the *Politics* not to create an ideal type of political order, as did Plato in the *Republic*. Rather, he seems to be writing a book that will give practical advice to rulers of any particular political system in order to allow them to govern effectively. This is certainly not an 'advisor to the Prince' type of work, such as Machiavelli's *The Prince*. Aristotle states quite clearly in chapter 9 of Book III that the polity is a place for people not just to live together, but to live well together and to engage in noble actions. To simply allow a ruler to rule is not Aristotle's concern, but to propose ways in which different kinds of political systems can be the best possible systems is what animates his work (Aristotle, 1996: 75).

So, what prevents a state from collapsing? There are many ways in which a revolution might come about, but the one that Aristotle devotes his attention to is equality. A state that has formal equality among its citizens is a state in which the people will not rise up in jealousy against each other or their rulers. But formal equality before the law cannot function if people do not really see themselves as equal. And that equality relies very heavily on their material well-being. This does not mean that there must be an exact material equality across all persons, but if there is radical inequality across the society this will most certainly result in political unrest. This leads Aristotle to focus on the importance of the middle class. In fact, even before discussing revolution, which he does extensively in Book V, he devotes a good part of Book IV to the importance of the middle class. Building on his belief that the mean is the most important standard to achieve virtue for either a person or a state, Aristotle notes:

> Thus it is manifest that the best political community is formed by citizens of the middle class, and that those states are likely to be well-administered in which the middle class is large, and stronger if possible than other classes, or at any rate than either singly; for the addition of the middle class turns the scale, and prevents either of the extremes from being dominant. (Aristotle, 1996: 108)

Aristotle does not give specific advice on how to create such a class, but he does highlight the importance of property ownership and ensuring that those who are extremely wealthy might be ostracized from a community in order to keep this balance in place. That is, he has a practical concern with ensuring economic equality in order to ensure that a political system functions effectively.

The second practical element of Aristotle's constitutionalism is education. Book III begins with an extensive discussion of citizenship, though without much detail on how to make good citizens. It is not until Books VII and VIII that Aristotle explores in some depth how to make good citizens. Book VII explores how to make citizens good, including provision of food and when to marry, while Book VIII turns to how to educate citizens. This last book is the shortest of all, and many scholars agree it seems unfinished. Yet it does state quite clearly what a good education entails, including reading, drawing, gymnastics and, surprisingly, music. Music is included not because it is practical in the way that the other subjects are but because it provides 'intellectual enjoyment in leisure' (Aristotle, 1996: 197). Aristotle here is highlighting that while we may think of education into citizenship as being about the practical arts of business or politics, what we enjoy in our leisure time and how we like to play is perhaps what will make us who we are. This is practical guidance in a different, but no less important, sense. That is, to be the type of citizen who can rule and be ruled requires attending to how we play and not just how we work.

This section has explored the practical nature of Aristotle's understanding of law and politics. And these practical dimensions link the law to the wider 'constitutional' order within which they sit. That is, the ancient notion of constitutionalism is not one that relies only a legal code or even a description of institutions and their relation to each other. Instead, it includes a social and broadly defined political dimension that relates back to those institutional forms. Aristotle's practical constitutionalism suggests that perhaps Kratochwil might have been too quick to locate Aristotle in the category of a theoretical thinker rather than a practical one. Admittedly, his practical suggestions rely on theoretical and idealist assumptions. But they do move us towards ways of being and acting in the world that might map more closely onto Kratochwil's praxis orientation.

Practical global constitutionalism

In concluding, I want to briefly suggest how Aristotle's practical constitutionalism might help us to understand law and politics at the global level. That is, can Aristotle provide us any resources for how we might think about global constitutionalism? And how would those resources speak to some of the ways in which Kratochwil has articulated his notion of praxis as a way to understand the international order?

Most certainly, economic inequality remains at the centre of all politics. Global inequality, however, is complex. According to some scholars, global inequality is in fact decreasing as a result of the increase in wealth of China and India, even while inequality within some societies is increasing. According to Branko Milanovic, globally the lowest classes have seen their incomes increase, the middle classes have seen their incomes decrease and the upper classes have seen their incomes skyrocket (Milanovic, 2016). This divergence in economic growth could explain why movements such as Occupy Now were largely based in developed countries, where the 2008 financial crisis hit middle classes much harder than it did the lower classes in developing countries.

How does this relate to Aristotle's emphasis on equality and the rule of law? First, according to neoliberal economics, the imposition of a liberal rule of law agenda will result in income increase for all (Hayek, 2009 [1960]). Yet the income increases for the lower classes in places such as China and India are not the result of simple neoliberal policies; indeed, the mixed economic and political practices in these countries with increasing incomes result from decidedly non-liberal economic and political systems. What does this mean for the analysis here? As Aristotle highlighted, the rule of law is not a single practice but relies on different political systems. Perhaps this is evidence for Aristotle's argument; some form of a rule of law is being put in place in developing countries, but it is not necessarily the neoliberal model assumed by many development economists. Instead, it is one that is nuanced and reflective of the societies where it is being put in place. This suggests that a global push towards a great neoliberal economic and political rule of law agenda may not be the best way to create greater equality and a strong middle class.

This also relates to debates among scholars writing about global constitutionalism. In the *Handbook on Global Constitutionalism*, scholars of law and economics provide different positions on whether or not neoliberal institutions such as the World Trade Organization, International Monetary Fund and World Bank are reflective of a stronger global constitutionalism or are simply tools by which powerful interests are advancing their own agendas. The former position is reflected in the contribution by Joel Trachtman, a leading scholar on global constitutionalism and economics (Trachtman, 2017), while the latter is represented by Gavin Anderson, a leading critical theorist of global constitutionalism (Anderson, 2017). Anderson's position is certainly not an Aristotelian one, but it captures the more critical position on global economics and its relation to the rule of law that the Aristotelian position I have set out suggests.

This is not the place to suggest practical solutions to the problems of global economics; instead, the point I wish to make is that rather than a neoliberal rule of law agenda solving the world's problems, a more nuanced, socially attentive and practical approach to creating a global middle class is necessary. This reflects Aristotle's key insights that equality matters for the rule of law to work and that the rule of law functions in different ways depending on the circumstances of different political and social systems.

What of education? Education is something that must be even more attuned to the local context; indeed, in countries such as the US, all educational policies are formulated at a local level. Is it at all possible to think about a global educational programme that might conform to Aristotle's practical approach? Briefly, I know of one that approximates it, though not with a focus on music. The United Nations Office on Drugs and Crime (UNODC) focuses much of its work on anti-corruption initiatives. These initiatives are framed through a strong rule of law discourse. In 2015, the UNODC launched the Doha Declaration, the outcome of one of its annual meetings. The declaration seeks to integrate development and a global rule of law agenda (UNOCD, 2015a). As a result of funding from the state of Qatar, UNODC initiated what it called an Education for Justice programme. This programme, designed to create modules for teachers around the world at primary, secondary and tertiary levels, focuses on a range of different topics.

The tertiary educational modules provide a small window into how a global educational programme might reflect the nuanced practical approach that Aristotle suggests.[6] The process by which the modules were written, evaluated and then promoted demonstrates how to combine the practical and theoretical, along with a balance between the local and universal. I was involved as a consultant in writing one module and evaluating 15 others. At an initial meeting in Vienna, a small group of consultants developed topics for the tertiary education strand. One topic we proposed was Integrity and Ethics, which focused on the wider ethical foundations that would support the anti-corruption and rule of law agenda. This topic was then broken down into 15 modules, with specific topics including, among others, Universalism, Gender and Business Ethics. UNODC then hired scholars from around the world to write each module, which included background information, teaching resources and pedagogical exercises. These modules were then assessed at two different meetings in Greece, again including an international group of scholars. The final versions of the modules were then put through a global peer review process, and then published online (UNODC, 2015b).

I wrote the module on Ethics and Universal Values (UNODC, 2015c). In that module, I used the example of how the Universal Declaration of Human Rights (UDHR) was written as a model for how a Universal Declaration of Human Values might be written and made prominent. This module suggested that some principles, such as human rights, can be both universal and particular at the same time, especially when they emerge from diverse intellectual and religious contexts (as the UDHR did; see Morsink, 1999). While I drafted the first version of this module, it really resulted from a process in which scholars and activists from around the world read, evaluated and challenged the assumptions and ideas found within it. For instance, the first draft used (not surprisingly) Aristotle as a key figure to understand how to negotiate the local and the global. In the course of the various rounds of evaluation, however, it was emphasized that this reflects only one tradition of thought. As a result, a discussion of the Chinese philosopher Mencius was added, whose insights into values provided a parallel but distinct approach to the question of universal values. In addition, some participants in the discussions around gender and ethics pushed back at assumptions about sexual orientation and transgender rights. This did not result in reference to these issues being dropped, but rather to an exploration of how such contested

---

[6]　See Lang (2020) for a discussion of how this initiative can help advance a form of practical universalism.

ideas might be integrated into teaching modules while giving local teachers the ability to develop and modify the lessons for their own purposes.

The promulgation of these modules is also an interesting exercise. Once they were written, UNODC began a process of rolling them out in different regional contexts, finding partners who were willing to host workshops with university educators from around the world. Workshops have been held in Europe, Latin America, Africa and Asia, with efforts underway to host some in North America and the Middle East. These promulgation efforts include those involved in writing and developing the modules demonstrating how such modules might be used in teaching contexts.

The process by which these modules were written, evaluated and promulgated is not perfect. But it does provide a small example of how a universal value – the rule of law or human rights – can be developed and promulgated in different social and political contexts. This is also a very practice-based approach to education, one that includes detail on how to teach such matters to diverse students around the world. It maps onto Aristotle's practical constitutionalism by highlighting education as a means by which to advance constitutional norms around the world.

Conclusion

As noted at the outset, this chapter is not a critique of Kratochwil's ideas as found in *Praxis*. Rather, it is an effort to highlight how Kratochwil's approach is perhaps reflective of Aristotle's practical constitutionalism. I have highlighted two dimensions of this practical constitutionalism as they relate to the rule of law, the economic and the educational. The small examples cited here suggest ways in which these ideas might be better understood, ones which reflect Kratochwil's focus on acting and knowing in a contested global context.

In conclusion, let me highlight one other dimension of praxis which arises from Aristotle and which might be encompassed in my conception of global constitutionalism. Aristotle famously argued that understanding social and political life requires attention to the ethical. Indeed, his works on ethics and politics are intimately related to each other (Adkins, 1984). As noted earlier, he compared constitutions of the classical world in order to find the best, both operatively and normatively. Aristotle was interested in understanding what form of political life would make the best person, a task that necessitates combining the ethical and the political. Kratochwil helps us to see this as well. In a chapter from Adler and Pouliot's book on the practice turn in IR theory, Kratochwil (2011b) points us to the benefits of turning to an Aristotelian conception of praxis. He points out that for Aristotle, praxis differs from other forms of activity, such as technical or artistic practices. Unlike these other dimensions of the human condition, '[s]ince we usually act in social contexts, others' interests and possible interferences have to be addressed. This adds a moral dimension to action distinguishing the latter from events, from the production of things, and from theoretical speculation' (Kratochwil, 2011b: 40).

It is this moral dimension of global legal and political life which requires more careful analysis. Kratochwil is correct to point us to this moral dimension, and Aristotle provides one way in which we might bring ethics and politics together. As anyone who has written about normative elements of international affairs knows, the common-sense understanding of international relations is that there is no place for ethics, because of either a vague form of moral relativism or realist assumptions about amorality. The practical global constitutionalism I have articulated here, especially the idea of global education, suggests one place where ethics might be operative. Rather than imposing rules on the global order, efforts to provide education in ethics that is both universal in its aspirations and yet particular in its application is perhaps a way we might think about inculcating a normative framework for international politics. Kratochwil's conception of praxis, leavened by an Aristotelian dimension, helps us move in this direction. Finding ways to incorporate those normative elements and highlighting where they already exist builds upon and extends the potential for a praxis-oriented approach to global politics.

References

Adkins, Arthur W.H. (1984) 'The connection between Aristotle's ethics and politics', *Political Theory* 12, 1, pp 29–49.

Anderson, Gavin (2017) 'Critical theory', in Anthony F. Lang, Jr and Antje Wiener (eds), *Handbook of Global Constitutionalism* (London: Edward Elgar Publishers), pp 140–51.

Arendt, Hannah (1968) *On Revolution* (New York: Penguin Books).

Aristotle (1941) *The Nichomachean Ethics*, trans. William D. Ross, in Richard McKeon (ed), *The Basic Works of Aristotle* (New York: Random House), pp 935–1126.

Aristotle (1996) *The Politics and The Constitution of Athens*, ed. and intro. by Stephen Everson (Cambridge: Cambridge University Press).

Gill, Stephen. and A. Claire Cutler, eds (2014) *New Constitutionalism and World Order* (Cambridge: Cambridge University Press).

Gurr, Ted R. (1970) *Why Men Rebel* (Princeton, NJ: Princeton University Press).

Hayek, Friedrich A. (2009 [1960]) *The Constitution of Liberty* (London: Routledge).

Koskenniemi, Martii (2006 [1989]) *From Apology to Utopia: The Structure of International Legal Argument* (Cambridge: Cambridge University Press).

Kratochwil, Friedrich (1989) *Rules, Norms and Decisions: On the Conditions of Practical and Legal Reasoning in International Relations and Domestic Affairs* (Cambridge: Cambridge University Press).

Kratochwil, Friedrich (2011a) *The Puzzles of Politics: Inquiries into the Genesis and Transformation of International Relations* (London: Routledge).

Kratochwil, Friedrich (2011b) 'Making sense of "international practices"', in Emanuel Adler and Vincent Pouliot (eds), *International Practices* (Cambridge: Cambridge University Press), pp 36–60.

Kratochwil, Friedrich (2014) *The Status of Law in World Society: Meditations on the Role and Rule of Law* (Cambridge: Cambridge University Press).

Kratochwil, Friedrich (2018) *Praxis: On Acting and Knowing* (Cambridge: Cambridge University Press).

Lang, Jr., Anthony F. (2020) 'Constructing universal values? A practical approach', *Ethics and International Affairs* 34, 3, 267–78.

Leroi, Armand M. (2014) *The Lagoon: How Aristotle Invented Science* (London: Bloomsbury).

McIlwain, Charles (2008 [1948]) *Constitutionalism: Ancient and Modern* (Indianapolis, IN: Liberty Fund Press).

Milanovic, Branko (2016) *Global Inequality: A New Approach for the Age of Globalization* (Cambridge, MA: Harvard University Press).

Morsink, Johannes (1999) *The Universal Declaration of Human Rights: Origins, Drafting, and Intent* (Philadelphia: University of Pennsylvania Press).

Onuf, Nicholas (1989) *World of Our Making: Rules and Rule in Social Theory and International Relations* (Columbia: University of South Carolina Press).

Trachtman, Joel (2017) 'Global commercial constitutionalization: the World Trade Organization', in Anthony F. Lang, Jr and Antje Wiener (eds), *Handbook on Global Constitutionalism* (London: Edward Elgar Publishers), pp 395–404.

UNODC (2015a) Doha Declaration on Integrating Crime Prevention and Criminal Justice into the wider United Nations Agenda to address Social And Economic Challenges and to promote the Rule of Law at the National And International Levels, and public Participation, available at: https://www.unodc.org/documents/congress//Declaration/V1504151_English.pdf, accessed 26 February 2021.

UNODC (2015b) Integrity and Ethics, Module Series Overview, available at: https://www.unodc.org/e4j/en/tertiary/integrity-ethics.html, accessed 26 February 2021.

UNODC (2015c) Integrity and Ethics, Module 2: Ethics and Universal Values, available at: https://www.unodc.org/e4j/en/integrity-ethics/module-2/index.html, accessed 26 February 2021.

8

Rules, Institutions and Decisions: Taking Distribution Seriously

Jan Klabbers

Introduction

This chapter is inspired by a simple observation. In the almost 500 pages of his recent work *Praxis*, Fritz Kratochwil pays little attention to the distributive role of rules (legal or otherwise), institutions and decisions (Kratochwil, 2018). This is not a criticism: it would be like criticizing Leo Messi for not playing basketball, or complaining that Lebron James does not play chess very often (assuming this to be the case). In all his work, Kratochwil has pioneered the constitutive role of rules, institutions and decisions, and he has more than made his mark on the study of international affairs. The fact remains, though, that while he has pioneered the constitutive effects of rules, institutions and decisions, he has rarely zoomed in on their distributive effects. That said, few others have done so beyond positing assumptions about the effectiveness of governments or markets. There are some exceptions: some scholars of (neo-)Marxist or (neo-)Gramscian persuasion (e.g. Cox, 1987), or the odd institutional economist (e.g. North, 1990), some revisionist historians and historiographers (e.g. Hobsbawm, 1975), and some international political economists (e.g. Strange, 1994); they all concentrate on issues of distribution in one way or another. But, by and large, in doing so they often neglect the specific role of rules, institutions or decisions. Put differently: for many, distributive results are results of political processes that are then cast in rules, institutions or decisions. Those rules and institutions are thought to reflect distributive outcomes rather than contribute to them: rules and institutions are often treated as the outcome of political processes, rather than key structures which help determine those very outcomes. For others, some branches of law address distribution as attaching to specific occurrences – tort law and insurance law may qualify as examples. But the role that rules, institutions and decisions play in achieving, channelling, promoting or facilitating particular distributive results remains under-illuminated; it is precisely here that my interest resides.

The ambition of this chapter is to start a conversation at precisely the point where others often sign off: on the distributive role of rules, institutions and decisions. My interest rests with the distributive effects of rules, institutions and decisions rather than with distribution per se – how is it that rules, institutions and decisions can best be conceptualized so as to take their distributive effects seriously? In what follows, I will briefly sketch that distributive effects are perennial. I will then develop the hypothesis that getting to the distributive effect of rules, institutions and decisions requires a dual intellectual operation. It requires, firstly, relaxing the strongly state-centric approach prevailing in the study of international affairs, in combination with, secondly, a realization that law, politics and economics should not be neatly separated but rather should be treated as single decision-making moments or units. On occasion, of course, there is considerable analytical merit in zooming in on the state or zooming in on the economics behind a particular decision. But it is also worthwhile to zoom out on occasion – doing so may reveal things that would remain hidden from a close-up view. Next, I will present an example or two, combining concrete (non-state) interests with the role of a concrete (non-state) institution, in this case the venerable Universal Postal Union, followed by the conclusion.

Rules and distribution

In November 2019, the British press reported that an inquiry into possibly illegal activities conducted by Prime Minister Boris Johnson, handing out financial benefits to favour a friend, was to be postponed until after elections had taken place (Townsend, 2019). The episode was reminiscent of an earlier one, in the run-up to the 2016 US elections, to announce an investigation into Hillary Clinton's use of her personal email address for official (and often classified) government business. In the end, the investigations exonerated Clinton, but by then Trump had already been elected (Comey, 2018: 191–204).

What the two episodes suggest is that even the seemingly most innocuous legal decisions tend to have a distributive effect: a decision to postpone investigation into Johnson's behaviour may well have affected the result of the elections, as his opponents were quick to point out. If he turns out to have acted corruptly, the voters could have been expected to punish him at the ballot box. The other side of the coin is, of course, that if a proper investigation would exonerate him, the voters might reward him or punish the opposition for what they may perceive as a witch hunt. Hence, even if the decision itself can have – and is likely to have – distributive effects, its actual effects can by no means clearly be anticipated. What the episodes also suggest is the relevance of timing: a decision to launch an investigation long after Johnson has left office would not nearly spawn as much discussion; a decision to investigate Clinton would not be nearly as controversial if not taken in the middle of a presidential election. Clearly, a decision on whether or not to investigate, taken at a specific moment, is expected to have serious effects, and it is expected to have such effects both by proponents and by opponents.

The more general point to emerge is that legal decisions about whether to do something or to refrain from doing something will benefit some and might come to harm others – or at least will be expected to benefit some and harm others. It is not always the case that one person's benefit automatically entails someone else's harm, or rather that there is a symmetry in the harms and benefits. A decision not to give someone a tourist visa will harm the applicant but without other applicants benefitting, unless, for example, a limited number of visas are available, in which case a competitor will have been eliminated.

This dynamic plays out at all levels. It plays out when a hospital needs to decide on which patient to prioritize for a kidney transplant, or when a municipality needs to decide which company gets to repave the city's bicycle lanes. It plays out when a foundation needs to decide on distributing scholarships, or when university management needs to assign offices or (more likely these days) cubicles. And it also plays out when the city or county decides on the boundaries of electoral districts, or when the country club decides which applicant member to accept, or when authorities decide whether to investigate allegations that could affect election results.

These decisions, all of them, have some distributive effect, and the examples suggest two things. First, they suggest that benefits may be tangible or intangible, and that the boundary between them might be porous. The local businessman applying for country club membership may do so in a quest for recognition as a legitimate member of the community, which in turn may be inspired by the thought that such recognition may be good for business – intangible and tangible benefits conspire here. Second, the examples suggest that the distributive effects may be all the more visible the scarcer the benefits are; it takes little imagination to realize that a hospital decision on a kidney transplant has winners and losers, because it is generally realized that the supply of suitable kidneys is extremely limited.

The previous examples all involve an organization of sorts, and this is hardly a coincidence. We tend to create institutions to help us make decisions on who gets to pave the city's bicycle lanes, who shall receive a scholarship and who shall be the recipient of a kidney. Those institutions, then, are constructed by rules and, at the same time, hemmed in by rules. Not even the nominally private country club can decide on a whim whom to accept: it may have to respect general laws (e.g. non-discrimination laws) and will in all likelihood have laid down some rules in its by-laws, for example on the sort of financial situation applicants must be in as well as the procedure for admission.

The reason for institutionalization will be obvious: leaving such decisions to individuals is bound quickly to lead to accusations of unfairness. Someone needs to make a decision on the scholarship or the kidney transplant, but it is considered unwise to leave it to any particular individual, and thus rules and institutions are created to streamline the process. The rules will provide, for example, that no one should be arbitrarily excluded, or that applications must be submitted before a particular cut-off date, and that decision-makers shall recuse themselves if they are somehow related to one of the applicants. The institutions are set up precisely to prevent the final decision being made solely by the uncle of one of the applicants, or her father, mentor or other relation (Elster, 1992).

As a general proposition, then, all organizations end up distributing costs and benefits, whether they were intended to do so or not. This also applies to organizations with a distinctively public task. The fire department, in situations of scarce resources, may have to decide which fire to quell first. The police department, likewise, may have to decide which burglar to pursue or which murder to solve first. Prosecutors typically need to decide on which cases to investigate or prosecute, based at least in part on available resources. Administrative agencies such as food or drug administrations need to decide which standards to apply to food or drug products, and whether those standards are met in specific cases. And all such decisions have a distributive effect of sorts: they work to someone's disadvantage, or to someone's advantage, or, often, both: they come with winners and losers.

Curiously, political theory and jurisprudence have paid relatively little attention to the distributive role of rules and institutions compared with the level of attention paid to their constitutive effects (Kratochwil, 1989). To the extent that distributive effects are noted, attention tends to come in two guises. It comes either in the form of work on the distributive justice (*vel non*) underlying entire political communities (e.g. Rawls, 1971) or in the form of discussions of individual provisions or the policies of particular organizations (e.g. Stiglitz, 2002). By contrast, the distributive effects of rules and institutions as such (qua rules, qua institutions: the meso-level, if you will, and independent of institutional policies) are usually given less attention. When complaining about the International Monetary Fund (IMF) or the World Bank, for example, the complaint is usually based on their policies rather than the institutional biases inherent in their structures, in the way they are set up by legal rules.

It remains mysterious what causes this lack of attention, other than perhaps the realization that a singular focus on distribution as the outcome of political processes (usually associated with Eastonian systems theory; Easton, 1965) remains incomplete in the absence of examination of distributive configurations in the 'original position'. Eastonian systems theory, while considerably more subtle and comprehensive than I can here reflect, viewed political decision-making processes as systems for the authoritative allocation of values but paid somewhat less attention to how values were allocated prior to decision-making processes, or to the respective power positions of participants in those processes.

One reason for the relative lack of attention to the distributive effects of rules and institutions might be that individual authors can be methodologically radical, but socially conservative; they might be perfectly willing to undermine received academic wisdom but are less interested in the larger social or economic questions. This is probably not untrue, but it is a little too facile to be of much use: surely one does not need to be a social progressive to be interested in distributive outcomes. Social conservatives too might be interested and, additionally, social conservatism is a broad church: David Hume, for example, is often considered socially conservative but was generally said to be rather scornful of the (also socially conservative) Whigs (Hardin, 2007).

On a deeper level, one possible explanation for the relative absence of work on the distributive effects of rules and institutions may reside in the division of thinking into separate academic disciplines. Within those disciplines, rules and institutions are the province of, predominantly, legal theory and several branches of philosophy, both normative and analytical. Distributive questions, by contrast, are the province of other branches, of economics perhaps, or empirical social sciences and political (or institutional) economy. Despite several generations' worth of calls for interdisciplinary scholarship, scholars who work in both traditions are scarce.

Those preoccupied with rules tend to look at the formal qualities of rules or at why people might obey rules or, more generally, at the role of rules in society (Schauer, 1991). Rules are generally viewed as serving the role of guideposts, as having a signalling function, telling people what to do and what not to do with a view to achieving or maintaining some kind of order. Those preoccupied with distribution, by contrast, may underestimate the influence of rules and institutions. Companies performing well may be the result of good market conditions, or the unique vision of company leadership, rather than the existence of rules or institutions. At best, rules and institutions are considered tangentially related, in much the same way that political realists tend to view international law as largely epiphenomenal. Both groups, moreover, have a habit of working mostly in the rarefied atmosphere of ideal theory which, as some suggest (Coady, 2008; Guess, 2008), almost by definition may diminish any budding interest in the distributive effects of actual rules and institutions.

The challenge, then, for both jurisprudence and political theory, is to develop ways of thinking that would fruitfully combine the constructivist effects of rules and institutions (for there can be little doubt that society is socially constructed, on a deep level, and in part through rules and institutions) with their distributive effects. Admittedly, there has been a recent move towards a political economy of the law, but this turns out to have relatively little analytical traction (e.g. Mattei and Haskell, 2015). It suggests that institutions and rules help cause inequalities but typically refrains from explaining why this happens and how exactly it occurs. Instead, it tends to fall into the trap of identifying agency 'with the efficacious pursuit of one's own power and position' (Laidlaw, 2014: 6). Hence, the question Amartya Sen threw up a decade ago still has some validity. Sen asked himself, and his readership, 'whether we can leave matters to the choice of institutions (obviously chosen with an eye to results to the extent that they enter the negotiations and agreements) but without questioning the status of the agreements and of the institutions *once* the arrangements have been chosen, no matter what the actual consequences prove to be' (Sen, 2009: 84). And the answer, it should be clear, is in the negative.

Two intellectual operations

International affairs are usually construed as affairs involving states. This is not, in and of itself, inaccurate: a history of the world, at least since the 17th century, can be told as a history of the interactions between states (Spruyt, 1994), with pivotal moments including the Westphalia Peace and the creation of the League of Nations and the United Nations. It is commonplace to do so, and to analyse international political developments and international law through the prism of the state – indeed, the very word 'international' suggests the lexical and epistemological priority of the state.

The emerging picture is not obviously wrong (states, after all, are of considerable importance, if only because everyone constantly repeats that they are of considerable importance), but it is a little limited. A history of the world can also be discussed in terms of empires or classes (Wallerstein, 1974), civil society, transnational cultural movements or intergovernmental organizations (Iriye, 2002; Rosenberg, 2012).

A state-centric approach tends to ignore other actors and agents, sometimes even completely so (e.g. Ferguson, 2006). This also applies to the role of the hundreds of international organizations in existence, which is, by and large, ignored or at best seen as representing aggregates of state interests. The idea that the World Bank, the UN High Commissioner for Refugees and the International Maritime Organization are important agents in their own right has yet to gain a firm foothold – and where such a role is recognized, it is often lamented for 'undermining' state sovereignty, even in the academic literature (e.g. Johnson, 2014).

Thus, the focus usually rests on states – the study of international affairs, from whatever discipline precisely, tends to be hugely state-centric, with the state given pride of place as the central agent. This overshadows a different, and equally fundamental, aspect of the role of the state: the state as conducting agent, in much the same way as copper metal conducts electricity – states are important also as intermediaries.[1]

States play, admittedly, a seemingly central role in international affairs. Treaties are typically (if no longer exclusively) concluded by states and among states. International organizations are established (if no longer exclusively; Andonova, 2017) by states banding together for some purpose or other. States play a 'figurehead' role: with governments coming and going and domestic power configurations, however conceptualized, perpetually shifting, the state is the only constant and thus useful for the performance of formal, legal acts. But the state is not just agent, it is also structure or forum, a site for political struggle: it would be wrong to identify the legal acts solely with the state without ever considering that the state's position may result from political struggle (struggles for resources, struggles for outcomes) among different groups and factions within the state. This role of the state as site for struggle is generally acknowledged but, surprisingly perhaps, not all that often reflected in the ensuing analysis.

Likewise, there are no rules of international law that affect (or even that can affect) solely states in their capacity as abstract actors. Instead, rules of international law and international regulation, like law generally, are intended to affect individuals and industries. Not even the rules regulating diplomatic relations are applicable only between states, and the idea that war would be limited to a meeting between state organs (armies) always was a perversely state-centric conceit.

As a result, states have long struggled (and are still struggling) to define the place of international law in their domestic legal orders. They realize that rules typically affect industries and individuals, but they are reluctant to give in. The Permanent Court of International Justice held in the late 1920s that international provisions could be 'directly effective' if their authors so intended (PCIJ, 1928). Moreover, leading theoreticians already in the late 19th century concluded that the matter is in the hands of states

---

[1] There is a semantic (but not substantive) similarity here with the recently developed concept of orchestration by international organizations (orchestras are directed by conductors, after all), whereby agents would engage other agents in harmonious action (Abbott et al, 2015).

at any rate: the domestic constitution determines whether and how to apply international law (Triepel, 1899). Hence, states have two tools available to fend off international law being directly applied in relations among their citizens. First, the constitution may not allow for it, and second, even where it does, the phrasing of provisions may stand in the way of 'direct effect' (Klabbers, 2020: 327–31).

All this suggests a strong role for the state not only as agent, but also as conductor, both outward and inward. States may endorse certain interests on the international level and may protect certain interests against international interference, even after signing up to international commitments. This adds considerable nuance to the central, quasi-independent role of the state that both legal scholars and political scientists have adopted. This quasi-independent role is understandable in that it makes parsimonious theorizing possible, and zooming in on state agency can be a useful heuristic. It becomes problematic, however, when abstract political positions come to be attributed to those states, such as when suggesting that states are for or against 'multilateralism', or for or against 'international law'. This then often prompts the observer to twist and contort. As an example, Talmon contrasts the attitude of the US under Trump to that under earlier administrations (Talmon, 2019: 646). To his mind, previously the US was 'a steadfast defender' of international law, only violating its obligations 'if economic, political, or strategic interests demanded it to do so'. But this, of course, begs the question: if the US violated its obligations when its interests compelled it to do so, should the focus not come to rest then on those interests (economic, political, strategic), instead of a perceived (or imagined) *Völkerrechtsfreundlichkeit*? And those interests are served by institutions, rules and decisions.

Rules, institutions and decisions never operate in a vacuum. Political and economic decision-making is undergirded by legal rules, which are based in turn on assumptions and *topoi* (a Kratochwilian term if ever there was one) about law and what it aims to do. Bringing this to the fore, together with a realization of the conducting role of the state, may help us understand why the world comes to look as it does, why some interests always seem to win out; why some tend to win, and others tend to lose. These two intellectual operations together may clarify things that otherwise often remain obscure.

The distributive role of international organizations

In this section, I would like to outline a distributive role for international organizations (Klabbers, 2019a). International organizations, as traditional theory holds it, are set up by states to perform a particular function or set of functions, ostensibly 'public' in nature. They exercise powers delegated to them by their member states, so the dominant theory holds, acting as agents for their (collective) principals (Hawkins et al, 2006; Klabbers, 2015). Again, this is not entirely inaccurate and fine as far as things go, but things do not go very far.

It is unlikely that states wake up one morning and decide to regulate postal relations, or set up an entity to fix world sugar prices, or protect the copyrights of struggling poets. And yet this is often how the picture is somewhat hazily presented. States somehow think it is a good idea to set up a World Bank, or an International Bureau for Weights and Measures, or a League of Nations. These initiatives are often presented as coming out of the blue or, at best, as having been inspired by dramatic political events, with the League of Nations arising out of the ashes of World War I, and the World Bank embodying a response to the destruction caused by World War II. As David Kennedy astutely summarizes the prevailing spirit with respect to the major and most visible institutions: 'Thinking about the origins of international institutions seems to demand a vision of war, of peace, and of the process by which war gives way to peace' (Kennedy, 1987: 845). By contrast, thinking about the origins of international institutions rarely involves a vision of whose benefits they serve; the classic question '*cui bono?*' tends to remain ignored.

While connecting the League of Nations and the World Bank to the world wars is plausible enough, it is also clear that no dramatic event or global rupture explains the creation of the International Bureau of Weights and Measures or, for that matter, the creation of most international organizations. In most cases, a plausible explanation must be found elsewhere. International organizations, in such a view, emerge as the products of the imagination of individuals, and they emerge in order to secure the economic interests of particular factions.

Take, for example, the case of the Universal Postal Union (UPU), one of the oldest and most venerable international organizations, having been set up in 1874. The UPU, it is fair to say, exists predominantly because, in the early 1860s, the US postmaster general, Mr Montgomery Blair, realized that postal traffic and postal rates made little sense. He noted that there were at least several different routes for a parcel to be sent from the US to Europe, incurring different costs, and he noticed that different countries entertained different methods for calculating costs: either by size, weight, duration of the voyage or length of the voyage. In short, Mr Blair found that the situation was messy; and later, it has been estimated that 1,200 different rates existed in Europe alone in the mid-19th century (Luard, 1977: 12). Blair convinced his government to talk to other governments in order to convene an international meeting to discuss these matters in 1863. Nothing much happened for a few years, but by then Blair had found an ally in Germany. His German counterpart, Mr Stephan, took up the issue with his government; another meeting was convened, and it was more or less agreed to set up a union to regulate and manage postal relations. At this moment, the Franco-Prussian War intervened, but once the war had come to an end, the Union was established in 1874 (Sly, 1927).

The UPU is often seen as a textbook example of a purely technical organization, and indeed, the story of its genesis suggests it was mostly created with a view to overcoming technical obstacles. And yet, if not exactly deceptive, that picture remains incomplete without an appreciation of the politics behind the UPU – global postal politics, so to speak. As the story of its creation suggests, different states entertained different methods for calculating the costs of postal traffic; as a result, settling on a single method benefitted some and disadvantaged others – those less prepared for using the new ways of doing postal business. In fact, over the years, the setting of postal tariffs ('terminal dues', in jargon) has come to be influenced by all sorts of political factors, including the relative economic capacities of the various member states of the UPU: senders from less developed states pay, relatively, less for international postal traffic than do senders from wealthy industrialized nations. Technological developments too have left their mark; the popularization of airmail after World War II, for example, led to intense negotiations with representatives of the airline industry, who were united in the International Air Transport Association (Luard, 1977: 15).

If this already showed the interface between the management of public affairs and the private sector, well aware of the costs and benefits involved, it was still relatively innocent as long as postal traffic consisted mainly of vacation postcards and letters to grandparents abroad. In more recent years, postal relations have taken on new dimensions due to (ironically perhaps) the emergence of the internet and, with it, the emergence of e-commerce. This entails that people can shop online and get the goods delivered at their doorstep, and this in turn implies that the costs of transportation and shipping become a factor – indeed, huge parts of global trade are delivered these days by postal modes. The result is, graphically put, that it may be cheaper to send a parcel from anywhere in China to San Francisco than it is to send it from Seattle to San Francisco. In this light, it is no surprise that the Trump administration announced in 2018 that the US would withdraw from the UPU. Clearly, the material interests of (some) US-based companies were under threat. The threat of withdrawal concentrated the minds of the representatives of other states and of the UPU, and in the autumn of 2019, just before the US withdrawal was to take effect, the UPU announced that an extraordinary conference had resulted in a compromise, persuading the US to stay in (UPU, 2019).

Discussing this purely in state-centric terms is unsatisfactory, a position that also transpires from other examples. In 2017, the same Trump administration had announced its withdrawal from UNESCO, further feeding impressions of anti-internationalism. And yet, during his tenure, the Trump administration joined the BIE (the International Exhibition Office) and contemplated joining the UN World Tourism Organization. In both cases, it is not too difficult to discern material interests behind the action. The US government considered that the US tourism industry would benefit from membership of the World Tourism Organization, while there would not be much of a price to pay – a general feature of international organizations already flagged by early theorists (Reinsch, 1911). Likewise, accession to the BIE was informed by the candidacy of Minneapolis to organize Global Expo 2023 – appointing the organization of Global Expos is the main material benefit the BIE has to offer and is considered to generate a boost for local business. As it happens, the US moved in vain: the prize went to Buenos Aires instead (Charnovitz, 2017).

Similar stories can be told for many – possibly most – international organizations. They tend to emerge because someone has a project and manages to garner sufficient political support among sufficiently powerful states to set up a vehicle for the project in the form of an international organization – for given their epistemological priority in international affairs, the constituent documents of institutions still need to be concluded between states. Few (if any) international organizations have emerged solely from a public-spirited ethos; for many, their source is a combination of someone's material interests and felicitous momentum. The International Copyright Union, nowadays known as the World Intellectual Property Organization, was relentlessly lobbied for by popular 19th-century novelists, among whom the likes of Victor Hugo and Louisa May Alcott stand out. The much younger Union for the Protection of New Varieties of Plants (UPOV), dedicated to the protection of intellectual property rights over new plant varieties, in turn was established under impulses from agricultural companies once it had become clear, at some point in the 1950s, that plant varieties would become big business (Raustiala and Victor, 2004). The International Sugar Union, at one point possibly the most 'progressive' international organization around in that it could set binding prices (Sayre, 1919), served to protect the interests of the UK sugar-producing colonies and the companies heavily invested in them (Fakhri, 2014).

Discussion on the post-war creation of a world trade regime revolved around disputes between the US and the UK about the latter's 'imperial preference'. Likewise, the well-known rivalry between the US and the UK about plans for the IMF and the World Bank, while often presented in terms of either a clash of personalities (John M. Keynes vs Harry D. White) or of abstract economic philosophy (inflationary state intervention vs deflationary laissez-faire), owed much to the obvious interests of their respective private sectors after World War II (Gardner, 1980).

The International Labour Organization, a response of sorts to the Russian Revolution, served to even out industrial competition by improving the conditions of labour especially in the colonies, as happily acknowledged by one of its creators, British delegate George Barnes (Barnes, 1926: 37, 45). Even the first health organizations arising in the mid-19th century (often in the form of regional sanitary bureaux) owed little to any public ethos: their aim was to prevent the spread of contagious disease to the Global North, rather than to improve global health conditions per se (Klabbers, 2019c).

If the establishment of an international organization and its priorities may already manifest a distributive element, and if admission (or withdrawal) may likewise be inspired by distributive concerns, so too is the everyday operation of international organizations. This holds true on the most mundane level. International organizations are employers, and they hire some while they do not hire others. They procure goods and services, and in choosing service or goods providers, they benefit some at the expense of others. Some organizations are mandated to provide services, and to do so for a fee; one example is how the European Organization for the Safety of Air Navigation (better known as Eurocontrol) collects route charges from airlines flying over much of Europe (Wurm, 2010). Among the tasks of the financial institutions and development banks is to make a healthy profit on the financing of projects – profits that can flow back to the major shareholders, that is, the wealthier member states (Woods, 2006). Others, especially in the global health domain, have started to cooperate with the private sector in various forms in a bid to attract additional funding. And yet others are bereft of compulsory member state contributions and thus are forced to sell their expertise on the market, therewith functioning much like a private company, albeit often with public status (Klabbers, 2019b).

Most important of all, the decisions that are the bread and butter (the term is chosen advisedly) of international organizations tend to have distributive effects, and often this is an inevitable consequence of the fact that the organization is supposed to take decisions in the first place.

Entities such as Palestine and Kosovo have in recent years applied for membership of various organizations, including organizations that bring little by way of tangible benefits. Joining UNESCO, as Palestine did, is bound to cost more money that it brings in, but it comes with one enormous bonus: it can be seen as a sign of political recognition by much of the international community. Likewise, Kosovo applied to join (and did join) the Permanent Court of Arbitration and the World Customs Organization not so much for material gain, but as salvos in its struggle for political recognition.

And then there are the regular substantive decisions to be taken by international organizations. The International Telecommunication Union distributes bandwidths, radio frequencies and satellite positions; there is much to gain here for telecommunications industries, and historically this has been realized since its creation in 1865 as the International Telegraphic Union (ITU). The ITU served as the axis around which the first telecommunications revolved (Murphy, 1994). Likewise, decisions of the World Health Organization (WHO) tend to have distributive effects, however unintentional or tangential. One of the briefs of the WHO is to declare a global health pandemic when circumstances so demand. When it does so, however, it is bound to affect the interests of those pharmaceutical companies whose vaccines are not yet marketable, as well as the interests of airlines and possibly the tourism industry – the 2020 COVID-19 crisis is a powerful example, but by no means unique (Alvarez, 2016).

The World Meteorological Organization (WMO) is not immune to the politics of distribution and redistribution either. This is most obviously visible with respect to the strong emotions provoked by the Intergovernmental Panel on Climate Change, a joint venture of the WMO and the UN Environment Programme, but also in myriad other ways. Decisions to announce a disaster risk reduction programme in one member state but not in another will have distributive effects, not just in respect of those states but also in respect of people and industries within them, as will a decision to establish a capacity development programme in some location. And much the same applies to disarmament organizations. The Organisation for the Prohibition of Chemical Weapons, for example, controls international transfers of chemicals, allowing some and disallowing others. Likewise, it may indicate risks involved in particular chemicals that are widely used for normal industrial purposes but can be turned into chemical weapons or can be used in the production of chemical weapons. Here, too, the organization's work will benefit some and not benefit others.

Conclusion

Almost four decades ago, a young Fritz Kratochwil ended his passionate plea for the adoption of a Humean perspective on the study of international affairs by pointing out that this field of study could benefit from a greater understanding of the role of international organizations. 'Instead of simply focusing on state actors and their bargaining, and adding on – as an afterthought – the marginal impact of international organizations in such an arena, the focus on convention and various allocation mechanisms enlarges the agenda of international organization and frees it from the fetters of purely institutional descriptive analysis' (Kratochwil, 2011: 31).[2]

In the intervening years, not much has changed. International organizations are still typically studied from state-centric perspectives and on the basis of state-centric premises and assumptions by political scientists and international

---

[2] The piece first saw the light as a working paper at Princeton's World Order Studies programme, in 1981.

lawyers alike, and without much attention for their roles as 'allocation mechanisms'. This may allow for elegant theoretical modelling but does so at the cost of a deeper and more accurate understanding. And this, in turn, may well affect the social world around us: it is probably no exaggeration to claim that the popularity of nationalist movements in much of the Western world owes something to fundamental misrepresentations of the roles (and limits thereof) of international organizations in global governance.

References

Abbott, Kenneth W., Philipp Genschel, Duncan Snidal and Bernhard Zangl, eds (2015) *International Organizations as Orchestrators* (Cambridge: Cambridge University Press).

Alvarez, José E. (2016) *The Impact of International Organizations on International Law* (Leiden: Martinus Nijhoff).

Andonova, Liliana B. (2017) *Governance Entrepreneurs: International Organizations and the Rise of Global Public–Private Partnerships* (Cambridge: Cambridge University Press).

Barnes, George N. (1926) *History of the International Labour Office* (London: Williams and Norgate).

Charnovitz, Steve (2017) Why the International Exhibitions Bureau should choose Minneapolis for Global Expo 2023, SSRN, available at: https://ssrn.com/abstract=3053623, accessed 30 December 2019.

Coady, Cecil Anthony J. (2008) *Messy Morality: The Challenge of Politics* (Oxford: Clarendon Press).

Comey, James (2018) *A Higher Loyalty: Truth, Lies, and Friendship* (New York: Macmillan).

Cox, Robert W. (1987) *Production, Power and World Order* (New York: Columbia University Press).

Easton, David (1965) *A Systems Analysis of Political Life* (New York: Wiley & Sons).

Elster, Jon (1992) *Local Justice: How Institutions Allocate Scarce Goods and Necessary Burdens* (New York: Russell Sage Foundation).

Fakhri, Michael (2014) *Sugar and the Making of International Trade Law* (Cambridge: Cambridge University Press).

Ferguson, Niall (2006) *The War of the World* (London: Penguin).

Gardner, Richard N. (1980) *Sterling–Dollar Diplomacy in Current Perspective: The Origins and Prospects of Our International Economic Order* (2nd edn) (New York: Columbia University Press).

Geuss, Raymond (2008) *Philosophy and Real Politics* (Princeton, NJ: Princeton University Press).

Hardin, Russell (2007) *David Hume: Moral and Political Theorist* (Oxford: Oxford University Press).

Hawkins, Darren G., David A. Lake, Daniel L. Nielson and Michael J. Tierney, eds (2006) *Delegation and Agency in International Organizations* (Cambridge: Cambridge University Press).

Hobsbawm, Eric (1975) *The Age of Capital 1848–1875* (London: Abacus).

Iriye, Akira (2002) *Global Community: The Role of International Organizations in the Making of the Contemporary World* (Berkeley: University of California Press).

Johnson, Tana (2014) *Organizational Progeny* (Oxford: Oxford University Press).

Kennedy, David (1987) 'The move to institutions', *Cardozo Law Review* 8, pp 841–988.

Klabbers, Jan (2015) 'The EJIL Foreword: the transformation of international organizations law', *European Journal of International Law* 26, pp 9–82.

Klabbers, Jan (2019a) 'International organizations and the problem of privity: towards a supra-functionalist approach', in George Politakis, Tomi Kohiyama and Thomas Lieby (eds), *ILO 100: Law for Social Justice* (Geneva: International Labour Office), pp 629–46.

Klabbers, Jan (2019b) 'Notes on the ideology of international organizations law: the International Organization for Migration, state-making, and the market for migration', *Leiden Journal of International Law* 32, pp 383–400.

Klabbers Jan (2019c) 'The normative gap in international organizations law: the case of the World Health Organization', *International Organizations Law Review* 16, pp 272–98.

Klabbers, Jan (2020) *International Law* (3rd edn) (Cambridge: Cambridge University Press).

Kratochwil, Friedrich (1989) *Rules, Norms, and Decisions: On the Conditions of Practical and Legal Reasoning in International Relations and Domestic Affairs* (Cambridge: Cambridge University Press).

Kratochwil, Friedrich (2011) 'The Humean perspective on international relations', in F. Kratochwil, *The Puzzles of Politics* (Abingdon: Routledge), pp 15–37.

Kratochwil, Friedrich (2018) *Praxis: On Acting and Knowing* (Cambridge: Cambridge University Press).

Laidlaw, James (2014) *The Subject of Virtue: An Anthropology of Ethics of Freedom* (Cambridge: Cambridge University Press).

Luard, Evan (1977) *International Agencies: The Emerging Framework of Interdependence* (London: Macmillan).

Mattei, Ugo and John D. Haskell, eds (2015) *Research Handbook on Political Economy and the Law* (Cheltenham: Edward Elgar).

Murphy, Craig N. (1994) *International Organization and Industrial Change: Global Governance since 1850* (Cambridge: Polity).

North, Douglass C. (1990) *Institutions, Institutional Change and Economic Performance* (Cambridge: Cambridge University Press).

PCIJ (Permanent Court of International Justice) (1928) *Jurisdiction of the Courts of Danzig*, advisory opinion, Publ. PCIJ, Series B, no 15.

Raustiala, Kal and D. Victor (2004) 'The regime complex for plant genetic resources', *International Organization* 58, pp 277–309.

Rawls, John (1971) *A Theory of Justice* (Oxford: Oxford University Press).

Reinsch, Paul S. (1911) *Public International Unions, Their Work and Organization: A Study in International Administrative Law* (Boston, MA: Ginn & Co).

Rosenberg, Emily S. (2012) *Transnational Currents in a Shrinking World 1870–1945* (Cambridge, MA: Harvard University Press).

Sayre, Francis B. (1919) *Experiments in International Administration* (New York: Harper).

Schauer, Fred (1991) *Playing by the Rules: A Philosophical Examination of Rule-Based Decision-Making in Law and in Life* (Oxford: Clarendon Press).

Sen, Amartya (2009) *The Idea of Justice* (Cambridge, MA: Harvard University Press).

Sly, John F. (1927) 'The genesis of the Universal Postal Union', *International Conciliation* 233, pp 395–436.

Spruyt, Hendrik (1994) *The Sovereign State and Its Competitors* (Princeton, NJ: Princeton University Press).

Stiglitz, Joseph (2002) *Globalization and Its Discontents* (London: Penguin).

Strange, Susan (1994) *States and Markets* (2nd edn) (London: Bloomsbury).

Talmon, Stefan (2019) 'The United States under President Trump: gravedigger of international law', *Chinese Journal of International Law* 18, pp 645–68.

Townsend, Mark (2019) 'Fury as decision on police watchdog inquiry into PM shelved until after election', *The Guardian*, 9 November, available at: https://www.theguardian.com/politics/2019/nov/09/boris-john son-jennifer-arcuri-iopc-delay-announcement-investigation, accessed 30 December 2019.

Triepel, Heinrich (1899) *Völkerrecht und Landesrecht* (Leipzig: Hirschfeld).

UPU (Universal Postal Union) (2019) 'US officially revokes intent to withdraw from postal union during Washington D.C. visit of UPU's Director General', available at: https://www.upu.int/en/News/2019/10/ US-officially-revokes-intent-to-withdraw-from-postal-union-during-Was hington-D-C-visit-of-UPU's-Dir, accessed 23 February 2021.

Wallerstein, Immanuel (1974) *The Modern World System*, Vol. I (New York: Academic Press).

Woods, Ngaire (2006) *The Globalizers: The IMF, the World Bank, and their Borrowers* (Ithaca, NY: Cornell University Press).

Wurm, Jakob (2010) 'Asking national courts to correct the over-flight charges of Eurocontrol', in August Reinisch (ed), *Challenging Acts of International Organizations Before National Courts* (Oxford: Oxford University Press), pp 157–77.

PART III

Biology, Contingency and History

9

I Think, Therefore IR? Psychology, Biology and the Notion of Praxis

James W. Davis

Introduction

In his spirited defence of a thick constructivist approach to the study of international relations, Friedrich Kratochwil repeatedly invites us to adopt the perspective of the first-person plural. Without a conception of 'we', there is no language or discourse, no possibility for authority or justice, no collective sense of right and wrong. But how does the constructed 'we' relate to the psychological and biological agent, 'I', who is engaged in practice?[1]

For Kratochwil, 'we-intentionality' cannot be reduced to the antecedent beliefs or feelings of individuals. For as long as members of a group accept the legitimacy of decisions made on their behalf, groups can have 'beliefs' that previously were not held by any of the members individually. Collective intentionality presupposes a conception of the 'we' to which the individual attaches some value or meaning (Kratochwil, 2018: 26).

At first glance the argument is compelling enough, yet it begs the question of the origins of the group in the first place. If, as Kratochwil (Kratochwil, 2018: 28) is quick to assert, the Hobbesian contract cannot emerge in a state of nature characterized by generalized distrust, are we to start our analysis of social organization from the assumption of generalized trust and the absence of any individuals motivated to abuse it for egoistic purposes?

---

[1] The following discussion blends two aspects of the first-person singular. A fuller discussion would address the relationship of the 'I' to the 'me', which George Herbert Mead understood to be the self after it has internalized the views of others (Mead and Morris, 1967).

A related objective is to draw our attention to the ways in which language not only describes but also constitutes the social world. Most social facts are reproduced via concepts that find their articulation in language and derive their meaning from malleable practice. The implications for social science epistemology are significant. '[E]specially in the social world, the question of what "is" ("this note is legal tender") runs from the mind to the world (mind dependence), instead of the other way around as conceptualized by positivist "theories"' (Kratochwil, 2018: 7). Yet it is worth reminding ourselves that the mind is a property of individuals, even as Kratochwil takes pains to point out, we can recognize collective intentionality without postulating something like a collective mind.[2] Thus, his assertion that a concern with a coherent account – which avoids the two extremes of reducing collective intentionality to the aggregate of individual intentionality or the assumption of a disembodied group mind – is an instance of misplaced concreteness seems beside the point as it does not answer the question of how 'we' intentionality is formed in the individual mind (Kratochwil, 2018: 26). The question, as Kratochwil (2018: 36) himself puts it, is how emotions and feelings are related to social practices, in particular language.

With no claims to providing a coherent answer to these conundrums, in what follows I want to explore the link between the first-person singular and plural – the 'I' and the 'we' – from the perspective of contemporary work in biology, cognitive psychology and neuroscience. In doing so, I suggest that Kratochwil's thick constructivism at once is too radical and too conservative. It is too radical because it neglects the fact that the feelings, sentiments and emotions that provide the motivations for much of the behaviour he seeks to explain are not 'floating freely' (to borrow a term from a proponent of a rather 'thin' constructivism) but are embodied in and experienced by biological agents. Someone has to 'feel' the rights and wrongs that give rise to the discourse on grievances central to meaning-making in society, and feeling is a function of biology. At the same time, widespread variation within and among cultures – in particular with respect to when and how biological agents experience feelings such as anger, guilt, shame or pride – allows us to dispense with crude claims of biological determinism. Biology and culture are mutually implicated. Each constrains and conditions the effects of the other.

Reminding ourselves that sentiments and feelings are embodied in biological agents directs our attention to the fact that human biology is the product of genetic adaptations to environmental and reproductive challenges faced by our forebears, some of which influence our behaviour. At first glance

---

[2]   For an argument that communities of praxis are characterized by a form of collective cognition, see Adler (2019).

perhaps ironic, it is our emerging understanding of the genetic bases of social behaviour that leads me to suggest that Kratochwil's constructivism may be too conservative. Though some elements of culture likely are the product of long-term evolutionary adaptations to the physical environments within which humans have lived, other evolutionary adaptions likely were induced by culture. Less widely appreciated is the fact that variation in individual behaviour can be the result of biological changes induced by the individual's social environment. Understood either as a form of praxis or as the more general category to which praxis belongs, culture can change the biology of individual human beings in ways that produce non-trivial behavioural patterns. Moreover, evidence is mounting that these biologically produced behavioural effects can persist across generations.

Though a comprehensive treatment of the various strands of research is not possible here, in what follows I summarize some of the relevant findings in contemporary psychology, neuroscience and evolutionary biology and then turn to the ways in which the links between the 'I' and the 'we' suggest a much broader research agenda for the sort of 'thick' constructivism championed by Kratochwil.

The psychology of feelings, cognition and behaviour

Emotions, and their relationship to linguistic concepts, which are collective representations and thus the stuff of constructivism, are central to Kratochwil's conception of the 'we'. In contrast to environmental pressures or institutional constraints that may compel cohesion among individuals with similar interests from the outside, Kratochwil's 'language dependent feelings' act as a sort of social glue that bonds the group from within: 'feelings of remorse, shame, admiration, and dignity have to do with *who* and *what we are*' (Kratochwil, 2018: 36). But how do emotions relate to individual behaviour and how does group membership lead to individual feelings of remorse, shame, admiration and the like?

In both popular and scholarly discussions, emotional behaviour frequently is juxtaposed to rational decision-making.[3] Conceiving feelings to be distinct from cognition, adherents to this position regard emotions as hindrances to rational responses in situations of choice. The belief was evident in the answer Donald Trump's ghost writer provided when asked about the former president's cognitive style: '[h]e feels things and he thinks that the things he feels are thoughts' (Davis et al, 2017). When it comes to leaders, we fear

---

[3] The following discussions of cognition, evolution and genetics summarize more extensive arguments found in Davis and McDermott (2020).

the 'hot head', preferring individuals who can 'keep cool' under stress (see, e.g., Buckley and Ramzy, 2017).

The juxtaposition of emotional and rational – or indeed reasoned – decision-making no longer holds sway among psychologists and neuroscientists. Although certain intense emotions can confound productive decision-making (albeit often in quite systematic fashion), in most situations emotions are essential to sound, indeed rational, decision-making.[4] Without emotions, the notion of 'preference maximization' makes no sense. For what is a preference if not an affective attachment to one option in the light of others?

Rational choice models of decision-making routinely discuss the ordering of preferences with reference to the 'utility' some outcome would provide. Yet in Bernoulli's original articulation of the concept, utility was closely linked to the pleasure derived from a prospective outcome (see Bernoulli, 1954). Eschewing any reference to emotions, such models are at a loss to provide a plausible explanation for the origin of preferences. Some assert that preferences reflect the obvious and unmediated implications of the actors' environment. Thus, for neo-realists, a preference for 'security' replaces the emotion of 'fear' as the 'rational' response to anarchy (Waltz, 1979). Meanwhile, neoliberal theorists either postulate some universal interest – such as 'welfare', usually reduced to wealth – with preferences referring merely to an ordering of options on the basis of a subjective assessment of associated expected net benefits, or they relegate actor preferences to a domain that is defined as beyond the scope of their theory (for good discussions of the issues, see Legro [1996] and Moravcsik [1997]).

Advances in psychology and neuroscience support the link between emotions and preferences. Moreover, the evidence is consistent with the proposition that emotions are prior to preferences and that preferences do not require prior cognitive assessments of utility. Rather, preferences are the product of our evolutionary and personal developmental history.[5] Although observable variation of preferences within groups provides evidence that the environment's effects are not strong enough to produce strict uniformity, they are nonetheless significant.

Preferences imply emotions, and emotions, it seems, do not require cognition. The converse, however, is not the case. When emotional faculties are seriously impaired, individuals are incapable of making decisions on the basis of the kind of cost–benefit calculations central to rational choice models. The original studies were clinical in nature and based on patients with damage to the brain's ventromedial prefrontal cortex. These patients

---

[4]   For an extended discussion of the findings outlined here, see McDermott (2004).

[5]   See Zajonc (1980, 1984), Kunst-Wilson and Zajonc (1980) and Zajonc and Markus (1982). Zajonc's arguments are not without their critics (see, e.g., Lazarus [1982, 1984]).

frequently were unable to access and integrate emotions, an impairment that inhibited their ability to negotiate the decisions required in daily life. Without emotions to guide their decisions, otherwise intelligent persons with no impairments of memory, alertness or language skills often engage in a form of infinite regress, calculating and re-calculating the advantages and disadvantages of various choices, unable to settle on any particular option. Moreover, if they do decide, a seeming inability to envision the future consequences of current choices leads these individuals to opt for short-term gratification at the expense of longer-term gain (see Damasio, 1996; Damasio et al, 1994; see also Bechara et al, 1997, 2000). The overwhelming wealth of evidence led Damasio and his colleagues to conclude that emotions are a precondition, rather than a hindrance, to effective reasoning (Vogel, 1997).

If emotions are central to understanding how we reason and choose, then understanding the social origins and effects of different types of emotions on preferences, decision-making and social behaviour is an area where constructivists and psychologically oriented scholars of international relations and foreign policy should collaborate. Both psychology and constructivism share an interest in understanding how emotions influence behaviour, in particular how they serve as a form of social glue among individual members of a group. Each perspective provides an important component to the enterprise.

Aided by cognate research in the field of neuroscience, psychologists have developed a fuller understanding of the structures and processes of the human brain. In addition to the interplay between emotions and cognition that characterizes human brains in general, we now have a better understanding of the way the individual human brain develops in response to its social environment, the latter constituting the central focus of constructivist research.

Evolutionary legacy

Our brains are the product of evolution and represent functional adaptations to the challenges faced by our forebears. And from an evolutionary standpoint, it makes sense that the brain would privilege emotions – such as fear or lust – over higher-order abstract reasoning. To put it simply, the survival of the individual and his or her genes depended on it. Advances in neural imaging have helped us better understand the spatial biology of the brain and how emotions relate to cognition. Neural fibres (efferents) from the peripheral senses flow more or less directly to the amygdala, the seat of the brain's emotional processing. The amygdala serves as a sort of 'gatekeeper', deciding which stimuli should be sent to the prefrontal cortex for further analysis. Rational analysis only takes place if the person feels emotionally and physically secure (LeDoux, 1996; Anderson and Phelps,

2000; Nader et al, 2000; LeDoux, 2012). Again, this makes sense from an evolutionary perspective. Deliberation is not conducive to survival when the latter depends on fight-or-flight decisions. The primacy of affect over reason explains why the fear produced by unexpected noises often precedes the identification of the source of the noise (Damasio, 1996: 159).

Emotions also affect our memory in ways that structure subsequent perception and behaviour. Our memories of emotional reactions often are distinct from our memories of the details of the situation that originally produced them. Thus, we often know we didn't like something or someone, even if we can't remember why (Bargh, 1984). In the field of international affairs, we can expect strong emotions produced by an experience with a particular leader or country to be enduring and difficult to shake, even when the current situation no longer resembles the original encounter. Such mechanisms may also extend to our assessments of foreign policy strategies. If, for example, the failure of a particular strategy gave rise to strong emotions in the past, the mere thought of such an option may evoke an emotional response before anyone has had time to deliberate its suitability to a contemporary challenge. Damasio postulates that sensory information is physically embodied in the form of emotions. These 'somatic markers' influence subsequent decisions by providing a feeling for who or what is likely to produce pleasure or pain (Damasio, 1996).

Such findings relate to long-standing subjects of interest to students of international relations and foreign policy. Take, for example, the well-documented phenomenon of analogous reasoning by foreign policy decision-makers (May, 1973; Neustadt and May, 1986; Khong, 1992). Researchers have not only found that individuals gravitate towards analogies of events that were salient in their political youth, but also documented strong cohort effects. Thus, members of the Vietnam generation share a certain collective memory that is different from those who came of age during the Gulf War or post 9/11. The somatic marker hypothesis would suggest that strong memory of political events in early adulthood is produced not only because these were vivid and novel, but also because they aroused strong emotions. The impact of analogies is enhanced as the memory of these events revives the original emotional response.

From culture to cognition

Applying insights from cognitive psychology to the study of foreign policy decision-making, scholars such as Robert Jervis, Richard Ned Lebow and Janice Gross Stein have demonstrated how the perceptions of foreign policy decision-makers are influenced by pre-existing beliefs, images and theories. In an effort to reduce complexity, resolve ambiguity and avoid the psychological discomfort produced by the pervasive need to confront value trade-offs, decision-makers subconsciously resort to a variety of cognitive shortcuts that bias inferences in systematic ways. They exhibit a strong predisposition to perceive what they already know or expect; they tend to ignore or discount information that contradicts prior beliefs; and they assimilate ambiguous information to pre-existing beliefs (see Jervis, 1976; Lebow, 1981; Jervis et al, 1989).

Understanding misperception as a discrepancy between individual perceptions and 'reality' and individual, if systematic, deviations from the normative precepts of rational choice models of information processing, early work on the psychology of foreign policy decision-making was not concerned with the cultural origins of the baselines against which individual deviations could be established.[6] But as I have discussed at length elsewhere, the conceptual categories into which perceptions are assimilated vary widely across cultures and languages. Whether we are speaking of sounds or visual or tactile stimuli, individuals experience and interpret these in quite different ways depending on their socialization (see Davis, 2005: 10–60). Though most human beings are born with a very similar neural apparatus, non-trivial portions of the individual's neural development are conditioned by culturally determined stimuli, with subsequent important effects on higher-order cognitive processes such as reasoning.

Take, for example, the development of our auditory apparatus. Numerous studies have demonstrated that newborn babies are able to distinguish among phonemes that are not found in the language of their parents and that their parents can no longer 'hear'. Thus, babies born to English speaking parents in Canada could distinguish among phonetic contrasts in both English and Czech. If only exposed to English, however, they rapidly lost the ability to differentiate meaningful phonetic segments in Czech. While it appears that infants engage in prelinguistic categorization of sounds in ways that are relevant to the phonemic distinctions of adult speech, languages differ with regard to which phonemic categories they use and the location of the acoustic boundaries among these categories. As infants come to master their native language, the brain is modified in ways that allow it to distinguish between meaningful and irrelevant acoustic cues. Within eight to ten months of age, the infant brain is already losing the ability to distinguish among sounds not found in the languages to which it is exposed (see Miller and Eimas, 1983; Bahrick and Pickens, 1988; Mehler and Dupoux, 1994; Nelson, 1996).

Returning to one of the premises animating Kratochwil's deliberations, answering the question of 'what is' in social life does require us to move from the mind to the world. But in important ways, the mind itself is a product of the social world. How might this relate to questions of practice at the

---

[6]   On the various interpretations of the term 'misperception', see Levy (2003).

centre of Kratochwil's tome? One obvious answer relates to the possibility for multiple descriptive and normative frames of the 'same' situation. While Kratochwil is certainly right to point out that practical arguments require us to move beyond mere cognition, in many cases cognition itself has already been constrained (or enabled) by culture. Cultural practice provides the very conceptual categories within which cognition itself takes place by directing our attention to some aspects of the situation at the expense of others. And as the example of infant language acquisition makes clear, these processes are subconscious and part of the deep structure of our cognitive apparatus.

Behavioural genetics

The cognitive paradigm drew our attention to the ways in which the environment interacts with the decision-maker's mind to bias choice. Aided by the availability of rapid and relatively inexpensive sequencing technologies, a new generation of political scientists have begun to examine how the individual's genetic make-up interacts with the environment – social and physical – to influence behaviour. Although it is unlikely that any single gene can explain complex social behaviour, it is also unlikely that the influence of heritable traits on behaviour is insignificant. More likely is the possibility that multiple genes acting in concert across numerous causal pathways come to influence behaviour in systematic ways. The burgeoning field of epigenetics adds dimension, nuance and further complexity to this examination by focusing on the ways in which environmental factors can influence gene expression, which in turn can affect downstream behaviour through processes such as hormone release.[7]

Though the fields of behavioural genetics and behavioural epigenetics are truly in their infancy, researchers have already produced findings with potential application to questions of social order, international relations and foreign policy decision-making. Take, for example, the open question of the origins of trust that is so central to Kratochwil's critique of the Hobbesian account of the social contract and liberal theories of international institutions.[8] True, generalized trust seems conducive to cooperation. The provision of public goods has been shown to be more effective when levels of 'generalized' or 'social' trust are higher (Fehr and Gintis, 2007). When levels of generalized trust are higher, social and economic transactions are more

---

[7] For examples of the various causal pathways, see Boomsma et al (1999), Meyer–Lindberg et al (2006) and Ebstein et al (2010).

[8] For a somewhat similar critique of the standard liberal explanation for international institutions, see Rathbun (2012).

efficient and the costs of policing compliance and punishing transgressions are lower than in situations of generalized mistrust (Mansbridge, 1999).

Previous scholarship explained variations in people's basic inclination to trust others in terms of environmental factors, including the individual's education, socio-economic status and socialization (Nie et al, 1996; Alesina and La Ferrara, 2002; Uslaner, 2002). These findings have been challenged by genetic studies focusing on monozygotic and dizygotic twins. For example, Sturgis and his colleagues set out to estimate the relative influence of genetic and environmental factors on subject scores on a multi-item trust scale. In contrast to those studies emphasizing the effects of socialization, they found that environmental factors experienced in common by sibling pairs produced no discernible effects. Only those environmental factors unique to the individual had a measurable effect on that individual's level of social trust. But the majority of the observed variance was accounted for by additive genetic factors (Sturgis et al, 2010). Though nature and nurture condition the individual's propensity to trust others, across the populations used for these studies, the former accounts for more of the observed variance than the latter.[9]

Cultural epigenetics?

Genetic-based explanations provide a counterpoint to social science models that attribute behavioural variation to changes in one's environment or different positions individuals are said to occupy in some theoretically defined structure. Yet insofar as they are evolutionary in nature, genetic explanations are not completely reductionist. Much of our genetic make-up reflects adaptive responses to environmental challenges. Similarly, the new field of epigenetics proceeds from the premise that behaviour emerges from the interaction of our genes with the environment. The difference is that epigenetics focuses not only on the genes we have inherited, but on how environmental factors affect their operation and thereby condition downstream behaviour. A focus on genetics runs counter to the overwhelming tendency of social science to attribute behavioural variation to environmental factors alone. If social science has tended to privilege nurture over nature, the new field of behavioural epigenetics starts from the premise that behaviour emerges from factors at the interface between genes and environment. The focus is not only on what genes you have, but on how things 'around the gene' affect their operation and thereby downstream behaviour. Moreover, in some situations, genes and the environment can be thought of as mutually

---

[9]   For a sampling of research attributing dispositions to genetics, see Arvey et al (1989), Bouchard et al (2004) and Alford et al (2005).

constitutive, the social environment both cause and consequence of genetically influenced behaviours (McDermott and Hatemi, 2014).

Epigenetics is the study of the processes whereby genetic information is made available or unavailable for use in other biological processes. Disease, exposure to toxic chemicals or high levels of stress can have the effect of 'turning on' or 'turning off' specific genes. This in turn can affect other biochemical processes, with effects that eventually reach the level of behaviour. 'Histone acetylation' refers to processes whereby DNA segments become more accessible, gene expression is enhanced and the production of proteins associated with those genes is increased. 'Methylation', by contrast, inhibits access to DNA segments, decreases gene expression and subsequently reduces the production of associated proteins. These processes are ongoing and not unidirectional. For at least a subset of genes, environmental influences and experience can lead to methylation, demethylation and remethylation. The result is persistent functional change in the nervous system (see Powledge, 2011; Moore, 2017).

For example, laboratory studies of variations in the behaviour of mother rats towards their offspring discovered that denying newborn pups exposure to the frequent licking and grooming that is characteristic of mother rat behaviour produced highly methylated DNA segments within the cells of the brain's hippocampus. The consequent decrease in the production of a protein associated with stress regulation in turn produced adult rats that were significantly more fearful when exposed to stress compared with those rats that experienced maternal attention (Francis et al, 1999; Weaver et al, 2004; Weaver, 2007; Murgatroyd et al, 2009). Analogous effects have been documented in humans, with the hippocampal cells of adults who experienced abuse as children also exhibiting methylation in the region of the DNA association with the production of the protein (glucocorticoid receptor) important for the regulation of stress (McGowan et al, 2009; Palumbo et al, 2018). Moreover, studies of children who were institutionalized in Romanian orphanages and deprived of socio-emotional attention exhibited similar developmental deficits (Chugani et al, 2001; Eluvathingal et al, 2006).

But are the effects of such processes really of interest to social scientists, or indeed students of international relations? It seems hardly a stretch to hypothesize that parents exposed to ongoing civil or inter-state war will have relatively less time to devote to the social and emotional care of infants and children than parents in more peaceful settings. If such deprivations prove pervasive and durable, they probably enhance the prospect that significant populations within society will exhibit developmental pathologies with significant implications for subsequent levels of social cohesion. Although well-established social transmission belts, such as generalized tit-for-tat strategies or more thick processes of socialization, may provide a sufficient basis for the perpetuation of anti-social behaviours, evidence is mounting that socially triggered epigenetic effects are heritable, a finding that suggests biological transmission of cultural attributes (or at least behavioural tendencies) across generations (Axelrod, 1984). For example, the daughters of Finnish women who were evacuated from their homes and separated from their families as children between 1941 and 1945 during Finland's war with the Soviet Union share the same high risk for mental illness as their mothers. By contrast, their cousins born to mothers not evacuated display an incidence of mental illness characteristic of the overall population (Santavirta et al, 2018). Similarly, women who were pregnant during the Dutch famine at the end of World War II gave birth to children who displayed much higher rates of diabetes, and this effect appears to exert itself across at least two generations (Painter et al, 2008).

Even when the direct effects of epigenetic processes on behaviour are limited in scope and domain, collective responses to the underlying pathologies might produce societal-level effects. For example, public health interventions designed to redress rising levels of diabetes – perhaps in the form of information campaigns designating certain foods as 'good' or 'bad' – if successful, could change long-standing cultural practices.

Social science is only beginning to contemplate the ways in which epigenetic mechanisms can help explain phenomena of interest. It remains an open question whether the explanations generated with reference to such processes will bring insights beyond those of existing social science models and theories. Careful attention to scope conditions is called for. For whereas the effects discussed previously appear to transmit across generations, early studies of epigenetic effects on social preferences suggest they may be of more limited durability (see, e.g., Hatemi, 2013). And, as mentioned earlier, scholars should resist the temptation to match a particular behaviour to a specific gene. Even when positive, the correlation between isolated genes and social traits most often accounts for only a small portion of observed behavioural variance (see Duncan and Keller, 2011).

Nonetheless, a focus on the ways in which socially constructed environmental conditions interact with biological processes at the level of individuals to produce genetic changes that subsequently influence aggregate social behaviour and thereby potentially culture allows us to dispense with simplistic nature versus nurture debates. The emerging fields of behavioural genetics and epigenetics point to the more promising framework of biological and social co-evolution.

Practising praxis

To repeat an often misapplied aphorism: there is a difference between theory and praxis. Being an expert in physics and aerodynamics is not much help on the tennis court. When trying to learn a new sport, *practice*, not theory, makes perfect (or at least is a necessary if not sufficient condition thereof). Neuroscientific advances have enhanced our understanding of how dexterity develops and point to a complex interaction between repeated play and neurological processes involving various areas of the brain, many of which require sleep in order to operate effectively. Both the size and the structure of the human brain change in response to environmental demands as action sequences are imprinted in synaptic connections in ways that allow even complex moves to become automated or habitual (see, e.g., Draganski et al, 2004; Meister and Buffalo, 2017).

While Kratochwil (2018: 425) is correct to note that praxis cannot be reduced to habit – for then innovation would not be possible – the relationship between habits and innovation is more symbiotic than his critique implies. Firstly, it appears that variability is essential to learning. To master a practice requires us to try it out in different ways. Secondly, innovation presupposes dexterity. One cannot improve upon that which one has not already mastered to some degree. Thirdly, by providing functional and reflex-like behaviours that help us to successfully navigate complex environments, habits actually free up cognitive resources, allowing for critical reflection over both the substance and form of praxis (Meister and Buffalo, 2017).

Psychobiology of praxis

There can be no 'we' without individuals, but contemporary research in psychology, biology and neuroscience provides strong evidence that the 'I' is constituted by the 'we' in non-trivial ways. 'Co-constitution' seems a more apt methodological position than either reductionism (methodological individualism) or holism. While biology surely constrains what human beings can do, it is not immutable. And cultural variety is not merely a conditioned response to physical and social environmental challenges. Praxis is more than a store of lessons, scripts or standards that provide the thinking individual with functional responses to the complexities of social life and the terms according to which discourses over social questions may occur. It also (re-)structures the biological organism and in doing so both enables and constrains behaviour, which includes thinking and choice.

Because the thick constructivism defended by Kratochwil is silent as to the psychobiology of human agents, it is apt both to exaggerate our ability to make and remake the social world and to overlook the biological effects produced by the individual's social environment. This silence is ironic given Kratochwil's indebtedness to Hume, who was concerned with the 'anatomy of the mind' (Hume, 1896 [1739]: 326) and distinguished between 'impressions', a category that for him included emotions, and 'ideas', which he considered to be the product of thinking and reasoning (Hume,

1896 [1739]: 1–4).[10] But because both constructivism and psychology share the conviction that to understand international relations requires us to understand how individuals perceive and construct reality, the study of praxis can only benefit from a sustained dialogue between these two modes of inquiry. How might collaboration proceed? In what follows, I briefly sketch out a hypothesized relationship between culture and psychology and in doing so try to show how 'we' and 'I' relate along some of the dimensions discussed previously.

Human beings perceive their world, experiences and fantasies in terms of a limited set of concepts and schemas, as otherwise we would be overwhelmed by the sheer volume of stimuli and impressions. Among the various categories used by individuals to make sense of their world are those pertaining to social groups. The cognitive imperative to classify individuals, including the self, into groups then gives rise to a social identity. Because social categories not only describe group attributes but also prescribe appropriate group behaviour, social identities imply behavioural consequences. The mechanism leading from categorization to behaviour is identification. One can belong to a particular group on the basis of some defining features without self-identifying as a member of the group. Hence, identification with a group is a psychological phenomenon, and social identity is that part of an individual's self-concept that derives from knowledge of membership in a social group. With identification comes affect, as the individual begins to attach emotional significance to group membership (Niedenthal and Brauer, 2012). When emotional attachments move beyond mere membership to include the symbols and values that are meaningful to the group as a whole, the first-person singular and plural merge and the 'I' becomes 'we'. Evidence of this process will be apparent in the emotional responses of individuals when group symbols, values, members or the group as a whole are the focus of praise or condemnation (Leonard et al, 2010; van Zomeren et al, 2010). In the first instance the individual will experience the emotion of pride, in the second, anger or fear. Because social categories have reference to the self, social categorization induces social comparison. Favourable or unfavourable comparisons to other groups can induce affective responses analogous to those produced by perceived threats or support for group symbols and values.[11]

If the human brain is predisposed to (self-)categorize, the world rarely provides ready-made and obvious categories. Of particular interest from the standpoint of a study of praxis is the fact that most objects or experiences are multidimensional and thus can be categorized in any number of ways. The

---

[10] I am grateful to Nicholas Onuf for alerting me to this irony.

[11] For the full articulation of the mechanism summarized here, see Larson (2012).

question then shifts from the object or experience itself to the purposes of the attempt at categorization (Kratochwil, 2018: 378). What is the problem to be solved? Similarly, nature usually does not present us with a clearly defined list of dimensions according to which we can (or should) compare our group with others.[12] To gain leverage over these questions requires the insights and methods of constructivism.

The foregoing sketch implies that there is no inherent dichotomy between psychology's focus on the individual's subjective experience of the world and constructivism's emphasis on the intersubjective component of social reality. Instead, emphasizing the co-constitution of the 'I' and the 'we' directs our attention to the ways in which subjectivity and intersubjectivity relate to and reinforce each other.

Paul Kowert (2012) offers a more specific articulation of the general argument in his exploration of the deontic force of obligations. How an idea or belief comes to exert a deontic force on actors, Kowert argues, is a question of both intersubjective understandings and the way the brain works. If we are to move beyond a mere instrumental conception of compliance, where the effects of rules and norms are produced via actors' calculations of the benefits of compliance as compared with the likely costs of non-compliance (usually conceived in terms of externally imposed negative sanctions), we necessarily must move beyond discourses based on intersubjective understandings to individual psychology. To understand an individual's sense of obligation requires us to link processes of reasoned judgement to the evocation of emotions, a position Kowert (2012: 35) associates with Hume. Again, linguistically oriented constructivists and psychologists each contribute insights that foster a better understanding of the issue involved:

> [N]ormativity depends on creating feelings of obligation. For emotions to generate obligation, they must be linked to beliefs, and these beliefs must be capable of being articulated in certain ways. The constructivist interest in shared beliefs and in language thus gets an important part of the story right. Obligation does indeed require belief. Yet not all beliefs are normative (any more than all choices are rational): The functioning of language on the one hand and emotion on the other endows certain beliefs with normative force. (Kowert, 2012: 37)

---

[12] There is, however, evidence that evolution has predisposed humans to prefer some 'types' over others, especially when considering reproductive mates. Although some judgements show cultural variation, the evidence suggests that other predispositions are pre-cultural. See, for example, Jones and Hill (1993), Thornhill and Gangestad (1993) and Rhodes et al (2001).

A sense of obligation, then, is the result of a non-idiosyncratic characterization of some situation involving objects and/or events to which the individual has attached some feelings. To say that we cannot reduce shared understandings of situations, objects or events to the pre-linguistic drives or instincts of individuals does not negate the proposition that it is individual emotional reactions to these that provide obligations their moral or deontic force. Shared understandings provide us the *content* of obligations, but for obligations to produce effects, they must be meaningful for individuals (Kowert, 2012: 50). It is precisely via the internalization of intersubjective understandings that subjective experiences produce emotional responses that subsequently influence individual choice. In this way, psychology puts the group – or the collective 'we' in Kratochwil's formulation – into the individual 'I'.[13] It is this social identity that is then subject to manipulation through the various special rites and ceremonies created by communities for purposes of mobilizing memories and their associated emotions (Kratochwil, 2018: 33).

Conclusion

Friedrich Kratochwil's *Praxis* is the culmination of a lifetime of scholarly critical reflection. In it, he returns to early topics and themes, such as the development of a Humean perspective on International Relations (IR) and the need for methods of analysis adequate to the task of analysing the origins, reproduction and effects of conventions as social rather than natural kinds (Kratochwil, 1981, 1984). Though many of the themes are familiar to the generations of scholars influenced by his early work, they no longer seem exotic or radical. A giant of the constructivist turn in IR scholarship, Kratochwil (Kratochwil, 1989, 1994, 2006) is directly responsible for the (near) mainstream status now accorded the many research programmes directed at understanding, inter alia, the role of intersubjective understandings; history and memory; legal and moral reasoning; as well as questions of identity, in international life. And owing to the 'practice turn', the claim that knowing is not merely a question of subsuming individual cases under general laws or principles – but also about *knowing how* to proceed with goal-directed activity in the light of unknowable and ever changing circumstances – while not universally accepted, continues to attract adherents (Kratochwil, 2018: 414–16).

But what does it mean to 'keep going' when the signposts of constructivist praxis and the attendant 'rules of the road' are not only extended to help us navigate new terrain but *de-* or *re-*based in ways that fundamentally subvert the original purposes of the conventions? The intersubjectivity of standards

---

[13] For a concise review of the relevant research in psychology, see Smith and Mackie (2016).

may provide some defence against idiosyncratic justifications, but how are we to adapt when symbols and rituals are instrumentalized to conjure the 'we' in pursuit of tyranny (Kratochwil, 2018: 463)? When priests and pastors increasingly are exposed as imposters and even the most senior judges are suspected of being little more than artful penmen, selected on the basis of their willingness to serve the needs of the politician, appeals to the law or morals will not do, as these are precisely the objects of debasement.

Given the current state of national and international affairs, it seems no accident that Kratochwil ends his tome with some thoughts on the future of politics. Echoing Hannah Arendt, he wonders how to inspire new political projects that would allow free people to reconcile their individual and collective projects (Kratochwil, 2018: 472). It is a question many readers will share and are likely to repeat after having read this monumental reflection: how *do* 'we' recover collective intentionality in pursuit of a common understanding of the good life, and what can 'I' do?

References

Adler, Emanuel (2019) *World Ordering: A Social Theory of Cognitive Evolution* (Cambridge: Cambridge University Press).

Alesina, Alberto and Eliana La Ferrara (2002) 'Who trusts others?', *Journal of Public Economy* 85, 2, pp 207–34.

Alford, John R., Carolyn L. Funk and John R. Hibbing (2005) 'Are political orientations genetically transmitted?', *American Political Science Review* 99, 2, pp 153–7.

Anderson, Adam K. and Elizabeth A. Phelps (2000) 'Perceiving emotion: there's more than meets the eye', *Biology* 10, 15, 551–4.

Arvey, Richard D., Thomas J. Bouchard, Nancy L. Segal and Lauren M. Abraham (1989) 'Job satisfaction: environmental and genetic components', *Journal of Applied Psychology* 74, 2, pp 187–92.

Axelrod, Robert (1984) *The Evolution of Cooperation* (New York: Basic Books).

Bahrick, Lorraine E. and Jeffrey N. Pickens (1988) 'Classification of bimodal English and Spanish language passages by infants', *Infant Behavior and Development* 11, 3, pp 277–96.

Bargh, John A. (1984) 'Automatic and conscious processing of social information', in Robert S. Wyer and Thomas K. Scrull (eds), *Handbook of Social Cognition* (3rd edn) (Hillsdale, NJ: Erlbaum), pp 1–43.

Bechara, Antoine, Hanna Damasio, Daniel Tranel and Antonio R. Damasio (1997) 'Deciding advantageously before knowing the advantageous strategy', *Science* 275, 5304, pp 1293–5.

Bechara, Antoine, Daniel Tranel and Hanna Damasio (2000) 'Characterization of the decision-making deficit of patients with ventromedial prefrontal cortex lesions', *Brain* 123, 11, pp 2189–202.

Bernoulli, Daniel (1954) 'Exposition of a new theory on the measurement of risk', *Econometrica* 22, 1, pp 23–36.

Boomsma, Dorret I., J.C. de Geus Eco, G. Carolina van Baal and Judith R. Koopmans (1999) 'A religious upbringing reduces the influence of genetic factors on disinhibition: evidence for interaction between genotype and environment on personality', *Twin Research* 2, 2, pp 115–25.

Bouchard, Thomas J., Nancy L. Segal, Auke Tellegen, Matthew McGue, Margaret Keyes and Robert Krueger (2004) 'Evidence for the construct validity and heritability of the Wilson–Patterson Conservatism Scale: a reared-apart twins study of social attitudes', *Journal of Personality and Individual Differences* 34, 6, pp 959–69.

Buckley, Chris and Austin Ramzy (2017) 'China's state media slams Trump's "emotional venting" on Twitter', *New York Times*, 2 August, p A5.

Chugani, Harry T., Michael E. Behen, Otto Muzik, Csaba Juhász, Ferenc Nagy and Diane C. Chugani (2001) 'Local brain functional activity following early deprivation: a study of postinstitutionalized Romanian orphans', *Neuroimage* 14, 6, pp 1290–301.

Damasio, Antonio R. (1996) *Descartes' Error: Emotion, Reason, and the Human Brain* (New York: Putnam and Sons).

Damasio, Hanna, Thomas Grabowski, Randall Frank, Albert M. Galaburda and Antonio R. Damasio (1994) 'The return of Phineas Gage: the skull of a famous patient yields clues about the brain', *Science* 264, 5162, pp 1102–5.

Davis, James W. (2005) *Terms of Inquiry: On the Theory and Practice of Political Science* (Baltimore, MD: Johns Hopkins University Press).

Davis, James W. and Rose McDermott (2020) 'The past, present, and future of behavioral IR', *International Organization* 75, 1, pp 147–7.

Davis, James W., Symone D. Sanders, Tony Schwartz and Evgeny Morozov (2017) 100 days of President Trump – 47th St. Gallen Symposium, Panel Discussion at the 47th Annual St. Gallen Symposium, 4 May, available at: https://www.youtube.com/watch?v=qFaLrN_jwcU, accessed 26 February 2021.

Draganski, Bogdan, Christian Gaser, Volker Busch, Gerhard Schuierer, Ulrich Bogdahn and Arne May (2004) 'Changes in grey matter induced by training', *Nature* 427, pp 311–12.

Duncan, Laramie E. and Matthew C. Keller (2011) 'A critical review of the first 10 years of candidate gene-by-environment interaction research in psychiatry', *American Journal of Psychiatry* 168, 10, pp 1041–9.

Ebstein, Richard P., Salomon Israel, Soo Hong Chew, Songfa Zhong and Ariel Knafo (2010) 'Genetics of human social behavior', *Neuron* 65, 6, pp 383–408.

Eluvathingal, Thomas J., Harry T. Chugani, Michael E. Behen, Csaba Juhász, Otto Muzik, Mohsin Maqbool, Diane C. Chugani and Malek Makki (2006) 'Abnormal brain connectivity in children after early severe socioemotional deprivation: a diffusion tensor imaging study', *Pediatrics* 117, 6, pp 2093–100.

Fehr, Ernst and Herbert Gintis (2007) 'Human motivation and social cooperation: experimental and analytical foundations', *Annual Review of Sociology* 33, pp 43–64.

Francis, Darlene, Josie Diorio, Dong Liu and Michael J. Meaney (1999) 'Nongenetic transmission across generations of maternal behavior and stress responses in the rat', *Science* 286, 5422, pp 1155–8.

Hatemi, Peter K. (2013) 'The influence of major life events on economic attitudes in a world of gene–environment interplay', *American Journal of Political Science* 57, 4, pp 987–1007.

Hume, David (1896 [1739]) *A Treatise of Human Nature* (Oxford: Clarendon Press).

Jervis, Robert (1976) *Perception and Misperception in International Politics* (Princeton, NJ: Princeton University Press).

Jervis, Robert, Richard Ned Lebow and Janice Gross Stein (1989) *Psychology and Deterrence* (Baltimore, MD: Johns Hopkins University Press).

Jones, Doug and Kim Hill (1993) 'Criteria of facial attractiveness in five populations', *Human Nature* 4, 3, pp 271–96.

Khong, Yuen Foong (1992) *Analogies at War: Korea, Munich, Dien Bien Phu, and the Vietnam Decisions of 1965* (Princeton, NJ: Princeton University Press).

Kowert, Paul A. (2012) 'Completing the ideational triangle: identity, choice, and obligation in international relations', in Vaughn P. Shannon and Paul A. Kowert (eds), *Psychology and Constructivism in International Relations: An Ideational Alliance* (Ann Arbor: University of Michigan Press), pp 30–53.

Kratochwil, Friedrich (1981) *The Humean Conception of International Relations* (Princeton, NJ: Princeton University, Center of International Studies).

Kratochwil, Friedrich (1984) 'Errors have their advantage', *International Organization* 38, 2, pp 305–20.

Kratochwil, Friedrich (1989) *Rules, Norms and Decisions: On the Conditions of Practical and Legal Reasoning in International Relations and Domestic Affairs* (Cambridge: Cambridge University Press).

Kratochwil, Friedrich (1994) 'The limits of contract', *European Journal of International Law* 5, 4, pp 465–91.

Kratochwil, Friedrich (2006) 'History, action and identity: revisiting the "second" great debate and assessing its importance for social theory', *European Journal of International Relations* 12, 1, pp 5–29.

Kratochwil, Friedrich (2018) *Praxis: On Acting and Knowing* (Cambridge: Cambridge University Press).

Kunst-Wilson, William R. and Robert B. Zajonc (1980) 'Affective discrimination of stimuli that cannot be recognized', *Science* 207, 4430, pp 557–8.

Larson, Deborah Welch (2012) 'How identities form and change: supplementing constructivism with social psychology', in Vaughn P. Shannon and Paul A. Kowert (eds), *Psychology and Constructivism in International Relations: An Ideational Alliance* (Ann Arbor: University of Michigan Press), pp 57–75.

Lazarus Richard S. (1982) 'Thoughts on the relation between emotion and cognition', *American Psychologist* 37, 9, pp 1019–24.

Lazarus, Richard S. (1984) 'On the primacy of affect', *American Psychologist* 39, 2, pp 124–9.

Lebow, Richard Ned (1981) *Between Peace and War: The Nature of International Crises* (Baltimore, MD: Johns Hopkins University Press).

LeDoux, Joseph E. (1996) *The Emotional Brain* (New York: Simon and Schuster).

LeDoux, Joseph E. (2012) 'Rethinking the emotional brain', *Neuron* 73, 4, pp 653–76.

Legro, Jeffrey W. (1996) 'Culture and preferences in the international cooperation two-step', *American Political Science Review* 90, 1, pp 118–37.

Leonard, Diana J., Wesley G. Moons, Diane M. Mackie and Elliot R. Smith (2010) ' "We're mad as hell and we're not going to take it anymore": anger self-stereotyping and collective action', *Group Processes and Intergroup Relations* 14, 1, pp 99–111.

Levy, Jack S. (2003) 'Political psychology and foreign policy', in David O. Sears, Leonie Huddy and Robert Jervis (eds), *Oxford Handbook of Political Psychology* (Oxford: Oxford University Press), pp 261–3.

Mansbridge, Jane (1999) 'Altruistic trust', in Mark E. Warren (ed), *Democracy and Trust* (Cambridge: Cambridge University Press), pp 290–309.

May, Ernest R. (1973) *'Lessons' of the Past: The Use and Misuse of History in American Foreign Policy* (New York: Oxford University Press).

McDermott, Rose (2004) 'The feeling of rationality: the meaning of neuroscientific advances for political science', *Perspectives on Politics* 2, 4, pp 691–706.

McDermott, Rose and Peter K. Hatemi (2014) 'Political ecology: on the mutual formation of biology and culture', *Political Psychology* 35, 1, pp 111–27.

McGowan, Patrick, Aya Sasaki, Ana C. D'Alessio, Sergiy Dymov, Benoit Labonté and Moshe Szyf (2009) 'Epigenetic regulation of the glucocorticoid receptor in human brain associates with childhood abuse', *Nature Neuroscience* 12, 3, pp 342–8.

Mead, George H. and Charles W. Morris (1967) *Mind, Self and Society from the Standpoint of a Social Behaviorist* (Chicago, IL: University of Chicago Press).

Mehler, Jacques and Emmanuel Dupoux (1994) *What Infants Know* (Cambridge: Blackwell).

Meister, Miriam L.R. and Elizabeth A. Buffalo (2017) 'Memory', in P. Michael Conn (ed), *Conn's Translational Neuroscience* (Cambridge, MA: Academic Press), pp 693–708.

Meyer-Lindberg, Andreas, Carolyn B. Mervis and Karen Faith Berman (2006) 'Neural mechanisms in Williams's Syndrome: a unique window to genetic influences on cognition and behavior', *Nature Reviews Neuroscience* 7, 5, pp 380–93.

Miller, Joanne L. and Peter D. Eimas (1983) 'Studies on the categorization of speech by infants', *Cognition* 13, 2, pp 135–65.

Moore, David S. (2017) 'Behavioral epigenetics', *WIREs System Biology and Medicine* 9, 1, pp 1–8.

Moravcsik, Andrew (1997) 'Taking preferences seriously: a liberal theory of international politics', *International Organization* 51, 4, pp 513–53.

Murgatroyd, Chris, Alexandre V. Patchev, Yonghe Wu, Vincenzo Micale, Yvonne Bockmühl, Dieter Fischer, Florian Holsboer, Carsten T. Wotjak, Osborne F.X. Almeida and Dietmar Spengler (2009) 'Dynamic DNA methylation programs persistent adverse effects of early-life stress', *Nature Neuroscience* 12, 12, pp 1559–66.

Nader, Karim, Glenn E. Schafe and Joseph E. LeDoux (2000) 'Fear memories require protein synthesis in the amygdala for reconsolidation after retrieval', *Nature* 406, pp 722–6.

Nelson, Katherine (1996) *Language in Cognitive Development: Emergence of the Mediated Mind* (Cambridge: Cambridge University Press).

Neustadt, Richard E. and Ernest R. May (1986) *Thinking in Time: The Uses of History for Decision-Makers* (New York: Free Press).

Nie, Norman H., Jane Junn and Kenneth Stehlik-Barry (1996) *Education and Democratic Citizenship in America* (Chicago, IL: University of Chicago Press).

Niedenthal, Paula M. and Markus Brauer (2012) 'Social functionality of human emotion', *Annual Review of Psychology* 63, pp 259–85.

Painter, Rebecca C., Clive Osmond, Peter Gluckman, Mark Hanson, D.I.W. Phillips and Tessa J. Roseboom (2008) 'Transgenerational effects of prenatal exposure to the Dutch famine on neonatal adiposity and health in later life', *BJOG: An International Journal of Obstetrics and Gynaecology* 15, 10, pp 1243–9.

Palumbo, Sara, Veronica Mariotti, Caterina Iofrida and Silvia Pellegrini (2018) 'Genes and aggressive behavior: epigenetic mechanisms underlying individual susceptibility to aversive environments', *Frontiers in Behavioral Neuroscience* 12, 117, pp 1–8.

Powledge, Tabitha M. (2011) 'Behavioral epigenetics: how nurture shapes nature', *BioScience* 61, 8, pp 588–92.

Rathbun, Brian (2012) *Trust in International Cooperation: The Creation of International Security Institutions and the Domestic Politics of American Multilateralism* (Cambridge: Cambridge University Press).

Rhodes, Gillian, Sakiko Yoshikawa, Alison Clark, Kieran Lee, Ryan McKay and Shigeru Akamatsu (2001) 'Attractiveness of facial averageness and symmetry in non-Western cultures: in search of biologically based standards of beauty', *Perception* 30, 5, pp 611–25.

Santavirta, Thorsten, Nina Santavirta and Stephen E. Gilman (2018) 'Association of the World War II Finnish evacuation of children with psychiatric hospitalization in the next generation', *JAMA Psychiatry* 75, 1, pp 21–7.

Smith, Eliot R. and Diane M. Mackie (2016) 'Group-level emotions', *Current Opinion in Psychology* 11, pp 15–19.

Sturgis, Patrick, Sanna Read, Peter K. Hatemi, Gu Zhu, Tim Trull, Margaret J. Wright and Nicholas G. Martin (2010) 'A genetic basis for social trust?', *Political Behavior* 32, 2, pp 205–30.

Thornhill, Randy and Steven W. Gangestad (1993) 'Human facial beauty', *Human Nature* 4, 3, pp 237–69.

Uslaner, Eric M. (2002) *The Moral Foundations of Trust* (Cambridge: Cambridge University Press).

van Zomeren, Martijn, Russell Spears and Colin Wayne Leach (2010) 'Exploring psychological mechanisms of collective action: does relevance of group identity influence how people cope with collective disadvantage?', *British Journal of Social Psychology* 47 , 2, pp 353–72.

Vogel, Gretchen (1997) 'Scientists probe feelings behind decision making', *Science* 275, 5304, pp 1269.

Waltz, Kenneth N. (1979) *Theory of International Politics* (Reading, MA: Addison-Wesley).

Weaver, Ian C.G. (2007) 'Epigenetic programming by maternal behavior and pharmacological intervention. Nature versus nurture: let's call the whole thing off', *Epigenetics* 2, 1, pp 22–8.

Weaver, Ian C.G., Nadia Cervoni, Frances A. Champagne, Ana C. D'Alessio, Shakti Sharma, Jonathan R. Seckl, Sergiy Dymov, Moshe Szyf and Michael J. Meaney (2004) 'Epigenetic programming by maternal behavior', *Nature Neuroscience* 7, 9, pp 847–54.

Zajonc, Robert B. (1980) 'Feeling and thinking: preferences need no inferences', *American Psychologist* 35, 2, pp 151–75.

Zajonc, Robert B. (1984) 'On the primacy of affect', *American Psychologist* 39, 2, pp 117–23.

Zajonc, Robert B. and Hazel Markus (1982) 'Affective and cognitive factors in preferences', *Journal of Consumer Research* 9, 2, pp 123–31.

10

Practice, Intersubjectivity and the Problem of Contingency

Oliver Kessler

Introduction

Kratochwil's monograph *Praxis: On Acting and Knowing* is a healthy corrective to many current debates in general and about and within constructivism in particular (Kratochwil, 2018). In fact, it can be read as a fundamental critique of what constructivism has become as most contributors don't even get the basic questions right. If we take textbook introductions as the 'common sense' of what constructivism is all about, then every single introduction I looked at highlighted 'the study of norms' as its key concern. Sometimes it was even – along with the agent-structure problem – the *only* issue deemed relevant (Burchhill et al, 2013; Jackson and Sørensen, 2015; Berenskoetter, 2018: 446).

Naturally, there are certainly good reasons for any constructivist to be interested in norms. When they started to develop this approach, both Kratochwil and Onuf drew heavily on international law (Kratochwil, 1989; Onuf, 2008). Its semantic field of norms, rules, sanctions and obligations provided (and still does) an avenue to challenge the then dominant positivism in International Relations (IR). Data and the identification of empirical 'regularities' are simply unable to deal with normativity and counterfactual validity. A dimension that was in subsequent debates moved somewhat to the background as 'empirical' analyses of 'norms' have dominated the discourse in recent years – a move that is awkwardly reproduced by those who now look for a 'new constructivism' through practice theories and thereby eclipse any interest in counterfactual validity (McCourt, 2016: 475).

So, while there are thus good reasons to be interested in norms, already the title highlights that it is simply wrong to equate constructivism *with* norms.

Here, constructivism is associated not with the concept of norms per se, but the problem of *action*, a problem best circumscribed by a conjunction of Hume's notion of common sense (Kratochwil, 2018: chapter 8) and the problem of knowledge (Kratochwil, 2018: chapter 9). Starting from here shows that those who took norms as the explanans simply barked up the wrong tree. If anything, future textbook introductions to constructivism need to start from 'action' and carefully lay out how its intersubjective quality is actually fundamentally different from both individual rational choice and the empiricism inscribed in the current search for 'practices' (see Kratochwil, 2018: 391).

This chapter takes Kratochwil's notion of acting as vantage point to further explore the problem of intersubjectivity. It seeks to clarify the difference between positive and constructivist approaches in relation to expectations, common sense and 'how to go on'. It argues that their key difference is how they conceptualize contingency. From here, differences can be made visible and different notions of intersubjectivity can be identified. At the very least, and through a discussion of game theory, this chapter highlights that the problem of intersubjectivity is not to be confused with the physical presence of two or several actors. While the presence of several actors can be shared by both, a constructivist conceptualization of intersubjectivity also presupposes a concept of a *contingent social reality*. While behavioural or positive approaches are able to include either the problem of contingency or problem of the social into, we enter the terrain of constructivism only when both are considered at the same time. The focus on contingency also highlights a particular reading of Kratochwil's book: It is fair to say that while knowing, acting and common sense are given considerable attention, the concept of contingency remains somehow hidden in the background. Of course, as Kratochwil would often say, there might be a good reason for this. However, I do hope that my discussion may shed some light on the limits of positive approaches and help future debates to get the question right.

In order to make good on my claims, this chapter unfolds in three steps. In a first step, it takes Kratochwil's discussion on game theory as vantage point to highlight the problem of intersubjectivity, where I identify two distinct notions: a thin version that operates in-between existing actors (intersubjectivity) and a thick version where this intersubjectivity actually constitutes a distinct complexity that encompasses and constitutes the actors in the first place. The second section explores the contours of this thick version of intersubjectivity by exploring the use of the concept 'society' in *Praxis*. To separate this set of questions from the mere 'contingency' in-between actors (double contingency), I use the term triple contingency. The third section explores the different mechanisms of sense-making in dyadic and triadic constellations and argues that questions of knowledge, expertise and power are differently constituted in these two settings – a point where

Kratochwil's *Praxis* certainly points to important avenues, but where much work is still to be done.

On the problem of cooperation in game theory and beyond

As soon as one opens Kratochwil's *Praxis*, one is instantly confronted with some of the most challenging questions of social theory. One of these is the problem of cooperation, a question he traces from Aristotle to Hobbes and finally to modern game theory. Kratochwil does not dispute the insights that game theorists were able to generate with their distinction of collective versus individual rationality, the importance of iteration, the shadow of the future, and the importance of the tit-for-tat strategy. At the same time, however, he is very critical when game theory is understood as *the* approach for understanding the role, structure and constitution of cooperation in society, as he summarizes:

> Virtually all evidence from social psychology indicates that reputation is gained and lost in ways fundamentally different from those suggested by rational choice models. Studies on compliance and deviance support our suspicions that sanctions cannot actually play the role assigned to them by rationalistic models, precisely because issues of interpretation enter the picture and signals are hardly ever unambiguous because they can be misused. Equally misleading seems to be the assumption that coercion works in the same way irrespective of whether we deal with individuals or collectivities, and that therefore the absence of an enforcer is the main problem in the 'anarchical' realm of international relations. (Kratochwil, 2018: 60)

It is interesting to note that Kratochwil pursues a slightly different avenue than the usual critique outlining that the shadow of the future is not really a shadow or to show that game theory cannot explain tit for tat as an adequate strategy from within game theory. There are some remarks on that as well, of course. However, this kind of critique on game theory is eventually as old as game theory itself and we may not need to iterate some of the points here. What is more surprising and quite unique is that Kratochwil actually wonders what concept of society might be inscribed in game theory. Kratochwil argues that rational choice needs to imagine society as a system of dyadic decisions. He shows that such a concept of society actually misses out several crucial dimensions of any notion of society. Next to the question of sanctioning, blaming and commitment within society, a set of problems that for Kratochwil is only insufficiently addressed in game theory, there is a question of *expectations*, where Kratochwil emphasizes:

When we act in a society, we do so because we have certain expectations, for instance that the bus will arrive, or that I can put out my garbage tonight because it will be collected in the morning. In other words, we presumably orient ourselves towards future actions of others, that is, count on something which has not yet occurred and is 'unknown'. (Kratochwil, 2018: 59)

I will come back to the importance of this reference to the unknown later, but for now let me stay with the notion of *expectations*. At first, one could get the impression that while positive approaches deal with individual expectations, constructivist approaches deal with the problem of expectations of expectations. This line of argument, though, leads to conceptual ambiguities that leave the distinction of positive and constructivist approaches in the air and hence runs the danger of motivating some odd debates about game theory and constructivism. Kratochwil's discussion on game theory might help to clarify some of the problems – if read in particular ways.

I think Kratochwil's critique of game theory can be easily misread and too easily refuted without actually acknowledging the important points. The reason for this is that Kratochwil discusses rational choice as an approach by means of simple simultaneous *games* where *two* actors have to make mutually interdependent decisions. Here, he criticizes game theory for some of its shortcomings: games are said to assume full information; game theory is based on the exit strategy and is unable to account for voice and loyalty; game theorists necessarily entertain a dyadic notion of society; and game theory is said to be unable to account for expectations of expectations (Kratochwil, 2018: 58ff). At first sight, economists could quite easily refute some of these claims. In fact, games don't need to assume full information; games may also address questions of loyalty and voice; and game theory does talk about expectations of expectations. In order to show that these rejoinders would miss the actual point, let me go through some of them in turn.

The first point to look at concerns the knowledge structure in games: game theorists have meanwhile explored different avenues to better understand the strategic consequence of ignorance. Firstly, there are games of *imperfect* information, where one actor does not know which alternative the other actor has chosen or what the pay-off function is and only finds out after a decision has been made: some number in the decision tree is missing. To solve these games, economists have developed several strategies with the infamous backward induction the best known of them (Selten, 1965: 301). In games of *incomplete* information, one actor does not know *who* the other actor is: with whom am I dealing here? In particular, the work of John Harsanyi has pointed out that it is possible to transform games of incomplete information into ones of imperfect information once we allow for different possible *types of actors* and have nature choose one of them through some kind of lottery (Harsanyi, 1967: 159).[1] Hence, to argue that games *necessarily* presuppose full knowledge can be slightly misleading.

Secondly, Kratochwil points to the important literature on exit options and their impact on the outcomes of games. Does that mean that game theory is unable to deal with loyalty and voice? The first thing to note here is that signalling games do explore the importance of language and hence could be said to touch upon 'voice'. New developments in contract theory (Hart and Moore, 1999: 115) might even be said to contribute to hierarchy and hence loyalty when we deal with moral hazard in teams (Holmström, 1982: 324). Even though this take on voice and loyalty eventually has hardly anything to do with what Albert Hirschman had in mind (Hirschman 1970), at least the answer is not as straightforward as one could expect, and some counter-argument cannot be easily dismissed out of hand.[2] Last but not least, one of the key insights of game theory is that the expectations of the expectations of others matter decisively for possible equilibria, as the classic example of the stag hunt illustrates. In the face of multiple possible equilibria, norms can play a crucial role as they can 'lock in' certain equilibria and stabilize cooperation.

So, in a way, game and contract theory does address questions of uncertainty, norms and intersubjectivity and, at first sight, Kratochwil's discussion seems to misfire. What is even worse is that now it seems that very positivist game theorists seem to share the same 'semantic field' as constructivists. Could it be that 'constructivists' have lost the debate and positivists are equally able to address exactly the same set of questions? Is it really that in the end meta-theoretical debates were overheated and finally boil down to nothing? Doesn't game theory equally explore exactly that notion of society understood as expectations of expectations 'rather than being merely guided by purely "personal" experience' (Kratochwil, 2018: 59)? Of course, to answer affirmatively would do away with crucial epistemological differences. These differences between positivist and constructivist approaches to 'intersubjective' questions, however, have to

---

[1] Meanwhile, the literature on contract theory makes it possible to analyse how *ignorance* of the game structure itself changes possible equilibria. While game theory takes the game structure as a given, contract theory analyses how actors negotiate the game structure on the basis of asymmetric information. Furthermore, even contracts are considered to be incomplete (Hart and Moore, 1999: 115).

[2] As a third point, Kratochwil points out that game theorists observe dyadic decisions and therefore entertain a notion of society that is composed of dyadic relationships only. Also in this context, in particular contract theorists have expanded their range of observed relations and looked for three decision and n-decision theories, as the literature on folk theorems aptly points out. Kratochwil is, of course, aware of this literature, as he referred to it back in 1989 (Kratochwil, 1989).

arise from somewhere else rather than merely 'expectation' or 'existence' or 'ignorance'. In the following discussion I suggest that the difference can (and must) be located at different notions of contingency. I think that from here, we can differentiate two rather distinct notions of intersubjectivity and hence reconstruct the difference between positivist and constructivist approaches in a more nuanced way. To make visible the importance of contingency, it is useful to turn to the question of the 'unknown' mentioned earlier. As Kratochwil points out, at the core of game theory lies the notion of expected utility. Without expected utility, the entire construct of modern microeconomics in all its variants and guises would collapse. As is certainly known, expected utility argues that when actors deal with a decision that addresses an uncertain future, they maximize not actual but *expected* utility calculated by the product of a possible state of the world, a probability distribution over these possible states of the world and respective output functions in relation to the manifestation of a possible state of the world. Of course, we need not iterate that economists have also constructed all sorts of extensions and modifications about the possible knowledge structure within the expected utility calculus, for example. In addition, nobody doubts that expected utility is a powerful tool and can help explain various 'obvious' paradoxes and inconsistencies in decision theory.

What is more important is the fact that expected utility is unable to deal with 'the unknown' in the sense of an unstructured future. Let us go back to the distinction between incomplete and imperfect information. The transformation was possible as soon as we allowed for an objective (!) probability distribution over possible types of actors. For expected utility to work, there has to be a full and complete probability distribution and hence a closed action space in place. As measure theory tells us, it is impossible to have additive probabilities over possible states of the world when the action space is open. Therefore, the problem setting at hand needs to be sufficiently well structured. This means that in such circumstances it has to be specified *in advance what, for whom and when something is unknown*. The observer knows what the players don't. In other words, expected utility operates on the presumption that it is possible to *know what is unknown*, that is, the contingency of not knowing the other player is 'tamed' and limited by the assumed objectivity of types of actors. On this basis, individual strategies can be formulated and calculated.

To emphasize this point: with a well-structured decision problem and the 'pretence of knowledge' at hand, all models based on expected utility ultimately reduce and explain the intersubjective dimension by the set or combination of *individual* strategies. It is in the end the individual who updates beliefs on the basis of received signals; it is the individual who formulates a best (or second-best) strategy. It is the mutual compatibility of *individual decision processes* that constitutes equilibria. The intersubjective is nothing more than a set of *individual decisions* (given a certain set of expectations). In particular through the notion of equilibrium, the very problem of 'intersubjectivity' is solved by assumption: apparent objective equilibrium conditions align subjective 'expectations' but do so only at the cost of eclipsing the very *diagnostic processes* ('how to go on') that the unknown motivates.

This 'how to go on', in the sense in which Kratochwil uses it, is thus not to be confused with search costs or similar concepts: it only makes sense if it never comes to a halt and hence we free ourselves from equilibria and probability distributions. Hence, I believe that constructivist research questions only start when we move away from this positivist notion of intersubjectivity and allow for *true* uncertainty (Kratochwil's 'unknown future'). Only then are expectations not reduced to the level of the individual but allow for *generalized or institutional* expectations (Kratochwil, 2018: 61). The notion of intersubjectivity that is at play here is broader and more encompassing than what the rational approach has to offer. The expectations we hold in Kratochwil's quote are not directed against another actor per se, but they are directed at institutions such as public transport, waste systems, railways, schools and so forth. Norms operate on this level of generalized expectations and not just on the basis of expected utility. Yet norms are not the explanans, but an explanandum for problems of 'intersubjectivity' understood as 'double contingency'. Otherwise, we would never open the door: it is the general expectation that one is allowed to enter, and not expected utility from the one inside, that motivates the call 'come in'.

To conclude the discussion in this section: we started with Kratochwil's critique on game theory. This section tried to show that the target of his critique has less to do with the specific information structure or specific developments in contract theory. Instead, the critique targets the way rational choice conceptualizes 'expectations of expectations' that – via objective equilibrium conditions – reduce the problem of intersubjectivity to a set of individual best answers. Constructivism, meanwhile, starts only when we take this 'inter' in intersubjectivity seriously. Before we move back to the questions of intersubjectivity and institutions, the next section explores some of the differences through the notion of contingency.

Contingency and the logic of social facts

Through a discussion of Kratochwil's take on game theory, the previous section suggested that positivist approaches based on expected utility calculus always reduce the problem of intersubjectivity (or *expectation of expectation*) to a combination of individual strategies. Intersubjectivity as a concept is not as clear as one may wish and in itself cannot sustain the distinction between positive and constructivist approaches. Something else has to do the explaining. As Kratochwil points out, collective intentionality is not simply an aggregation of individual actions or individually held beliefs (Kratochwil, 2018: 25–6), just as the *volonté de tous* is just not the *volonté générale*.

This section seeks to explore further this distinction by means of a conceptual reorientation. Instead of again talking about rational choice or thick and thin versions of constructivism, I recast some of the debates by means of 'different notions of contingency'. Let me start with the notion of contingency itself. Contingency can be broadly defined as the space between the impossible and necessity (Luhmann, 1997: 1130). Now, this leaves open what can be considered contingent. Here, we can say that expected utility theory as discussed earlier has shown us that the *future* can be contingent. In the context of expected utility, I argued that sense-making is actually reduced to the individual actor who has to formulate the best possible answer given the options by the other actors. Which one of the set of possible states of the world will manifest can actually be understood like a ball being drawn within a lottery.

Another notion of contingency enters the picture when not the future (as object) but the presence and actions of another (possible) actor are accepted to be contingent. In this setting, the process of sense-making works differently as there is no pre-established equilibrium condition that could bring the processes of differentiation, role-taking and 'expectations of expectations' to an end. To explore the difference from the rational approach, let us start with the classic definition of *double* contingency (alas, two 'actants') by Talcott Parsons. Double contingency can be described as a situation where ego and alter meet and then establish signs and links to figure out who the other actor actually is (see Vanderstraten, 2002: 77ff). As Parsons and Shils argued:

> In interaction ego and alter are each objects of orientation for the other. The basic differences from orientations to non-social objects are two. First, since the outcome of ego's action (e.g. success in the attainment of a goal) is contingent on alter's reaction to what ego does, ego becomes oriented not only to alter's probable overt behavior but also to what ego interprets to be alter's expectations relative to ego's behavior, since ego expects that alter's expectations will influence alter's behavior. Second, in an integrated system, this orientation to the expectations of the other is reciprocal or complementary. (Parsons and Shils, 1951: 105)

This quote nicely captures how expectations of expectations are not reducible to individual best answers but are 'constitutive' of the mutual sense-making processes among actors. Not only the future but the mutual positionality – including one's own position – is considered to be contingent. Within the context of game theory, the actors precede or are ontologically prior to the strategic interaction. Within the context of double contingency, the mutual 'recognition as actor' (as social fact) is contingent.

The change from a contingent future to the actors' positions also changes the concept of language and communication, where now it is also possible to understand why the linguistic turn is so important for constructivism. Within game theory, language and communication is used in a classic sender–receiver model, where economists are able to tell us quite a lot about the strategic use of words, learning, search costs, belief updating, cheap talk and signals. However, language is always used strategically and part of a semantic field of rationality and equilibrium where the meaning of these concepts is 'external to' the analysed structures or dynamics. The linguistic turn, as highlighted by Kratochwil, moves beyond these confines and therefore changes the 'image' of language: here, language escapes the straitjacket of bivalent semiotics where it could only serve as 'tags' for things, that is, where it can be used by single actors to denote things and hence be used strategically. In particular modalities, conditionals, conjunctions and disjunctions that allow us to 'connect' sentences cannot be reduced to the individual level but indicate a distinct complexity of language that is open and subject to change (Kratochwil, 1989: 23). For these operations to work, they need to be understood intersubjectively, where conventions and norms stabilize the meaning of words. Language only works *because* it is intersubjective and cannot be reduced to a set of individually best answers.

This brings us now into a position to see how these two notions of contingency approach the problem of norms. In rational approaches, norms are condensed into an objective force that manifests itself in front of individual actors. The question 'why should an actor follow a norm' or 'which norms matter', as widely discussed in the compliance literature, already points to the individual choice underneath that problem, as it is the individual (state) who is left with a choice to either follow or deviate from a specific norm (Hurd, 1999: 379–408). Whether or not a norm 'matters' or is being followed, then, can be understood in terms of a set of expectations and pay-off matrices. Questions of power, interest and legitimacy ultimately only change the pay-off structures in the game.

From a constructivist perspective, this conceptualization of norms misses out an important dimension, as norms constitute the rules of the game in the first place: norms tell us who actors might be and what counts as cost or benefit. Norms allow actors to make sense of each other's behaviour where common sense, conventions and rules stabilize expectations as these actors 'go on'. Hence, norms allow for the 'link across the abyss', as Karin Fierke nicely framed it (see Fierke, 2002: 332), and allow for the stabilization of perspectives, conventions, common sense and thus sense-making – a point that is shared by Wendt and his first contact argument. As he explained, when actors meet for the first time without any prior contact, identity formations are relational and the product of processes rather than properties of individual actors. It is only through *inter*action that 'stabilized' expectations emerge and actors are able to ascribe meaning to each other's actions.

Kratochwil's concept of contingency (and the formation of expectations of expectations) goes even further as it addresses institutional facts as discussed earlier: institutions predetermine possible 'identities' or roles that actors can 'take on'. Like the notion of the language game indicates, we cannot take on the position of a goalie in chess – just like we cannot end a soccer game by checkmate. The games simply don't work that way as their constitutive rules don't allow for these options. It just doesn't work. This also holds true for 'world society' as a whole: we never enter situations as 'human beings' per se. Instead, we always communicate and act through roles that come with a pre-stabilized set of expectations on how to relate to others – from 'being a good kid' to 'being a good student', from 'being a good patient' or professor, customer, banker or father or any other role we have to take.

The concept of *roles* or *role-taking* indicates that possible positions are already pre-stabilized: one cannot enter a bus and decide to be a patient, just as it is impossible to play offside in chess. Even in speech act theory, one cannot say 'I do' as referee or judge and thereby get married. This pre-stabilization of possible perspectives not only highlights specific mechanisms of inclusion and exclusion, but it shows that a *third element* is needed (Simmel, 1908: 50; Strydom, 2001: 50). Only in triadic relations is it possible to exchange actors and still keep 'social structures' intact. Only then is it possible to actually have pre-stabilized roles that do not disappear once an actor decides to leave.

Take the example of disappointed expectations for a moment. If I expected good behaviour or trust from a friend and my friend failed to live up to them, then I might consider not talking to that person in the future and hence terminate our relationship. That brings the friendship to an end. When the bus does not arrive as expected, I may decide to ride a bicycle the next time, but that does not make public transport go away. The institutions still continue. In other words, institutions fix expectations and allow for non-learning from disappointments, as Kratochwil confirms (Kratochwil, 2018: 59). At the same time, however, they only allow me to form certain expectations on the basis of certain *institutionally defined positions* and roles (Kratochwil, 2018: 61). Two actors may decide on whatever they like, that is, differentiate themselves as enemies, as an interest group, or as friends; but institutions create possible perspectives, positions and voices that exist independently of the physical presence of actors per se. In other words, institutional facts 'constitute' certain roles as a set of condensed expectations. We can expect the bus to come because we are *passengers*; we can expect medical treatment in a hospital as *patients*. Students form expectations about their professors not as John, Mary or Tina – but as students. Professors form expectations about their students by being in a certain position provided by the *institution of the university*. Take away the university and you take away students and professors as possible positions or roles with their specific behaviours, tasks, positionality, expectations and expected everyday behaviour. The next section explores this avenue further and comes back to the issue of expectations, uncertainty and 'institutions'.

A Humean approach to uncertainty? Institutions as discovery process

The previous section highlighted Kratochwil's references to double contingency in order to separate 'genuine' double contingency from the rational notion of intersubjectivity as a 'set of individual best answers'. It also pointed out that there is a necessary element of 'the third' in order to understand institutions. In this section, I explore this distinction between double and triple contingency for the problem of 'praxis', contingency and the issue of uncertainty.

As Patrick Jackson (Chapter 14, this volume) points out, it is interesting to note that *Praxis* marks a return by Kratochwil to his very first publication: the promise of a Humean approach to international studies (Kratochwil, 1981). Hume features prominently in particular in the chapter on 'Knowing and Doubting' (Kratochwil, 2018: 352ff). As always, Kratochwil advances his discussion by pointing to alternative interpretations, several additional sidetracks, further avenues and references to his specific context of Calvinism and the Scottish Enlightenment. There are so many unexplored avenues in his discussion that one can only hope that Kratochwil will write a whole book on Hume. There is certainly enough material condensed in these chapters already. That said, I can only provide an interpretation and cannot claim any expertise on Hume's writing itself.

Generally speaking, Hume is presented as a philosopher who mediated between the Scylla of scepticism and the Charybdis of Cartesian doubt. The Hume Kratochwil presents can be read as a precursor to modern process philosophy of the late 20th century. Here, the human mind is not an essence that can serve as an identity between nature and thought (identity principle). Hume therefore de-ontologizes both 'things' and 'mind' – the two ends of scholastic thought. In-between, we find an autonomy of practical reasoning, a pragmatic intuition based on the particular situation one finds oneself in. We find a variety of methods, disciplines and resistance to unifying schemes as we always find ourselves within specific situations. On the one hand, this implies that the kind of self-reflection à la Descartes is simply impossible. As Kant later elaborated this Humean intuition, we don't have direct access to our thought but can only think about it when we already make ourselves an *object* of it. The Cartesian doubt simply cannot carry the weight that Descartes ascribed to it. On the other hand, there is no grand design, no ontological fix in the form of either 'god' or 'reason' which could hold possible worlds together either. As Kratochwil continues:

> This new perspective dramatically changed the role of philosophy, which no longer can pretend to stand outside of a common life, claiming an authority independent of all beliefs, customs, and even 'prejudices'. Instead philosophy had to recognise its responsibility by not reflecting from the outside, taking social life as an object, but by realizing its purpose and potential as a critical voice within the institutionalized interactions and the discourses of a society on problems of common concerns. (Kratochwil, 2018: 352)

This primacy of 'practical reason' situated between Scylla and Charybdis opens for Kratochwil the possibility to detect an interest of Hume in the 'historical emergence of conventions that define a common life in which man is not only a participant, but shaped by it' (Kratochwil, 2018: 358). Kratochwil detects in Hume an interest in the 'intersubjective' production of meaning through the concept of 'common sense'. For example, for Hume causality is not reducible to 'matter' but 'is nothing but the effects of custom on the imagination' (Kratochwil, 2018: 367). Similarly, we learn about conventions in relation to improvisations, causality, ritual dances, aesthetics and rules. We learn about how we find out what is the case, how our quests never come to an end, and how the idea of an original social contract simply doesn't work.

While Hume is presented as a figure who already captured and dealt with the 'double contingency problem' (Kratochwil, 2018: 366), one cannot deny that Kratochwil here focuses on how common sense and intersubjectivity presuppose a de-ontological concept of the human mind in particular, a concept that is clearly incompatible with any idea of utility maximization (Kratochwil, 2018: 362). Recast in the vocabulary proposed in the previous section, it seems to me that Kratochwil's discussion explores the boundaries and intersection of double (common sense) and single contingency (individual imagination). What is less discussed is the particular logic of institutional facts and the functionally differentiated generalized set of expectations – as was the case in his first chapter in 1989. In his chapters, questions of social imaginaries, disciplinary confined knowledge or the 'functionally differentiated social systems' are to be found only in the background of the discussions. All I want to suggest here is that by highlighting all three dimensions, we can further specify specific constellations of how the unknown, expectations and knowledge relate to each other.

Combining a 'Humean' notion of common sense with the problem of contingency gives us three avenues for understanding 'common sense': the confines of single contingency are encapsulated within the literature on decision under uncertainty that brings together rational and behavioural approaches (Tversky and Kahneman, 1974; Kahneman and Tversky, 2013). This literature is particularly interested in understanding how uncertainty influences certain strategies and how 'uncertainty' can then be reduced through 'institutions'. In situations of uncertainty, common sense and norms may serve as positive heuristics for individual decision problems. The first section has already pointed to some of the boundaries of this approach, in particular in relation to questions related to intersubjective processes. Yet here, common sense serves as an 'interlocking' device to facilitate coordination of individual strategies. Common sense, norms and conventions are under continuous threat of losing this function, as it might become rational to deviate from them.

The problem of double contingency is, of course, explored at length in Kratochwil's discussion, as just indicated. Kratochwil's quote that *in society* we 'count on something which has not yet occurred and is "unknown"' points to a rationality beyond the confines of calculus, probability and utility (Kratochwil, 2018: 59). Instead, this kind of uncertainty is continuously processed, that is, it is continuously reduced but instantly regenerated as we 'go on'. Common sense or norms are not simply there, an objective entity, but common sense is continuously reproduced. Common sense in dyadic relations can be said to relate to specific relational dimensions among actors: it mediates between them and gives them the possibility to communicate. Common sense stabilizes the meaning of terms and perspectives. When we take into consideration the third element, expectations are not directed towards an uncertain future or another actor but target an institutionalized, impersonal net of expectations. Here, common sense already operates through constitutive rules that limit possible moves and perspectives. Common sense here also touches upon the question of who is a member of society and who isn't, whose voice gets to be heard and who is to be silenced. Here, common sense and the generality of rules are established from situations where roles, disciplines and imaginaries are already in place. For example, institutional facts such as money already structure and delimit the possible situatedness, the possible roles actors can take on to participate in social interactions. On the individual level, we might form expectations on how much money is used for various items, the income and expenditure and hence the 'personal' balance sheet. On the intersubjective level, money is embedded in conventions, rules, ritual dances and a certain aesthetics. Here, expectations are interpersonal and also then come with specific relations among actors. On the third level, we address money as an institutional fact based on constitutive rules that allow money to work *as* money. Here, expectations are directed to the institution itself and not located in-between actors.

To conclude, this section suggested that terms such as common sense, norms and conventions may change their meaning depending on which kind of 'contingency' is being observed. The discussion in this section was not intended to advance an argument that they are incompatible, but I do think they point to a different set of questions and problems: in single contingency, we encounter predominantly the problem of deviation and uncertainty reduction; in double contingency, questions of identity and relations enter the picture. In situations of triple contingency, the knowledge actors have is not only directed towards another actor when it comes to promises or contract, but it is also directed towards the institutions themselves, that is, the constitutive rules of the games. Here we encounter also 'functionally' specific boundaries, questions of disciplines and professions and their particular way to identify positions, how to formulate arguments, how to structure knowledge claims and try to persuade the opponent. As Kratochwil hides 'Hume's snide remarks' in a footnote, ' "[d]isputes are multiplied as if everything was uncertain; and these disputes are managed with the greatest warmth, as if everything was certain. Amidst all this bustle 'tis not reason which carries the prize, but eloquence"' (Kratochwil, 2018: 357, quoting Hume, 2000: 3). Exactly this eloquence is not 'natural' but dependent on systemic rationalities: to be eloquent in market relations is differently constituted than when it comes to justice or security. It is here where disciplines, persuasion and rhetoric interact and where constructivists eventually still have a lot to say on how these emerged, how knowledge in disciplines or professions is structured, including what is left out, and how arguments are formulated. This may allow us to push the Humean approach to an understanding of *institutions as discovery process* where institutional facts are processed and are subject to the 'dialectics' of stability and change.

Conclusion

The exploration into constructivism as an approach to international studies finds itself in an awkward if not rather fragile situation. First of all, there is an eventually rightful abandonment if not an emerging hostility towards the big 'isms'. To even have an ism in the title runs the danger of anachronism. The isms are associated with gatekeeping, hierarchical organization of science, but most of all as a somewhat scholastic enterprise at the cost of more 'empirically' relevant, problem-oriented research. The isms are associated with what could be considered the ivory tower politics of academia, while practice and empirically oriented research is not only more relevant but can legitimate its relevance by its impact on policy-making and its more pragmatic stance: it is more important to provide advice and care about empirical problems even if that comes at the price of 'theoretical' eclecticism.

However, there is also, as Kratochwil so aptly points out, a certain eagerness for everybody to move out of the constructivist house, so that one wonders who is actually still in it? There is a current trend to expand, renew or reconstitute the constructivist project *beyond* norms, agent-structure or ideas and to leave behind these old dogmas. In particular, the turn to practices and the turn to quantum provide two alternatives that are said to promise a new set of questions. It is interesting to note that nowadays it is important to emphasize discontinuity and 'difference' where the semantic field of 'turns' always works to attract citations. Yet these attempts assume that it is *agent-structure and norms* that we need to move away from, that is, they already take as a given that constructivism *apparently is about norms* and that our previous avenues suffer from specific problems that can now be overcome and finally left behind. It is certainly a very liberating and self-gratifying enterprise to see oneself constructing something new and to see one's name associated with one's own turns. In a sense, everybody should have a turn of their own. Yet my chapter argues that Kratochwil's *Praxis* highlights the need to get the basics right first – and that the new constructivism on the basis of practice theories actually leads us astray. The problem is not enough empirics; the problem is our lack of understanding of theory.

I pursued this question via a rewriting of the problem of action in terms of contingency. Through a discussion of the term 'expectation of expectations', I outlined two distinct notions of intersubjectivity: one that reduces that inter to a set of individual best answers, and an understanding that allows for the constitution of actors. This chapter then continued by outlining the difference between social and society where double contingency alone is insufficient to capture the different dynamics. I tried to trace these changes by looking at uncertainty, knowledge and expectations in detail.

References

Berenskoetter, Felix (2018) 'E pluribus unum? How textbooks cover theories', in Andreas Gofas, Ianna Hamati-Ataya and Nicholas G. Onuf (eds), *The SAGE Handbook of the History, Philosophy and Sociology of International Relations* (London: SAGE), pp 446–66.

Burchill, Scott, Andrew Linklater, Richard Devetak, Jack Donnelly, Terry Nardin, Matthew Paterson, Christian Reus-Smit and Jacqui True (2013) *Theories of International Relations* (5th edn) (Basingstoke: Palgrave Macmillan).

Fierke, Karin M. (2002) 'Links across the abyss: language and logic in international relations', *International Studies Quarterly* 46, 3, pp 331–54.

Harsanyi, John C. (1967) 'Games with incomplete information played by "Bayesian" players, I–III Part I. The basic model', *Management Science* 14, 3, pp 159–82.

Hart, Oliver and John Moore (1999) 'Foundations of incomplete contracts', *Review of Economic Studies* 66, 1, pp 115–38.

Hirschman, Albert O. (1970) *Exit, Voice, and Loyalty: Responses to Decline in Firms, Organizations, and States* (Cambridge, MA: Harvard University Press).

Holmström, Bengt (1982) 'Moral hazard in teams', *Bell Journal of Economics* 13, pp 324–40.

Hurd, Ian (1999) 'Legitimacy and authority in international politics', *International Organization* 53, 2, pp 379–408.

Jackson, Richard and Georg Sørensen (2015) *Introduction to International Relations: Theories and Approaches* (6th edn) (Oxford: Oxford University Press).

Kahneman, Daniel and Amos Tversky (2013) 'Choices, values, and frames', in Leonard C. MacLean and William T. Ziemba (eds) *Handbook of the Fundamentals of Financial Decision Making: Part I* (Singapore: World Scientific), pp 269–78.

Kratochwil, Friedrich (1981) *The Humean Conception of International Relations* (Princeton, NJ: Princeton University Press).

Kratochwil, Friedrich (1989) *Rules, Norms and Decisions: On the Conditions of Practical and Legal Reasoning in International Relations and Domestic Affairs* (Cambridge: Cambridge University Press).

Kratochwil, Friedrich (2018) *Praxis: On Acting and Knowing* (Cambridge: Cambridge University Press).

Luhmann, Niklas (1997) *Die Gesellschaft der Gesellschaft* (Berlin: Suhrkamp Verlag).

McCourt, David M. (2016) 'Practice theory and relationalism as the new constructivism', *International Studies Quarterly* 60, 3, pp 475–85.

Onuf, Nicholas (2008) *International Legal Theory: Essays and Engagements 1966–2006* (London: Routledge).

Parsons, Talcott and Edwards Shils (1951) *Towards a General Theory of Social Action: Theoretical Foundations for the Social Sciences* (Cambridge, MA: Harvard University Press).

Selten, Reinhard (1965) 'Spieltheoretische Behandlung eines Oligopolmodells mit Nachfrageträgheit', *Zeitgeschichte Staatswissenschaften* 12, pp 301–24.

Simmel, Georg (1908) *Soziologie* (Leipzig: Duncker and Humblot).

Strydom, Piet (2001) 'The problem of triple contingency in Habermas', *Sociological Theory* 19, 2, pp 165–86.

Tversky, Amos and Daniel Kahneman (1974) 'Judgment under uncertainty: heuristics and biases', *Science* 185, 4157, pp 1124–31.

Vanderstraten, Ralf (2002) 'Parsons, Luhmann and the theorem of double contingency', *Journal of Classical Sociology* 2, 1, pp 77–92.

11

The Praxis of Change and Theory

Mathias Albert

Introduction

The present chapter discusses the account of historical change and the (seeming) rejection of theory in Friedrich Kratochwil's *Praxis* (Kratochwil, 2018). It argues that Kratochwil's sophisticated account both of historical change and of theory leads him to treat them as different sides of the same coin, resulting in the fact that when tossing that coin, usually only one side can be seen in the end, but not the other. The argument to be made in the following is that this conceptualization of historical change and theory as basically mutually exclusive is not necessary, although at first glance it might seem to follow from some of Kratochwil's basic assumptions. Of course, making an argument in order to show that one would have arrived at different results if only one had started out on the basis of different assumptions would be fairly superfluous. However, the point to be made here is a different one: I argue that the conclusions drawn by Kratochwil would not be necessary were he to add a few ingredients to his account and become a little more relaxed regarding the use of others – a few tablespoons of theories of social differentiation and social evolution in order to describe modern society and its development, a little less baking time in the oven of law, and a consideration of how the dish should best be presented if it were to be sold where it rightfully belongs, that is, in a Michelin-starred restaurant rather than the eclectic mix of fast-food fare so often savoured around the International Relations (IR) campfires. This is another way of saying that probably one of the issues with *Praxis* is that when it comes to theory, its biggest problem might be that it mainly has in mind that special fare called 'IR theory' – but that this is exactly the fare not to Kratochwil's liking, that is, the one that might have filled generations of IR students with academic carbohydrates, but which often doesn't even pass muster for a decent home-cooked meal (*Hausmannskost*).[1]

Kratochwil's *Praxis* is a great book. This needs to be mentioned because the present chapter will only recount those parts of it that are required for making the argument about historical change and theory.[2] In doing this, it might thus appear far more critical of the entire work than it is intended to be. As proof of the latter I am relieved to be able to refer to a review of the book that I wrote a while ago (Albert, 2019). Before proceeding with the argument, two caveats are in order: firstly, in the following the argument will be limited to a reading of *Praxis*. Although it does not ignore Kratochwil's previous work, it is not an exegesis of how that work has developed and fed into *Praxis*. Rather, it engages with *Praxis* largely on its own, and in this sense it is hoped that it also avoids delving into a 'Festschrift' mode.[3] Secondly, much of the argument to be developed engages with Kratochwil's extremely ambivalent relation to particular parts of social theory, and most notably systems theory. However, it will not fall into the trap of arguing that this is a basic flaw in Kratochwil's work but will strictly limit itself to some substantive points that can be developed in an imagined dialogue between *Praxis* and aspects of systems theory as they pertain to the issues of historical change and theory.

The argument of this chapter is structured as follows: a first section will provide a highly condensed, and possibly highly parochial, summary of change and theory in *Praxis*. As the role of change in particular can hardly be understood without reference to the basic assumptions regarding the constitution of the social, chapters 2 and 3 (on 'Constituting' and 'Changing') will play the main role in this context. The status and location of 'theory' are probably less easy to pin down, which already points to the deeply ambivalent use of the term in *Praxis*, an ambivalence that is probably due to a lack of distinction between 'IR theory' and other uses and concepts of 'theory'. The second section will then question the explicit or implicit accounts of social constitution, particularly with a view to social differentiation as a defining characteristic of social systems. It will be argued that while Kratochwil's account is quite clear in this respect, there seems to be a bias towards the

---

[1] It should be mentioned that Friedrich Kratochwil has a reputation for being an excellent cook.

[2] *Praxis* is also a book that touches upon so many issues and literatures that each of its arguments could be dealt with by referring to a bibliography of many pages. I deliberately develop the argument here without doing this, but also – and hoping to not come across as presumptuous by doing so – deliberately point to a number of my own works where I think they mark productive similarities and differences to the arguments made in *Praxis*.

[3] Again, I am relieved to be on the safe side here again as the Festschrift contribution was provided, together with Yosef Lapid, quite a while ago; see Albert and Lapid (2010).

legal system being primary among others under the condition of functional differentiation. The third section argues that such a privileging of the legal system might not necessarily be legitimate from a view of 'pure' functional differentiation but could indeed be upheld as an empirical argument about social evolution. For that purpose, Kratochwil's arguments about change would need to be twisted in the direction of a theory of social evolution. The fourth section will argue that such a twist would in fact equip him with theory but would also remove him quite a bit from the shallows of IR theory – the latter probably being the place from where his theory aversion stems in the first place.

Constituting and changing

For the purposes of the present argument, the chapters on 'Constituting' and 'Changing' provide the key to understanding some of the basic underlying concepts of *Praxis*, and indeed to Kratochwil's thinking in general. While the reading of these underlying concepts necessarily will be somewhat parochial, it needs to be emphasized at the outset that such parochialism is not simply an aberration on the side of the reader, but rather something that is invited by some basic characteristics of Kratochwil's writing in general, and of *Praxis* in particular. As professed by Kratochwil (2018: 5), his mode of presentation is close to that of a complex monumental painting. This makes it more difficult for the reader to digest than a 'standard' IR text, the latter often resembling more a technical drawing than a monumental painting, in that it invites aesthetic judgement in addition to critical reasoning.[4] The present reading thus also at least partially proceeds on the grounds of judging what is to some degree a work of art rather than an argument geared towards coherence!

When it comes to the constitution of the social in *Praxis*, two things stand out as largely unquestioned: firstly, 'the social' *is* society; secondly, society is *not* defined through its normative integration. These two things need to be emphasized since the first has consequences for Kratochwil's conceptualization of change and order, while the second is somewhat counter-intuitive given Kratochwil's focus on the pre-eminent role of norms and law in society. Seeing the social as society puts Kratochwil's work squarely in the rather particular German tradition of *Gesellschaftstheorie*. While also a form of social theory, the difference is remarkable in that it assumes that society constitutes a meaningful social whole. Where Kratochwil, following the Luhmannian trait, parts with classical sociology is in not seeing society

---

[4] But then: where Alexander Wendt in his book on *Quantum Mind and Social Theory* claimed his argument to be too elegant not to be true (2015: 288), Kratochwil's is probably too true in order to be elegant.

as an integrated whole where integration is accomplished through common norms, a collective identity, a *Gemeinschaft* and so forth. Rather, society is not about the integration of a 'unit', but about drawing boundaries. 'Such an approach owes much to Luhmann's Modern System Theory (MST), although I shall not simply adopt it, because important parts of the political problematique disappear if one makes that choice' (Kratochwil, 2018: 48).

The difference between 'owing much' and 'not simply adopting' because of the 'political problematique' will be the subject of the remainder of this chapter. Before expanding on this difference, however, it is worth noting that Kratochwil *avoids* further specifying society, most notably as 'national', 'international' or 'world' society. This is particularly noteworthy in contrast to Luhmann's understanding, where society includes every communication and thus everything social: in this sense society cannot be anything else but world society, and its boundaries are between the system of society constituted by communication, on the one hand, and natural and psychic systems in its environment, on the other hand.[5]

In contrast, Kratochwil's account is certainly about *society*, but it remains unspecific as to whether this should be seen as a world, an international or a national society. Ultimately, this seems to be taken less as an issue stemming from a theoretical consideration (as in Luhmann), and more as one that derives from empirical considerations of what constitutes a relevant framework of reference: society's boundaries in this sense are drawn by the interrelated validity claims of norms. This is a point that merits some consideration: indeed, Kratochwil parts with the classical sociological image of society being *normatively integrated* and adopts an image in which society is differentiated from its environment on the basis of its constitution by norms.[6] The latter, however, does not imply that society would be socially integrated by norms. Rather, the integration on the basis of norms is a systemic one at best: 'society is entirely a symbolic construct and, this being so, no simple deitic procedure or observation will do ... the meaning of a concept is not a function of its reference *but of its use*' (Kratochwil, 2018: 54). In that context, the function of norms merely consists in the permanent processual relating of ever shifting elements, and not in establishing '*order as a result of an overall design in which various parts are harmoniously related to*

---

[5] Psychic systems, that is, meaning-processing systems of individual consciousness, are *not* part of society, as they are not directly accessible for communication; individuals are relevant only as addresses of communication – this is the background of the often ill-understood idea in systems theory that persons are not 'part' of, let alone constitutive of, society. For an overview of Luhmann's extensive works, the most accessible main ones translated into English are probably Luhmann (1995) and Luhmann (2012).

[6] See Schimank and Volkmann (1999) for a good overview of the difference between the integration and the differentiation view of society.

each other' (Kratochwil, 2018: 55). Society, thus understood, only exists and can only be disclosed 'through its "archeology", not through a definitional exercise' (Kratochwil, 2018: 55). While it remains unspecified as to whether, and to what degree, such an archaeology primarily involves, for example, the study of historical power relations or of historical semantics, or of how these are bound together, there is at least one distinct consequence of this understanding: that only that is treated as society which has attained some degree of historical-structural relevance (and that can be observed, and observes itself, accordingly). This probably explains why society is not specified further as, most notably, 'international' or 'world society', as these composite terms arguably play only a limited role historically, their use mostly being confined to academic discourse.[7] It is, however, somewhat surprising that after its stage appearance in chapter 2, save some supernumerary appearances, 'society' drops out of *Praxis* almost completely. This, at least, is how it seems at first glance: as will be argued at the end of this chapter, in fact it remains hidden in the background and forms the theoretical bond within and behind *Praxis*. Kratochwil's failure to bring it to the foreground might actually create an impression of an argument that seems to have scripting issues.

The dropping out of society as a 'social whole' (Albert and Buzan, 2013) also relieves the argument of having to come up with more abstract accounts or theories of change. In fact, it finds indulgence in referring to Weber when stating that while 'transformative changes are part and parcel of our social world and ... cannot and should not be neglected in our analysis' (Kratochwil, 2018: 75), 'it seems significant that Weber has no entry for "society" in his discussion of the basic concepts of sociology' (Kratochwil, 2018: 75). This reference, however, serves the function of a relief operation that allows the entire chapter on 'Changing' to proceed without further specifying the accounts of social change that are contained in the preceding chapter, instead jumping right to an account of *specific* processes of transformative change, grouped under 'On "Sovereign Authority"' (chapter 3, section 2) and 'Jurisdiction and Organization' (chapter 3, section 3). This creates the impression that these are the most important processes of transformative change in the context of Kratochwil's argument. However, while the most important processes of transformative change have been identified, there remains a big elephant in the hallways of this argument, namely the question of *what* exactly it is that is undergoing change. The remainder of this chapter will attempt to identify this 'what'.

---

[7]   The exception here might be international society, which – in seemingly defying the conventions of sociological thought – makes frequent appearances in political language as 'international community'.

Constitution and social differentiation

Probably one of the main critical issues with *Praxis*, and one that provides grounds both for fertile debate as well as for some of the difficulties in following the argument, is that it does not follow a simple, two-step approach, that is, one that proceeds from the more general to the more specific. The argumentative figure is not one in which a more general point would be made about the constitution of society, only then to ask where and how something like an 'international system' might fit in there. Rather, the more general points are always interspersed with points about application and applicability to international relations broadly speaking. This is the case for a systematic reason: it is what is ultimately required by a view that does *not* see itself as being about specific social systems 'only', let alone about world society as the highest-order social system, but a view that *wants* to be about praxis understood as the inclusion of agency into a systemic view. It remains the big undecided question in Kratochwil's book, and probably in all his works, whether this particular desire represents a world view that lies at the bottom of its author's thoughts, or whether it could rather be seen as the *result* of all these thoughts taken together. My strong suspicion is that it is the former, but towards the end of the present chapter I will also outline to what degree it could be seen as the latter, although that move probably requires a bit of salvaging of Kratochwil from Kratochwil.

Regarding the constitution of society, the main points made in *Praxis* are that society must be understood not as an integrated whole in and for itself, but rather as something always reproduced in distinction to an environment; and that society historically has been characterized by forms of social differentiation. Social differentiation is where Kratochwil explicitly draws on Luhmann (see Luhmann, 1982, 2013: 1–108): (a) he adopts his characterization of the historical succession of forms of social differentiation; (b) he parts with him regarding the conclusions to be drawn from the notion that functionally differentiated society has no function 'at the top', so to speak; and (c) he is in good company with him regarding some lack of clarity regarding the relation between different forms of social differentiation in terms of their historical evolution.

Regarding (a), there is little disagreement between Kratochwil and Luhmann (or other theorists of social differentiation, for that matter) that historically three forms of social differentiation emerged one after the other: segmentation was followed by stratification, which was in turn followed by functional differentiation (with some argument remaining as to the role of centre–periphery differentiation as a distinct form in this context) (see Albert et al, 2013). There is also, following Kratochwil's acknowledgement that society must not be seen as an integrated unity per se, agreement that social differentiation is not something that somehow 'happens' to a pre-existing unity. Rather, the unity of society appears as such only through its internal differentiation. This is the main difference from concepts of society in classical sociology, most notably up until Habermas's insistence on the integrative function of the 'lifeworld' (Habermas, 1981: 173–294), which cannot think of functional differentiation as anything but a process that drives society apart – a tendency that, then again, has to be countered by a collective identity or a *Gemeinschaft*. While not denying that the operative autonomy of functionally differentiated social systems causes all kinds of problems, however, the main gist of an emergence view of social differentiation is that particularly modern society appears as such only because it is functionally differentiated. The problems that emerge are addressed through complex mechanisms of coordination, which in Luhmann's thinking are achieved through the rather difficult form of 'structural coupling', which describes the way in which operatively autonomous function systems are tied together (Luhmann, 2013: 108–15): 'structural coupling sets the parameters for evolution. The operationally closed systems can innovate, or fail to do so, as long as their own reproduction remains possible. To that extent the occupation of niches and differentiation, not general homogenization or simple adaptation, are the results of evolution' (Luhmann, 2013: 72). Yet this is the point where Kratochwil parts company with Luhmann.

Regarding (b), the parting mentioned is aptly summarized in one central sentence: 'it becomes obvious that the autonomy of functional systems always presupposes the existence of law. Law protects the autonomy of the systems by "ruling out" certain challenges to the legitimacy of their operations' (Kratochwil, 2018: 72–3). This is a fundamental point, yet also one which requires a quite detailed reading: Luhmann usually criticizes the view, quite common in most Western social and political thought, that the political system is somehow more important than other function systems, given its function to provide the capacity for collectively binding decisions (cf Luhmann, 2000). It might seem that Kratochwil makes a similar claim, with the difference of claiming precedence for the legal rather than the political system. However, this is not what he actually says: he does not strictly say that the legal system is 'more important' than other functionally differentiated social systems; what he says is that it is functional differentiation as a central characteristic of (modern) society that '*presupposes*' the law. I argue that this is not so much a systematic claim contra Luhmann, but rather a historical one, and that systematically it would only be a problem to the most devout orthodox reader of systems theory. However, in order to make this point, a little detour – via (c) – is required.

Regarding (c), as mentioned, what Kratochwil shares with Luhmann is the general account of an historical sequence of segmentation, stratification and functional differentiation as the main characteristic forms of differentiation of society. The difference from Luhmann seems to pertain to the further internal differentiation under the condition of a primacy of one form of differentiation. Here, Kratochwil claims that 'Luhmann's systems theory ... still has to come to terms with the fact that some of the most important organizational features of our social life function on the basis of territorial limits, or according to membership criteria' (Kratochwil, 2018: 73). On this level of abstraction, this amounts to either a misreading of Luhmann by Kratochwil, or possibly an ignorance of important parts of the former's work by the latter: Luhmann would not claim that territorial limits, understood as an expression of segmentation, are unimportant. Quite to the contrary, he repeatedly emphasizes that both the political and the legal systems *internally* are primarily segmented territorially (cf Luhmann, 2000: 69–139, 189–227).[8] However, in Luhmann's reading, this segmentation pertains to the internal differentiation of function systems: in order to function and be recognized as such, they first require the functional differentiation of society. What Kratochwil, in other words, seems to be questioning might in the end be nothing but the very primacy of functional differentiation. This conclusion, however, may not be a necessary one. What saving the argument about the particular role of law in spite of functional differentiation might require, however, is a criticism of Luhmann's account that is different from Kratochwil's, and one that rather pertains to what might, for lack of a more elegant phrase, be called the 'pure sequentiality of forms of social differentiation'. The diagnosis of the consecutive appearance of segmentation, stratification and functional differentiation is both a diagnosis of nothing less than world historical proportions, and a diagnosis that very much relies on the underlying figure of, firstly, the emergence of modern society as the characteristic feature of Western modernity, and, secondly, the global expansion of that society. While the gist of the argument can hardly be disputed on the basis of either anthropological or historical evidence, its problem is that it is in danger of ignoring, or at least sidelining, the complex historical multiplicity and a-synchronicity of evolutionary dynamics that point us to an ongoing 'competition' of forms of social differentiation: while for the sake of theoretical purity it might be nicer to have one form of social differentiation rule as 'primary', history often begs to differ from theoretical purity. Segmentation, stratification and functional differentiation all exist, and there could be reasons to claim that the historical 'newcomer', that is,

---

[8] In addition, it should be mentioned that Kratochwil here also inserts an explicit reference to organizations and their membership criteria: for Luhmann, organizations are a specific type of social system (in addition to interaction systems and society). And they are differentiated against their environment through membership (cf Luhmann, 2013: 141–54). While certainly such membership criteria themselves could be territorially defined (e.g. only people who live within the boundaries of a specific community can become part of the *Gesangsverein*), this is by no means necessary.

functional differentiation, is the main characteristic of modern society that otherwise could not have appeared (to itself) as such. However, this does not necessarily mean that the other forms of differentiation could always be relegated to some form of secondary differentiation *within* function systems only. They often also 'compete' with functional differentiation.[9] In order to see how such a view on social differentiation might actually take us quite some way in terms of thinking about the role of law in a way similar to, but theoretically also somewhat different from, Kratochwil, it is necessary to take a closer look at accounts of change in that context. Before doing so, however, it should be emphasized that the following argument will also be about something that might appear to be a mere detail at first, but which upon closer inspection might actually have a crucial role to play in terms of historical-systematic argument: Kratochwil does not dispute that society is functionally differentiated, nor does he claim that law as a functionally differentiated realm or system in that capacity is somehow more important than other function systems such as politics or the economic system; but what he claims is that law works on an entirely different plane of the structuring of social reality, in that functional differentiation – as the difference through which only a unity of society appears as such – somehow presupposes the law.

Change: 'of what?' and 'how?'

One could argue that there is a big rupture between the chapters about 'Constituting' and 'Change' in *Praxis*. Whatever its relation might be to concepts such as 'world society', 'international society' and so forth, it is clear that 'Constituting' is about society as an embodiment of the social on a high order of structuration, as well as about an extremely long-term perspective. It is, as insinuated by the title, about the constitution of the social world in a quite basic sense. This is not the case with 'Change': it is not a chapter that takes up the issue of how to conceptualize change in the social world in a general way. It is not a chapter, for example, about the comparative merits or disadvantages of various motives of *Geschichtsphilosophie*, of theories of social evolution, of event history, of historical semantics and so forth. It is a chapter that, first of all, gives an account of change of *something specific*, and it

---

[9]   A quite telling point here is Luhmann's difficulties in coming to terms with the conditions of people living in *favelas*, which to him appeared to exist outside of function systems. His solution was to think about another form of a 'meta-'social differentiation in addition to segmentation, stratification, and functional differentiation (cf Luhmann, 2013: 24–7), a move probably prompted by a desire to keep the primacy of functional differentiation in relation to the other two forms of social differentiation intact in a situation where one arguably could otherwise just claim that it is stratification and segmentation combined, pure and simple.

is a chapter that entails at least hints of an account of *how* change takes place in that context. Particularly the former account provides some additional information *in concreto* as to the conceptualization of social differentiation discussed earlier.

Clearly, what changes in 'Change' is not society as a whole, and it is also not an account of change spanning the millennia. What changes is what, with all due reservations, can somehow be called 'the international', the 'international system', 'world politics' and so forth – it seems quite telling that this is nowhere spelled out explicitly. This is not at all surprising given that Kratochwil's account of change is an account *ex negativo*: it is primarily about the avoidance of a more or less standard, state-centric IR journey from Hobbes and Machiavelli, over the Peace of Westphalia, to a structurally static (structurally realist) view of an international system. It seems crucial to note, and I will come back to this point, that while (a) Kratochwil narrates the standard IR story *very differently*, (b) in an important sense he shares with that story something about which he *largely remains silent as well*.

Regarding (a), focusing on 'Westphalia' as something like the 'founding myth' of a (modern) international system of states, Kratochwil follows others who have pointed out that what might count as '*international* relations' for a long time even after 1648 was still primarily just a complex dynastic feudal order. He notes that von Pufendorf, as 'the first historian of the state system[,] writes his history as one of the "ruling houses" rather than that of states' (Kratochwil, 2018: 88–9). His substantive account of change seems worth quoting here at length:

[I]n a way it is true that from the Westphalian settlement emerged a 'state system', but it was certainly not one in the form assumed by neo-realists. The order that came into existence did not consist of homogenous units facing each other in an anarchical arena. Rather, the *res publica Christiana* was highly heterogeneous and showed some interesting overlaps: At its core it consisted of a reconstituted loose association of entities of various degrees of independence, the Empire. In one of its decision-making bodies, the Diet, outside members such as Sweden and later – through the accession of the House of Hanover to the British throne – even the English sovereign played an important role. Some of the members of this association 'contracted out' their defense, quite contrary to the assumed generative logic of anarchy, but even *de jure* questions of sovereign equality remained highly contested. Here, Leibniz's futile attempt to convince his contemporaries of a right of all sovereigns to send and receive ambassadors is highly instructive. Contrary to the logic of his argument this position was not even accepted by the most statist member: France. (Kratochwil, 2018: 89)

What is changing here are constitutive elements of political order particularly in relation to the concept of sovereignty. Of course, Kratochwil's perspective is more comprehensive and long-term, rather than just a focus on the time around the Peace of Westphalia. What is most important, however, is that he clearly professes an understanding of the evolution of the concept of sovereignty over time that marks his account as one of *transformative change*. This is a history not of interacting sovereigns, where change only occurs in shifting distributions of capabilities (or the disappearance of old and the appearance of new units). Change is always transformative as it changes, or at least has the potential to change, *both the constitution of society as well as the rules of the game.*

Regarding (b), despite this concentration on transformative change, something interesting happens between the chapters on 'Constituting' and 'Change'. While it is clear that change happens within a society that is not static, but that is both transformed and constituted by change, gone in the 'Change' chapter are reflections about the constitution of society in a larger sense, or about the relation between forms of social differentiation and change. Rather, '*international relations*' appears as the main character at centre stage. It certainly does not make this appearance playing the part of the realist messenger who tells us that nothing has changed since the Peloponnesian War – but it does make an appearance with the quite remarkable self-confidence of someone not in need of any further introduction. What we get from Kratochwil is a clear sense that this appearance can only take place in the context of a performance during which the entire stage of the political is always in the process of being redesigned and rebuilt. Nevertheless, in the midst of this ongoing change, 'the international' miraculously seems simply to belong there, like some kind of institutionalized *deus ex machina*. The deliberations on sovereignty are used to address 'transformative change in the international system' (Kratochwil, 2018: 93), yet we do not learn how the latter managed to appear in the scheme of things. Rather, there are again only negative hints: the international 'arena' is *not* seen as a system in which states claim exclusive jurisdiction over their territory (Kratochwil, 2018: 93), and then, through its intimate link to the sovereignty principle, it somehow seems different from function systems that do not challenge that principle (Kratochwil, 2018: 93). What, then, is the 'international', or the 'international system', for Kratochwil?

While there is no straightforward – at least no explicit – answer within *Praxis* itself, it seems clear that Kratochwil does not go down the pure path of a theory of differentiation that would identify the system of world politics as a subsystem of the political system of world society. It is somehow more and bigger than that: it is inimically linked to the foundations of authority, and, through that, to law. I would in fact go so far as to say that although for Kratochwil the international is certainly not the same as society, it is co-extensive to it. The lack of a more systematic demarcation notwithstanding, his account of change of the international is always also an account of change of, and within, society. Without doubt, for *how* change occurs, law (and how it changes) is central in this account, but the exact figure of that 'how' lies hidden behind the fireworks of dense argumentation. There is a theoretical account of change here, but it is not in the form of a substantive motive of *Geschichtsphilosophie*: there is no meaning of history that would be given through the enactment of law (or, as a possible alternative in *Praxis*, through the virtues of those that 'do' praxis). What there is, however, is some kind of *constitutive social evolution of and through law*, and I would argue that this account of change actually – without Kratochwil being anywhere close to acknowledging this – is an account that at its core conjoins a theoretical argument about change with an empirical argument. The theoretical argument about change is that change occurs as social evolution – that is, change without any reference to any *Geschichtsphilosophie* whatsoever, but also change that is more than an enumeration of historical events. The empirical argument is that for quite some time already – and at least since before the massive onset of functional differentiation – it is *law* that has provided the most important boundary conditions for social evolution. This argument shares a lot with Brunkhorst's social evolutionary account of legal revolutions (Brunkhorst, 2014), and it would certainly be worth entering into a more detailed dialogue between Kratochwil and Brunkhorst. At this stage, I can only sketch why such a dialogue makes sense in the present context: Brunkhorst argues that all great revolutions have been legal revolutions. Starting with the Papal Revolution with its beginnings in the 11th century, these legal revolutions created the conditions for the emergence and later prospering of functional differentiation. However, legal *revolutions* setting important boundary conditions of social evolution in no way prohibited the *evolution* of law in the context of an operatively autonomous legal system which in that operative autonomy is functionally differentiated from politics, the economy, science and so forth. It is such a reading that probably shows a way to salvage Kratochwil's thesis that functional differentiation presupposes the law, and to reconcile it with Luhmann's ideas about autopoiesis, a theory of historical change, and the important empirical observation about the evolution of authority, sovereignty, the law and the international in that context: law partakes in functional differentiation as much as everything else in society (pace the observation that segmentation still trumps everything else in terms of an internal differentiation of legal systems). But the great legal revolutions of the past one thousand years or so set the boundary conditions for the evolutionary trajectories of society that are deeply characterized by the emergence of functional differentiation as probably the most important form, yet in the end merely one of three coexisting and co-struggling forms, of social differentiation.

Conclusion: Praxis and theory

The preceding observations ascribe a coherence to the arguments in *Praxis* which they might not appear to have when taken literally. Of course, it is completely open for discussion whether such a coherence, particularly in the terms proposed here, is in fact there or not, or whether it might not simply be the result of a highly parochial Albertian quest for harmony and coherence. But if one follows that route of argument, then it seems safe to say that for all its wanderings hither and tither, *Praxis* ultimately qualifies as an important piece of *Gesellschaftstheorie*.

This is a reading that would probably be resented by Kratochwil as far as it seems to put him in bed with theorists, that is, exactly the type he wants to get rid of in order to pursue the virtues of practical judgement and of acting. But I think it is also exactly here where he might need to be salvaged just a bit from himself (whether he likes it or not): Kratochwil is absolutely right, both in *Praxis* and in his previous writings, to criticize the many vices and shortcomings (both substantively and, alas, more often than not also intellectually) of what is labelled as 'IR theory'. His lamentation about the fashionable literature on practices in IR can probably be read as a verdict about the entirety of IR theory as well: 'What one sorely misses in the contemporary debate is precisely the critical examination of the silent and not so silent presuppositions of thought' (Kratochwil, 2018: 392). This is the basic motive that leads him to discount theory and emphasize that what is needed is exactly the critical examination mentioned in the interest of studying praxis. However, the details of the wording are again very important here. When Kratochwil professes that he does 'not believe that theory-building is what we should be doing when we study praxis' (Kratochwil, 2018: 441), what he *does not* say is that one should not be studying praxis on the basis of theory. What he says is that theory-building is not the purpose of studying praxis – and what he likely primarily means is that it is particularly the exercise of *IR* theory-building that should not be done (or possibly only by some aficionados in the private sphere of their own basement; after all, by Kratochwilian standards most IR theory resembles less a thorough exercise of theory-building than an exercise in theoretical pottering).

For all it might claim to the contrary, *Praxis* is also a book of theory, and Kratochwil is a theorist. Yet it is about complex social theory served as a multi-course meal and prepared by a great chef. While the present chapter might have come across at some points as an attempt to 'correct' or 'better' Kratochwil, there actually is no issue of right or wrong involved here. Presented here are ideas about how Kratochwil's argument *could* be framed or constructed in a slightly different yet highly consequential fashion. The point made, really, is in pointing out the differences between how he proceeds in making his argument, on the one hand, and the consequences if he were to make this argument by taking my proposed modifications on board, on the other.[10] But still: all this not only plays on a difference between Kratochwil's argument and mine, but also points to that persistent ambiguity, that simultaneous lust and deeply embedded reluctance on the part of Kratochwil himself, when – throughout all his works – it comes to engaging with systems theory. Why this is the case I have given up trying to find out. But then I guess that probably Fritz himself couldn't come up with the answer.

References

Albert, Mathias (2019) 'Friedrich Kratochwil, *Praxis: On Acting and Knowing*, and Silviya Lechner and Meryn Frost, *Practice Theory and International Relations*', *International Affairs* 95, 2, pp 469–70.

Albert, Mathias and Barry Buzan (2013) 'International Relations theory and the "social whole": encounters and gaps between IR and Sociology', *International Political Sociology* 7, 2, pp 117–35.

Albert, Mathias and Yosef Lapid (2010) 'The "inter" according to Fritz: rethinking IR's proverbial toolbox', in Rodney Bruce Hall, Oliver Kessler, Cecelia Lynch and Nicholas Onuf (eds), *On Rules, Politics, and Knowledge: Friedrich Kratochwil, International Relations, and Domestic Affairs* (London: Palgrave), pp 242–51.

Albert, Mathias, Barry Buzan and Michael Zürn (2013) 'Introduction: Differentiation theory and International Relations', in Mathias Albert, Barry Buzan and Michael Zürn (eds), *Bringing Sociology to International Relations: World Politics as Differentiation Theory* (Cambridge: Cambridge University Press), pp 1–24.

Brunkhorst, Hauke (2014) *Critical Theory of Legal Revolutions* (New York: Bloomsbury Academic).

Habermas, Jürgen (1981) *Theorie des kommunikativen Handelns*, Vol. 2 (Frankfurt am Main: Suhrkamp).

Kratochwil, Friedrich (2018) *Praxis: On Acting and Knowing* (Cambridge: Cambridge University Press).

Luhmann, Niklas (1982) *The Differentiation of Society* (New York: Columbia University Press).

Luhmann, Niklas (1995 [1984]) *Social Systems* (Stanford, CA: Stanford University Press).

Luhmann, Niklas (2000) *Die Politik der Gesellschaft* (Frankfurt am Main: Suhrkamp).

---

[10] I owe this very 'pragmatist' point to Gunther Hellmann.

Luhmann, Niklas (2012 [1997]) *Theory of Society*, Vol. 1 Stanford, CA: Stanford University Press.

Luhmann, Niklas (2013 [1997]) *Theory of Society*, Vol. 2 (Stanford, CA: Stanford University Press).

Schimank, Uwe and Ute Volkmann (1999) *Gesellschaftliche Differenzierung* (Bielefeld: Transcript).

Wendt, Alexander (2015) *Quantum Mind and Social Science: Unifying Physical and Social Ontology* (Cambridge: Cambridge University Press).

12

Thinking on Time: How Scholarly Praxis Can Sustain, Subvert and Transform Social Reality

Jörg Friedrichs

Introduction

One purpose of scholarly praxis in social science is to have effects on social realities. Depending on our normative orientation, we may want to stabilize, subvert and transform the status quo. How can we do so? The conventional answer is that we need positivist approaches because, to intervene effectively in things social, we must know the regularities or even 'laws' governing them. In this chapter, I leave to one side the question of whether positivism has as much explanatory power and real-world relevance as proponents claim. Instead, I show how reflexive approaches are more relevant than conventional wisdom suggests. My focus is on approaches where scholars reflect in the context of the present about the past, with a vision for the future on their minds. To show how the scholarly praxis of *thinking on time* can stabilize, subvert and transform social realities, we need a hermeneutical framework that connects our contemporary lifeworlds as scholars with the historical lifeworlds of the people we study, while also taking account of the zeitgeist, or wider social realities, that influence us and that we may want to influence.

Originally, hermeneutics was the art of interpreting text. Today, it has become the art of interpretation *tout court*: not just texts but cultural artefacts; and not just cultural artefacts but human action and social interaction. What unites hermeneutical approaches is the realization that interpretation always mediates between one context and another (Gadamer, 1975 [1960]).[1] If this is true, then to understand an act of interpretation we need to

---

[1] For helpful introductions, see Bauman (1978), Bleicher (1980) and Yanov (2006).

understand not only the context to which an interpreter turns their gaze but also the context from which the interpreter operates. To account for an act of interpretation, we must grasp not only what it refers to but also the interpreter's positionality – what Anthony Giddens (1982) calls 'double hermeneutics'. In what follows, I move from double to triple hermeneutics. Giddens is right that we operate from a *research context* to envisage a *referent context*, but we do so in the wider context of our society and epoch – what I call the *cultural horizon*. Based on this tripartite conceptual framework, I show how engaging the cultural horizon can serve stabilizing, subversive and transformative purposes.

To begin with, I show that Weberian interpretive sociology leans towards stabilization. Its *cognitive* aim is to understand the referent context, while keeping the *normative* framework of the cultural horizon. Nietzschean and Foucauldian genealogy, by contrast, leans towards subversion. Their aim is not so much to understand the referent context but rather to destabilize the cultural horizon. Before his critical turn, the young Nietzsche (1980 [1874]) was interested in cultural transformation: how might knowledge of the past help society project itself from the present into the future? This ties in with an older strand in philosophy. Already in the 18th century, Hume tried to harness history in order to help society reinvent itself – what Kratochwil (2018: 419) calls the 'dialectics of time'. Reflexive approaches turn out to be far more relevant to social order than conventional wisdom suggests. Scholarly praxis in social science can stabilize, subvert and transform social reality.

Triple hermeneutics

Reed (2010) suggests that, in research and scholarship, 'two social contexts come together: the context of investigation, consisting of the social world of the investigator, and the context of explanation, consisting of the social world of the actors who are the subject of study' (Reed, 2010: 20). According to Reed, a hermeneutic approach sees the two contexts in a dynamic relationship and is sensitive to both. 'In social science, the role of meaning in structuring human action takes place both in the context of investigation and the context of explanation' (Reed, 2010: 36).

As already mentioned, Giddens (1982: 11–14) calls this 'double hermeneutics'. The concept is helpful, but it misses a crucial point. Reflexive work does not just happen in cultural and normative isolation, between a context of investigation and a context of explanation. It happens within the constraining and enabling environment of our society and epoch – the cultural horizon. To account for the cultural horizon, we must move from double to triple hermeneutics. As we will see, doing so does not only help us to model reflexive approaches but also to show how, by engaging the

Figure 12.1: Triple hermeneutics

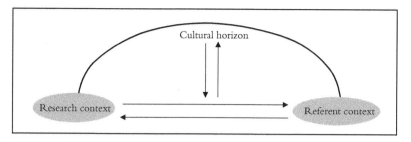

cultural horizon, reflexive approaches can serve stabilizing, subversive and transformative purposes.

Scholarship happens, firstly, from a vantage point – the *research context*. Think of the epistemic habits and normative orientations shaping our academic communities and disciplines. Secondly, the 'object world' of social research is actually a 'subject world' of humans sharing some epistemic habits and normative orientations while clashing over others – the *referent context*. Thirdly, scholarship happens under the influence of, and scholars may want to influence, the epistemic habits and normative orientations prevalent in their society and epoch – the *cultural horizon* (Figure 12.1).[2]

In light of this, we may define reflexive research as research in its broadest terms that does not objectify; instead, it reflects on knowledge production as constituted by the interplay of a research and a referent context, as well as the way such knowledge production is informed by, and informs, a cultural horizon. While this applies not only to temporal analysis but also to ethnographic work, my focus in this chapter remains thinking on time.[3]

Interpretive social science

Let us start with social research that seeks to sustain, rather than subvert or transform, social reality. Max Weber's interpretive social science allows for *cognitive* innovation (Weber, 2004 [1921]: 313–33) while aiming at *normative* stabilization (Weber, 2004 [1904]). Weber suggests social scientists should appreciate the epistemic significance of social phenomena stretching the

---

[2] As depicted in Figure 12.1, the research context and the referent context can be distant from one another and stretch the boundaries of the cultural horizon. This is obviously not always the case but, from a hermeneutic perspective, it is where social research becomes interesting: when scholars choose a topic in order to bridge lifeworlds and/or engage the cultural horizon.

[3] Regarding applicability to ethnographic work, see the final footnote of this chapter.

cultural horizon, but they should do so in a way that stabilizes rather than challenges the normative orientations within that horizon.

This means that, in *cognitive* terms, social scientists should aim to understand the meanings and values shared by the people and groups being studied (referent context). In *normative* terms, however, they should act under the guidance of the values accepted by their society and epoch (cultural horizon). Doing so will free them from personal and group-specific compulsions that might otherwise overwhelm their ability to conduct disinterested research (research context).[4] Non-judgemental (*werturteilsfreie*) social science thus demands a dual form of self-transcendence from scholars and their communities. On the one hand, scholars should set aside their cognitive presuppositions and derive the meaning of cultural phenomena from the referent context. On the other hand, scholars should also set aside their particularistic value commitments and defer to the normative values of the 'social and cultural life that surrounds us' (Weber, 2004 [1904]: 375).

A parenthesis on Weberian ideal types may help to clarify this further.[5] Ideal types are conceptual devices to enable 'success in revealing cultural phenomena' (Weber, 2004 [1904]: 389). They are mental constructs with the heuristic value of helping us to grasp empirical evidence. To serve that purpose, they must be adequate to the social situations under study, which Weber sees as historical and intersubjective. Social scientists should develop ideal types that are in tune with the way the historical subjects under study would have felt, reasoned, acted and interacted – in the referent context.

When it comes to the values guiding their research, however, social scientists should *not* derive these from the referent context (Weber, 2004 [1904]: 393). Instead, they should act under the moral guidance of the society and epoch in which their research is taking place – the cultural horizon. Only when those values change should researchers revise their conceptual apparatus to accommodate the emerging new values and world views. 'In the sciences of human culture the construction of concepts depends on the posing of problems, and the latter change with the content of the culture itself' (Weber, 2004 [1904]: 399).

An ideal type 'is formed by one-sided accentuation of one or several viewpoints and through the synthesis of a great many diffuse, discrete, more or less present and occasionally absent individual phenomena, which are arranged according to those one-sidedly emphasized viewpoints into a unified analytical construct [*einheitliches Gedankenbild*]'.[6] It is 'a purely ideal *limiting* concept [*Grenzbegriff*], against which reality is *compared*, so

---

4   Weber thereby establishes the fact–value dichotomy, viz. 'objectivity' or 'value freedom' of social science.
5   For a primer on Weberian ideal types, see Swedberg (2018).
6   Author's translation from the original (Weber, 2004 [1904]: 387–8).

that particular significant component parts of its empirical content can for the sake of clarification be *measured*' (Weber, 2004 [1904]: 390; original emphasis). The practical task is to 'determin[e] in each individual case how close to, or far from, reality such an ideal type is' (Weber, 2004 [1904]: 388). Ideal types are 'concepts and judgments that are not empirical reality, nor represent such reality, but which allow it to be ordered in thought in a valid manner' (Weber, 2004 [1904]: 401).

In terms of triple hermeneutics, if ideal types reflect the meanings in the referent context on the one hand, and the values in the cultural horizon on the other,[7] then what the social scientist does – in the research context – is to connect the cognitive lifeworlds of the people under study with the moral lifeworld of his or her own society and epoch. There is a creative element to this, as ideal types 'attempt, on the basis of prevailing knowledge and using the conceptual constructs available to us, to bring order into the prevailing chaos of facts that we have drawn into a field circumscribed by our interest' (Weber, 2004 [1904]: 398).

As the parenthesis on Weberian ideal types and 'non-judgemental' research confirms, his kind of interpretive social science is cognitively progressive but normatively conservative. It expands our cognitive horizon in terms of intersubjective meanings accessible to us, while deflecting the normative destabilization that might otherwise follow from an attempt to understand alien value systems. The net effect is that interpretive social science stabilizes the cultural horizon and thereby sustains the normative or moral status quo.

Critical genealogy

If interpretive social science aims to stabilize the cultural horizon, then critical genealogy aims to undermine it. Nietzsche's goal in the *Genealogy of Morality* (1994 [1887]) is to question, critique and subvert established values. 'Under what conditions did man invent the value judgments good and evil, and what value do they themselves have?' (Nietzsche, 1994 [1887]: 5). Taking issue with conventional genealogy and the prevailing 'slave morality' or 'morality of pity', Nietzsche asserts: 'We need a critique of moral values, the value of these values should itself, for once, be examined – and so we need to know about the conditions and circumstances under which the values grew up, developed, and changed' (Nietzsche, 1994 [1887]: 8).

---

[7] Note the following complication: any reference context contains not only meanings but also value judgements. Yet Weber finds it misguided for the historian 'to draw his judgement from the material, i.e. to allow the "idea" in the sense of the *ideal* to emerge from the "*idea*" in the sense of the "ideal type"' (Weber, 2004 [1904]: 393–4; original emphasis).

For Nietzsche, conventional genealogy produces nothing but morality tales. It constructs historical 'origins' that are supposed to serve shared moral 'ends'. Nietzsche debunks conventional genealogy, as practised by Paul Rée and other contemporary authors, because he is dissatisfied with the prevailing moral order. He wishes to show that the values of the present are not the result of noble origins and that they do not serve a higher purpose. Instead, they are the imprints left by successive manifestations of arbitrary power.

> Anything in existence, having somehow come about, is continually interpreted anew, requisitioned anew, transformed and redirected to a new purpose by a power superior to it; everything that occurs in the organic world consists of overpowering, dominating, and in their turn, overpowering and dominating consist of re-interpretation, adjustment, in the process of which their former 'meaning' and 'purpose' must necessarily be obscured or completely obliterated. (Nietzsche, 1994 [1887]: 55)

In principle, Nietzsche does not see anything wrong with this. On the contrary, morality and other expressions of power are 'just a sign that the will to power has achieved mastery over something less powerful' (Nietzsche, 1994 [1887]: 55). According to Nietzsche there is nothing wrong with this because the will to power is the essence of life. It is spontaneous, arbitrary, aggressive, expansive and formative. For instance, it drives the primordial agency of strong and powerful leaders. Operating through such leaders, the will to power dictates who 'we' are and where 'our' values come from. In so doing, it directs our collective identity and moral order. While docile subalterns may experience this as progress, it inevitably appears 'in the form of the will and way to greater power and always [emerges] victorious at the cost of countless smaller forces' (Nietzsche, 1994 [1887]: 56).

In principle, and as indicated, Nietzsche *celebrates* power. Yet he takes issue with its specific contemporary manifestation. The reason is that, in his view, contemporary values are not the imprint of superior power but of degenerate 'slave morality'. He therefore calls for genealogies as critical counter-histories to debunk the illusion that the present morality has a rightful origin and unimpeachable 'end'. To achieve this, the genealogist reconstructs the succession of arbitrary imprints of arbitrary power. Nietzsche's goal is to overturn the false 'morality of pity' and awaken the aristocratic will to power from its slumber, so that humanity may stand invigorated and reach its highest evolutionary potential (*Übermensch*).

Thus, the purpose of critical genealogy is moral subversion. The whole point is to undermine and eventually overturn the taken-for-granted status quo. The method poses as 'historical' (Nietzsche, 1994 [1887]: 56) but, in reality, it shows little regard for the factual accuracy of historical claims. Like its mirror image, conventional genealogy, critical genealogy replaces careful historical reconstruction with morality tales, or just-so stories. 'To produce the shock and confusion that are needed to help subjects to disengage from what they have become, textual techniques of estrangement and confrontation with the unfamiliar about oneself have to be used' (Saar, 2008: 310). It is worth turning the genealogical gaze on the author himself. Nietzsche (1994 [1887]: 5) claims noble origins for his critical genealogy. He asserts that it springs from a primordial will to knowledge that was present in him already as a teenager, when he would refuse to accept established notions of good an evil. He introduces his critical genealogy as a reaction to Paul Rée's 'English' genealogy. 'I have, perhaps, never read anything to which I said "no", sentence by sentence and deduction by deduction, as I did to this book: but completely without annoyance or impatience' (Nietzsche, 1994 [1887]: 6).

This is baloney. Rée was not an English but a Jewish German philosopher. When writing the *Genealogy of Morality* (1887), Nietzsche was desperately trying to get over the humiliating experience of a *ménage à trois* with Rée and Lou Salomé (Prideaux, 2018). Probably in order to express what the relationship felt like, Nietzsche had arranged a famous picture. The photograph (see http://commons.wikimedia.org/wiki/File:Nietzsche_paul-ree_lou-von-salome188.jpg) speaks volumes regarding Nietzsche's claim that his motivation for developing critical genealogy was a primordial and disinterested will to knowledge. It also speaks volumes of a philosopher who, like no other, spoke against resentment and quipped: 'You go to women? Do not forget the whip.'

Genealogy reloaded

In the early 1970s, Michel Foucault (1977 [1971]) borrowed the method of critical genealogy from Nietzsche. Like his predecessor, he saw genealogies as critical counter-histories to subvert a moral order seen as oppressive. Yet Foucault diverges radically from Nietzsche in his ethical impulse.

Nietzsche, for one, is committed to the will to power. He takes issue with 'slave morality'. For him, the purpose of genealogy is to re-empower the masters. Foucault, by contrast, takes issue with disciplinary power. He is committed to marginal subjects engaged in local resistance against 'sovereign' or centralizing power and knowledge. Foucault thus ends up detesting what Nietzsche celebrates and celebrating what Nietzsche detests. Where Nietzsche is committed to the heroic agency of the strong, Foucault is committed to the decentred subjectivity of the weak. One is tempted to say that, if Nietzsche is the Antichrist, then Foucault is the anti-Nietzsche.[8]

Foucault (2008 [1976]) presents genealogies as *anti-sciences*. They deconstruct the progress narratives produced by disciplinary power and its epistemic expression, disciplinary science. In doing so, genealogies expose the latent brutality and totalizing nature of the prevailing power–knowledge nexus in terms of normalizing domination and subjugation. Knowledge is power, and power is knowledge. This should spur local criticism and the insurrection of marginal, buried and unqualified forms of knowledge. This, in turn, should galvanize alliances between critical academics and activists, professionals and marginalized people.

The strategy, in typically leftist fashion, is to exploit contradictions that have built up in 'the system' – between disciplinary science on the one hand, and a-theoretical practices and anti-disciplinary resentment on the other. Foucault hopes that this might lead to 'the possibility of a new form of right [*droit*], one which must indeed be anti-disciplinarian, but at the same time liberated from the principle of sovereignty' (Foucault, 2008 [1976]: 325). Political emancipation should follow from moral-epistemic emancipation.

The tactic is de-normalization. One focuses on a social phenomenon that seems normal or true, turns it into a problem and then shows 'how it came about in the light of contingency and power' (Vuketic, 2011: 1301). Genealogies deconstruct conventional progress narratives by debunking the secret workings of power and disciplinary knowledge, in order to empower the agency of marginalized groups and enable a different future.

As we have done with Nietzsche at the end of the last section, let us turn the genealogical gaze on the author. Foucault had experienced the neo-Marxist and anarchist ferment of the post-war French intellectual left. He and other neo-Marxists and quasi-anarchists harboured anti-authoritarian resentment. They entertained an insurgent *will to counter-power* against repression seen as lurking everywhere. When the revolt of 1968 did not turn into a revolution, and when the gains in terms of emancipation did not lead to the hoped-for utopia, Foucault and his fellow travellers started overhauling their conceptual apparatus regarding 'power', 'repression' and so forth. They developed a more totalizing understanding of power, while at the same time theorizing subversion from the margins.

---

[8]   Despite the different ethical impulse, Foucault and Nietzsche suffer from similar contradictions. On the one hand, they see power in impersonal terms. On the other, they see it as a surrogate agent: the 'will to power' (Nietzsche), or power with its 'strategies' (Foucault). On the one hand, they reject subject philosophy. On the other, they want to liberate subjects: the *Übermensch* (Nietzsche), or marginalized people (Foucault).

Despite their different goals, Foucauldian and Nietzschean genealogy have much in common. Both present morality tales, or just-so stories, to subvert a normative order seen as oppressive (cultural horizon). Both claim historical erudition while running roughshod over factual detail and lived experience (referent context). Both suffer from blind spots and offer little clarity on how to imagine the desired future (research context).[9]

History for life

Before his turn to critical genealogy, the young Nietzsche was interested in cultural transformation: how might knowledge of the past help society project itself from the present into the future? In *The Advantage and Disadvantage of History for Life*, published 13 years before *Genealogy of Morality*, Nietzsche (1980 [1874]) reflects on the costs and benefits that different forms of historical knowledge may have for 'life', enabling a society and its leaders to move ahead and shape their destiny. Clearly, this was a transformational-reformist rather than a subversive-revolutionary pursuit.

At the time, a trivialized version of German historicism was paying great attention to the minutiae of chronological detail. Nietzsche was concerned that such historiographic scrupulousness might jettison society's vital interest in drawing *on the past* in pursuit of what 'we' *in the present* want *for the future*. To bring this home, he draws a distinction between *antiquarian* and *monumental* history, that is, history as the recollection of either memorable facts or memorable deeds. As far as antiquarian history is concerned, Nietzsche somewhat appreciates the idea that we must remember or even reminisce about where we come from so that we can preserve what we have. However, he sees the danger that this might turn us into philistines, rejecting any deviation from ossified patterns as a betrayal of who 'we' are and persecuting anyone who might challenge 'us' in our set ways.

All of this impulse against antiquarian history is geared against the lures of same old, same old: 'What has been will be again, what has been done will be done again; there is nothing new under the sun' (Ecclesiastes 1:9). Precisely because this would seem to be 'against life', Nietzsche commends monumental history – drawing on the past as a prop room, not so much to re-enact familiar episodes but rather in a creative quest to propel society into the future by finding examples of greatness and memorable deeds. The goal is to make history subservient to 'life', supportive of the vital interests of a community of fate.

---

[9] Incidentally, Nietzsche was fully aware that this kind of critical historiography risks sacrificing accuracy on the altar of a cultural revolution that is bound to remain elusive; watch out for the next footnote.

Nietzsche's bottom line is that allowing the referent context to drive the agenda (antiquarian history) means using history *against* life. Using history *for* life means reminiscing about some features of history while forgetting others, harnessing memorable events and facts (monumental history) for what 'we' want to achieve – not only as scholars, in the research context, but also as agents, free to shape and re-shape our cultural horizon.[10]

We may summarize the takeaway as follows. History 'is always remembered from a certain situation in the present, for which things past have now relevance. Thus the "recollecting" of the past, putting it in a frame, bestows importance on some earlier actions and events by connecting the past through the present with our personal and political projects' (Kratochwil, 2018: 326). Or, in terms of triple hermeneutics: reflexive historiography should serve our vital interest in progress and renewal. Hypertrophic attention to past events (referent context) must not overwhelm the ability of strong and creative decision-makers and citizen-scholars (research context) to draw on history in ways that enable us to reform and transform society (cultural horizon).

Dialectics of history

Nietzsche's 'history for life' ties in with an older strand in philosophy. Already in the 18th century, David Hume developed an elaborate method of harnessing history for social renewal by means of problem-focused anamnesis – what Kratochwil (2018: 419) calls the 'dialectics of time'.

To the scholar of political science, Hume is an unlikely author to come up in the context of reflexive 'thinking in time'. Hume is usually cited as an arch-positivist, the originator of the 'Humean empiricist concept of cause' (Kurki, 2006: 215). Yet Hume is different things to different people (Harris, 2015). Some scholars see him as a precursor of hermeneutics who grounds the 'science of morality' on 'sympathy' rather than 'constant conjunction' (Farr, 1978; Bohlin, 2009). Others see him as the proponent of a humanist 'philosophy of common life' who has studied moral conventions as social constructs which, over time, emerge in a society (Livingston, 1984).

In this view, Hume regards morality and social order as artificial because the conventions and 'laws' of the social world arise from interaction. Accordingly,

---

10 Alongside monumental and antiquarian history, Nietzsche contemplates a third kind: critical history. Using critical history *against* life means that the present judges the past in a negative fashion; using it *for* life means that the present judges the past in the interest of a better future. Nietzsche (1994 [1887]) went down precisely that route 13 years later, in the *Genealogy of Morality*. By then, Nietzsche had morphed from a reformist into a revolutionary thinker and saw himself as blazing the trail for some imaginary future *Übermensch* to leave behind the shackles of Judaeo-Christian 'slave morality', 'herd morality', 'morality of pity' and so on.

the scholar needs to understand them as historically developed and socially constructed. Understanding moral conventions as arising from social praxis opens an avenue to Humean sympathy, 'from the enlargement of the circle of people we converse with, and from a familiarity with different common worlds' (Kratochwil, 2018: 376), immersing ourselves in the social realities of people who are separated from us in various ways but for whom we are still able to develop sympathy. Despite some nuances, Hume's theory of sympathy is similar to the one developed by his contemporary Adam Smith (Sayre-McCord, 2013).

How do moral conventions develop? In his *Treatise of Human Nature*, Hume draws a distinction between 'violent' and 'calm' passions (Hume, 2007 [1738], Book 2, Part III, Sect. 3–4). The transition from violent to calm passions is a key step not only for the human being but also for the body politic. It happens gradually, in ways that a biographer or historian may trace (Livingston, 1984; Baier, 1991). Thus, when individuals and collectives experience arousing disturbances, order is re-established, or established in the first place, via a process of disciplining violent passions and turning them into calm passions. Over time, this enables the emergence of moral habits and conventions that constrain action but also enable unconventional moves when required (Kratochwil, 2018: chapter 9).

As Kratochwil (2018) notes, Hume's (1983 [1754–61]) monumental *History of England* is a case in point. In the first couple of volumes, dedicated to the pre-Reformation period, Hume shows how the slow accretion of conventions enabled a viable degree of social cohesion and political consensus. He then shows how, especially during the civil war era, theological disputes upended this consensus. Finally, Hume shows how the Glorious Revolution of 1688 enabled a return to a viable settlement.

In a way that is surely intentional, this historiographical plot vindicates a passage in Hume's *Treatise of Human Nature*. In that passage, Hume (2007 [1738], Book 3, Part II, Sect. 10, para 17–19) seems to suggest that the settlement of 1688 was viable because it combined shrewd compromise on dynastic and constitutional matters with a creative update of time-honoured consensus, 'linking the recent unprecedented changes to the hitherto existing traditions and customs' and creating the cherished institution of parliamentary sovereignty in the process (Kratochwil, 2018: 388).[11]

Despite his conservative leanings, Hume was a political reformist at heart. The radicalism of the civil war era posed a threat to established order. The

---

[11] This moral vision lies at the foundation of a living tradition. In an address to the University of Bristol, Winston Churchill stated in 1938: 'The central principle of Civilization is the subordination of the ruling authority to the settled customs of the people and to their will as expressed in the Constitution.' See Churchill, 'What we mean by "civilization"', available at: https://winstonchurchill.hillsdale.edu/churchill-understanding-civilization/, accessed 3 January 2020.

challenge, therefore, was to find a compromise. Hume was able to embrace the Glorious Revolution because, under a new guise, it re-enacted time-honoured moral conventions. It was a revolution in the original sense of *re-volvere*: moving back on track.[12]

Kratochwil calls this the 'dialectic of time', 'dialectic of action', or 'dialectic between present, past, and future'. This dialectic enables us to become more aware of contingency and, thereby, gain a renewed sense of freedom. 'Precisely because we know that things could have been different, the more we deepen our understanding of the past the more we begin to sense the opportunities forgone and thereby become aware of our own potential as agents' (Kratochwil, 2018: 315).

> [History] is always viewed from a particular *vantage point of the present*. It is this present problem that informs the selection of what is considered worth remembering. To that extent historical reflection is not some collection of interesting facts one could do without, but is intrinsic to our notions of agency and identity. In approaching history not in terms of fixity of the past, but through the modality of remembering, we become aware of the 'possible.' In this way individuals and collectivities can transcend the confinements imposed by [the] system, and find new ways of mastering their destiny. (Kratochwil, 2018: 349)

Our interest in the past 'arises from a problem of the present, which calls forth a specific recollection to which meaning is assigned'. Yet 'the dialectic of action requires not only a remembered past, but also a selection and a construction of a projected future' (Kratochwil, 2018: 406). Thereby, we become part of a shared story that has not only a past but also a present and a future.[13]

Especially in moments of crisis, such reflexivity may enable transformation and renewal. We must expand our circles beyond the confines of our social and political environment in order to develop sympathy with our forebears and, thereby, with contemporaries who think differently. If historical reflection can show how, in the past, people have converted violent passions into moral conventions, it becomes easier to envisage how we might do so in the present, for the future.

---

[12] The word 'revolution' has taken on a different meaning since the French Revolution of 1789.

[13] Historiography is not mere chronology, nor is it purely premised on causes, regularities or even 'laws' of history. Without denying the importance of chronology and causation, historiography is a narration *plotted* in manifold ways: not only 'then' and 'because' but also 'whereas', 'in spite of', 'in order to', 'lest' and other reasons for or against particular courses of action, as well as ways to make sense of them.

To sum up, in terms of triple hermeneutics, social order is viable when 'violent passions' have become 'calm passions', supporting shared understandings and moral conventions (cultural horizon). Especially in times of crisis, this amounts to a crucial task for citizen-scholars. We must leave our comfort zone (research context) and study the tortuous ways by which social order has emerged in the past (referent context), so as to understand how it can re-remerge in a reformed or transformed, yet morally recognizable, way.

Conclusion

Positivism holds the promise that we can know reality and act on that knowledge: *give me a lever and a place to stand, and I shall move the earth.* If we can know the regularities of social life in a way that is analogous to the way we know the laws of physics, then this should enable us to act in similar ways: *give me evidence-based policies and the power to act, and I shall change society.*

The premise, of course, is that social reality is akin to physical reality. This does not seem to be the case, so positivism stands on shaky ground. It remains irresistible to those whose aim is to engineer social change. From an epistemological standpoint, however, positivism seems overrated. This chapter suggests that reflexive approaches, by contrast, are often underrated. By engaging the cultural horizon, they can have sustaining, subversive and transformative effects.

Conservative approaches such as Weber's interpretive social science have sustaining effects. They help us expand and stabilize the cognitive horizon of our culture without questioning its normative underpinnings. The implications are more important than meets the eye. A society in which interpretive approaches thrive would be firm in its values but eager to understand, and slow to judge, social contexts that stretch our comfort zone. For instance, we would be less inclined to topple monuments of historical figures fallen in disgrace or pursue regime change in faraway lands. Interpretive approaches enable us to understand and appreciate contexts where people (used to) think and act differently.

Critical approaches such as genealogy have subversive effects. They are too negative to show the way forward, but we should not underestimate their corrosive power. Nietzsche's contempt for the 'morality of pity' was grist for the mill of fascist movements wreaking havoc in the 20th century. Foucault's suspicion of disciplinary power has rallied a cultural left eager to discipline its adversaries, for example by delegitimizing 'White privilege' and prescribing 'anti-bias training'. It would be unfair to blame any of this directly on Nietzsche or Foucault, but critical approaches are more effective in terms of subverting social order than a complacent attitude might suggest.

Reformist approaches may have transformative effects. In connecting the past with the present and future, they aim to find a reasonable compromise between what a historical drama meant to the actors and what it may mean for us today – enabling us to write, or dare we say *make*, our own history. In expanding our circles of sympathy and conversation, it connects people from different intellectual and political walks of life – enabling the reconstruction of moral conventions that can carry social order in challenging times. By cultivating violent passion into calm moral sentiment, reformist approaches may help our deeply divided societies overcome polarization.[14]

References

Agar, Michael H. (1996) *The Professional Stranger: An Informal Introduction to Ethnography* (2nd edn) (San Diego, CA: Academic Press).

Baier, Annette C. (1991) *A Progress of Sentiments: Reflections on Hume's Treatise* (Cambridge, MA: Harvard University Press).

Bauman, Zygmunt (1978) *Hermeneutics and Social Science: Approaches to Understanding* (London: Hutchinson).

Bleicher, Josef (1980) *Contemporary Hermeneutics: Hermeneutics as Method, Philosophy, and Critique* (London: Routledge).

Bohlin, Henrik (2009) 'Sympathy, understanding, and hermeneutics in Hume's *Treatise*', *Hume Studies* 35, 1, pp 135–70.

Farr, James (1978) 'Hume, hermeneutics, and history: a "sympathetic" account', *History and Theory* 12, 3, pp 285–310.

Foucault, Michel (1977 [1971]) 'Nietzsche, genealogy, history', in Michel Foucault and Donald F. Boucard (eds), *Language, Counter-Memory, Practice: Selected Essays and Interviews* (Ithaca, NY: Cornell University Press), pp 139–64.

Foucault, Michel (2008 [1976]) 'Two lectures', in Steven C. Roach (ed), *Critical Theory and International Relations: A Reader* (New York: Routledge), pp 317–26.

Gadamer, Hans-Georg (1975 [1960]) *Truth and Method* (London: Sheed and Ward).

Giddens, Anthony (1982) *Profiles and Critiques in Social Theory* (London: Macmillan).

Harris, James A. (2015) *Hume: An Intellectual Biography* (Cambridge: Cambridge University Press).

Hume, David (1983 [1754–61]) *The History of England: From the Invasion of Julius Caesar to the Revolution in 1688* (Indianapolis, IN: Liberty Classics).

---

[14] Expanding the circles of understanding and conversation with strangers in our own time and age is every bit as important for social renewal as developing 'sympathy' with our forebears. Understanding people who are different in the here and now is as valuable as understanding the past. Ethnography (Agar, 1996) can expand our cultural horizon every bit as much as historiography. At the end of the day, 'thinking on time' is another way of thinking about people.

Hume, David (2007 [1738]) *A Treatise of Human Nature* ed. David F. Norton and Mary J. Morton (Oxford: Oxford University Press).

Kratochwil, Friedrich (2018) *Praxis: On Acting and Knowing* (Cambridge: Cambridge University Press).

Kurki, Milja (2006) 'Causes of a divided discipline: rethinking the concept of cause in International Relations theory', *Review of International Studies* 32, 2, pp 189–216.

Livingston, Donald W. (1984) *Hume's Philosophy of Common Life* (Chicago, IL: Chicago University Press).

Nietzsche, Friedrich (1980 [1874]) *On the Advantage and Disadvantage of History for Life* (Indianapolis, IN: Hackett).

Nietzsche, Friedrich (1994 [1887]) *On the Genealogy of Morality* (Cambridge: Cambridge University Press).

Prideaux, Sue (2018) *I Am Dynamite! A Life of Friedrich Nietzsche* (London: Faber and Faber).

Reed, Isaac Ariail (2010) 'Epistemology contextualized: social-scientific knowledge in a post-positivist era', *Sociological Theory* 28, 1, pp 20–39.

Saar, Martin (2008) 'Understanding genealogy: history, power, and the self', *Journal of the Philosophy of History* 2, 3, pp 295–314.

Sayre-McCord, Geoffrey (2013) 'Hume and Smith on sympathy, approbation, and moral judgment', *Social Philosophy and Policy* 30, 1, pp 208–36.

Swedberg, Richard (2018) 'How to use Max Weber's ideal type in sociological analysis', *Journal of Classical Sociology* 18, 3, pp 181–206.

Vuketic, Srdjan (2011). 'Genealogy as a research tool in International Relations', *Review of International Studies* 37, 3, pp 1295–312.

Weber, Max (2004 [1904]) 'The "objectivity" of knowledge in social science and social policy', in Sam Whimster (ed), *The Essential Weber: A Reader* (London: Routledge), pp 387–404.

Weber, Max (2004 [1921]) 'Basic sociological concepts', in Sam Whimster (ed), *The Essential Weber: A Reader* (London: Routledge), pp 359–404.

Yanov, Dvora (2006) 'Thinking interpretively: philosophical presuppositions and the human sciences', in Dvora Yanov and Peregrine Schwartz-Shea (eds), *Interpretation and Method: Empirical Research Methods and the Interpretive Turn* (Armonk, NY: M.E. Sharpe), pp 5–26.

PART IV

Theorizing as Intervention

13

Practising Academic Intervention: An Agonistic Reading of *Praxis*

Antje Wiener

Introduction

As the ink of the special issue on *The Status of Law in World Society: Meditations on the Role and Rule of Law* (Kratochwil, 2014) is barely dry (Peltonen and Traisbach, 2020), this chapter follows yet another invitation to engage with Friedrich Kratochwil's seminal work in International Relations (IR) and International Law in celebration of his most recent monograph titled *Praxis* (Kratochwil, 2018). In this chapter, I turn to Kratochwil's veritable gusto in performing academic interventions to explore the purpose and effect of his by now seminal practice of deeply engaging with the work of others by way of intertextual interaction. While some detect a certain 'grumpiness' (Welsh, 2020), this chapter argues that his academic interventions on IR theory and International Law, are of a notable game-changing quality. As the following will demonstrate, based on an agonistic reading of these interventions, this quality is characterized by two moves: firstly, a *normative* call for more critical engagement with the claims of other IR theorists, for 'values and committing to them have to be an intrinsic concern for social analysis that cannot be sacrificed on the altar of scientific objectivity as otherwise we lose, so to speak, the "object" we are supposed to study' (Kratochwil, 2020: 1); and secondly, the development of a *practice*-based approach to constructive critique through academic intervention. According to Kratochwil, this kind of practical engagement works best through praxis, which involves the practices of thoroughly scrutinizing and contesting the theoretical claims of others. This constructive critique in the social sciences is not value-free, to be sure, for 'it makes at least prima facie sense to be sceptical about the possibility of a value-free "scientific" approach to problems of *praxis* since values are constitutive for our interests, and following rules is linked to "commitments" and the validity of norms, not to causality' (Kratochwil, 2020: 1, emphasis added).

This chapter argues that throughout his academic career Kratochwil's own scholarly action has been developed to a fine point. In the process, his repertoire for academic intervention has been constituted by the writings of those IR theorists whose work he finds to be misleading their readers, thereby often distorting the potential of the discipline. It is this approach to critical engagement with other(s') texts that this chapter will highlight and explore as a distinct practice of academic intervention. To Kratochwil, practising social sciences must be precisely the opposite of complying with calls 'to provide rather promptly the "solutions" to our problems', and, as he stresses 'anyone not delivering them, or even refusing to do so, becomes easily an incompetent and a party-pooper to boot, whose "negativity" might even justify yanking his licence to practice social science' (Kratochwil, 2020: 8). By taking a closer look at Kratochwil's academic interventions, I demonstrate the effects of this practice, illustrated by his most recent book. Developing the argument against the backdrop of Kratochwil's career and drawing on excerpts from *Praxis*, this chapter presents 'acting through *praxis*' as a practice of academic intervention that is mindful of the dynamic of the 'hermeneutic cycle between facts and norms' (Kratochwil, 2020: 7) with a twofold effect. For it is both critical *and* facilitative. The chapter seeks to bring these constitutive and political effects of praxis to the fore. To demonstrate them the following undertakes an agonistic reading of Kratochwil's *Praxis*. Following Mark Wenman, I understand '"agonism" to imply both the necessary interdependence of social relations and also the constitutive nature of strife' (Wenman, 2003: 167, referring to Connolly, 1995, and Tully, 1995).

As per the editors' invitation, I address praxis as an enabling foil that invites us to engage critically with Kratochwil's lifelong academic interventions which carry the theme of 'rules, norms and decisions' in international relations (Kratochwil, 1989; for earlier contributions, see Kratochwil, 1984; Kratochwil and Ruggie, 1986). Given the beneficial effects that these interventions had for the development of this author's thinking and academic progression, the following offers an appreciative reading of these academic interventions. The wider context of this reading is set by critical constructivist scholarship in the discipline of IR, while the more immediate context is set by the privileged 'thinking space' that was provided by the workshop that preceded this book manuscript. The latter was conceived as an opportunity to read and engage with Kratochwil's contemplations of human action, through interactions, inviting the participants to critically reflect upon their own motivation for undertaking academic research. This said, the following raises three guiding questions:

1. To what end and for what purpose do scholars engage in academic research (*motivation*)?
2. How do we identify our respective standpoint as researchers vis-à-vis the real world (coming *from somewhere*)?
3. Do academics acknowledge their privilege of accumulating knowledge and recognize the social responsibility to use it (*academic intervention*)?

The chapter addresses these questions in three further sections. The first section introduces the concept of academic intervention as a principled practice that is based on the positions of privilege and responsibility. The second section turns to the method of agonistic reading and the central importance that is assigned to 'conflict' according to this approach. The third section then undertakes an exemplary agonistic reading of Kratochwil's *Praxis* in order to illustrate the approach and its impact for future research by new generations of IR scholarship.

Practising academic intervention from the positions of privilege and responsibility

Broadly speaking, academic interventions comprise the bulk of academic output on a global scale and therefore do not represent a helpful categorical distinction as such. However, I suggest that an agonistic reading that defines academic intervention as a principled practice facilitates explorative research with a view to pinpointing the potential effects of these interventions. The effects may be political or normative. As will be detailed later, responsible academic intervention sets out to depict political inequality, moral injustice or material exclusion from partaking in processes of development and progress in the world. In practice, it aims to reflexively counter these conditions, for example by generating better theories and/or proposing measures to counter these real-world issues. The social sciences identify a range of such practices of principled academic interventions. Given the limited space of an edited volume, a few examples may suffice here. For example, the public policy literature speaks of 'reciprocal elucidation' (Tully, 2002). It highlights conditions of unequal access to contestation vis-à-vis the norms that govern them and suggests accounting for 'multiplicity' as a challenge to modern constitutionalism. Against this background, research seeks to identify novel conditions of 'contemporary constitutionalism' that allow for reconnecting and rewriting the interrelations between 'civic activity' and 'civil orders' in late modern political orders (Tully, 1995, 2002, 2008a, 2008b; Owen and Tully, 2007; Owen 2019a, 2019b).

In the light of the unequal conditions that set the reciprocal relation between *being* in the world, on the one hand, and *governing* society, on the other, principled academic intervention has been practised as 'staging global multilogues' (Wiener, 2018). This intervention identifies conflicts about norms and then zooms in on sites where affected stakeholders engage in contestation under unequal conditions. To constitute a space for visible public engagement, these stakeholder groups are then placed on a global stage where their discursive input in global normative change is made visible. This type of academic intervention is centred on local discursive interventions that are constrained by unequal access to contestation. To counter this lack of opportunity for political participation, it gives a voice to those who have a stake in a given global norm conflict (Wiener, 2018, especially chapter 8). In sum, a growing critical scholarship has foregrounded the necessity and purpose of academic intervention with the public philosophy in a new key project (Tully, 2008a, 2008b; as well as Laden and Owen, 2007; Karmis et al, forthcoming), the Global IR project (Acharya, 2014, 2016, 2018; Hurrell, 2016; Tickner, 2016; Acharya and Buzan, 2019), the post-critical IR project that invites IR scholars to address the consequences of critical approaches to IR more specifically, asking us to engage in 'explicit discussions of how we might make (critical) impact in and on the world' (Austin, 2018: 1); or the grounded normative theory (GNT) project that brings political theorists, IR theorists and feminist theory together in order to 'theorise with those who struggle' (Ackerly et al, 2021). Last and by no means least, another example is offered by the growing literature of feminist and post-colonial work that calls for rereading societal constellations with reference to the condition of intersectionality and offers novel perspectives with a view to rewrite the emergence of international order(s) on a global scale (Spivak, 1988; Chakrabarty, 2008; Wilkens, 2017).

More specifically, Kratochwil's academic interventions highlight the two dimensions. This involves, firstly, generating knowledge through critical interventions with the text of others and thereby recovering lost 'thinking space' and putting these on the academic map. Secondly, and relatedly, this remapping has played a facilitative role over the years, for it has allowed generations of younger, less prominent scholars a legitimate 'space' from where they, in turn, were able to engage in knowledge generation themselves. That is, on the one hand, and most visibly, his academic interventions consistently advanced knowledge in the social sciences – bringing hidden gems to the fore, as it were. And by keeping his 'voice' up, both literally and with a continuous presence in print with the top journals of the discipline, on the other hand, Kratochwil has succeeded in maintaining the presence and accessibility of that very thinking space, thereby enabling and encouraging critical thinking for subsequent generations of IR scholars.

The two effects are interrelated steps in the process of joint knowledge generation, to be sure. To the general IR scholarship, the former effect will be more obvious, while to those of us who were fellow spatio-temporal travellers, the latter facilitative effect has often turned out to be the crucial – even career-making or career-turning – intervention. After all, up to the 2000s, IR was a discipline that moved forward by means of paradigm battles that did not care for making prisoners (Farrell, 2002). Kratochwil recalls

> tedious epistemological debates over the last three decades when logical positivism was bolted together with empiricism, grafted upon Kuhnian notions of paradigms, was modified by Lakatosian 'generative problem shifts' and pepped up by some notions of 'instrumentalism' *a la* Milton Friedman, in order to realise that such constructions are neither able to provide an accurate account of scientific 'progress' nor define usable demarcation criteria for distinguishing 'science' from other activities. (Kratochwil, 2007: 25–6)

Against the background of the dominant narrative which pitched the discipline as an 'American social science' (Hoffmann, 1977; cf Zürn, 1994; Wæver, 1998: 687; Acharya, 2014), Kratochwil's manifold academic interventions were decisive for creating the 'thinking space' and 'reference frame' that allowed for innovative and critical thinking and enabled critical IR scholarship to thrive.

Against the often overbearing institutional and substantive constraints that were set by the 'American' narrative – nurtured by recurring paradigm battles and the long-uncontested steadfast belief in a 'Westphalian' international order, this thinking space enabled innovative research on change that raised questions about the mainstream's state-centric assumptions (Wæver, 1996; Zalewski, 1996; Tickner, 2001; Ackerly and True, 2008). To Kratochwil and many other critics it was obvious that 'the "debates" turn out to be largely *ex post facto* constructions provided by the historical narrative rather than by the events themselves' (Kratochwil, 2007: 26–7). Over the decades, Kratochwil has chosen his critical interventions carefully. He engaged in questioning the fundamental research assumptions and theoretical claims advanced by (neo-)realist colleagues and held their authors to account. In the process, doors into academia were opened for generations of younger scholars who, especially in the 1980s and 1990s, had to be constantly mindful of the powerful hegemony of the positivist language of the so-called mainstream in US-based IR theory. In Kratochwil's own scathingly clear words, in the 2000s,

> the vast majority of students are still being 'trained' (not to say indoctrinated) in 'the scientific method' no matter what area or problem

they want to investigate. Apparently, as in the case of the Midas muffler, 'one size fits all'. Why? Because we (the authors) say so! Similarly, the power structure within the profession and reflected in the 'top departments' has remained predictably stable. (Kratochwil, 2007: 27)

To bring the effects to the fore, the following sections recall Kratochwil's academic interventions along the two core dimensions of his work. The first consists in the project of studying human action and its effect on the transformation of norms, rules and orders through redrawing the disciplinary boundaries of international studies. And the second consists in opening and expanding access to thinking space that enabled subsequent generations to engage in critical questions about international studies and advance knowledge building on these interdisciplinary strands of theoretical engagement. To that end, academic intervention is defined as 'making use of knowledge in a responsible and purposeful way'. Having access to this knowledge and knowing how to use it effectively places academics in a position of privilege, and this privilege comes with the duty of using that knowledge responsibly. The concept of academic intervention therefore implies taking account of the tools available to us as researchers who engage in 'acting and knowing' (Friedrichs and Kratochwil, 2009; Kratochwil, 2018; for responsible intervention compare also 'diplomatic intervention', Fierke, 2007; and more generally, the debates about the responsibility to protect, Ulbert et al, 2017; Hansen-Magnusson and Vetterlein, 2021).

Following public philosophy, in principle, academic interventions are identified according to two types of action that are distinguished by an individual's *access* to knowledge, which enables scholars to act in a dual role, namely, as learned scholars and political activists. These access conditions are set by the socio-cultural grounding of that action (acting from somewhere). As 'learned citizens', academics are able to use and generate knowledge about the rules and norms that are constitutive of civil order while at the same time enjoying the freedom to act as 'struggling citizens' who engage in civic activities in order to change that order (Laden and Owen, 2007; Tully, 2008a; Owen, 2019a). While, in principle, both categories of citizens are related through their position as potential contestants in the same conflict, their respective positions remain to be activated based on a strategic decision to 'enter into the dialogue with citizens engaged in struggles against various forms of injustice and oppression' (Tully, 2008a: 3).

According to James Tully, one way of activating the relation between these distinct positions involves establishing 'pedagogical relationships of *reciprocal elucidation* between academic research and the civic activities of fellow citizens' (Tully, 2008a: 3, emphasis added; Tully, 2002). In *Praxis*, the chapter on 'Acting' (Kratochwil, 2018: chapter 10) makes a similar point when referring to 'the "vocation" of pragmatism, which "demands that we recognize our scholarship as political tools … [which] are integral to the constitution of the global public"' (Kratochwil, 2018: 426; citing Abraham and Abramson, 2017: 19) That is, as scholars we are not only in the position to obtain and develop knowledge, but we are also enabled to apply that knowledge in our respective academic interventions. Performed in public, and notwithstanding qualitatively distinct types of intervention (e.g. theoretical or activist), academic intervention is therefore always *per se* political.[1] In addition to the socio-cultural ground of academic intervention, scholars choose their epistemological standpoint, whether foregrounding it or not (Jackson, 2008). It follows that academic interventions are value-based, they carry socio-cultural capabilities, and they are political.

At the hands *of the few*, academic intervention is therefore conceived as a potentially powerful tool that has a constitutive effect *on the many*, for 'all theories are "for" someone and naturalising the social world mystifies power through an hegemonic discourse' (Kratochwil, 2007: 25). Academic intervention therefore has a political effect and works beyond academia, influencing societal change, cultural narratives and strategic framing about how to see the world in the making (Onuf, 1989). Whether acting in public or in a more exclusive intertextual space, therefore, practising scholarship is about 'change'. Notably, academic intervention always reflects a position of privilege and responsibility. This includes both types of academic practice, that is, critical discursive intervention, for example, when engaging with other 'learned citizens' or their work; and direct discursive intervention, for example, when acting in support of 'struggling citizens'. Assessing the effect of academic intervention means taking account of the position of *privilege* which is enabled by scholarly access to knowledge. The position of privilege is constituted by norms as social facts. It involves distinct *societal conditions* that are enabled or constrained by *access* to education in the widest possible sense, including facilitative and enabling conditions of learning and practising scholarship. In turn, the position of *responsibility* reflects the scholar's awareness of the potentially powerful effects that are generated by using their privileged knowledge.

The position of responsibility is constituted by ethical values, such as, for example, acknowledging the power of knowledge with regard to constituting public goods such as norms, institutions or order. It follows

---

[1] Note that this reference to the public follows an agonistic definition which centres on the practice of contestation and the fundamental contestedness of norms (as opposed to the Habermasian definition of the 'public sphere' that sets the legitimate boundaries for discursive intervention). The next section will discuss this distinction in more detail.

that taking account of the political power of scholarship therefore involves the principled normative task of dedicating appropriate attention to the step of foregrounding the researcher's moral standpoint and purpose prior to an academic intervention (Haverland and Yanow, 2012). This task echoes, to a certain extent, Max Weber's emphasis on context and ethical principles which were developed in *Politics as Vocation* (Weber, 1919). As Weber notes, the context of a project matters[2] as much as an agent's awareness of two kinds of ethics as the key moral principles.[3] Famously, Weber centres on two kinds of ethics, i.e., the 'ethics of responsibility' and the 'ethics of conviction'. Notably, the 'ethics of responsibility pays attention only to the actual consequences of what is done' (Owen and Strong, 2004: xli). This implies that an ethics of conviction that is *not* sustained by an ethics of responsibility represents an insufficient condition for practising politics as vocation. Weber's perception of the two ethics thus highlights a politician's responsibility regarding the potential effects of her or his decisions, for as he stresses, 'it does no good in politics to say you did not intend the (unfortunate) consequences of your action' (Owen and Strong, 2004: xli).

Weber's insistence on the relational effect of these two principles offers an important cue with regard to this chapter's argument for foregrounding the epistemological standpoint and intention prior to engaging in the practice of academic intervention. It acknowledges the use of scholarship as a powerful tool towards societal change. As critical IR scholars have pointed out, putting the principle into practice can be achieved by way of 'foregrounding epistemological assumptions' and 'logics of enquiry' (Jackson, 2008; Haverland and Yanow, 2012). That is, all academic interventions are by definition public interactions by those holding an academic position, regardless of whether these are practised in the very space of academic institutions or in other thinking spaces. Against this backdrop, it is remarkable that the political effect of these interventions has so far rarely been made explicit (Abraham and Abramson, 2017). Addressing this gap involves foregrounding the epistemological standpoint and, relatedly, the

---

2   As Weber notes, given his profession as a political economist, his research customarily begins with the external conditions of the research object. For the lecture on *Science as Vocation*, these are set by the respective academic contexts. In turn, for the lecture on *Politics as Vocation*, this context is set by the state. See Weber's *Science as Vocation* lecture on 7 November 1917 (page 1, translated print edition, Owen and Strong, 2004), as well as his *Politics as Vocation* lecture where he argues that 'the modern state is an institutional form of rule that has successfully fought to create a monopoly of the legitimate physical force as a means of government within a particular territory' (Weber, 1919: 38).

3   The responsibility that mattered for politics (and politicians), he argued, came in two types: '(O)ne he calls the "ethic of responsibility,"' the other the 'ethic of conviction' (Owen and Strong, 2004: xli).

methodological approach and method vis-à-vis other scholars and/or those who are in struggle.[4] To fill the research gap, therefore, this chapter identifies the two positions from which academic interventions are practised and illustrates their effect with reference to Kratochwil's *Praxis*.

An agonistic reading of *Praxis*

Before analysing Kratochwil's academic interventions based on an agonistic reading of *Praxis*, this section turns to that method in some more detail. As Royer notes,

> agonists agree on three fundamental points: First, agonists do not only stress the ineradicability of conflict (although they do so, of course) but insist on the ethical and political value of certain forms of struggle, competition and conflict; secondly, agonism is based on the fundamental value of human plurality as a constitutive element of social and political life; and thirdly, agonists share a tragic vision of political life. By stressing these three fundamental elements, agonists have developed distinctive insights into the nature, the role and the purpose of politics and, indeed, a constitutional order. (Royer, 2019: 6–7; citing Wenman, 2013: 28–58)

To simplify somewhat, if an agonistic approach rests on the assumption that 'conflict is a form of justice' (Havercroft, 2017: 101), and the assumption about the conflict–justice relation builds on the expectation that, as moments of contestation, conflictive discursive encounters help reveal 'difference' in opinion or point of view, then an agonistic reading of the work of others leads straight into the 'messy midst' of doing theory. Given the underlying assumption that conflict entails the dynamic potential for enhancing justice in global society, the objective consists in identifying conflictive engagements and exploring the normative conditions and constructive potentials for change towards enhancing 'justice' (in this context read as putting the record straight). In this regard, political agonism 'offers a particular interpretation and understanding of the nature, the role and the purpose of politics. As a critique of more "conventional" political theories, it challenges consensus-oriented and rationalistic versions of liberal and democratic thought from a radically democratic perspective' (Royer, 2019: 6).[5]

---

[4]   Compare here also the methodology of 'grounded normative theory' that intends to 'theorise with those who are in struggle' (Ackerly et al, 2021).

[5]   Royer is here drawing on Conolly, Tully, Honig, Mouffe and Wenman respectively.

An agonistic reading of Kratochwil's academic interventions reveals his notable disdain for scholars who shy away from 'messy details' (Kratochwil, 2018: 15). This applies especially to those self-proclaimed IR theorists who claim to advance ever more parsimonious theories or methodological approaches (or both) with every other paper they produce. Instead, he contends, the more veritable goal of doing theory does not consist in providing a better 'picture of the whole' based on a more compelling new theory or, low and behold, yet another novel methodological approach (Kratochwil, 2018: 15), but in engaging with the messy details instead. This regularly leads him to a starting point in the 'midst' in order to provide 'systemic reflection on the observations of various disciplines' (Kratochwil, 2018: 18; Kurowska, 2020). The meta-theoretical stance for that endeavour is that of 'thick' constructivism and its 'ontological assumptions concerning human action – or *praxis* to use the classical concept' (Kratochwil, 2018: 18–19). He likens his preferred 'mode of presentation' as coming 'closer to a painting in which the picture includes also elements which are not directly part of the central "theme"' (Kratochwil, 2018: 5).

The approach which often matches Tully's concern with digging out the cultural practices swept underneath the 'blanket of modernity' in order to recognize diversity (Tully, 1995) comes to the fore in Kratochwil's interventions in *Praxis*. As he notes,

> [n]ot surprisingly, calls for supplying a new 'picture of the whole' can be heard everywhere. There are the visions of a cosmopolitan order based on the reform of existing institutions, which have captured the imagination of some international bureaucrats, academics, and 'mission junkies' (public or private). Networks and global civil society also invent new projects for the political agenda. Finally, there are the attempts to capture our present predicament by means of the familiar grand narrative of realism concerning the 'rise and decline' of states, nations, civilizations, or whatever.
>
> I do not want to engage here these different speculations, which … often rely more on seductive but highly problematic metaphors of a telos promising emancipation and redemption, rather than on actual analysis. Instead, I want to call attention to another flaw in those interpretations, which is even more striking. Virtually all the 'visions' take for granted that the Western conceptual baggage is appropriate for providing orientation, even though it clearly prevents us from even seeing, or 'naming,' some of the fundamental ruptures or transformations that are occurring in front of our eyes. (Kratochwil, 2018: 15)

The remainder of this section turns to Kratochwil's engagements with other IR colleagues' theoretical writings.

Responsible academic intervention begins by detailing the research objective and identifying the purpose of this intervention, for example, as a means to counter injustice, inequality or 'ignorance' (Kratochwil, 2018). With *Praxis*, Kratochwil offers a prime example of how to operate in acknowledgement of the two principled positions. His central point about 'acting and knowing' (Kratochwil, 2018) represents an exemplary contribution to addressing 'academic intervention' as a critical long-term project insofar as it aims to bring knowledge to bear in order to counter ignorance, especially about the Western narrative which has dominated IR in the 20th century. Zooming in on Kratochwil's academic interventions facilitates a detailed understanding of how each of the practices addressed by *Praxis* (that is, constituting, changing, showing, guiding, sanctioning, punishing, remembering and forgetting, knowing and doubting, acting, as well as judging and communicating) offers a distinct focus on academic intervention by doing critical theory (Kratochwil, 2018: chapters 2–11). As observers and commentators have frequently noted, Kratochwil's academic interventions are marked by poignant intertextual interaction with (at times self-declared) IR theorists (Welsh, 2020).

Notably, these interventions also reveal that Kratochwil is not out to make an argument for more or better theory. Instead, *Praxis* represents a book-length treatise engaging with 'international studies' in order to identify 'transformative changes' in the larger context of world society. Kratochwil is less concerned with IR as a discipline. Instead, his interdisciplinary endeavour decidedly ignores the constraints posed by the often quite narrow, paradigmatically defined disciplinary boundaries of IR theory. Instead, Kratochwil argues, IR scholarship would benefit from a wider perspective on a larger scale. This involves 'redrawing the boundaries of the established disciplines', including comparative politics, international law, economics and political theory (Kratochwil, 2018: 7). As Kratochwil summarizes, for example,

> although our hopes in a comprehensive 'theory' of international relations have been disappointed, perhaps interdisciplinary research is able to provide a new map that would enable us to orient ourselves more successfully in this turbulent world. Thus we could perhaps be true to our conviction that all true knowledge has to be theoretical, while letting go – for the moment – of the idea of a general theory of international relations. (Kratochwil, 2018: 17)

In detail, with these intertextual academic interventions Kratochwil engages in the purposeful task of holding his realist learned colleagues to account. This is exemplified by addressing the effect of the textual academic interventions of others and thereby pointing out the lamentable consequences of 'writing' as 'doing'. For example, in *Praxis*, each chapter begins with an elaboration of how and on what grounds Kratochwil aims to engage with his learned sparring partners. He then proceeds with holding them to account against their own claims.

Through his very academic intervention, he then continues to frame his exploration into different dimensions of international studies. As an example of this practice, compare Kratochwil's presentation of a learned colleague's erroneous reference to Hume in 'Knowing and Doubting' (Kratochwil, 2018: chapter 9). Here, the colleague's claim is presented against the background of common standards of academic intervention that are quite widely shared in the epistemic community that is constituted by a certain type of IR scholarship. Kratochwil begins his intervention by reminding his readers that

> debates in IR frequently exhibit a certain artificiality. Precisely because they often lack the necessary philosophical background, IR scholars often use the writings of one of the founders of a school in their field as a 'proxy measure,' or they select one philosopher as their more or less unquestioned authority, so that his insights can now be 'applied' to the discipline. What then takes up most of the discussion is who in the discipline said what, and placing the different participants in the ever more finely subdivided spaces of a quadrant (actually drawn out in a table or implied). (Kratochwil, 2018: 350)

With this context established, in the subsequent paragraph he then offers an example of this kind of strategic presentation that he clearly views as manipulative framing. To do so, he summarizes the learned colleague's claim that is made 'in a recent book, which wants to "reclaim causal analysis" in IR' and whose author, in order to do that, 'identifies the "Humean syndrome" in a variety of writers in IR and claims that the dangers of this Humeanism can only be mastered if we return to a "causal ontology" and allow for "more holistic" (or more varied) explanatory accounts' (Kratochwil, 2018: 351).

Against this background, he then critically highlights some shortfalls, noting that

> since apparently rational choicers, as well as reflexivists of various stripes, have symptoms of this disease, only 'scientific realists' seem reliable as they have acquired the necessary immunity. The latter are basing their arguments largely on Roy Bhaskar's 'realist' philosophy of science – nobly suppressing the fact that their guru had left their camp long before his untimely death. Kurki's analysis then sits uneasily with her own analysis of Aristotle and the latter's notion of a variety of 'causes'. (Kratochwil, 2018: 351)

Following from this account of a learned colleague's claims, Kratochwil identifies the other's misleading effect on their readers, for which in the following his own academic intervention will hold the other to account: '[I]n constructing as a sparring partner a Humean "theory" that never was – picking and choosing bits and pieces from Hume's writings – distortion is rampant and develops its own dynamic, instead of providing a fuller and "more holistic account" of knowledge and human action' (Kratochwil, 2018: 351). Picking up from the intervention, Kratochwil then turns to laying out the parameters that will guide his own academic intervention in reply:

> I shall here use Hume as my guide in advocating a fuller (causal) account for the analysis of praxis without giving the material or efficient cause the pride of place. For this I use Humean texts as my basis, instead of relying on a specific interpretation of a follower (or critic). I do this because I believe that Hume provides the only well-articulated approach to the study of the social world and its historical character that does not fall victim to most of the errors which the ontological tradition brings along in its conceptual baggage. (Kratochwil, 2018: 352)

And so it goes.

Conclusion

As the illustrative agonistic reading in the previous section shows, Kratochwil's academic interventions are undertaken with an almost palpable urge – and often with gusto. The analysis follows Kratochwil's own sensitizing reading of the field to locate specific conflictive claims. Once these conflicts are located, he then zooms in on these thinking spaces to contest them by taking a different, usually philosophically more sophisticated, vantage point. And, finally, he zooms out beyond disciplinary boundaries to present novel questions to the social sciences, thereby effectively re-contextualizing specific issue- or problem-based research questions from the disciplinary context in IR to the more general scale of the social sciences.[6] Zooming in on Kratochwil's numerous academic interventions and probing them against Robert Cox's seminal claim that theory is 'always for someone and for some purpose' (Cox, 1981: 128) demonstrates the important contribution of principled academic interventions. They make a powerful point about the very purpose of academic research, namely, to advance enlightenment by 'putting the

---

[6] For the sequence of these methodological steps, compare Blumer (1954), Bueger (2014), Bueger and Gadinger (2015), Hofius (2016) and Wiener (2018).

record straight'. As Kratochwil has pointed out tirelessly, this does not translate into presenting 'facts' and 'simple solutions'. Instead, it requires thinking through and making sense as a dynamic process that involves reconnecting past trajectories with present questions. This project, then, developed from a clearly defined, principled starting point which led him to engage with what is 'underneath' the surface, recalling trajectories of thought, recovering philosophical thought and marking new thinking spaces. The effect of these interventions leads beyond this point, of course. For through his work, Kratochwil has progressively advanced novel ways of doing IR theory through contesting the claims of others.

This concluding paragraph returns to the three guiding questions raised in the introduction against the backdrop of Kratochwil's scholarship, especially his most recent book on praxis:

1. To what end and for what purpose do scholars engage in academic research (*motivation*)?

As noted in the introductory sections, to those who acknowledge the position of privilege and responsibility, the motivation for academic intervention includes a number of aims such as countering injustice or inequality. To Kratochwil this aim is mediated through engagement with the text of others in order to hold them to account, and then to move on from there by accounting for a world that is less universal, lean and value-free and more driven by the constructive force of the messy multiplicity that emerges and that is ultimately constitutive for offering novel options.

2. How do we identify our respective standpoint as researchers vis-à-vis the real world (coming *from somewhere*)?

As Kratochwil highlights in his 'observation' about the state of the art of critical theory after 25 years in IR, 'critical theory has always pointed out that the "view from nowhere" is impossible' (Kratochwil, 2007: 25). So where then do we go to begin from 'somewhere'? Kratochwil warns against the temptation to construct a 'tradition', as it is likely to become a lead story that carries undeclared conceptions, terms and categories, the origins of which are most likely lost in translation. Instead, he advocates an approach that engages right from 'the midst', beginning with observation. And, given the 'multiplicity' underlying both perceptions of the real world and constructions of theories, inevitably, research then must begin from observing observations. According to *Praxis*, the observations ought to begin from observing praxis as emerging from the middle and laying out the effects with regard to rethinking theories and understanding change in the wider world.

3. Do academics acknowledge their privilege of accumulating knowledge and recognize the social responsibility to use it (*academic intervention*)?

Engaging with this ethical question about the purpose and effect of theorizing, as a practice of academic intervention, is of central concern to Kratochwil. It is expressed most clearly in his dismantling of academic power games and the related structures that are reconstituted by the crude one-upmanship of battles over epistemological preferences. This final quote may summarize the point:

> Andrew Moravcsik, articulating the objection of many 'mainstreamers', that the main difference between, for example, constructivists and the adherents of mainstream approaches (counting at least some of their constructivists and exponents of critical theorising) is that the latter believe in testing while the others go about their business in a somewhat woolly-headed fashion, is getting the story precisely wrong. (Kratochwil, 2007: 30; quoting Moravcsik, 2003: 131)

Clearly, to Kratochwil, responsible academic intervention consists in contesting and scrutinizing the temptation of others to generalize in order to manifest 'the view from nowhere'. Therefore, he has taken on scholars who are either oblivious about the responsibility that comes with academic intervention or who fail (or refuse) to realize that their respective epistemological standpoints require foreclosing. As this chapter highlighted, research positions not only come from 'somewhere', they also always rest on a position of privilege and therefore, relatedly, of responsibility. As illustrated with reference to *Praxis*, this chapter argued that over the decades, Fritz Kratochwil's steadfast academic interventions have consistently shown that and how this privileged position of the few comes with a responsibility to generate, facilitate and communicate knowledge to the many.

Acknowledgements

For very helpful comments, I thank the participants at the 2019 Frankfurt Workshop on *Praxis*, Maren Hofius as commentator at the annual conference of the IR section of the German Political Science Association (DVPW) 2020, the editors, as well as Fritz Kratochwil. Thanks to research assistance at the University of Hamburg are in order for David Weiß, Deborah Kirchgässner, Paula Bäurich, Antonia Meiswinkel and Lars Feuerlein.

References

Abraham, Kevi Joseph and Yehonatan Abramson (2017) 'A pragmatist vocation for International Relations: the (global) public and its problems', *European Journal of International Relations* 23, 1, pp 26–48.

Acharya, Amitav (2014) 'Global International Relations (IR) and regional worlds: a new agenda for International Studies', *International Studies Quarterly* 58, 4, pp 647–59.

Acharya, Amitav (2016) 'Advancing global IR: challenges, contentions, and contributions', *International Studies Review* 18, 1, pp 4–15.

Acharya, Amitav (2018) *Constructing Global Order: Agency and Change in World Politics* (Cambridge: Cambridge University Press).

Acharya, Amitav and Barry Buzan (2019) *The Making of Global International Relations Origins and Evolution of IR at its Centenary* (Cambridge: Cambridge University Press).

Ackerly, Brooke and Jacqui True (2008) 'Reflexivity in practice: power and ethics in feminist research on International Relations', *International Studies Review* 10, 4, pp 693–707.

Ackerly, Brooke, Luis Cabrera, Fonna Forman, Genevieve Fuji Johnson, Chris Tenove and Antje Wiener (2021) 'Unearthing grounded normative theory: practices and commitments of empirical research in political theory', *Critical Review of Social and Political Philosophy* 24, 1, pp 1–27.

Austin, Jonathan Luke (2018) 'Post-critical theory – an introduction', Paper prepared for presentation at the Post-Critical IR Theory Workshop, Copenhagen.

Blumer, Herbert (1954) 'What is wrong with social theory?', *American Sociological Review* 19, 1, pp 3–10.

Bueger, Christian (2014) 'Pathways to practice: praxiography and international politics', *European Political Science Review* 6, 3, pp 383–406.

Bueger, Christian and Frank Gadinger (2015) 'The play of international practice', *International Studies Quarterly* 59, 3, pp 449–60.

Chakrabarty, Dipesh (2008) *Provincializing Europe: Postcolonial Thought and Historical Difference* (Princeton, NJ: Princeton University Press).

Connolly, William E. (1995) *The Ethos of Pluralization* (Minneapolis: University of Minnesota Press).

Cox, Robert W. (1981) 'Social forces, states and world orders: beyond International Relations theory', *Millennium* 10, 2, pp 126–55.

Farrell, Theo (2002) 'Constructivist security studies: portrait of a research program', *International Studies Review* 4, 1, pp 49–72.

Fierke, Karin M. (2007) 'Constructivism', in Tim Dunne, Milja Kurki and Steve Smith (eds), *International Relations Theories: Discipline and Diversity* (Oxford: Oxford University Press), pp 166–84.

Friedrichs, Jörg and Friedrich Kratochwil (2009) 'On acting and knowing: how pragmatism can advance International Relations research and methodology', *International Organization* 63, 4, pp 701–31.

Hansen-Magnusson, Hannes and Antje Vetterlein, eds (2021) *Handbook on Responsibility in World Politics* (London: Routledge).

Havercroft, Jonathan (2017) 'Perpetual struggle', *Polity* 49, 1, pp 100–8.

Haverland, Markus and Dvora Yanow (2012) 'A hitchhiker's guide to the public administration research universe: surviving conversations on methodologies and methods', *Public Administration Review* 72, 3, pp 401–8.

Hoffmann, Stanley (1977) 'An American social science: International Relations', *Deadalus* 106, 3, pp 41–60.

Hofius, Maren (2016) 'Community at the border or the boundaries of community? The case of EU field diplomats', *Review of International Studies* 42, 5, pp 939–67.

Hurrell, Andrew (2016) 'Beyond critique: how to study global IR', *International Studies Review* 18, 1, pp 149–51.

Jackson, Patrick Thaddeus (2008) *Social Science as a Vocation: Weber, Pragmatism, and Experiential Inquiry*, Theory Talks #44, available at: http://www.theory-talks.org/2011/11/theory-talk-44.html, accessed 13 January 2021.

Karmis, Dimitri and Jocelyn Maclure, eds (forthcoming) *Civic Freedom in an Age of Diversity: The Public Philosophy of James Tully* (Montreal: McGill-Queen's University Press).

Kratochwil, Friedrich (1984) 'The force of prescriptions', *International Organization* 38, 4, pp 685–708.

Kratochwil, Friedrich (1989) *Rules, Norms, and Decisions: On the Conditions of Practical and Legal Reasoning in International Relations and Domestic Affairs* (Cambridge: Cambridge University Press).

Kratochwil, Friedrich (2007) 'Looking back from somewhere: reflections on what remains "critical" in critical theory', *Review of International Studies* 33, 1, pp 25–46.

Kratochwil, Friedrich (2014) *The Status of Law in World Society: Meditations on the Role and Rule of Law* (Cambridge: Cambridge University Press).

Kratochwil, Friedrich (2018) *Praxis: On Acting and Knowing* (Cambridge: Cambridge University Press).

Kratochwil, Friedrich (2020) 'On engagement and distance in social analysis: a reply to my critics', Forum on Friedrich Kratochwil's *The Status of Law in Global Society*, *International Theory*, pp 1–15, available at: https://doi.org/10.1017/S1752971920000615, accessed 26 February 2021.

Kratochwil, Friedrich and John Gerard Ruggie (1986) 'International organization: a state of the art on an art of the state', *International Organization* 40, 4, pp 753–75.

Kurowska, Xymena (2020) 'Politics as *Realitätsprinzip* in the debate on constitutions and fragmented orders: remarks on meditation 3 "On constitutions and fragmented orders"', Forum on Friedrich Kratochwil's *The Status of Law in Global Society*, *International Theory*, pp 1–8, available at: https://doi.org/10.1017/S1752971920000573, accessed 26 February 2021.

Laden, Anthony Simon and David Owen (2007) *Multiculturalism and Political Theory* (Cambridge: Cambridge University Press).

Moravcsik, Andrew (2003) 'Theory synthesis in International Relations: real not metaphysical, in forum: are dialogue and synthesis possible in International Relations?' *International Studies Review* 5, pp 123–56.

Onuf, Nicholas Greenwood (1989) *World of Our Making: Rules and Rule in Social Theory and International Relations* (Columbia: University of South Carolina Press).

Owen, David (2019a) 'Refugees, EU citizenship and the Common European Asylum System: a normative dilemma for EU integration', *Ethical Theory and Moral Practice* 22, pp 347–69.

Owen, David (2019b) 'Migration, structural injustice and domination: on 'race', mobility and transnational positional difference', *Journal of Ethnic and Migration Studies* 46, 12, pp 2585–601.

Owen, David and Tracy B. Strong (2004) *Max Weber: The Vocation Lectures* (Indianapolis, IN and Cambridge: Hackett Publishing).

Owen, David and James Tully (2007) 'Redistribution and recognition: two approaches', in Anthony S. Laden and David Owen (eds), *Multiculturalism and Political Theory* (Cambridge: Cambridge University Press), pp 265–91.

Peltonen, Hannes and Knut Traisbach (2020) 'In the midst of theory *and* practice: a foreword', Forum on Friedrich Kratochwil's *The Status of Law in Global Society*, *International Theory*, pp. 1–2, available at: https://doi.org/10.1017/S1752971920000536, accessed 26 February 2021.

Royer, Christof (2019) 'Between constitutional order and agonistic freedom: toward an agonistic global constitutionalism', paper presented at Scholars Workshop: New Thinking in Global Constitutionalism, WZB Berlin Social Science Center, 6 July.

Spivak, Gayatri Chakravorty (1988) 'Can the subaltern speak?', in Cary Nelson and Lawrence Grossberg (eds), *Marxism and the Interpretation of Culture* (Urbana: University of Illinois Press), pp 271–313.

Tickner, J. Ann (2001) *Gendering World Politics: Issues and Approaches in the Post-Cold War Era* (New York: Columbia University Press).

Tickner, J. Ann (2016) 'Knowledge is power: challenging IR's Eurocentric narrative', *International Studies Review* 18, 1, pp 157–9.

Tully, James (1995) *Strange Multiplicity: Constitutionalism in an Age of Diversity* (Cambridge: Cambridge University Press).

Tully, James (2002) 'Political philosophy as a critical activity', *Political Theory* 30, 4, pp 533–55.

Tully, James (2008a) *Public Philosophy in a New Key: Volume 1, Democracy and Civic Freedom* (Cambridge: Cambridge University Press).

Tully, James (2008b) *Public Philosophy in a New Key: Volume 2, Imperialism and Civic Freedom* (Cambridge: Cambridge University Press).

Ulbert, Cornelia, Peter Finkenbusch, Elena Sondermann and Tobias Debiel, eds (2017) *Moral Agency and the Politics of Responsibility* (London: Routledge).

Wæver, Ole (1996) 'The rise and fall of the inter-paradigm debate', in Steve Smith, Ken Booth and Marysia Zalewski (eds), *International Theory: Positivism and Beyond* (Cambridge: Cambridge University Press), pp 149–85.

Wæver, Ole (1998) 'Explaining Europe by decoding discourses', in Anders Wivel (ed), *Explaining European Integration* (Copenhagen: Copenhagen Political Studies Press), pp 100–46.

Weber, Max (1919) *Politik als Beruf [Politics as a vocation]* (Berlin: Duncker and Humblot).

Welsh, Jennifer M. (2020) 'Unsettling times for human rights: remarks on meditation 7 "The politics of rights"', Forum on Friedrich Kratochwil's *The Status of Law in Global Society*, *International Theory*, pp. 1–7, available at: https://doi.org/10.1017/S1752971920000597, accessed 26 February 2021.

Wenman, Mark (2003) '"Agonistic pluralism" and three archetypal forms of politics', *Contemporary Political Theory* 2, pp 165–86.

Wenman, Mark (2013) *Agonistic Democracy: Constituent Power in the Era of Globalisation* (Cambridge: Cambridge University Press).

Wiener, Antje (2018) *Contestation and Constitution of Norms in Global International Relations* (Cambridge: Cambridge University Press).

Wilkens, Jan (2017) 'Postcolonialism in International Relations', in Renée Marlin-Bennett (ed), *Oxford Research Encyclopedia of International Studies* (Oxford: Oxford University Press).

Zalewski, Marysia (1996) 'All these theories yet the bodies keep piling up': theory, theorists, theorising', in Stephen Murray Smith, Ken Booth and Marysia Zalewski (eds), *International Theory: Positivism and Beyond* (Cambridge: Cambridge University Press), pp 340–53.

Zürn, Michael (1994) 'We can do much better! Aber muß es auf Amerikanisch sein? Zum Vergleich der Disziplin "Internationale Beziehungen" in den USA und in Deutschland', *Zeitschrift für Internationale Beziehungen* 1, 1, pp 91–114.

14

Between Science and Politics: Friedrich Kratochwil's Praxis of 'Going On'

Patrick Thaddeus Jackson

Introduction

Friedrich Kratochwil's first professional article – published in 1971, the year before I was born – was a conceptual exploration of the relationship between politics and political science. After canvassing a number of different attempts to define politics, he settles on an account that emphasizes the centrality of unsolvable problems to politics, and he relates that unsolvability to the 'incompatibility of value-orientations' between various parties (Kratochwil, 1971: 121). As a result, he suggests, the challenge of both politics and political science is to find a language in which 'specific critical problems', such as the nuclear arms race between the US and the USSR, can be defined and addressed (Kratochwil, 1971: 122). Assuming, or advocating, a complete homogenizing of values doesn't get us as far as efforts to define a situation in ways that make possible at least minimal amounts of cooperation. Here the *wissenschaftlich* study of politics, particularly of international politics, can make a contribution to clarifying the areas of common concern even for otherwise diametrically opposed actors and communities.

In the conclusion of his latest and most synoptic work – the *summa Kratochwilia*, so to speak – we find much the same concern on display. We who are 'not engaged in making practical politics, but who, as critical observers in the privileged position of academia, surely have something to say and to contribute to the understanding of praxis', Kratochwil notes, but we won't get far by imagining that we can exhaustively determine what political actors ought to be doing. Instead, we need a project of 'seeking to establish an order that allows us to "go on" in that mode of communication that is a "conversation"'. This is

> the precondition for common action ... without reviving a genuine political language and caring again about what comes into existence by a communication that focuses on forming an *inter-esse* – rather than engaging in interminable arguments about 'ultimate' values or human rights – the chances for a politics of freedom seem dim indeed. (Kratochwil, 2018: 475–6)

There is a remarkable continuity here, over almost 50 years of scholarship. The role of systematic scholarship is not, and for Kratochwil never has been, to develop ideal theory from which supposedly necessary consequences for political action could be derived. Instead, he has long been concerned to clarify the conditions of praxis: how we creatively and collectively make and remake the world through our meaningful dealings with one another. This orientation has always placed him outside the neo-positivist project of explaining by testing hypothetical correlations that dominates so much of US-centred anglophone 'International Relations' (IR); it also places him outside those projects in political philosophy which seek to develop general standards for evaluating arrangements and courses of action, whether on the domestic or on the international level. In both of those projects, the goal of the exercise is for scholars to *correct* or *improve* political practice, bringing supposedly superior general knowledge to bear in dictating to actors of various types how they *ought* to act.[1] Such a vision of scholarly activity has animated the American Political Science Association since its founding in 1903 (Ross, 1994: 181; Jackson, 2014: 274–6), and in this as in so many other areas, global anglophone 'IR' retains substantial traces of its historical organization as a subfield of the discipline of US Political Science.

That vision has never been Kratochwil's, however, and that raises an intriguing question: if we take his alternative account of practical knowing – praxis – seriously, what *is* the role for academics and for the scholarship that they produce? How *should* we academics be engaging political issues,[2] if we are not supposed to legislate solutions from our perch outside the

---

[1]   In this way, the *logical* generality of ideal theory meets the *empirical* generality of neo-positivist covering laws, and it does so in such a way that *both* forms of generality serve as a basis upon which 'experts' can make policy pronouncements. What sets these two forms of reasoning together is nothing conceptual – they are very different ways of knowing, after all – but a *practical* habit of citing something general as a basis for a specific recommendation. More on this later.

[2]   Throughout this chapter I will assume that my audience is composed, for the most part, of academics. If I were writing for practitioners outside the academy, I would almost certainly formulate my claims somewhat differently.

rough and tumble of partisan political contests? I think the implications of Kratochwil's position place him in the company of Max Weber and John Dewey when it comes to answering this question, although in a somewhat distinct or even deviant place from the usual and dominant understanding of both of these authors' work. With Dewey, Kratochwil would celebrate the role of academics and academic scholarship in forming new publics united by a concern with some pressing practical problem, but that role has to be understood not as political organizing so much as what we might call the *intellectual constitution* of a public. With Weber, Kratochwil would highlight the distinctiveness of scholarly input *into* politics from a place provisionally isolated *from* politics – the academy – and highlight the ways that such input is able to serve as a parametric basis for subsequent contestation rather than collapsing into just another partisan political position.

But Weber's identification of the contribution of *Wissenschaft* to the formation of a responsible politician was more or less exclusively confined to the scholarly identification of *causal* relationships from which likely consequences could be ascertained, and Kratochwil has been clear throughout his career that norms *do not function as causes* in the neo-positivist, efficient-causal sense (for example, and perhaps most famously, Kratochwil, 1984: 316–18; and Kratochwil and Ruggie, 1986: 767–8). It is therefore necessary to look to the *other* component of Weberian *Verantwortungspolitik* to see what academic scholarship in a broadly interpretive – that is to say, non-causal – mode could contribute to practical political life. After all, Weber's responsible politician is suspended between *two* imperatives: the likely consequences of their actions, and the ethical imperatives from which they derive their 'passion'. With Kratochwil, I want to suggest that there also is a distinctive scholarly role to be played in deriving and elaborating those ethical imperatives, not by miraculously finishing any of the inherently incomplete projects of ideal or nomothetic theorizing that continue to litter the academic landscape, but instead through a 'Wittgensteinian redescription of practical action' (Kratochwil, 2014: 266) that clarifies and sharpens our sense of the challenges involved in 'going on'. This kind of broadly interpretive scholarship intellectually constitutes the public to which the politician is then responsible.

In order to read Kratochwil on these points and draw out the distinctive aspects of his position, I will place him in dialogue with three interlocutors – not necessarily as direct sources of influence on Kratochwil, but as thinkers wrestling with some of the same issues as he does. I begin with Weber, as there is a fundamental similarity between Weber's diagnosis of the problem that arises when we look to contemplative, scholarly knowledge to resolve the problems of political contestation, and Kratochwil's scepticism about political expertise. Their solutions diverge insofar as Kratochwil's account of practical reason opens the possibility of something other than the 'clash of gods' that Weber sees as the inevitable outcome of differences in value commitments. I then place Kratochwil in conversation with Dewey, as the publicity of practical reason plays a similar role in their accounts – although Kratochwil is less sanguine about the possibilities of rational planning than Dewey was. Kratochwil's emphasis on ongoing *dilemmas* leads me finally to place him in dialogue with Andrew Abbott's 'fractal' approach to conceptual dichotomies, which re-centres the always unfinished character of social and political projects in a way that lets us understand how academic scholars in particular should stop lamenting the loss of ideal circumstances which we never had access to in the first place and focus instead on how to 'go on' under our actual circumstances.[3]

Responsible politicians

Political actors, Weber argues in his famous essay on the vocation for politics, should have a sense of responsibility, a feeling of 'being answerable to', as a core component of their vocation. Without this sense of responsibility, a politician is ineffectual, because their passion for some cause doesn't serve to animate and direct their actions, and their sense of measured proportion simply devolves into a calculating adaptation to and exploitation of existing realities. The cause that a politician serves gives political successes their meaning and purpose (Weber, 2004: 76) and connects the politician's efforts to something broader than their own enrichment. At the same time, the politician's sense of responsibility to their cause, whatever that cause is, allows them to endure the 'strong slow boring of hard boards, with a mixture of passion and proportion at the same time', which constitutes, for Weber, the truest vocation for politics (Weber, 2004: 88, translation modified).

Weber's greatest fear is that a politician will succumb to either pure passion or pure calculation and thus forgo their actual vocation in favour of either an 'ethics of conviction' or a vainglorious pursuit of power for its own sake rather than for its utility in achieving an end. The latter outcome is produced by losing a sense of responsibility to a cause. Absent a morally compelling purpose that undergirds an ethically desirable end, nothing remains but more or less efficient means of employing the coercive techniques of state

---

[3] My reading of Kratochwil's work is thus also in dialogue with Stefano Guzzini's (2010) reconstruction of Kratochwil's thought. Where Guzzini emphasizes Kratochwil's quest for coherence across the parallel domains of theory and methodology and how that quest places him outside of the anglophone mainstream, I emphasize Kratochwil's consistent exploration of a sense of the social world that differs from that on offer in most mainstream anglophone International Studies scholarship. This is ultimately a very subtle nuance, probably having more to do with the different perspectives of a European and an American reconstruction of a thinker who has spanned both worlds throughout his career.

rule for arbitrary and idiosyncratic goals. Perhaps chief among those goals is staying in office, so as to continue to benefit from whatever spoils one derives from occupying that position.[4] The former outcome – the 'ethics of conviction' – is generated when a politician ignores the tragic necessity of using the immoral means of state coercion to achieve *any* end, even the most praiseworthy:

> Can the ethical demands on politics really be indifferent to the fact that politics works with a specific means: power, behind which stands *violence*? Don't we see that the Bolshevist and Spartacist ideologues are achieving the *same* results as any militaristic dictator precisely because they are using this tool of politics? ... How are we to distinguish between the polemics of most of the representatives of the supposedly new ethics against their opponents, and those of any other demagogue? By their noble intentions! we are told. Good. But here we are talking about means, and the nobility of ultimate intentions is also claimed by their opponents with just as much sincerity. (Weber, 2004: 78)

Because of the necessity to use coercive force in political action, Weber argues, a responsible politician *cannot* follow an ethics of conviction in which the moral value of the ultimate end gives the politician licence to ignore the '(foreseeable) *results*' of their actions (Weber, 2004: 79) – because that road leads either to abandoning political action altogether because of its immoral means, or to justifying any and every action in terms of the purpose pursued. Either way, the specific responsibility of the politician both *to* their cause and *for* the consequences of their actions – the unity of passion and a sense of proportion – is sacrificed. Even though Weber also notes that it is 'authentically human and moving' when a responsible politician reaches a point where they adopt an ethics of conviction to say, after Martin Luther, 'here I stand, I can do no other' (Weber, 2004: 86), it is clear that, for Weber, this is an extreme limit to political action rather than its core.

It would thus appear that a Weberian politician needs to know two things in order to properly exercise their vocation. On the one hand, they need to be able to foresee the consequences of their actions – not perfectly, but in a way that allows a deliberate consideration of what particular courses of action might lead to. On the other hand, they need a grounding in some vision of the goal to be achieved, a morally compelling cause that

---

[4]   Any similarity between my characterization of the politician without a sense of responsibility and the theoretical assumptions of most rational choice accounts of political behaviour is entirely intentional.

can anchor their actions and give them meaning and purpose. Logically speaking, neither of those can be generated from within the sphere of politics, where the pursuit and exercise of coercive power is the continual means. Both consequential knowledge (that is, knowledge of cause and effect) and moral knowledge (that is, knowledge of right and wrong) have to serve as a check on the pursuit and exercise of coercive power, and as such they need to emanate from somewhere *beyond* politics. A politician who simply announced a moral purpose or produced their own forecast of outcomes would, and quite rightly, be quickly accused of inventing something that served their own interests rather than any ends towards which that purpose or forecast ostensibly pointed. The very *grammar* (in a Wittgensteinian sense) of such claims – claims about the ethical value of a course of action, and claims about the epistemic validity of a forecast – is that they are evaluable in terms of, or using standards other than, the question of whether they serve the political interests of one or another politician or political faction. This is how such claims can be compelling for 'us' rather than just for you or for me (Rescher, 1997: 14–16). To put this a little differently, they cannot be *political* claims, lest they lose any of their influence in politics.

In Weber's account, politicians get their forecasts from academics with a vocation for science.[5] Unlike people with a vocation for politics, people with a vocation for *Wissenschaft* abide not by the demands of acquiring and exercising power, but instead by a different set of commitments: 'Presupposed in every piece of scientific work is the validity of the rules of logic and method: the general foundations of our orientation in the world' (Weber, 1994: 13). This presupposition in turn gives rise to a distinct way of using words, with a quite different goal:

> [T]he taking of practical-political positions and the scientific analysis of political forms and party positions are two very different things. If you speak about democracy at a public meeting, you do not make a secret of your personal position; on the contrary, you have to take one side or the other explicitly, that is your damned duty and responsibility. In that context the words you use are not tools of scientific analysis, but political advertisements against the positions of others ... in short, weapons. (Weber, 2004: 14)

---

5   Note that the German word *Wissenschaft* is considerably broader than the English word 'science' and means something like systematic, scholarly inquiry. So 'a scholar with a vocation for science' would be somewhat redundant. I use the locution 'an academic with the vocation for science' because not everyone with an academic position displays the kind of vocation that Weber is talking about here; indeed, some are more political than others.

A scientific analysis does not yield a categorical pronouncement about what ought to be done in a given circumstance; that would be an instance of political speech. Instead, a scientific analysis yields a more modest elaboration of the consequences – both logical and causal – of the adoption of particular value commitments. This is both because scientific work cannot answer questions about ultimate value (the science of theology, Weber points out, is the rationalization of the feeling of being saved, and not a proof of salvation) and because the clarity that scientific analysis brings only demonstrates the necessity of choosing between irreconcilable values. In particular, instruction in scientific analysis can make one aware of the 'unavoidable means' that are required to bring about particular ends, even though those means may be morally questionable, thus posing the question: 'does the end "sanctify" the means or not?' (Weber, 2004: 19).[6]

Weber's analysis is therefore primarily an effort to limit the reach of scientific reason,[7] upholding and foregrounding the tragic necessity of choice between irreconcilable values at the core of political and social action. Kratochwil certainly shares this scepticism about the capacity of scientific reason to put an end to difficult choices, and he operates in a decidedly Weberian manner when using his analyses of law and language to puncture the pretensions of putatively universal norms and foundational moral imperatives. He warns of the 'open invitation for imperial projects' that a universalist crusade for a notion such as 'human rights' appears to issue, including the dangers of 'an "activist" judiciary – hardly rooted in a constitutional structure and a functioning political process – or by great powers, perhaps even by a coalition of the willing, who feel empowered by the universalist nature of their goals' to engage in all manner of authoritarian abuses (Kratochwil, 2013: 18–19). And he is particularly sceptical of 'the reformist bent animating much of legal scholarship', which, under contemporary conditions, leads to a situation in which 'anything deemed desirable becomes a "right," without much concern for specifying the corresponding duty holders' (Kratochwil, 2014: 115). A political project of limiting state authority thus arms itself with scholarly claims and portrays itself as a *release* from difficult choices in a way that Weber too would seek to analytically puncture.

---

6   Several English translations of this sentence overlook Weber's deliberate use of the word *heiligt* and the academic scare quotes with which he surrounds it and thus render this as a question about whether the ends *justify* the means. The religious resonance (even if it is a resonance that has been somewhat 'de-sacralized' in everyday German, as Stefano Guzzini pointed out to me) seems to me to be much more important than any connection to a superficial Machiavellianism.

7   I have discussed the very deliberately neo-Kantian aspects of this project in Jackson (2017b).

But Kratochwil's strategy for such a critique of illusion differs from Weber's. Weber focuses on the necessary use of the immoral means of state coercion in order to achieve even moral ends; Kratochwil instead focuses on the logical impossibility of foundational moral claims putting an end to difficult political decisions in the first place:

> '[H]umanity' is an … ambiguous symbol as it usually does not stand for 'all people' existing, but for a specific way of life … It is through politics that we not only decide which goods are 'public,' that is are goods 'for' a public, but also determine who is entitled to enjoy them and who is left outside … Here questions of membership and of making binding and effective decisions arise. Law then becomes the sediment of such decisions and a powerful instrument of rule. (Kratochwil, 2014: 188)

For that reason, the invocation of putatively foundational moral principles (such as 'human rights') is *never* a universal imperative but *always* a particular usage that derives its operative meaning from the locally specific 'sediment of [prior] decisions'. Difficult choices remain and leave their traces even in our efforts to resolve them by appealing to some 'higher' values.

Part of the difference between Weber and Kratochwil on this point is due to the fact that Weber doesn't think that systematic, scientific scholarship does anything but work out the consequences of value commitments, and although those consequences can be both logical and causal, the consequences Weber thinks are most relevant to a responsible politician are the *causal* consequences. Jurisprudence, Weber suggests, can only tell us that 'if one wants to achieve a certain result, then according to the norms of our legal thinking this legal rule is the appropriate means of achieving it' (Weber, 1994: 14). But that, in turn, is only binding on someone for whom upholding the rule of law is a paramount value, especially when confronted with undesirable consequences of adhering to the law; the status of legality has no special value for the responsible politician but is one among many other considerations that have to be assessed in terms of their practical consequences. Knowing whether something is legal is far less important to the Weberian politician than knowing what *effects* might arise from pursuing a legal course of action – or, for that matter, knowing what effects might arise from pursuing an illegal course of action.

This is compounded by Weber's strict insistence on locating ethical imperatives in religious systems of morality, and in particular in Christian admonitions about refraining from the use of violence. Weber's key example of an ethical imperative in both of his vocation lectures is the Sermon on the Mount,[8] a key piece of Christian ethical teaching which, among other

---

8   Chapters 5–7 in the Gospel of Matthew, one of the four canonical Christian gospels.

things, specifically praises 'peacemakers' and admonishes listeners to love their enemies and pray for them, and to 'turn the other cheek' when struck rather than offering resistance. Weber declares that this is an 'undignified' ethic viewed from the worldly perspective, because not resisting evil may well make one complicit in its victory (Weber, 1994: 17). But even more strikingly, it runs directly against the organization of the contemporary sovereign territorial state, which rests on a claimed monopoly of the legitimate use of physical force within a particular territory, *unlike other forms of rule*. This last qualification is significant, because it localizes, so to speak, the tension between the Christian ethical imperative not to use force and the irreducible linkage between politics and coercive force. What makes Weber's diagnosis so powerful is precisely that it is located, empirically and historically, within a *particular* tradition of political and ethical thought and practice, and Weber's responsible politician is a *particular* solution to problems arising in that tradition. If the organization of politics were different, or if ethics were different – say, if politics didn't involve coercive force, or if our moral cosmology didn't praise peace and condemn violence – then the tension Weber argues is always at the heart of a responsible politics would simply evaporate.

Similarly, if there were sources of ethical imperatives that were not so closely linked to religious moral cosmologies, scholarship on values might not be so strictly limited to elaborating the logical consequences of commitments based in faith. This possibility is key to Kratochwil's solution to the Weberian 'clash of gods', Weber's evocative terminology for the conflict of irreconcilable value commitments. Kratochwil recognizes, in a way that Weber does not, that 'after all, we *do* debate value questions and the reason is not accidental' (Kratochwil, 1995: 34). Weber would regard such debates as unresolvable conflicts and highlight the limitations of reason when it comes to trying to resolve them; he is scornful of such efforts, comparing them to the exercise of trying to 'scientifically' demonstrate the superiority of German or French culture (Weber, 2004: 23). But while Kratochwil agrees that our debates about values don't have any hidden telos that would deliver us from the realm of political contestation – we never arrive at a utopian kingdom of ends in which all speech situations are ideal and all rational beings join in consensus about the highest good – that does not make our debates nothing but a war of words. Instead, our debates are ways of figuring out how to live with one another, drawing on what we might call – borrowing terminology from John Shotter (1993: 170–2) – the rhetorical resources of the 'living tradition' in which we find ourselves. Scholarly reflection, far from providing universal moral solutions to political questions, elucidates the ambiguities and dilemmas characteristic of our tradition and can thus perform a role in politics that Weber doesn't specifically envision: making plain to the politician the necessity of choosing not merely between ethical imperatives and causal consequences, but between *different moral accounts* and their correspondingly diverse ethical framings.

In other words, Kratochwil understands the political situation as being even more complex than Weber argues that it is: not just a tension between *one* set of value commitments and the *one* unavoidable necessity of coercive force, but between *many* value commitments and courses of action. Here it matters a great deal, I think, that Kratochwil is interested first and foremost in *international* affairs, and in international law in particular. The challenge of the coexistence of diverse and distinct ways of morally ordering the world poses itself in such a context in ways that, perhaps, might be overlooked from an elite position within a single sovereign territorial state sitting near the top of a global hierarchy, which is the position from which Weber inevitably wrote and spoke.[9] Indeed, the problem of the coexistence of different moral cosmologies, so to speak, is provisionally resolved by the principle of sovereignty, which displaces such differences to a place outside the state's boundaries and makes possible the homogenization of the realm inside those boundaries (Walker, 1993; Inayatullah and Blaney, 2004). *In practice*, Weber can assume that the members of the domestic public to whom he is speaking share, more or less, a consistent set of (Christian) value commitments with respect to the use of force. There is no special challenge involved in their coexistence as a community because they are presumptively already coexisting. The plurality of value commitments poses a *logical* problem for Weber, making unavailable a purely rational solution to the tension between the values held by the political community and the necessary coercion utilized by efforts to rule that community.

But as Kratochwil points out, 'the ambiguity of whether international law was to allow for the coexistence of vastly different systems with different political projects, or whether it represented a missionary endeavour for a specific way of life, has always been part of the tradition of international law' (Kratochwil, 2014: 166), and as such this question of living with moral plurality has always been internal to the study of international affairs. Weber is concerned to prevent crusades, and to reign in naked ambition; his point about the plurality of the highest values is that reason alone cannot adjudicate between them. Kratochwil agrees that reason alone cannot provide the solution, but he is by contrast concerned with figuring out how we can 'go on' together, *despite* the lack of a value consensus based in pure reason. His position is therefore productive, or better, *reconstructive* (Dewey, 1978; Friedrichs and Kratochwil, 2009), where Weber's stance is decidedly negative.

---

[9] This is, of course, situated within the very intellectual tradition that gave birth to the realpolitik/realist tradition in anglophone International Studies (Shilliam, 2007; Jackson, 2014).

Constituting the public

In this way, Kratochwil's position comes close to that of John Dewey. For Dewey, political activity is about coordinating and organizing rather than commanding and coercing. The challenges of politics are 'a practical problem of human beings living in association with one another' (Dewey, 1985b: 255), and Dewey's emphasis is on the nature of those problems rather than on the character of the officials who play a role in solving those problems. The public, for Dewey, 'consists of all those who are affected by the indirect consequences of transactions to such an extent that it is deemed necessary to have those consequences systematically cared for' (Dewey, 1985b: 245). Those indirect consequences – where, for example, a commercial exchange between you and me, say when I hire you to build a fence to keep my cattle from wandering off, prevents other people from bringing *their* cattle to the water source now enclosed with a fence – are what call for regulation, by producing a public composed of people who are being affected by something they had no part in bringing about. Precisely *how* that problem is to be solved is less important to Dewey than recalling *that* the problem is what called for regulation and government in the first place:

> Means of transit and communication affect not only those who utilize them but all who are dependent in any way upon what is transported, whether as producers or consumers. The increase of easy and rapid intercommunication means that production takes place more and more for distant markets and it puts a premium upon mass-production. Thus it becomes a disputed question whether railroads as well as highways should not be administered by public officials, and in any case some measure of official regulation is instituted, as they become settled bases of social life. (Dewey, 1985b: 273)

Indeed, Dewey suggests that solutions to problems like this – whether railroads and roads need public officials to administer them, given the indirect effects of actions such as building a road or laying railroad tracks – can only be ascertained in practice, experimentally, through 'continuous inquiry, continuous in the sense of being connected as well as persistent', which 'can provide the material of enduring opinion about public matters' (Dewey, 1985b: 346). There is no *ex ante* solution to an actual problem, and no way to decide in advance of practical engagement in the situation whether publicly administering roads is better than letting private owners do so.

There is, however, little or no coercion in Dewey's account of political life. This is likely due to Dewey's understanding of a public as something that comes into being more or less automatically because of indirect consequences: a public exists whenever such consequences exist. The problem, though, which even Dewey recognizes, is that the factual *existence* of a public – which, in virtue of the common problem faced by all its members, has an interest in solving that problem – isn't always enough to actually activate that public in a politically relevant way.

> Indirect, extensive, enduring and serious consequences of conjoint and interacting behavior call a public into existence having a common interest in controlling these consequences. But the machine age has so enormously expanded, multiplied, intensified and complicated the scope of the indirect consequences, has formed such immense and consolidated unions in action, on an impersonal rather than a community basis, that the resultant public cannot identify and distinguish itself. And this discovery is obviously an antecedent condition of any effective organization on its part. (Dewey, 1985b: 314)

It is therefore possible to *know* that a public exists even if that public *does not know itself to be a public*. This, in turn, sets up what Dewey calls the 'prime difficulty ... of discovering the means by which a scattered, mobile and manifold public may so recognize itself as to define and express its interests' (Dewey, 1985b: 327). By Dewey's own logic, this cannot be a means that comes into being by the same channels as a public does. A public, for Dewey, is a constellation of people united by the set of effects that they have in common, whether they realize it or not; the common interest that they have is in regulating those effects, not in constituting themselves as a public. Despite some trenchant observations about the role of communication in producing a community (Dewey, 1985b: 329–31), there is a gap between the existence of a public and the constitution of that public.

The bridging of that gap involves the active production of a public by demonstrating to the relevant people that they *do in fact constitute a public*. Dewey has great confidence in the capacity of artists to do this – '[a]rtists have always been the real purveyors of news, for it is not the outward happening in itself which is new, but the kindling by it of emotion, perception and appreciation' (Dewey, 1985b: 350). However, especially given the technical complexity of life in industrialized societies, there would seem to be a role for other kinds of detached observers too: observers who could trace out the complex consequences of various configurations and arrangements of action and thus generate awareness of a need to regulate and coordinate them. Clearly such observations would need a standard of validity that could not be reduced to solving a problem that *the observers* were facing and trying to solve; otherwise, publics would be produced as a by-product of other processes and as a solution to other problems, and not because the members of that public themselves were facing problems. Dewey's answer to this conundrum presumes that people are engaged in 'continuous inquiry' (Dewey, 1985b: 346) so that they will recognize valid arguments about indirect consequences when they hear them, but even he admits that '[i]nquiry, indeed, is a work which devolves upon experts' (Dewey, 1985b: 365) and not on every person equally.

This opens a role for scholars that is quite distinct from Weber's notion that the principal contribution of systematic scholarship is to force political actors to confront the consequences of their commitments and their actions. Instead, scholars and scholarship can articulate the basis on which a public – a number of affected people sharing an interest in governing the phenomenon affecting them – can coalesce and put pressure on the formally political actors (office holders and other public officials) to act. In this role, the scholar's influence on the politician is indirect rather than direct; the point is not to urge *the politician* to see the gap between value commitments and coercive means, but rather to urge *other people* to recognize themselves as sharing an interest, so that they can urge the politician to enact appropriate policies. By virtue of their position outside the rough and tumble of practical politics, and because they are deeply immersed in research on their topic, scholars can diagnose complex problems and propose solutions which may elude the grasp of people going about their everyday lives, and they can do so on a *non-partisan* basis: from outside politics narrowly understood, just as in Weber.[10] What changes here is mainly the audience, since Weber limits the scholar's public role more or less to the university classroom, whereas Dewey envisions a more expansive engagement.

Dewey and Weber also remain close together on the question of the *kind* of knowledge that a scholar can and should impart: consequential knowledge of cause and effect. What the scholar brings to the public, in Dewey's account, is an analysis of what is producing the difficulties and problems experienced by members of that public, and a recommendation for addressing those difficulties and resolving those problems. In accord with his broader pragmatist stance, Dewey doesn't really maintain a separate moral or ethical register; ethical claims and moral values in his approach are candidates for experimental inquiry in the same way that other claims are and should be evaluated based on their widespread practical effects.[11] The result is that Dewey's politicians don't have the same kind of tension-filled existence as Weber's do, because there is no overarching challenge of standing between irreconcilable opposites. Instead, there is a lack of proper rational

---

[10] Dewey would likely agree with Weber that the first duty of a scholar is to 'serve only the thing' and to be focused first and foremost on the topic of their research (Weber, 1994: 7).

[11] Space does not permit a fuller exploration of the complexity of Dewey's approach to ethics, which while taking consequences seriously, remains somewhat distinct from a narrow consequentialism. For a detailed examination of ethical issues in pragmatism generally, see Cochran (1999).

planning, which indicates, in Dewey's dated but very revealing formulation, a certain lack of civilized progress: 'A savage finds his way skillfully through a wilderness by reading certain obscure indications; civilized man builds a highway that shows the road to all' (Dewey, 1985a: 126). The value of rational planning is never really questioned in Dewey's work, and because Dewey's notion of politics is less necessarily coercive than Weber's is, the developmental telos here is towards an ever increasing control of causal forces, towards ever increasing 'civilization'.

Perhaps with the benefit of hindsight, Kratochwil is more sceptical of rational progress than Dewey is, although he largely agrees with Dewey that politics *can* be something other than merely a set of tragic choices. Kratochwil points out that increasing regulation, especially regulation that does not come courtesy of a formal political process with oversight and accountability, can in fact disempower people, who then are increasingly '"subjected" to virtual laws made in virtual spaces' and who have a tendency to retreat from 'a serious engagement with public issues' in favour of 'spend[ing] their time with like-minded people' and celebrating their shared private – but not public – interests (Kratochwil, 2014: 198). In that way, an overarching emphasis on the consequences of regulation, as is the case in the rapid promulgation of standards and conventions by firms and other private entities (someone has to decide this pressing issue, and we can move faster than the state authorities can!) might result in our losing sight of the value commitments that supposedly anchored the whole process. Kratochwil diagnoses the state of our present politics as resulting not from a lack of rationality but from a lack of *authority*, in the classic sense of a moral purpose in terms of which political activity might make sense and be legitimated: a common good, a *res publica*. If anything, we suffer from *too much* instrumental rationality, not too little.

Kratochwil's account of law makes this point extremely clearly. Because we often labour under the spell of ideal theory, he points out, we presume that law is supposed to be a direct elaboration of some set of universal principles, for example 'justice' or 'human rights'. This overlooks the actual, practical *function* of law, which is 'to settle certain issues so that we can go on and not be constantly burdened with showing why the application of a certain rule ... "truly" serve[s] the common good and [is] compatible with morality in general' (Kratochwil, 2014: 259). At the same time, such provisional settling is, or should be, something other than an arbitrary imposition:

[T]he discussion of 'rights' is always only part of the story, as the complex interaction of facts and norms, and not only of the structure of norms (rules vs. principles, conflict among rules and so forth) is at issue. To that extent the decisions to bring different norms into play involve judgments and appraisals that remain contestable. But this does not mean that such decisions are 'arbitrary,' that is unconstrained, although the 'right answer' thesis cannot be maintained either. (Kratochwil, 2014: 236)

To determine the legality of some course of action is not a simple deduction from either facts or principles but is instead a creative act in which 'authoritative sources and materials' are handed down 'for the resolution of the problems at hand'. As such, 'traditions are not simply "there" as is suggested by the large collection of "data" … They record *actions* rather than mere events, and they are "made" in the sense that they are "recollected" or remembered rather than just found' (Kratochwil, 2014: 69). Working within a tradition means bringing the historical inheritance of that tradition to bear on contemporary challenges, a process which involves grasping and reconstructing that inheritance in order to make it relevant – and, in so doing, shaping that inheritance itself. The stability of meaning, even legal meaning, 'must be maintained from context to context and preserved over time through the repetitive agency of speakers … through repeated use' (Medina, 2004: 355), making it something other than a more or less automatic adjustment to the technical requirements of the problem to be solved. Indeed, the problem situation *itself* is clarified and defined as people work on it (Dewey, 1985a: 205–6), and that process of definition and clarification always involves a subtle interplay of the stock of existing conceptual material that people hand down to themselves in making sense of the problem in the first place, and the consequences of doing so: a process of *situated creativity* (Joas, 1997; Jackson, 2009).

As such, Kratochwil's analysis of law highlights a second role for scholars, beyond the provision of causal explanations which might give politicians recipes for producing their preferred outcomes, and which might also make those politicians confront what they have to do in order to achieve those outcomes.[12] Kratochwil's reminder that 'law is not only a coordination device, regulating the interactions among "rational" self-interested actors, but also a vehicle of sense-making whose constitutive function is deeply embedded in our historical experiences and our political imagination' (Kratochwil, 2013: 13) is an implicit critique of the Deweyian emphasis on an ever increasing anticipatory control of consequences as the sole standard of desirable political action. Instead, the work of law – and the work of those engaging with making and interpreting the law, which is to say, *all of us* in law-governed societies, albeit in different ways depending on our social positions and roles – is an active process of discerning how we should 'go on' appropriately. The community aspect is paramount here, because 'the

---

[12] I elaborate the 'recipe' character of causal explanation in Jackson (2017a).

"view from nowhere" – God's view, in modernity recast as an epistemological ideal – remains unavailable to us', and always will be (Kratochwil, 2014: 204). The identification of value commitments cannot happen through the elaboration of universal standards, *even if the language deployed is without reference to any particular community*. Such putatively universal appeals always implicitly reference a community – a public, in the Deweyian sense – and its traditions of sense-making in practice, and derive their authority from that community's tacitly shared moral principles and ethical values.[13] Legal disputes are therefore a way that 'we', as a community, provisionally work out disagreements about values.

Scholars in this context can play one of two roles. They can wade into the fray, bringing their supposedly superior grasp of the moral issues involved to bear in defence of one or another side of a dispute. This kind of alliance between 'experts' in the law and 'enthusiasts' seeking to advance their cause produces, Kratochwil observes, the conditions for a 'professionalized' governance practice 'focusing on "policy" rather than representation, applying efficiency and "best practices" criteria rather than focusing on issues of positioning' in the name of 'a less ideological approach to problem-solving' (Kratochwil, 2014: 119). Alternatively, scholars can present themselves not as experts, but as contemplative thinkers, elaborating the issues involved and the values implicated in different possible solutions to a problem (and indeed, in different definitions of a problem). Explicating values also means shoring up a community, helping people realize that they *should* care about some issue and *should* work to address it, simply because 'our' values call for such a course of action. In so doing, scholars provide not a set of imperative instructions for action, but a voice in an ongoing dialogue – a dialogue that cannot be resolved in purely rational terms, but which will inevitably be resolved *in practice*, by the community.

The scholarly vocation

But it does not follow that scholars should abandon the academy and commit themselves to 'actively organize the public through a shared method of critical inquiry' (Abraham and Abramson, 2017: 40). As Kratochwil points out, the first duty of scholars is 'to play devil's advocate' and stick to the 'duties of an epistemic community' (Kratochwil, 2018: 426). In practice,

---

[13] There is a strong parallel here to Emanuel Adler's (2019) most recent articulation of cognitive evolution as a process whereby a community of practice selectively retains distinct ways of doing things over time, including ways of valuing actions and outcomes, and thus (re)produces itself as a particular community. Even putatively universal values, Adler points out, have to be selectively retained by a particular community in order to be effective.

Figure 14.1: The fractal diagram

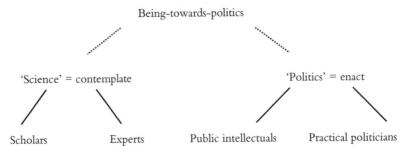

this means that the scholarly contribution to the constitution of a public is at best an *indirect* contribution, providing the intellectual resources on which proximate producers of an actually existing and actually aware public can draw in organizing people. In so doing, these organizers act not purely as politicians, but as *public intellectuals*, in a very specific sense of that term. What anchors their public intellectual role is the work of scholars proper, whose vocation is to think things through and to help others to do the same – especially in the rarefied, provisionally separated out atmosphere of the classroom. To be a scholar aware of their public role is a different thing from being a public intellectual.

I find it helpful to think these issues through with the help of a device that I borrow from Andrew Abbott (2001): the fractal diagram.[14]

Abbott's key insight is that, in practice, dichotomous distinctions display a tendency to 'fractalize' and replicate themselves at different levels of resolution, and the resulting positions are 'indexical' and related to a local context, rather than acting as timeless conceptual categories. The Weberian distinction between *Wissenschaft* and *Politik* is presented as, in essence, a binary distinction between the vocation to contemplate politics to try to understand it, and the vocation to enact programmes through political action. But if we look more closely, we see that the same distinction then fractally recurs *within* each camp, producing the four ideal-typical positions pictured in Figure 14.1. At the far left we find the pure(st) contemplators, concerned almost exclusively with scientific validity; at the far right, we find the pure(st) enactors, the politicians that Weber worried would succumb to an 'ethics of conviction' or a naked grab for power for its own sake. *Between* these two poles we find the scientist who is concerned to deliver instructional messages to the wider world (the expert) and the

---

[14] This specific diagram is not one that Abbott himself offers, but one that I have produced through an application of his insights about dichotomous distinctions in practice.

politician who seeks to theorize their experience 'from within' and urge action on that basis (the public intellectual). While the expert seeks to simply demonstrate an optimal solution, the public intellectual calls a public into being by practically articulating the common threads that tie its prospective members together.[15] The content of specific claims varies depending on the relative positions of the speaker and the audience; words spoken by a scholar and an expert might carry different weight, and a politician's use of the same words might not come with the same commitment to epistemic validity. The diagram gives us an ideal-typical instrument for making sense of concrete speech acts, a kind of provisional classification that elucidates the intention (in the sense of Anscombe, 1963) of acting from different positions.[16]

These fractal distinctions shed some additional light on the question of how scholars ought to relate to practitioners. If we follow Kratochwil in abandoning the project of ideal theory, it follows that the 'expert' position is not one that we can occupy when it comes to issues involving moral values. We *can* occupy that position as long as we confine ourselves to advancing causal arguments about the likely consequences of different courses of action, because then we are resting on the epistemic authority of our specialized research to compel practical politicians to acknowledge necessary tensions between their means and their ends – precisely the role that Weber envisioned for scientists with respect to politics. In fact, because the 'experts' and the 'practical politicians' are, so to speak, the 'local enactors' of their respective branches of the fractal tree, they share a positional similarity that we can see on display in the calls from practitioners to scholars for relevant solutions to their immediate problems, and in the persistent efforts to 'bridge the gap' (George, 1993) between scholarly experts and practitioners by working on issues of vocabulary and communication. Here the presumption is that the experts and the politicians are working with a fundamental similarity of aims. As we have seen, neither Weber nor Kratochwil considers the matter to be so simple.

---

[15] Note that the distinctions here are distinctions between *positions*, and not between actually existing concrete *persons*. A single person might, at different times in their career, occupy different positions on the fractal tree. Not all experts have to start off as scientists, nor do all public intellectuals have to come biographically from the political arena. My point here is to elucidate the consequences of occupying a particular position; my analysis is ideal-typical, and not empirical-historical.

[16] In this way, the fractal diagram itself is the kind of thing that would almost certainly only be produced by a scholar. It is a provisional freezing of a set of ongoing relations of location and distinction so as to produce an ideal-typical mapping of different ways that one might comport oneself towards politics. Concretely, actually, these categories are never as fixed and stable as the diagram might make them appear.

But the more important thrust of Kratochwil's thinking, as I have argued throughout this chapter, is the identification of an alternate, *interpretive* – and thus non-causal – pathway for scholars and scholarship. Just because ethical imperatives emanating from a moral cosmology present themselves as universal or categorical instructions does not mean that we scholars can have nothing rationally to say about them, although we should never delude ourselves into thinking that we can produce purely rational solutions to conflicts of value. Instead, there is an important role for scholars to play in creatively deploying the inherited cultural materials of a community in such a way that they become and remain relevant for present predicaments. In that way, scholars can help a community think through what it *ought* to do and thus produce an authoritative baseline for subsequent action. A Deweyian public is then produced not merely by the identification of a shared interest in addressing some common effect, but by the development and circulation of an ethically compelling account of a problem and thereby an active constitution of the public that *should* work to address and solve it.

But we scholars cannot occupy the public intellectual position outright without, to some extent, abandoning our base in the academy. Indeed, the public intellectual *needs* the scholar, precisely because the relative detachment of the academic form of life underpins the possibility of abstracting from particular experiences in order to create knowledge claims that can travel beyond their original contexts: 'abstraction is liberation', as Dewey (1978: 166) once pointed out. This goes equally for causal *and* interpretive claims. The expert, armed with abstract causal claims worked into concrete causal explanations, can speak more or less directly to the practical politician; abstraction provides them with the basis on which to make specific recommendations. By contrast, the scholar provides the conceptual material which the public intellectual uses to enframe and understand their practical situation, and the situation of the community of which they are a part. Solving the problem is not the point of such scholarship; *defining* the problem and *envisioning* the relevant community while *refreshing* or *updating* its values is the point. And reminding us of *that* possibility is, I think, Kratochwil's most important contribution to the study of praxis.

Acknowledgements

Thanks to Gunther Hellmann and Jens Steffek for helpful feedback on an earlier, much draftier, draft. Thanks to Ian Reynolds, Stefano Guzzini and Eva Johais for comments and feedback on a much more complete draft.

References

Abbott, Andrew (2001) *Chaos of Disciplines* (Chicago, IL: University of Chicago Press).

Abraham, Kavi Joseph, and Yoni Abramson (2017) 'A pragmatist vocation for International Relations: the (global) public and its problems', *European Journal of International Relations* 23, 1, pp 26–48.

Adler, Emanuel (2019) *World Ordering: A Social Theory of Cognitive Evolution* (Cambridge: Cambridge University Press).

Anscombe, Elizabeth (1963) *Intention* (Cambridge, MA: Harvard University Press).

Cochran, Molly (1999) *Normative Theory in International Relations: A Pragmatic Approach* (Cambridge: Cambridge University Press).

Dewey, John (1978 [1920]) *Reconstruction in Philosophy (The Middle Works of John Dewey, 1899–1924, volume 12, 1920)* (Carbondale and Edwardsville: Southern Illinois University Press).

Dewey, John (1985a [1933]) *How We Think, revised edition (The Later Works of John Dewey, 1925–1953, volume 8, 1933)* (Carbondale and Edwardsville: Southern Illinois University Press).

Dewey, John (1985b [1927]) *The Public and Its Problems (The Later Works of John Dewey, 1925–1953, volume 2, 1925–1927)* (Carbondale and Edwardsville: Southern Illinois University Press).

Friedrichs, Jörg, and Friedrich Kratochwil (2009) 'On acting and knowing: how pragmatism can advance International Relations research and methodology', *International Organization* 63, 4, pp 701–31.

George, Alexander (1993) *Bridging the Gap: Theory and Practice in Foreign Policy* (Washington, DC: United States Institute of Peace Press).

Guzzini, Stefano (2010) 'Imposing coherence: the central role of practice in Friedrich Kratochwil's theorising of politics, international relations and science', *Journal of International Relations and Development* 13, 3, pp 301–22.

Inayatullah, Naeem and David Blaney (2004) *International Relations and the Problem of Difference* (London: Routledge).

Jackson, Patrick Thaddeus (2009) 'Situated creativity, or, the cash value of a pragmatist wager for IR', *International Studies Review* 11, 3, pp 656–9.

Jackson, Patrick Thaddeus (2014) 'Rationalizing realpolitik: US International Relations as a liberal field', in Neil Gross and Solon Simmons (eds), *Professors and Their Politics* (Baltimore, MD: Johns Hopkins University Press), pp 267–90.

Jackson, Patrick Thaddeus (2017a) 'Causal claims and causal explanation in international studies', *Journal of International Relations and Development* 20, pp 689–716.

Jackson, Patrick Thaddeus (2017b) 'The production of facts: ideal-typification and the preservation of politics', in Richard Ned Lebow (ed), *Max Weber and International Relations* (Cambridge: Cambridge University Press), pp 79–96.

Joas, Hans (1997) *The Creativity of Action* (Chicago, IL: University Of Chicago Press).

Kratochwil, Friedrich (1971) 'Politik und Politische Wissenschaften: Ein Diskussionsbeitrag zum Begriff des Politischen', *Zeitschrift für Politik* 18, 2, pp 113–23.

Kratochwil, Friedrich (1984) 'Errors have their advantage', *International Organization* 38, 2, pp 305–20.

Kratochwil, Friedrich (1995) 'Why Sisyphus is happy: reflections on the "third debate" and on theorizing as a vocation', *The Sejong Review* 3, 1, pp 3–36.

Kratochwil, Friedrich (2013) 'Politics, law, and the sacred: a conceptual analysis', *Journal of International Relations and Development* 16, 1, pp 1–24.

Kratochwil, Friedrich (2014) *The Status of Law in World Society: Meditations on the Role and Rule of Law* (Cambridge: Cambridge University Press).

Kratochwil, Friedrich (2018) *Praxis: On Acting and Knowing* (Cambridge: Cambridge University Press).

Kratochwil, Friedrich and John G. Ruggie (1986) 'International organization: a state of the art on an art of the state', *International Organization* 40, 4, pp 753–75.

Medina, Jose (2004) 'In defense of pragmatic contextualism: Wittgenstein and Dewey on meaning and agreement', *The Philosophical Forum* 35, 3, pp 341–69.

Rescher, Nicholas (1997) *Objectivity: The Obligations of Impersonal Reason* (Notre Dame, IN: University of Notre Dame Press).

Ross, Dorothy, ed (1994) 'Modernist social science in the land of the new/old', in *Modernist Impulses in the Human Sciences, 1870–1930* (Baltimore, MD: Johns Hopkins University Press), pp 171–89.

Shilliam, Robbie (2007) 'Morgenthau in context: German backwardness, German intellectuals and the rise and fall of a liberal project', *European Journal of International Relations* 13, 3, pp 299–327.

Shotter, John (1993) *Cultural Politics of Everyday Life* (Toronto: University of Toronto Press).

Walker, Rob (1993) *Inside/Outside: International Relations as Political Theory* (Cambridge: Cambridge University Press).

Weber, Max (2004) *The Vocation Lectures* (Indianapolis, IN: Hackett Press).

Weber, Max., Wolfgang J. Mommsen and Wolfgang Schlichter, eds (1994) *Wissenschaft als Beruf: Politik als Beruf* (Tübingen: J.C.B. Mohr).

15

Praxis, Humanism and the Quest for Wholeness

Jens Steffek

Introduction

This chapter suggests that we should read Fritz Kratochwil's praxis approach to the study of international relations (IR) and law as a humanist's quest for wholeness in a world full of reductionism and fragmentation. The humanist desire for wholeness that is present in Kratochwil's academic work remains largely disguised in the cloak of an epistemological stance. It underpins his concept of praxis and the related strategy of inquiry, an attempt to grasp human agency in all its facets. Kratochwil's recent book *Praxis* (Kratochwil, 2018) emerges from his long wrestling with the question of how we can obtain useful knowledge of the social world, and how we can make competent judgements on matters of IR. I read the book as a largely philosophical exercise in which IR and law furnish most of the examples that illustrate more general problems of generating and applying knowledge. In that respect the book follows the plot of *Rules, Norms, and Decisions* (Kratochwil, 1989).

For decades, Kratochwil's critical inquiries and polemics targeted mainly mainstream IR theory, although their implications were by no means limited to that field. He challenged the positivist American mainstream of the discipline on two grounds. Firstly, mainstream IR promotes reductionist conceptions of actors and situations of choice that paint a distorted picture of the social world. Secondly, due to their flawed ideal of parsimony, positivist theories and methods are unfit to explain (let alone understand) the social world adequately. Positivists just paper over the ambiguities and internal contradictions of human agency that are the real conundrums for us to address.

Praxis, then, suggests an alternative conceptualization of the social phenomena that international relations are made of, such as diplomacy, treaty-making, adjudication or warfare. This alternative approach does not have a name in the book. For convenience I call it the praxis approach. The praxis approach can be understood as a plea for strong contextualization. It requires us to consider the historical situatedness, contingencies and multiple constraints under which human beings act. It recommends a qualitative methodology that is sensitive to language use and the subjective world view of social actors. The goal is *nachvollziehendes Verstehen*, as proponents of a Weberian qualitative sociology would probably call it.[1] In this chapter, I explore Kratochwil's move from constructivism to praxis from a sympathetic but ultimately unconvinced perspective. I am sympathetic to it because I share Kratochwil's misgivings about the hubris and dogmatism of social scientists who pretend they can uncover eternal, law-like truths about the inner workings of politics and society. At the same time, I am struggling with what I perceive as an internal tension, if not contradiction, in the praxis approach that Kratochwil suggests as an alternative.

The praxis approach rests on the assumption that knowledge is not abstract but performative. Knowledge here resides in the act and is, in some way, part of it. At the same time, Kratochwil seems to suggest that social scientists can acquire solid knowledge about practices that they do not enact. If a concept of praxis is to be our guide, the question arises of how academic scholarship as an essentially world-observing activity can function. How can we gather knowledge *about* action when knowledge resides somehow *in* action? How can we understand human practices that we are not able to perform competently? This hermeneutic problem gestures to epistemological debates about the nature of qualitative inquiry and the logic of understanding that James Davis (Chapter 9) and Jörg Friedrichs (Chapter 12) address in this volume. In this chapter I take a slightly different route. I try to shed more light on the limitations of Kratochwil's praxis approach by focusing on the unresolved tension between the quest for wholeness and what I call the habit of distancing. Distancing occurs when scholars problematize and dissect the very words and concepts that actors engaged in their practices take for granted.

In the first part of the chapter, I discuss wholeness as a humanist ideal that Kratochwil endorses. It is visible in the canon of literature that Kratochwil cites, from Aristotle to Hume to 20th-century pragmatism. In its epistemic, world-disclosing variety, humanism suggests that human agency must be appreciated in all its facets and contradictions. It finds human wholeness

---

[1]   It is not easy to translate '*nachvollziehendes Verstehen*' into English; 'understanding through re-enacting' is probably the most appropriate choice.

threatened by the imperialism of scientific and instrumental rationality and the impoverished notion of human agency that it produces. My foil to develop this argument is George W. Morgan's book *The Human Predicament*, a scathing humanist critique of industrial modernity and the 'prosaic mentality' that underpins it (Morgan, 1968). In that book we find gloomy diagnoses of the late modern condition that are strikingly similar to Kratochwil's list of ills (Kratochwil, 2018: 452–68). It is an ethics of humanism that Morgan makes transparent here and that anticipates Kratochwil's calls for a 'vivere civile' and the old virtues of 'persuasion and friendship' (Kratochwil 2018: 474). Those virtues stand 'in lieu of a conclusion' (Kratochwil, 2018: 468) in *Praxis* but, in my reading, they do not follow neatly from the rest of the argument. In Kratochwil's final but still somewhat shy shift to ethics, his desire for wholeness (of the individual and the *body politic*) returns without the epistemological cloak.

In the second section of the chapter I explore the tensions between Kratochwil's desire for wholeness and his habit of scholarly detachment. Putting a plethora of words in inverted commas, Kratochwil prompts us to question all concepts that we usually take for granted, detaching ourselves from them in order to reflect upon them. I contend that this distancing from the language of action and its vocabulary inevitably removes us from the actors and their intuitive understanding of what it is they are doing. It puts limits on the 'conversation' that is Kratochwil's ideal because it catches scholars in the position of teachers and commentators. I conclude that the relentless distancing from the practices in the end prevents, rather than facilitates, the conversation that Kratochwil seeks. It also testifies to a manifest discontinuity between scholarly and everyday practices of 'going about a situation'. Social science, even at its most qualitative, is a distinctly modern way of dissecting and de-mystifying phenomena, in this case societies and their practices.

Humanism and the quest for wholeness

The central question in Kratochwil's book *Praxis* is how we can obtain useful knowledge, in the sense of a 'map that would enable us to orient ourselves more successfully in this turbulent world' (Kratochwil, 2018: 17). Much of his earlier writing spelled out how we will definitely not get there. As the arguments should be familiar, I can keep this discussion brief. At the most general level there is Kratochwil's rejection of a 'conception of science as a set of "true", a-temporal, and universal statements' (Kratochwil, 2000: 75). Kratochwil attacks the deductive Cartesian model of scientific inquiry and the logic of inference enshrined in modern-day manuals of how to do valid social research (see, e.g., King et al, 1994). In their conceptualization of actors and social action, American IR theories such as structural realism or rational institutionalism disfigure the *zoon politicon* to such an extent that cooperation morphs from a natural predisposition into a puzzle in need of explanation (Kratochwil, 2007: 2). Related to this is the failure of rationalism to acknowledge how rules and norms actually work in society (Kratochwil, 1984). Kratochwil's emphasis on norms and rules also hints to the importance of language as a world-disclosing and orienting device. Language has many uses and functions beyond representing objects and signalling preferences, as Kratochwil often explains with resort to Wittgenstein and speech-act theory (Kratochwil, 1989).

Not least, Kratochwil insists that human agency (and thus political change) can only be understood in relation to its specific historical context, a situatedness that 'the timeless wisdom of realism' stubbornly wants to ignore (Hall and Kratochwil, 1993; Koslowski and Kratochwil, 1994). Few colleagues made him as angry as the zealous world improvers (*Weltverbesserer*), that is, charlatans who claim they have discovered simple recipes to address wicked problems, or social engineers who pretend they could rebuild societies from scratch to make everyone happy. For Kratochwil, the organism of human society is incredibly complex and our interventions, even if high-minded, may have unforeseeable and unfortunate consequences.

I argue that a desire for wholeness inspires Kratochwil's attacks on IR realism, rationalism and other reductionist approaches to human agency. This desire finds its expression, strangely perhaps, at the level of epistemology. It is reflected in the canon of references that recur in Kratochwil's writings. They range from the Greek classics, in particular Homer and Aristotle, to David Hume, to 20th-century pragmatists. What stitches this rather unlikely canon together is humanism when we conceive it as an attitude that existed *avant la lettre*. The concept of humanism is a bit elusive, as it gestures vaguely to the value and unique qualities of human beings and, as an ethical stance, suggests kindness and benevolence towards them.[2] Regarding the philosophy of science, humanist ideals forbid reducing a human being to its parts, such as bodily functions, physical needs or intellect. The human being must be appreciated as a whole, mindful of its predetermined life in association where it can realize its full potential. This is what I mean by wholeness here. The concept bridges the individual and the societal levels, as only an intact society enables human beings to thrive.

A humanism thus conceived can be found in Aristotle's conceptions of humans as *zoon logon echon* and *zoon politicon*, along with his organic views of politics and the state, which Kratochwil likes to cite (Kratochwil,

---

[2]   Given Kratochwil's habit of citing the classics, we may be reminded of the German notion of *Humanismus*, which suggests that a solid knowledge of European antiquity is still key to understanding the modern world.

2018: 23–4). Praxis in the Aristotelian sense is the striving for a happy life (*eudaimonia*), which Kratochwil interprets as an art of making the right choices. This striving for a happy life has its own corresponding type of knowledge (Kratochwil, 2018: 393, 432). Aristotle's sweeping conception of praxis allows Kratochwil to introduce the 'big we' of humanity as a reference point for further epistemological discussions. The choice of the 'big we' implies that, whatever our differences, we all strive for the good life and happiness.

The epistemological implications of the ideal of wholeness come to the foreground more clearly in the work of David Hume, whose influence on Kratochwil's ideas can hardly be overstated (Kratochwil, 2010: 15–37; 2018: chapter 9). Hume rejected the rationalist and reductionist explanations of human action that many of his contemporaries fancied.[3] He famously attacked John Locke's suggestion that just two factors, pleasure (which is sought) and pain (which is avoided), could sufficiently explain human action. Hume pointed instead to the interplay of emotions and reasoning and thus suggested a more holistic understanding of human beings and their deeds (Kratochwil, 2018: 384). As a humanist, Hume believed that reason, and not any particular method, was the best means we have for discovering truth, but he conceded, with characteristic humility, that it was a very imperfect tool. Not least, Hume wanted to (re-)integrate scientists and laypeople in the quest for knowledge. As Kratochwil reads him, 'philosophy had to recognize its responsibility by not reflecting from the outside, taking social life as an object, but by realizing its purpose and potential as a critical voice *within* the institutionalized interactions and the discourses of a society on problems of common concern' (Kratochwil, 2018: 352, emphasis in original).

Kratochwil's more recent turn to pragmatism can be interpreted as a further episode of his humanist quest for wholeness. Leading pragmatists such as William James (1907: 254–8) and F.C.S. Schiller emphasized their connection to the humanist tradition. Schiller defined his own version of humanism as 'the perception that the philosophical problem concerns human beings striving to comprehend a world of human experience by the resources of human minds' (Schiller, 1907: 12). The fusion of pragmatism (originally a theory of science) and humanism here defines, first of all, an epistemological stance that seems to be very close to Kratochwil's own position. Pragmatism developed in opposition to world views and scientific practices that came

---

[3]   It is true that Hume and Aristotle can be associated with fragmenting tendencies as well. Hume contributed the fact/value distinction to the rise of modern science, and Aristotle paved the way for the distinction between the *vita activa* and the *vita contemplativa*. But when Kratochwil cites these two authors, a holistic approach to the social world usually is the point.

with the disenchantment and subsequent rationalization of the Western world since the Renaissance. Pragmatists, and also Kratochwil's praxis approach, in an important sense defy the idea that great 'ruptures' came with the modern age (Onuf, 2018: 33). They rather underline the enduring features of human reasoning. William James argued 'that our fundamental ways of thinking about things are discoveries of exceedingly remote ancestors, which have been able to preserve themselves throughout the experience of all subsequent time. They form one great stage of equilibrium in the human mind's development, the stage of common sense' (James, 1907: 170, emphasis in original).

Modernity, in contrast, dissolves the wholeness of humans and their society through an incessant specialization of activities and fragmentation of social domains. Modern science, as well, splintered into ever more disciplines and specialisms. The result is what Marx called alienation (*Entfremdung*). Men and women become strangers to themselves when they are reduced to a means of capitalist economic production (Kratochwil, 2018: 434). In a similar way, Max Weber feared that the increasing specialization of human beings in industrial modernity would leave them disfigured and soulless, mere levers in the machinery of the bureaucratic state (Weber, 1924: 413–14). Marx and Weber drew quite different conclusions from their findings, which Karl Löwith contrasted as follows:

> Marx wanted to find a way to abolish the specific human existence (i.e. existence as a specialist) characteristic of the rationalised world, and also to abolish the division of labour itself. Weber asked rather how man as such, within his inevitably 'fragmented' human existence, could nevertheless preserve the freedom for the self-responsibility of the individual. (Löwith, 1993: 78)

What Marx, Weber and the pragmatists share is a diagnosis of fragmentation and loss of wholeness. In response, Marx plotted a proletarian revolution, Weber sought refuge in heroism and the pragmatists called for a new science. The pragmatic approach also promised to bridge the boundaries of scientific disciplines with their limited purview. Kratochwil, who insisted time and again on the necessity of interdisciplinary research, certainly seconds this view (Kratochwil, 2018: 17). With its emphasis on experience as a world-disclosing activity, pragmatism erodes the distinction between scientific and non-scientific approaches to knowledge creation and, along the way, also the schism between the *vita activa* and the *vita contemplativa*. The influence of pragmatism is visible in Kratochwil's more recent work, which has edged away from the old focus on norms and rules as it has shifted more towards practices. A good example to illustrate this shift is the driving of a car as practice, where the 'decisive stage is getting acquainted with the practice of navigating through traffic' (Friedrichs and Kratochwil, 2009: 702). The abstract rules of the street code may be reasonably clear but still they are only a very imperfect guide. It is their local interpretation that matters. Learning the practice of driving is thus, at least beyond the mechanics of pressing the brake and turning the wheel, a highly context-dependent activity. Driving lessons learned in one place cannot be transferred easily to another. The constant interaction with other drivers and the anticipation of their actions give rise to quite different driving routines in the city of Naples and rural Nebraska (Friedrichs and Kratochwil, 2009).

What Kratochwil adopted from pragmatism is its fusion of acting and knowing, the idea 'that most of us have to act most of the time without having the privilege of basing our decisions on secure universally valid knowledge' (Kratochwil, 2007a: 11). We therefore develop the relevant knowledge as we go forward. Mary Follett put it nicely:

> We cannot assume that we possess a body of achieved ideas stamped in some mysterious way with the authority of reason and justice, but even were it true, the reason and justice of the past must give way to the reason and justice of the present. You cannot bottle up wisdom – it won't keep – but through our associated life it may be distilled afresh at every instant. (Follett, 1998 [1918]: 130)

The problem of bottling up wisdom seems to echo Kratochwil's concern that scientific questions are always time-bound and that scientific progress does not consist in a discovery of things out there. If there is progress at all in social science, it resides in our ability to reframe issues, to ask new and unprecedented questions.

Kratochwil also cites pragmatism because it 'recognizes that science as a process of knowledge production is a social practice determined by rules' (Kratochwil, 2007a: 12). Participation in that process, however, is not confined to scientists. Many pragmatists, probably most of all John Dewey, downplayed the distinction between scientific and practical deliberations. Dewey 'proposed a conception of science that not only placed it at the disposal of democracy but emphasized the intellectual affinities, even the continuities, between scientific method and everyday practices' (Wolin, 2004: 505; see also Evans, 2000: 314–15). Inquiry, as Dewey preferred to call it, was a method not for discovering truth but for making sense of situations. Experience is key here, and it is never just passively made but lived through (Dewey, 1981[1917]). Experience takes place in a 'community of inquiry' that stretches beyond professional inquirers in universities and research institutes.

Again, a desire for wholeness in an age of fragmentation stands in the background. 'The problem of modern society, as both Dewey and Jane

Addams diagnosed it, was the fragmentation of individuals. Because they were divorced from any participation in society as a whole, most members of society had no perception of how society functioned as an operating entity' (Stabile, 1984: 64). For Addams and Dewey, citizen education was the best remedy to that evil. It should enable citizens to participate more effectively and competently in the political process; to break down the barriers between governors, experts and lay people; and to bring practical knowledge to bear on political problems.

Pragmatists contend that there is no significant distinction between the 'big we' of human problem-solvers and the 'small we' of the scientific community. Social science, then, is not a peculiar and sectarian practice that must remain unfamiliar, in method and purpose, to most members of the 'big we'. Professionals and laypeople all take part in the enterprise of social progress. Consequently, the American pragmatists of the progressive age were avid world-improvers who conceived many reform projects. Jane Addams dedicated much of her life to campaigns for international peace, women's rights and social justice, and we cannot understand her seminal contributions to IR without that context (Addams, 1907). John Dewey, as a public intellectual, called for social progress, modernized education and the democratization of society.

In sharp contrast, Kratochwil's humanism is not connected to any political, world-changing project but remains in a philosophical, world-observing position (Kratochwil, 2018: 4). He would rather stick to individual virtues so old that they are best expressed in ancient Greek letters. A fellow traveller on that route was George W. Morgan, an American philosopher and pioneer of interdisciplinary studies at Brown University. His work is largely forgotten (and was probably never quite influential) but of interest here because his critique of industrial modernity, science and the project of the Enlightenment resembles Kratochwil's on many counts.

In his book *The Human Predicament*, Morgan finds a common denominator among the many features of modern decay. He calls it the 'prosaic mentality' (Morgan, 1968). The concept covers many, if not all, items on the long list of misgivings that Kratochwil has about the late modern world, most conspicuously the 'apparent loss of cultural resources for coping with our predicament' (Kratochwil, 2018: 469). The prosaic mentality that Morgan describes has engulfed all areas of modern social life, but the main culprit is the advance of the scientific method, its obsession with facts, objectivity, efficiency and neatly prescribed procedures. 'For the prosaic man', Morgan writes, 'each individual thing is basically another instance of something he has met already. ... When he finds an unfamiliar situation, it is at once assigned to a compartment or category that provides a standard explanation of it. Stock phrases and routine methods are instantly applied, and the thing is done with' (Morgan, 1968: 99).

Morgan expounds an alternative with the example of a historiography that is less concerned with establishing laws than with understanding unique events in the course of time. There is no manual for how to make such understanding work.

> When we say we understand something, we mean that in some way it makes sense to us. ... We have varied experiences of making sense of something, of accepting it as intelligible, of feeling that we understand it, of giving it our assent – and many of these, indeed most, cannot be cast into an explicit and adequate set of rules that we can follow step by step on other occasions. ... To be educated means, among other things, to be able to bring the proper mode of understanding to each occasion. (Morgan, 1968: 141–2)

The humanist epistemology of Morgan's approach is manifest, not least, in his insistence that we must encounter others with imagination and sympathy, a process he calls self-extension. 'Drawing on all our resources, all our actual experience, and on understanding previously gained from whatever sources, we try to present to ourselves and to apprehend others' being in the world: their life situations, their perspectives, their pressures and opportunities, and their desires and purposes' (Morgan, 1968: 149–50). This exercise in empathy is of use in everyday situations, and also in what we call social science, because Morgan does not see any categorical difference between the two endeavours.

Morgan's humanist epistemology does not seem far afield from Kratochwil's idea of praxis, although Morgan does not use that term. His humanism extends beyond the epistemological questions of how we gain knowledge of the outside world. Morgan outlines a way of making human beings whole again, and that is to familiarize them with all their mental faculties and, not least, emotions. Wholeness of individuals and of society are connected in that only whole individuals can re-establish rich and meaningful relations with others. 'The balance required for wholeness', Morgan writes in his concluding remarks, 'is one that is lived in the here and now of concrete occasions with their multifarious and often opposing claims, values and demands on the self' (Morgan, 1968: 330). Compared with Kratochwil's approach, Morgan's humanism more confidently steps beyond epistemological questions and is not shy about suggesting ways of healing, or redemption.

As a critique of industrial and scientific modernity, the quest for wholeness often seems to have something nostalgic about it. It implies that there must have been a point in time when conditions were better and when humans were still whole, even if it remains usually opaque when exactly that was. We may therefore be tempted to compare it to the romantic counter-movements in the arts and literature that refuted the rationalism and disenchantment that industrial and scientific modernity had brought about. Kratochwil is aware of this possible reading and is quick to assert that he is neither indulging in 'Schwärmerei' nor in an 'antiquarian interest for an idyllic past' (Kratochwil, 2018: 469, 474).

In any event, characteristic of pragmatism and the praxis approach is a desire to link up to the experiences and the common sense of 'normal people' who try to be effective in the world and to make good choices. The ambition is to reconcile (social) science with the 'big we' of humanity, and to reconcile the intellectual and more worldly purposes of human agency. The allure of pragmatism is that this difference should not matter much because, at the end of the day, we are all in the same boat of sense-making and problem-solving. Kratochwil and the pragmatists do not marshal much empirical evidence to show that there really is continuity in how scientists and more practically minded people go about their business. It rather comes as an assumption about human nature. The academic quest for knowledge of the world by definition is a practice like any other because it serves as orientation in the world that we (the 'big we') urgently need.

In the next section, I will question this assumption of continuity. I will start from my observation that the 'small we' of social scientists is a sectarian bunch of people, often enthralled by quite parochial problems that to outsiders may seem obscure. Kratochwil's writings always addressed primarily this group (or its IR theory sub-group) and its efforts to explain or understand the world. As far as I know, he never cared much for reaching out to the general public through op-eds in newspapers or television appearances. His scholarly books and articles – as we, as his keen readers, know – are no easy read for the uninitiated.

The habit of distancing

One of the remarkable features of Kratochwil's writing is his excessive use of inverted commas. From the linguistic point of view, inverted commas have different functions. One is to mark in a text what persons other than the author say or ask. When signalling direct speech in this way, they introduce a second voice to a text that the reader can distinguish from the author's. Inverted commas are also put around single words. In this function they warn the reader that a word is problematic or that its meaning in the text may deviate from familiar everyday parlance. Inverted commas could, for instance, flag a technical term that most people cannot be expected to know. A manual for engineers might not put the feeder tube of a machine in inverted commas, while it may well be a 'feeder tube' in a manual for consumers. Inverted commas can historicize when they are put around anachronistic expressions, especially when these words are used with a different meaning today. They can also indicate irony or that an author does not accept a given term or concept as valid. A liberal economist would probably put 'exploitation' in inverted commas when discussing a Marxist treatise, while a fellow Marxist would not.

The goal of the exercise is to problematize, and subsequently reflect upon, the meaning of a word or concept. Inverted commas break our reading routines as they *create a distance* between the author, the reader and the normal usage of a word. When using inverted commas in the distancing function, dosage matters a lot. 'The "normal" usage of the word' indicates a healthy dose of scepticism about the normality of that usage; 'the "normal" usage of the "word"' in one phrase may signal the beginning of a stylistic obsession but may be justifiable with due explanation; to write about 'the "normal" "usage" of the "word"' is whacky. We cannot distance ourselves from everything at the same time, it seems, but need to sow the seeds of doubt parsimoniously.

Even when not used to quote anybody directly, inverted commas still introduce a second voice to the text (Carduff, 2009: 157). It is a disciplining voice that comments, alerts and annotates from a distance. In contrast to scientific prose, where inverted commas in the distancing function are common, literary texts rarely ever use them. A poem with words in inverted commas is a strange idea. 'Shall I compare thee to a summer's day? Thou art more lovely and more "temperate"' (William Shakespeare, Sonnet 18, my inverted commas). I got it, an annoyed reader may despair, that Shakespeare is not referring to a woman's body temperature here but to her character – no need to point that out with inverted commas. In poetry, it seems, there is no room for a didactic second voice that interferes with the intimate conversation between the reader and the work. The presence of a second voice ruins poetry in much the same way as an explanation ruins a joke. It spoils the communicative practice in action by pointing out, and reflecting upon, the tacit understandings on which that very practice rests.

The distinction between a first and a second voice restates, in a way, the familiar dualism of an internal and external perspective, between actor and observer. That dualism is frequently interpreted as a problem of language use. 'Internalism, in brief, holds that the language of observation must match the language of action used inside the domain of a practice; externalism denies this' (Frost and Lechner, 2016: 301). The first voice speaks the language of action, the language of praxis. If knowledge resides in action, it must be inherent in this language and its use. The second voice is the observer's interpretative and sense-making voice, the voice of a controlling *Über-ich*. I do not think the second voice is necessarily using a different vocabulary, even if that may often be the case in today's jargon-ridden social sciences. The key difference is in the purpose of language use. While the first voice performs a practice in 'the language of action', the second voice is busy dissecting this practice for purposes of correction, clarification or explanation. It is not engaged in the original practice but commenting on it from a distance.

In the social sciences, the second voice is ubiquitous where words or concepts as used by the speakers in the real world are put to critical scrutiny. A classical social theorist who used inverted commas excessively was Max Weber. I do not think he did this to place some emphasis in his often rushed and breathless prose; he mostly used spaced print for that. Rather, he marked the distance between his language use as the author and the language of the subjects of his social analysis. The phenomenon has elicited quite some scholarly interest, even if it was largely restricted to the question of why he put the term 'objectivity' in inverted commas (McFalls, 2007; Palonen, 2010). With no prejudice to the question of what Weber really meant by objectivity, it seems safe to say that he put it in inverted commas when referring to 'that thing commonly called objectivity in the community of practice called science'. It seems also safe to conjecture that Weber did not fully share this common understanding of objectivity, for if he did, why the inverted commas?

In the social sciences, the use of inverted commas creates and maintains distance between the observer and the object of inquiry and its language use. Social science puts common words and concepts under the bright light of the dissecting table and takes them apart, thus inevitably breaking the bond with the community of practice and its implicit understandings. Kratochwil puts his inverted commas around technical terms of the social sciences that he does not (fully) accept, such as 'best practice', 'output legitimacy', 'global governance' or 'relative gains'. But on virtually every page of *Praxis* also basic words such as 'solution', 'failure', 'program', 'aggression', 'planning', 'novelty', 'enemy', 'morality', 'justice', 'history', 'victory', 'economics', 'law', 'public', 'approval', 'labor', 'exit', 'is' and 'ought', 'right' and 'wrong', 'soft' and 'hard' end up in inverted commas. Kratochwil's commentary on the language of international practices is a permanent distancing from what the actors, the practitioners, think they are doing with words. This commentary on language use often has disapproving undertones, denouncing a lack of reflection among those who employ those words carelessly.

The problem seems to be that practices work precisely because the practitioners have a tacit understanding of their words and concepts (their knowledge in action). In making the case for a practice perspective in IR, Vincent Pouliot pointed out that 'practices are the result of inarticulate, practical knowledge that makes what is to be done appear "self-evident" or commonsensical' (Pouliot, 2008: 258). Such practical knowledge is 'unreflexive and inarticulate through and through' (Pouliot, 2008: 265). I share Pouliot's view that practices only run smoothly when the knowledge in use remains tacit and unproblematic. Tacit here does not imply non-verbalized. Most social practices are to a large extent made of conversations.

Pouliot even draws on Kratochwil's earlier work on classic rhetoric to make that point, citing topoi and commonplaces as a typical feature of unquestioned practical language use. '[C]ommonplaces are tacit in nature: one discusses or acts with them but not about them' (Pouliot, 2008: 266).

To illustrate this point, let us imagine a lawyer who, in the midst of a treaty drafting process, says: 'Hang on, guys! Couldn't it be that what we call "law" here is just an instrument of the powerful to oppress the subaltern?' That lawyer would be reminded quickly that what was going on was treaty drafting, with its crystal-clear purpose and problem-solving orientation, and not David Kennedy's critical legal seminar. He could then either follow the advice and continue using law as unproblematic, thus staying in line with the requirements of accepted practice, or put law in inverted commas and, changing practice and habitus, leave the room for academia. The example shows how the appearance of a critical second voice, as I called it, disrupts the practice. This seems to confirm the common intuition that there is a practical and an academic way of using language, inspired and defined by very different purposes that are clear to the respective participants. How can Kratochwil claim that there is continuity between these activities?

Kratochwil's line of argument seems to run as follows and unfold again on the plane of epistemology. Social scientific inquiry, he argues, follows a mode of reasoning that Charles Sanders Peirce called 'abduction', which is 'a link of transmission between the empirical and the logical, between events and theory' (Bertilsson, 2004: 383). Abduction does not aim to establish a general theory (as through induction or deduction) but to determine what is the case in a given situation. It is amenable to the epistemology of praxis, because 'abduction is fundamentally based on a holistic understanding of the cases' (Friedrichs and Kratochwil, 2009: 719). Abduction, Friedrichs and Kratochwil suggest, is 'above all a more conscious and systematic version of the way by which humans have learned to solve problems and generate knowledge in their everyday lives' (Friedrichs and Kratochwil, 2009: 710). This is a strong claim of continuity between the practice of social science and the practices of the everyday. The members of the 'big we' and the 'small we' are both engaged in a world-disclosing enterprise and remain united by their practice of abduction.

That communality, if it exists, is a formal one, however. It is not substantial knowledge we share but a procedure, a way of going about things. Note that the pragmatists expected something more when they posited continuity between the expertise of scientists and lay people. Their expectation was that they would engage in joint problem-solving exercises and to that extent share a purpose. As IR scholars, however, we are writing about the behaviour of politicians, diplomats, soldiers, lawyers or economists without ever having performed their practices and shared their purposes. We never ran for election; we never conducted diplomatic negotiations; we (hopefully) never fought a battle in war; we never represented a plaintiff at court; and we never tried to predict next year's economic growth. In other words, we do not experience the practices we write about.

Let me illustrate the difference further with the example of driving a car that was mentioned earlier. As members of the 'small we' community of scholars, our purpose is not driving a car. What we want is to understand the patterns of car traffic, and we try to do that without a licence and without a clue about the technicalities involved in driving a car. We do not even plan to be driving in the future. We are making theories, or judging traffic situations without the hands-on experience and competences that derive from driving. We are specialists in explaining, interpreting and criticizing traffic, recognizing its patterns from afar, and this is our job. Kratochwil is right when he insists that this very peculiar business follows its own rules and negotiates its own truths. Paul Diesing put it beautifully:

> Social science produces a multiple, contradictory truth for our time— that is, a set of diversified perspectives and diagnoses of our changing, tangled, and contradictory society. These truths live in the practices and understandings of a research community, not in particular laws, and when that community peters out, its truth passes into history along with the society it tried to understand. (Diesing, 1991: 364)

Diesing offers here a good description of how social science works and what it can deliver. However, when discussing praxis or practices we need to differentiate between the practice of social science and the practices that social science studies. Abraham and Abramson do this when they distinguish an 'inward looking' and 'outward looking' perspective of practice theory (Abraham and Abramson, 2015: 28). Scholars who adopt the inward-looking perspective study their own profession with the help of practice theory, while the outward-looking perspective applies it to other realms of the social world.

Kratochwil's continuity thesis also sits uneasily with the idea that the ultimate goal of knowledge creation is not truth but usefulness. If this is correct, a wide gap opens between the actors' perspective on usefulness and the researcher's. Professionals want to succeed in their specific game and social scientists in theirs. As the two games are different, there is no common scale on which the usefulness of the generated knowledge could be measured. There are, to be sure, zones of overlap between what we would call professional and scientific activity – international law would be a case in point. But on the whole, there should be a reason why so few professionals of international relations take social science classes to enhance their problem-solving capacity and why so many go for an MBA or LLM degree instead. They look for the 'how to' kind of knowledge that helps them get on with their professional tasks.

Conclusion

In this chapter I took issue with the desire for wholeness that seems to animate Kratochwil's humanism. Kratochwil deploys the Aristotelian concept of praxis to reclaim a holistic type of knowledge for academic reflection. Drawing on Hume and American pragmatism, he tries to overcome the distinction between theory and practice, between knowing and acting, between the *vita activa* and the *vita contemplativa*. Such a holistic approach to the social world requires 'enlarging the self', as in Kratochwil (2018: 367), or 'self-extension', as Morgan (1968) calls it. While it is easy to accept empathy as a moral ideal for which to strive, it seems more difficult to understand how exactly 'enlarging the self' can help us make sense of the world and solve our problems. The idea seems to gesture at qualitative social research aimed at understanding, or the 'thick constructivism' found in Kratochwil's earlier writings (see Davis, Chapter 9, this volume). In *Praxis*, however, Kratochwil seems to go further, as he now emphasizes continuities between scholarly and practical reasoning.

In this chapter I presented a critique of this continuity assumption, prompted by the suspicion that it is a normative position in epistemological disguise. The humanist ideal of wholeness suggests that there *should be* no difference between how average people make their inquiries and how social scientists do. To show that this is really the case, Kratochwil cites Peirce's method of abduction, arguing that this is how the community of scientists (the 'small we') and human beings in general (the 'big we') tend to reason. There is not only an alleged continuity in method, but also a continuity in purpose, because 'we all' need to make sense of the situations we are in. Acting is knowing, and knowledge is (re-)produced in our practical experience. It is 'working together' on practical tasks that makes for meaningful community, engaging jointly in a practice and developing a tangible '*inter-esse*' (Kratochwil, 2018: 367).

While we may argue that, at a fundamental level, practices of inquiry and judgement follow similar patterns in everyday life and social science, I have my doubts about Kratochwil's strong claims about shared purposes and joint problem-solving. The same Peirce also argued that '[t]rue science is distinctively the study of useless things. For the useful things will get studied without the aid of scientific men' (Peirce, 1932: Vol. 1, para 76). He did not say this to discredit scientists, but just wanted to set apart those 'possessed by a passion to learn' from the vast majority of 'practical men, who carry on the business of the world' (Peirce, 1932: Vol. 1, para 43).

Most social scientists, and in particular theory-prone IR scholars, do not experience the situations that their inquiries are about but observe them from afar. Towards the end of *Praxis*, Kratochwil seems to acknowledge this when he portrays social scientists as 'critical observers in the privileged position of academics' who contribute to an order 'that allows us to "go on" in that mode of communication that is a "conversation"' (Kratochwil, 2018: 475). Yet even if acting together is a conversation rather than 'working together on joint tasks', our social scientific habit of distancing might get in the way. What social scientists speak is not the performative voice of practice. It is a distant, disciplining idiom that is constantly annotating, criticizing and correcting what others say and do. That *Über-ich* voice, as I argued in this chapter, disrupts the tacit understanding on which practices rest. The reflexive-critical stance of social scientists who dissect real-world practices to gain knowledge about them seems hard to reconcile with the habitual conduct of those practices that rely on tacit and unquestioned knowledge. Therefore, the prospects for re-establishing wholeness in a late modern, functionally differentiated world are dim. Ironically, perhaps, the sheer existence of social science as a breadwinning professional activity is among the forces that militate against it.

Acknowledgements

I am indebted to the participants of the Frankfurt conference, Gunther Hellmann and Nick Onuf, who kindly provided comments on an earlier draft of this chapter.

References

Abraham, Kavi J. and Yehonatan Abramson (2015) 'A pragmatist vocation for International Relations: the (global) public and its problems', *European Journal of International Relations* 23, 1, pp 26–48.

Addams, Jane (1907) *Newer Ideals of Peace* (New York: Macmillan).

Bertilsson, Thora M. (2004) 'The elementary forms of pragmatism: on different types of abduction', *European Journal of Social Theory* 7, 3, pp 371–89.

Carduff, Corinna (2009) 'Das einfache Anführungszeichen. Zeichen auf Distanz', in Christine Abbt and Tim Kammasch (eds), *Punkt, Punkt, Komma, Strich? Geste, Gestalt und Bedeutung Philosophischer Zeichensetzung* (Bielefeld: Transcript), pp 153–62.

Dewey, John (1981 [1917]) 'The need for a recovery of philosophy', in John J. McDermott (ed), *The Philosophy of John Dewey* (Chicago, IL: University of Chicago Press), pp 58–97.

Diesing, Paul (1991) *How Does Social Science Work? Reflections on Practice* (Pittsburgh, PA: University of Pittsburgh Press).

Evans, Karen G. (2000) 'Reclaiming John Dewey: democracy, inquiry, pragmatism, and public management', *Administration and Society* 32, 3, pp 308–28.

Follett, Mary (1998 [1918]) *The New State: Group Organization the Solution of Popular Government* (University Park, PA: Pennsylvania State University Press).

Friedrichs, Jörg, and Friedrich Kratochwil (2009) 'On acting and knowing: how pragmatism can advance International Relations research and methodology', *International* Organization 63, 4, pp 701–31.

Frost, Mervyn and Silviya Lechner (2016) 'Understanding international practices from the internal point of view', *Journal of International Political Theory* 12, 3, pp 299–319.

Hall, Rodney B. and Friedrich Kratochwil (1993) 'Medieval tales: neorealist "science" and the abuse of history', *International Organization* 47, 3, pp 479–91.

James, William (1907) *Pragmatism: A New Name for Some Old Ways of Thinking* (New York: Longmans, Green, and Co.).

King, Gary, Robert O. Keohane and Sidney Verba (1994) *Designing Social Inquiry Scientific Inference in Qualitative Research* (Princeton, NJ: Princeton University Press).

Koslowski, Rey and Friedrich Kratochwil (1994) 'Understanding change in international politics: the Soviet Empire's demise and the international system', *International Organization* 48, 2, pp 215–47.

Kratochwil, Friedrich (1984) 'The force of prescriptions', *International Organization* 38, 4, pp 685–708.

Kratochwil, Friedrich (1989) *Rules, Norms, and Decisions: On the Conditions of Practical and Legal Reasoning in International Relations and Domestic Affairs* (Cambridge: Cambridge University Press).

Kratochwil, Friedrich (2000) 'Constructing a new orthodoxy? Wendt's "Social Theory of International Politics" and the constructivist challenge', *Millennium* 29, 1, pp 73–101.

Kratochwil, Friedrich (2007) 'Of false promises and good bets: a plea for a pragmatic approach to theory building (the Tartu Lecture)', *Journal of International Relations and Development* 10, 1, pp 1–15.

Kratochwil, Friedrich (2010) *The Puzzles of Politics: Inquiries into the Genesis and Transformation of International Relations* (Abingdon: Routledge).

Kratochwil, Friedrich (2018) *Praxis: On Acting and Knowing* (Cambridge: Cambridge University Press).

Löwith, Karl (1993) *Max Weber and Karl Marx* (London: Routledge).

McFalls, Laurence, ed (2007) *Max Weber's 'Objectivity' Reconsidered* (Toronto: University of Toronto Press).

Morgan, George W. (1968) *The Human Predicament: Dissolution and Wholeness* (Providence, RI: Brown University Press).

Onuf, Nicholas G. (2018) *The Mighty Frame: Epochal Change and the Modern World* (Oxford: Oxford University Press).

Palonen, Kari (2010) *"Objektivität" als faires Spiel: Wissenschaft als Politik bei Max Weber* (Baden-Baden: Nomos).

Peirce, Charles S. (1932) *Collected Chapters of Charles Sanders Peirce. Vol. I, Principles of Philosophy* (Cambridge, MA: Harvard University Press).

Pouliot, Vincent (2008) 'The logic of practicality: A theory of practice of security communities', *International Organization* 62, 2, pp 257–88.

Schiller, F.C.S. (1907) *Studies in Humanism* (London: Macmillan).

Stabile, Donald (1984) *Prophets of Order: The Rise of the New Class, Technocracy and Socialism in America* (Boston, MA: South End Press).

Weber, Max (1924) 'Debattenrede auf der Tagung des Vereins für Sozialpolitik in Wien 1909 zu den Verhandlungen über "Die wirtschaftlichen Unternehmungen der Gemeinden"', in Max Weber (ed), *Gesammelte Aufsätze zur Soziologie und Sozialpolitik* (Tübingen: Mohr), pp 412–16.

Wolin, Sheldon S. (2004) *Politics and Vision: Continuity and Innovation in Western Political Thought* (Princeton, NJ: Princeton University Press).

PART V

Conversing with Critics

16

Acting, Representing, Ruling: A Conversation with My Critics on Social Reproduction and the Logic of Social Inquiry

Friedrich Kratochwil

Introduction

Coming last in this collection of essays on one's work is a privilege and a challenge. It is a privilege not only because one has now different texts articulating different facets of a common concern, but it is a privilege in that it shows that my attempts to rethink the issue of acting with all the conceptual baggage that comes with it has been useful for others, even if they (dis-)agree. Thus, the position alone could tempt one to provide just an overview and impose some weak order, familiar from the 'contrast and compare' genre. But one also could do worse, by creating the impression of a synthesis by opting for selective attention, in order to show how we all mean the same thing. Such an approach might be all the more tempting since we all seem to agree, due to the post-modern turn in social theory,[1] that *the world out there* does not provide us with unadulterated and free-standing facts which serve as last appeals.

These observations point to the challenge part of the task, especially for someone who has warned of last words and grand theories. Similarly, in insisting that we filter our experiences through categories and concepts defining what is normal and making sense, or what is deviant or out of bounds, I can deny neither that these 'bounds' are not only logical

---

[1] See the still seminal anthology by Seidman (1994).

distinctions – although they serve as criteria of intelligibility – nor that they are merely cognitive. Since they are norms, they not only state regularities but provide – through their counterfactual validity – for the enactments of 'rules' and the reproduction of social order, whereby alternatives are excluded and *dominum* is exercised *as rule*. Consequently, the notion of a 'full view' – attributed to theories when conceived from the point of the 'view from nowhere' – seems a doubly problematic metaphor for the social world where the observed order is based on rule-following and intersubjective understandings, some of which are clearly 'fictions' (such as corporations, or representations of a 'people', comprising also the dead and future generations), or they entail certain 'truths' that are *held and declared*, rather than found and available for inspection. Therefore, I think that both the notion of theory as a *full view of everything* and the idea of a universal, all-inclusive order – bolting together the visible and the invisible, the normative and the factual, the present, the past and the future – are incoherent. For starters, if order depends on distinctions and boundaries, every outside has to *exclude* something in order to mark an inside. Similarly, to conceive of order, especially social order, by a metaphorical extension of a homogeneous space in which there may be movement from here to there, but where no real transformative (historical) change can occur – as the past and the future are just like the present – is hardly plausible. Thus, I think the two *problematiques* are two sides of the same coin, which leads to the mistaken belief that knowledge consists in 'seeing' this totality into which everything is to be folded, but also that everything in it remains fixed.

In order to elaborate on this argument, I begin with an examination of two root metaphors of knowing – seeing vs grasping – which allows me to place the International Relations (IR) discussion about practices in the wider setting of the epistemological problem (section on 'Setting'). I then address the issue of institutionalized action and professional responsibility in the section 'What shall we do?' and conclude with some critical remarks on 'Law and its empire'.

Seeing and grasping

The plausibility of the previous 'hunch' rests on what we experience when we change the root metaphor for knowing, which relies on sight (evidence, idea, seeing), and shift to the different one of grasping ('*capire*', '*begreifen*') something. The latter involves us not only as passive observers, who just receive sense impressions, but as beings involved in what we perceive, by choosing a perspective, using instruments and controlling for what we think can be neglected. Such a switch in the root metaphor immediately confronts us also with the realization that in the case of thinking about order and social reproduction the term 'order' covers two rather different conceptions that partially overlap, but which point in different directions. One is the notion of the perfect order that is like a finished product open for our contemplation, so to speak the *ordo ordinatus* conception. But there is also the notion of an *order ordinans*, that is, of *ordering* conceived as a never ending effort to *create* order and ensure its reproduction in time.

Significantly, both stories are laid out in the first chapters of Genesis. The first few paragraphs of chapter 1 outline the *ordo ordinatus* position: 'and God saw that everything that he had made and behold, it was very good. ... And on the 7th day God finished his work ... and rested'. But just a few lines later, in the second chapter, another story line emerges with the creation of man, the seduction of the tree of knowledge, the fall of Adam and Eve and the expulsion from paradise. It introduces not only mortality but also the beginning of 'history'. Not only do the first couple have to leave paradise and 'make a life' through toil, but God also has now continuously to intervene in the course of events to protect his sacred line – listed meticulously in the *Chronicles* and continued by Matthew for the New Covenant ('Testament') – with which God makes the old and the new covenant. Part of this 'maintenance regime' is that the chosen people have to be reminded of their obligations through prophets, and God has even to use other peoples in order to keep his wayward tribes – which have through the Covenant become *a people* – in line.

I think Cecelia Lynch's (Chapter 3) interpretation points to some interesting further questions, aside from elaborating on prophecy as a mode of internally situated criticism, which she thinks my approach to praxis fits. Where she and I perhaps disagree is that the extension of prophecy in the tradition of Deutero-Isaiah and the emergence of an apocalyptic version in Daniel – taken up again in John's Book of Revelations – makes out of the situated criticism a message of universal redemption and damnation, with some unenviable consequences. The radicalization of the original prophetic perspective to one of a final convulsion and/or accounting fundamentally alters the function of earlier prophecies, which took issue with concrete problems of common concerns, in that the prophet reminded the people and their rulers of their obligations, rather than propagating a (catastrophic) vision of things to come. Now the shadow of the future casts its ominous spell over the present, especially since the return to an idyllic past is foreclosed. This has important implications for what we can know, what we shall do and what we can hope for in making sense for our individual and collective life.

In Kant's 'secularized' version of this story, redemption has become self-redemption accomplished by the human actor through individual moral action – rather than bestowed by the grace dispensed by God – which is the key problem from Augustine to Luther and the Reformation. The theme park of the paradise has thereby morphed into a kingdom of ends towards which mankind is moving. This construction creates new conceptual fault lines which are of interest to us. Thus, the old chestnut of medieval philosophy concerning the freedom of will and the role of grace (or divine election) reappears in the modern counterpoise of the *List der Natur*[2] – now standing in for God and his interventions maintaining order – and of the individual's free will. The latter requires the actors – if they really want to be free – to work in the 'interest of reason', imposing on all of us a *duty* to work towards that goal (Kant, 1991 [1795]: 114, 122). But then, again, the question of agency raises its ugly head. Since Kant does not trust the 'warped wood' of 'the human species' (Kant, 1991 [1784]: 46) to make the jump from nature as physis to morality and the kingdom of ends, his 'solution' of the free will determining itself can barely paper over the contradictions.

These introductory remarks shall only illustrate and justify my strategy of involving my critics in a further conversation, rather than provide a spectacle of 'gladiatorial fights' as Jörg Friedrichs once called it, and which is familiar from the theoretical debates in the field. The latter operate with the simple is/is not disjunction and with the winner takes all presumption as the 'end'[3] – which is of course an illusion, as the debates continue. But how are we then to think about action and our task as critical observers of the construction of the social world?

Friedrichs (Chapter 12) not only makes the case that as social analysts we are not condemned to be only apologists of the existing order pointing to the facticity of observational statements, nor do we have to become revolutionaries, as the prophecy/teleology of the history of humankind is equally distorting for analysing the problem of praxis. By using the framework of a triple hermeneutics – consisting of the issue of reference, that is, what we consider a problem; of interpretation (how it is perceived by the observer); and by our realizations that the observer is shaped by the cultural context in which they operate – Friedrichs opens up a fruitful discussion of the problem of social reproduction and action. It takes the issue of social reproduction out of the semantic field of 'sameness', which in a way justifies theory's mistaken claim of universality – since truth cannot be different from situation to situation – thereby easily mistaking action for just making the same thing again and again, as if all our actions were standardized moves like punching holes or hammering (remember the 'law of the hammer'!). But acting in time is different, as it entails yoking the present to past and future, and not just moving along a line from here to there, in an ahistorical continuum. Friedrichs elaborates on his triple hermeneutics by

---

[2]   See the more recent discussion of Kant's later works by Brand (2009, 2010), which critically evaluates the systemic coherence of the Kantian oeuvre. See also the harder criticism of Kant's political and legal writings by Horn (2014).

[3]   Here again the double meaning of 'end' as 'goal' and as 'finish' play on each other.

briefly discussing in an ideal-type fashion Nietzsche, Weber, Foucault and Hume, showing why social theory – if we take theory as critical reflection rather than merely as a distanced observation – is not like a simple tool, nor does it have a predetermined end (like a product, or a known future) but is a particular take by a theorist to come to terms with the problems of world-making and change.

Patrick T. Jackson (Chapter 14) and Hellmann (Chapter 5) carefully map out the similarities and differences between my attempts at thinking about praxis and those of the Western philosophical tradition, and of other participants and the disciplinary discourse of IR. Such a concern with the setting which frames our way of thinking and communicating is not simply a luxury adding adornment to the subject matter, which could be stated without reference to seminal contributions in the construction of the field; but, as we never can start from 'nowhere' and also not from an original position or a fictitious contract, these figures of thought emerge out of historical experiences and highlight the background, problems and concerns. Consequently, we are limited by the vocabularies we use, and thus clarifying their limitations and possibilities is the first order of business for analysts of the social world. This might limit our imagination – as we have to deal with situations and particular conjunctures – but it also limits our responsibility. We are not here to 'save the world' but to provide some orientation of how to lead a decent life individually and collectively, as best we can. Precisely because I am – for better or for worse – part of a privileged group of academics, I do have, above all, the obligation to engage critically with arguments made in this context, because we do 'learn' something by making distinctions and we become aware of their entrapments when, in dealing with political projects, we compare different concepts and semantics and trace their historical origins and trajectories before we come to conclusions and judge.

To that extent I appreciate fully Antje Wiener's (Chapter 13) thoughtful interpretation of my attempts as 'interventions' in the disciplinary debates which – while not changing the existing practices of politics in general or even those of academia – nevertheless created new opportunities for raising questions and thinking differently about what we are doing. That such a different 'thinking space' is not the same as providing prescriptions or 'practical advice' to the decision-makers is as clear as its importance is obvious. I certainly do not want to claim that my take on the problems is the only possible one, as different approaches amply demonstrate.[4]

As opposed to calling attention to such substantive concerns, the issues of fault – whether I failed to make myself clear or the critic misunderstood

---

[4] See Tetlock (2005), Tetlock and Gardner (2015), Tomasello (2003, 2009), Abbott (1988) and Kennedy (2016).

me, or erroneously objected – can take second place. Here Oliver Kessler's (Chapter 10) corrections on my critique of game theory – while at the same time not invalidating the major point I tried to make – is right. Acting in contingent circumstance requires a concept of intersubjectivity that is rather different from that of the rationalist approach. The latter limits itself to the individually conceived best answers while leaving the 'social' – which addresses the problem of *structures*, *situations* and *actors* – unattended.

I have tried to answer some of the more specific questions raised at the symposium in Frankfurt, which discussed the book *Praxis*, and also at a previous conference hosted by Jens Steffek in Darmstadt, which focused on the dilemma of 'being condemned as social scientists to provide mere "narratives" instead of "theories"', in a separate work which is in press (Kratochwil, 2021). In the following short remarks, I rather want to engage the writers in a further conversation instead of a detailed critique, which is hardly possible anyhow given the limitations imposed by the format. For that purpose, I want to concentrate on the topics outlined earlier.

The setting

My dissatisfaction with a 'science' of politics – and of international politics in particular – developed over the years, as Jackson so diligently documents by unearthing my first publication on different conceptualizations of politics. He thereby – surprisingly even for me – throws new light on the later 'ruptures' in my thinking that led me down the garden path to constructivism and a renewed interest in law and its role in social reproduction. The first intervention – co-authored with Ruggie (Kratochwil and Ruggie, 1986) – was to show why the methodologically tinged debates in the field were missing the mark, precisely because methodology and ontology were misaligned. The second was occasioned by my exposure to Hume's form of pragmatism – so aptly emphasized in Hellmann's chapter. As one of the constructivists of the first hour in the field of IR, I soon had to come to terms with the fact that some of the openings created by this intervention were foreclosed, precisely – and perversely – because constructivism became more or less the accepted third way of 'theorizing' after Marxism had dropped out of IR's 'paradigm' competition. One result was then a new round of rather arcane debates about the primacy of ontology or of methodology that killed many trees and spilled much ink, but which was pretty useless, as neither the disjunction nor the hierarchization of these problems but their co-constitution was the actual issue, as Hellmann rightly argues. Another problem was that the conceptual issues of the constructivist agenda became subject to what Yosef Lapid and I called exclusionary/inclusionary modes of control, as opposed to a theoretical reconstruction (Lapid and Kratochwil, 1986). Significantly, this article, in which we called attention to this sociology of knowledge problem, dealt with a 'substantive' problem, that is, the inability of the prevailing theoretical debates in IR to deal with the problem of nationalism. This was all the more astonishing since that field itself had chosen as one of its tags the 'inter-national' (instead of, e.g., calling itself world politics). As such, 'international politics' had, however, surprisingly little to say on both the nation and politics, not to mention power, which remained perhaps the most important concept, but remained – as Aristotle's 'fifth essence' (*quinta essetia*) – nebulous, even when 'operationalized' as capabilities.

Significant, though, was the fact that at this point Lapid and I still used the term 'theory', although we both thought in terms of a thorough reconstruction, rather than just an extended form of theorizing that would explain more of the variance.[5] If I had any illusions that a theoretical reconstruction was possible, they came to an end when Wendt's *Social Theory* appeared (Wendt, 1999). It managed – despite its considerable sophistication – to radically reduce the constructivist agenda by trying to convince the mainstream that constructivists were not the feared barbarians at the gate who wanted to storm the citadels of science, but that they could also do 'science'. Thus, the main focus of Wendt's inquiry became the 'profession', and much effort went into showing where different scholars fitted in a table, utilizing the apparently self-justifying dichotomies of materialism/idealism and holism/individualism (Kratochwil, 2000). Ironically, this exercise showed how the cognitive dominance of science, claiming to provide the universal yardstick for true knowledge, reinforces the social arrangements which make out of the scholar – committed to the pursuit of knowledge – a 'professional' who is supposed to provide useful knowledge. The result was a cognitive orthodoxy (although it included some different schools) which further weakened the critical inquiry of presuppositions and justifications of knowledge, so that even the creation of knowledge is nowadays recast in terms of 'practice' which orients itself on the template of production and *techne* rather than praxis.

Here I have some beef with Bueger's (Chapter 4) argument, and this objection has nothing to do with my rejection or failure to recognize that the organization of knowledge and of its dissemination is an important issue area that provided invaluable impulses for social thought. After all, although *The Practice Turn in Contemporary Theory*, edited by Schatzki et al (2000), as well the work of Jasanoff did not prepare the road for the emergence of 'constructivism' in IR – as here the work of Mead and others indebted to American pragmatism was instrumental, as Hellmann (Chapter 5) points out – it nevertheless contributed immensely to the heuristics and to the

---

[5]   See Patrick T. Jackson's superb discussion of the relevant issues (Jackson, 2011).

valorization of this approach. Furthermore, I am also not a definition fetishist who thinks that meaning is established solely by reference instead of being a language game. But acknowledging that 'theory' is a language game does not mean that no criteria are necessary for playing it and that one can go 'with the flow' (as one author, cited by Bueger, suggests). Is the 'attuning to the world', that is, 'to see, hear feel and taste it', a task for theorizing or practical reflection? This metaphorical stretching is particularly problematic, when the good old notion of the 'world out there' is still charged with doing most of the work by generating truths and by providing iconic matches, rather than being concerned with justifiable assurances, or appeals to aesthetic yardsticks.

Thus, a kind of happy inductivism prevails in contemporary practice studies (Schmidt, 2018) – without even having critically examined the exemplars which should be included or excluded. This is paralleled by a proliferation of categories in classifying the different ways of skinning the cat, without raising the question of whether we are dealing with fish or fowl, or 'just' ideas. The attempted clarification then consists largely in citing several taxonomies which one encounters in the literature. One can, of course, distinguish between those wanting to abandon the theory project and those who want to transform it; or one can distinguish between generalizers and singularizers in the 'theory building' game. But how does this classification then mesh with the other classification of modes of theorizing according to locale and purpose, which Bueger employs? Somehow, we seem to be in Borges's imaginative story of the classification of animals in Imperial China, where the distinctions concern male and female, animals which belong to the emperor or to others, or they are classified according to their being big or small, and so forth. Besides, as the example of classification according to traditional logic shows, the 'definition' of man as a featherless bi-ped is not 'wrong' logically speaking, as it focuses on one clearly identifiable property, but it is 'useless', as it generates no further interesting questions – such as defining man as the animal which associates by means of shared concepts (Aristotle). I am therefore a bit at a loss as to why singularizers will try to 'disrupt', while for generalizers the 'purpose of theorizing lies much more in producing order'. Why this should be so is not quite clear. Is the further implication that the 'full view' of order (theory) is already the same as realizing it? Then even Plato should be breathless. Practical experience as well as the Genesis example given previously seem rather to point in the other direction.

In short, is perhaps the attempt of getting as many relevant others under one roof not only distorting, but self-defeating, as differences are negated rather than mediated or perhaps even settled? Since I am credited with a style of theorizing that is less concerned with 'generalization and order and more with process and thinking', I am *faute de mieux* welcome in the theory tent. Okay, so be it, as long as it is clear that 'theory' can be used in a quite latitudinarian fashion, but that a rather different research programme follows from my approach than from the turn to practices, or from knowledge 'production', or syncretistic notions of 'wholeness'.

For this reason, I also have to clear up some things in Jens Steffek's (Chapter 15) chapter, knowing full well that, of course, the author of a text is not the only authoritative source for deciding what it means. I was astonished, nevertheless, that aside from the well-taken amusement about my – admittedly rather obsessive – use of quotation marks which defeat my own purpose of communicating in ordinary language, another charge was levelled at *Praxis*, that is, that it allegedly called for returning to a golden past in which we could recover the 'wholeness' that we have lost in modernity.

Since I have taken Steffek's advice and written – I hope more clearly – about the problem of distance and engagement in social analysis in a separate piece (Kratochwil, 2020), the second charge needs some further discussion. Here I am a bit surprised since neither my argument nor the examples I cite sit well with such an interpretation. As the example of Odysseus in the last chapter shows, this *nostos* is precisely not the happy end of a return to the old and familiar past. Instead, it recognizes that a new situation requires dealing with what transpired in the meantime and that a new order has to be established. Nor is Hume's argument about the Glorious Revolution, on which I rely, a paean to the return to the old freedoms of Englishmen. Instead, in following Hume I show why such presumably 'historical' constructions are particularly partisan and ideological examples of dubious historiography. Nor is my discussion about tradition – part of the examination of choice in which always the present, the past and the future interact – a plea for a return to an Arcadian utopia that never was. If anything, *Praxis* is an indictment against fantasies of a lost or prophesized wholeness. Even the present preoccupation with constant 'self-improvement' and of the quasi-religious delusions achieved through revivals or physical regimes in the *Praxis* book can hardly be understood as an endorsement of these practices.

So, what is the evidence for the second charge? I guess it is largely based on guilt by association. For that purpose George Morgan's (1968) book *The Human Predicament* provides for Steffek the link, since many of my criticisms have a 'striking similarity' to those of Morgan. Although I have used the term 'predicament' quite often, I am not familiar with Morgan's work. Since even Steffek considers him an obscure professor at Brown University who decried the decay of modernity, characterized by a 'prosaic mentality', my first question is why Morgan should provide the template. After all, the disenchantment of modernity has been a constant theme from Durkheim to Weber to Heidegger, Wittgenstein, Adorno, Taylor, Walzer, to name just a few, which I have read, and which have influenced my work.

Thus, putting an author's work into a context requires something more than just noting some coincidences with some other work, as such evidence is not even circumstantial. After all, Jackson does a yeoman's job in identifying the sources of my thinking without falling prey to the rather simplistic analogy that everything can be reduced to a 'disenchantment' with modernity, and Hellmann elaborates well on its pragmatist heritage – the 'third rupture' – which had important implications for my thinking. For Steffek, however, the actual key seems entirely personal, psychological and idiosyncratic, as it is more a *mood* that directs my attempts at world-making, rather than the dialogues I engage in with 'others', be they Aristotle, Peirce or Wittgenstein. Consequently, even my turn to pragmatism seems to prove for Steffek his point, since both my praxis approach and pragmatism 'defy the idea that great rupture came with the modern age'. This alleged common denial then justifies the inference that the nostalgic quest for a 'wholeness' aims at a world of 'virtues so old that they are best expressed in ancient Greek letters'. The latter expression is a hilarious gloss, but it provides illumination by low wattage, especially in the light of Steffek's counter-proposal to interpret our 'predicament': the normalcy of habit with which normal people go about their business. Needless to say, I do not find the bowdlerized form of Humean or Oakshottian habits that is now being sold to an IR audience (by Hopf and others) illuminating.

Mathias Albert's (Chapter 11) imaginative reconstruction of my struggle and my love/hate relationship with Luhmann might also be perhaps a bit exaggerated, but it does serve a good heuristic purpose, as his chapter raises one important methodological issue, and one more substantive one concerning theory building. The methodological issue concerns the issue of exaggeration and – *mirabile dictu* – its heuristic potential. After all, this is what we do when we create caricatures – and I mean this not at all in a derogatory fashion, since caricatures are quite different from simple distortions in that they highlight or bring out what otherwise might not be that obvious. For a constructivist who has always insisted that our work does not consist in just trying to represent as closely as possible a pre-existing reality, but what matters is how we bring this about by our doings and speaking – whereby this dichotomy collapses in the case of speech acts – such a technique of highlighting for heuristic purposes is well in tune with my approach. Similarly, as someone who believes that meaning is not primarily established by reference but by use, I also have to agree that the language game of theory is much more complicated than the traditional dichotomy suggests. To that extent I have no problem with the equivocal use of the term theory, as long as it is understood not as the pure and unadulterated 'view from nowhere'.

As to the more substantive point: it might be true that most of us start out as some type of Platonists. Later we perhaps free ourselves from it through the critical epistemology of the Enlightenment, only to end up as Marxists, structuralists or systems theorists à la Luhmann. Throughout we use terms such as culture or language or the 'world' in our explanations, and this seems to suggest that we all have a hard time – or seem to be unable to do without a device that serves as a last frame (à la Kant and his 'ideas', the 'world' being one of them) within which everything can find its place.

Here the close interaction of emotions and cognition might have more to it than we recognize at first blush. It explains why something that cannot find its place has to be met with the verdict *that it does not exist*, and that someone challenging our experience also calls into question our ability of judging and finding our way, individually and collectively. Here charges get generated. On the most innocent level, the charges are those of *idiocy* of yore – that is, being concerned only with one's own thing and not caring for the common world. But, as we know from experience, such insinuations can quickly change into charges of being unwilling to see, whereby the at first excusable error becomes stubbornness; a mistake is then no longer treated as a lapse or an inability, but as a sin or transgression that needs not only correction but punishment.

Those observations show that the semantic field connects different dimensions of cognition and emotions and provides various strategies of dealing with deviance or disappointment of our expectations. Against this right belief (the *orthe doxa*) heterodoxy is treated as a violation, in spite of the fact that the exclusion of a third possibility is even in strict Aristotelian logic limited to an impossibility 'at the same time' ('a' cannot be 'b'). But does this mean that, seen from a different perspective, 'a' can *never* be a 'b', as an independent variable can quickly become a dependent one (or vice versa) depending on the 'problem'? Things are even trickier, as Hellmann and Steffek (Chapter 1) suggest in the introduction by quoting the 'duck'/ 'rabbit' example used by Wittgenstein in calling attention to gestalt switches.

Since we all have such longings to know absolutely and once and for all, as expressed by Diotima in Plato's *Symposium* or by Goethe's *Faust*,[6] a latitudinarian attitude towards the use of the term 'theory' seems to recommend itself. Nevertheless, the last two examples deserve a short further gloss, since they show that the real issue is not that we (all?) have this longing but rather *what we do with it* – whether giving in to it allows us to orient ourselves or whether it leads us astray. In this context Kant's ironic gloss on the seduction of 'theory' starting from postulates and working its way down to the actual comes to mind.

---

[6] See Plato's *Symposium* (Plato, 2008: verse 208d, at p 46): 'I think that it is for the sake of immortal fame and this kind of glorious reputation that everyone strives to the utmost, and the better they are the more they strive: for they desire what is immortal'; and Goethe's *Faust* (Goethe 2014 [1808]: verse 382/83 at p 13): 'That is why I've turned to magic, in hope that with the help of spirit-power I might solve many mysteries, so that I need no longer toil and sweat to speak of what I do not know, can learn what, deep within it, binds the universe together'.

Mathematics gives us a splendid example of how far we can go with *a priori* cognition, independently of experience … Encouraged by such a proof of the power of reason, the drive for expansion sees no bounds. The light dove, in free flight cutting through the air the resistance of which bit feels, could get the idea that it could do even better in an airless space. (Kant, 1998: B8, A5 at p 129; emphasis in original)

Faust's belief that absolute doubt is more likely to lead to despair than to Cartesian certainty leads him to admit to being beguiled by the aura of the occult and the seductions of magic, and finally to his pact with the devil. While we, of course, have abolished the devil, the seductions of mood-altering drugs – and the flight from the actual to that of fantasy, by endless gaming or chatting on the net, or chasing the chimera of 'satisfaction' through mindless consumption – are still readily available. They seem to become ever more popular and are no longer limited to the fringes of society but are now found among members of the former middle class, who fear ending up in a precariat.[7]

This suggests to me that the liberal project of negative freedoms, as important as it is, is not enough for guaranteeing that this freedom *from* interference will also result in a freedom *for* creativity and self-realization. Even worse is that this flaw cannot simply be fixed by adding an ever-expanding catalogue of subjective rights as has become wont. Having emptied the world of praxis of content, in pursuing the ideal of formalization, or in the devotion to mindless activities, it has now to be filled up again by all those things we consider desirable and which we re-package now as individual 'rights'. This leads then to the odd construction that even constitutional issues are now formulated as individual human rights, such as 'the right to democracy'.

'What shall we do?' Some thoughts on institutionalized action, law and professional responsibility

Are we, then, as observers of what takes place before our eyes, condemned to accept this as 'reality', or even worse of 'singing' it into existence, when, as Steve Smith (2004) once called it, we no longer give the eye the pride of place? Let me get at the issue of what we shall and should do once more, by engaging with some of the contributors' suggestions.

---

[7] See the controversy surrounding the Sackler Foundation, which was set up by the family owning Purdue Pharma who have pushed opiates on people via a doctors' network. According to lawsuits filed by advocates, some 300,000 people have died over the years after becoming addicted to opiates. The US Centers for Disease Control and Prevention attributed 49,000 deaths in 2017 to the drug (see Perraudin and Neate, 2019).

As usual I have no final answer, but in thinking about it, several considerations come to my mind. Indeed, one of the themes running through several chapters is the issue of (professional) responsibility. This ranges from Chris Brown's (Chapter 6) unease with the lack of answers to the contemporary problems in my work, to James Davis's (Chapter 9) argument that in my analysis I might be too conservative and too radical at the same time, as there might be some grounding of our actions which social psychology or, even better, neuroscience provides; to Anthony Lang's (Chapter 7) criticism that a more complete reading of Aristotle's work, especially on education, would supply me with some valuable guidelines for building a constitutional order beyond the classical state; to Jan Klabbers's (Chapter 8) surprise as to why I have not really looked at issues of distributive justice, which has been a powerful force in modernity.

Let me begin with Brown (Chapter 6), which stresses mostly the Kantian dimension in the question of what acting is all about, and then engage with the other contributors. I shall use the problem of 'we', to which or for which we are accountable, as my point of departure. This has two important implications: one is that we have to realize that our questions are always formed by a context and thus there cannot be only the one right answer. The implication is, then, that we have to look primarily at the question side and what it tries to articulate and requires the addressee to respond to, rather than at the answers as if they could be free-standing. The second implication is the realization that many questions *cannot* be answered because – despite the depth of concern they articulate – they are formulated quasi-context-free: why something is there and not nothing, or 'what is it all about'. Then we do not get a definite answer, that is, one we can use for orientation – and we have to be satisfied with truisms, such as: 'do the right thing' – or we are getting involved in paradoxes. For Kant, such questions arise at the limits where 'reason is set against itself' and attempts to illuminate the unfathomable analogously to the tricks of the trade provided by the mind (*Verstand*) inevitably lead to paralogisms and paradoxes, or just simple nonsense (Kant, 1957: Part III).

I think Brown's discomfort precisely arises out of such an attempt to use the tools, or better the vocabulary, of understanding to answer the metaphysical question of what we ought to do as humans *tout court*. So yes, a theory in the social sciences is, and cannot be 'neutral' as it is always not only a theory *of*, but also *for something,* ensconcing historical victories and defeats, and establishing the normal ground from which one has to build up one's arguments. This not only enables some actors to do certain things but also immunizes them from responsibility in case their actions interfere with or have negative externalities for other actors, precisely because they can invoke the law and its universal applicability which is binding on all subjects.

There seem to be four interconnected issues that need further elucidation. First, there is the question of the 'in order to', the Aristotelian *hou heneka* that is determinative of action as we strive for something, rather than looking backward at a cause which will result in an effect. The second one is the baseline, which is of course not beyond doubt but depends on what the relevant facts and the rules for resolving the issue are. In this way, law also systemically creates injustices: someone who has given cash or a cheque to someone else in payment for a good cannot just cancel the cheque, and they might have no remedy if there was no guarantee for the good, as it was sold 'as is'.

This might sound like petty cash but it is here that the third and often neglected aspect of law comes to the fore: law's role in immunizing actors from responsibility for the harm they create, by allowing certain actions, such as enslaving certain people – especially if they are members not of one's own community but of other groups – or accepting that the harms done through normal market transactions will not be recognized as they are 'just' externalities (see Kratochwil, 2019). This then engenders, fourth, some further thought on the construction of the 'we' and of its representation (of making that which is absent present), as the 'will of all' transforms itself together with the actors into a common will and the individual – pace Rousseau – is transformed from a brute animal, governed by desires, into an intelligent and moral being (Rousseau, 1967: Bk I, chapter 8, at p 22).

Let us begin with the first issue, that is, the identification of the 'for' (the *hou heneka*) as the characteristic of the practical realm. When we act, we act 'in order to' rather than just react or engage in routines that provide outside observers with regularity descriptions. But making out of this observation that we should look for a *theory* of the good in Plato-like fashion has its problems, to which Aristotle first alerted us and which I take seriously. These 'visions', which in their contemporary versions unfortunately often run under the marketing label of cosmopolitanism,[8] have as their sparring partner suspect communitarians or downright reactionaries, people of yesterday and so forth. The paradox, then, is that despite the commitment to very real policy questions, the issue of how these problems and the different policy options arose, and whether any of the options discussed in the echo chambers of public opinion actually *address a problem that can be solved by*

---

[8] See, for example, Montesquieu's noble rhetoric (quoted in Kristeva, 1993: 28): 'If I knew something useful to myself and detrimental to my family I would reject it from my mind. If I knew something useful to my family but not to my homeland, I would try to forget it. If I knew something useful to my homeland and detrimental to Europe or else useful to Europe and detrimental to mankind, I would consider it a crime.' Here we finally seem to have found someone who, like Aristotle suspected, would have to be made a king (or expelled from the city) since he is so much better, as we seem able to imagine it. Unfortunately, dilemmas abound and going through life is not like putting together or taking apart Russian dolls.

individual or collective action, is easily displaced by the claim that we should or should not do something about it. Never mind that the 'it' remains often unclear precisely because of its strategic nature; success or failure crucially depend on the other's actions, not only on our intentions.

This realization brings into play the dialectic of restraint and constraint – of self-imposed discipline due to the experience that in strategic situations we hardly ever can get what we want, as we are constrained by what the opponent wants, and they in turn are constrained by our wishes. Unless they can be eliminated through the escalation to full-fledged conflict, they are also (it is hoped) aware of the dangerous possibility of their own elimination. Analogizing this mutual regress of reflections to some rare natural constraints is not really helpful. Here Brent Steele's (2019) searching and sophisticated analysis shows why this is so.

Distancing oneself from the strategic situation and taking a view from the 'outside' by, for example, pretending to know what the telos of humanity is changes the question substantially, reducing it again to an ends/means issue. It rather easily moves then from the questions of what we are to do about a particular problem to: why are you (not) on my or our side since I or we are defending the case of humanity; further, possible elaborations are insinuations, such as: you just want to ignore what is at stake, or: you want to 'sit out' the situation, thereby also undermining our ability to act collectively. While Brown, of course, does not take these last two steps, since they are *ad hominem*, such derailments are all the more likely not only if they are elicited in terms of a 'political' question on which we have to decide in terms of how it affects our conception of the common good, but if they are explicated in moral or legal terms.

In the moral discourse the 'we' then simply become instantiations of what all humans should do, and here again the tricky issue of priorities and trade-offs, of tragic conflicts among values and duties, is backgrounded by the supreme confidence that the proper values and their 'lexical ordering' à la Rawls will be enough to show the way. Choosing, therefore, a different vocabulary – that is, that of subjective human rights – might be more appropriate. It is, however, even more exacting if taken seriously. The notion of a right means not only that something is desirable, and we commit ourselves to its realization – subject to situative opportunities and re-assessments, as in the case of political goals – but that it can be claimed against the others in the community, or even beyond. To that extent, universalization of concerns transcends the usual boundaries of an established community which allocates the benefits and burdens by reference to the status of membership. It seems 'to stand to reason', then, that in secular times the old 'we are all Children of God' argument is transformed into the self-assertive vocabulary of subjective rights accruing to individuals qua their status as being human.

This move is not costless, however. Suddenly all concerns are 'politicized', but politicized in a special and rather strange way, in that they become universal concerns but without, for example, 'the peoples of the United Nations' becoming 'the people'. Thus, not only is the issue of how right- and duty-bearers are determined left hanging, as Onora O'Neill (2005) pointed out, but the question of 'universal concern' itself becomes problematic. Here Aristotle's arguments against Plato's community of wives and children come to mind, and also the questions of autonomy and domination raise their ugly head. Now 'humanity' can be invoked as the ultimate source of authorization – by anyone (?) having the guts and wherewithal to take this job and make it stick? Is thus the legacy of the French Revolution, which, as Kant acknowledged, 'can never be forgotten' (Kant, 1991 [1798]: 184), not only the rights revolution, but also the dynamic at whose 'end' a Napoleon stands? But would this not amount to endorsing the return of a politics as pure dominium, as *gloire* and subjection buttressed and justified by unadorned hero worship? Is populism really not such a new phenomenon as we think, since it recurs, although in different forms? Kant feared this drift (Kant, 1991 [1786)]), although he remained ambivalent when commenting on the events in France, and he died in 1804 before Napoleon (since his successful coup in 1799 the First Consul) returned from Africa and used Europe as his battleground. But he witnessed the Great Terror, and perhaps the rather ample room accorded to 'heteronomy' in the later Doctrine of Rights (*Rechtslehre* of 1797) is a reflection of this fear, in that the different 'publics' were not to meddle with the politics of the (of course) 'enlightened' sovereigns. Is this also the reason why popular participation was limited to a right of remonstrances, and to the principle that the subjects have to be informed about the laws (publicity) and that the cosmopolitan right only entailed a right of visit, not of residence abroad?[9]

This leads me to the fourth problem adumbrated earlier: another cluster of problems concerned with the definition of 'we' that is crucial for illuminating the social that transforms the conception of 'we' as an aggregate of individuals into a 'we' of the first-person plural. This 'we' can then be invoked for authorizing actions and assigning responsibility 'in the name of ...'. This is, of course, particularly crucial for states, but also for the international system through the creation of organizations, as well as for the state-transcending networks that have proliferated and are lumped together as non-governmental organizations of various kinds.

This problem of the 'we' is prominently raised by Davis (Chapter 9), and it is also the focus of K.M. Fierke's (Chapter 2) examination of 'making present what is absent', making actions and actors visible or invisible, or by

---

[9] For a searching criticism of Kant's alleged liberal project, see Horn (2014).

probing what we remember or forget and the responsibilities this entails for the scholar in a post-modern but also post-colonial epoch. This goes far beyond just paternalistically inviting some voices from the periphery in order 'to do' international relations, as it requires a different way of understanding world order problems (Getachev, 2019). The latter have little to do with the social Darwinist approach that underlies the Waltzian adapt-or-get-eliminated logic, or the popular learning thesis propagated by Tilly (1993) and Hoffmann (2015). Instead, a radical reorientation is necessary in that, for example, European exceptionalism (McNeill, 1963) or even its materialist interpretation in terms of the 'military revolution' thesis (Parker, 1988) need to be re-thought.[10] For not only a new historical understanding of the interactions among European powers and the rest of the world becomes necessary, we also have to deal with colonialism and imperialism and their aftermath, instead of just noticing the *extension* of the Westphalian system to the world (Anghie, 2004).

But let us return to the contributors. Klabbers's (Chapter 8) focus on the distributive consequences of institutions backgrounds the constitutive function of rules, which have been my main interest, not because I think that distributive questions do not matter, but because I increasingly became dissatisfied with the Rawlsian reduction of the problem of justice to one of distributive justice. Besides, Klabbers's main concern over the last few years has been how institutions matter in allowing for 'variation' in performance – to phrase it in social science lingo – and finding for the problem of leadership some answers in the revival of a virtue ethics. To that extent, making distributional issues the hinge for his comments was a bit surprising to me, although, of course, the activities he analyses are highly relevant for understanding the organizational revolution and its legacy for us.

I just wonder, however, whether the success story of formal institutions buttressed by an ideology of functionalism provides us with an adequate template to tackle the issues of praxis. Shall we again think about the problems of praxis in terms of an 'ideal' legislator à la Bentham who ensures the 'felicity' of people by applying a felicific calculus, that 'pushpin is as good as opera', and that the greatest happiness of the people is the ultimate yardstick that can and should be applied? I have my doubts, not because I am 'against' happiness but because this truism does very little work in an actual choice situation, as does the admonition: do the right thing! Was it not for good reasons that 'the law' always called attention to the fact that such a yardstick presupposes the commodification of different goods, and that recognizing the incommensurability of at least a few important ones was the precondition for individual freedom? And that we had better not lament the problem that

---

[10] For a devastating critique of this thesis, see Sharman (2019).

we do not have a general currency for all social issues,[11] but spend much time and energy in keeping different domains or spheres apart? The focus on distribution is certainly not irrelevant, but it presupposes answers first *about the goods* to be distributed and of the subjects or *actors among whom* it is distributed. That leads me back to the problem of the 'we'.

Contrary to Davis's intimation that I have no good concept of the *we*, as I do not investigate the formation of the we through the process of aggregation, I do take the 'we' seriously. Against any naturalism or mistaken methodological individualism I have always used the 'intersubjective' sphere for its explication, showing how the 'I' and the 'we' are constituted within a semantic field of common understandings (Kant's *sensus communis*, or Hume's common sense) and that the construction of a 'common weal' (*salus publica*) that marks the boundary between 'us' and 'them' is fundamental: to put it with Rorty, 'that is one of us', or with Walzer, 'they are like us but are not one of us', is a necessary implication of this recognition. As a matter of fact, Davis recognizes this indirectly. After the bow to science, which supposedly requires strict individualism and perhaps a physiological explanation of the 'we', in the second part of his chapter he references the symbolic interactionists. Here the process by which, through mutual role-taking, the 'I' of each interacting party gets formed supplies the answer. The same mode of analysis then allows us to see how a 'we' is formed when the interacting participants commit themselves to a concern that establishes a group in whose name action can be taken and responsibilities can be assigned. To the extent that individuation and socialization are the two sides of social reproduction, the idea of a pre-existing self is highly problematic. Consequently, the notion that society has to be explained, but not individuation (or identity formation) – as we all have virtually the same physiological make-up and can 'see' individuals but only indirectly observe society – could be a case of the fallacy of misplaced concreteness. Perhaps I do not understand him correctly, since he has argued previously to good effect that even colour concepts are not simple names for identical observations across cultures but are prototypes of what best represents, for example, the colour red, which varies from culture to culture (see Davis, 2005).

In this context, Hellmann's reference to pragmatists and particularly to John Dewey on the formation of 'publics' is also informative.

> Associated or joint action is a condition of the creation of community. But association itself is physical and organic while communal life is

---

[11] See the collection of seminal articles written on the problems of exchanges and power by David Baldwin, such as 'Money and Power', 'Power Analysis and World Politics' and 'Power and Social Exchange', all in Baldwin (1989).

moral, that is emotionally intellectually consciously contained ... For beings who observe and think and whose ideas are absorbed by impulses and become sentiments and interests 'we' is as inevitable as 'I'. But the 'we' and 'our' exist only when consequences of combined action are perceived and become object of desire and effort, just as 'I' and 'mine' appear on the scene only when a distinctive share in mutual action is continuously asserted or claimed. (Dewey, 1946: 151–2)

Thus, while interaction, role-taking and communication are obviously the necessary parts of individuation and socialization, for social reproduction to succeed something more has to happen, otherwise the episodic character of interactions and the specific interests among the parties involved is not able to manage the problem of shirking, or even of exit, which both inevitably arise when conditions change. Customers are not members; although they have rights, their rights are different! Members are supposed to have the conception of a continued interest that transcends episodes and requires some notion of a good that can only be produced jointly. But if they remain members of an interest group only, they are free to opt out, unless they morph into 'fans'. In that case their identification can become an all-consuming, perhaps even pathological, interest. Nevertheless, they cease to be actors and just become 'followers' as that provides the only reference point for action. They feel they have no choice but to root for their home team or follow their celebrity and live their life vicariously.

This realization also cautions us to apply 'constitutional thinking' – perhaps contrary to Lang's version of Aristotelianism – too readily to the global arena, despite the proliferation of regimes as islands of order. In a significant passage at the end of Book III of his *Politics*, Aristotle cautions us not to extend the concept of a political community without making much ado of settlements of different people, even if they share the same space and agree to common measures to prevent injustices and provide for security through an alliance. As if he were presciently addressing 'Project Europe', he states:

> [T]he state is not an association of people dwelling in the same place, established to prevent its members committing injustice against each other, and to promote transactions. Certainly all these features must be present if there is to be a state; but even the presence of every one of them does not make a state *ipso facto*. The state is an association intended to enable its members, in their households and the kinships, *to live well*.' (Aristotle, 1981: Bk. III, chapter 9, quote at pp 197–8; emphasis in original)

Such a conceptualization highlights the problem that beyond identification, the members must make *commitments* to the 'project' of remaining a group – exemplified by the transgenerational nature of an ongoing concern that has to be shored up by norms and defended against opportunistic deviance and holdout problems. As a project that is aspirational rather than 'real', it cannot be understood in terms of the execution of an existing design (production) or in terms of a step-by-step realization of a prophecy or teleology.

Furthermore, although communities are constituted by a common language, the notion of a common weal and a common sense do not coincide with the sharing of a particular language. Instead, the actual 'we' emerges from the historical circumstances by which the boundaries between the 'we' and the 'them' are drawn and normatively secured. We have to be part of a particular group whose communication is informed by a particular notion of a 'we', but for that we do not have to speak only one language – as multilingual communities exist, as do many separate communities who function on the basis of the same language – nor do the bounds of sense have to coincide with one language *tout court*. To that extent, the alleged attempt to derive or ground the particularity of such a perspective in a transcendental (universal) interest of communicative rationality, – as, for example, the early Habermas attempted – is unconvincing. Issues of intelligibility get mixed up with issues of identification and commitment, the former being part of the (Kantian) transcendental subject, the latter being the result of historically emerging customs and transformations that 'stick' – in the Humean sense – as they are *intersubjectively* (but not universally) reproduced.

But precisely because these boundaries are not given but represent a 'task', naturalizing them will not do. This, of course, puts us right back into the old Platonic cave,[12] and it is cold comfort when not only adherents of the unity of science approach propose such a return, but also some exponent of phenomenology, such as Husserl,[13] and the subsequent efforts for grounding our analysis of the social world in 'objective values', succumb to this temptation.

---

[12] To be fair to Plato, the *Republic* and the conception of a *kallipolis* was not his last word as his later ruminations in the puzzling *work* of the *Statesman,* and the 'second attempt' – the famous second voyage of the *Laws (deuterous plous)*.

[13] See, for example, Husserl (1982 [1929]). In his Introduction, Husserl makes no bones about his 'transcendental interest' – which seems quite at odds with the usual use of the term indicating an interest in the *phainomena* (as things appear) and affirms the Cartesian intent underlying his predecessor's efforts in the *Meditationes de prima philosophia* by postulating 'the need for a rational rebuilding that satisfies the idea of a philosophy as the all-inclusive unity of science'. Consequently, he announces a program that would 'provide complete and ultimate grounding on the basis of absolute insight behind which one cannot go back' (Husserl, 1982 [1929]: 2).

If we act *in order to* achieve something, we are not simple observers and, thus, the theoretical view of how things really distorts of what is at stake when we act. The *good* is not some everlasting part inhering in things but has to be realized through our actions in time. This does not mean that we act blindly, as there are criteria by which we and others can judge whether we act well or badly. The last horizon is then not 'being', but a life well lived, not contemplation of (eternal) truths; but it is also not a life in which we maximize something, such as the *greatest happiness*, as this would presuppose a common measure for all things and the readiness to exchange everything when the price is right (and this is not an empty or stretched metaphor). As Marx suggested, this commodification of different forms of acting well represents the fetishization of money constitutive of capitalism.[14]

Since I have dealt with this problem extensively in *Praxis*, let me pursue here a different line of argument, linking Aristotle's practical philosophy to modern language philosophy, that is, Wittgenstein and ordinary language philosophy. If we look at the 'episodic' character of action, this situatedness cannot be just interpreted as a lesser form of attaining the truth, which we can overcome by looking at what is universal or by making assumptions, so that we can predict. Such gambits simply miss the point of making practical choices because it is precisely this situative contingency we have to deal with. To that extent, the activity cannot be characterized by the regularity which a distant observer might register or by the fact that the execution of the rules requires one to be able to work with them, even though they might have become habitual and no explicit invocation is involved anymore. As the often ethereal discussions in international law about custom showed, we must cite a rule *opinio juris sive necessitatis* in order to show the 'existence' of a valid custom.

Some further questions of law and its empire

The upshot of the previous arguments is that when we utilize norms, we are not simply engaging in assertions of facts subject to truth conditions but we are justifying and explaining our actions by providing acceptable reasons for doing something. This is why my interest in law was originally kindled not by the particular political project of 'peace through law' but rather by the epistemological issues raised in the classical debate about 'prudence' and 'theory', since jurisprudence, for better or for worse, was the 'field' which had successfully defended its claim to autonomy until very

---

[14] Aristotle hints at this 'malformation' of a good life in his criticism of *chresmatics*, that is, a form of the economy in which one produces for the 'market' and by extension orients itself simply on 'money making' (Aristotle, 1981, Bk. I, chapters 8–10).

recently, when 'theories' invaded its domain (system theories and rational choice approaches).

Against these attempts I argued that providing reasons implies not only the utilization of norms for acting and understanding (first-person and third-person perspectives by means of intersubjectivity) but also the *realization of a background*, that is, *for whom and in what situation the norms shall be applicable* (the 'we' problem). The situative- (context-) dependent and the subject-dependent elements of norm use become most visible in institutional rules, such as 'x is legal tender', which means that 'x is y in circumstance z for all bs'. This sentence raises three issues: the first concerns the power of speech acts, which has been extensively discussed and which 'explains' the self-referential capacity of law to say what the law is (*juris dictio*). The second and third parts (relevant circumstances) and the 'for all "bs"' part, however, have unfortunately received less attention. Hans Lindahl has recently called attention to this problem (Lindahl, 2018), noting also the importance of the obscure notion of the a–legal, which the law might not officially recognize, as discussed earlier in the context of systematic injustices created by law in defining 'actionable claims'.

Here a recent searching investigation of property rights by Katharina Pistor (2019) provided a new perspective on the problem of ordering in the international arena. She showed how law creates wealth and inequality, which lead to fundamental ordering problems, putting a rather disenchanting gloss on the attempts at global governance, or the viability of global civil society to stem the tide of the systematic abuse of public law for 'private' purposes. Since there is simply no 'public',[15] what goes for a global legal order, such as the codification of the *lex mecatoria*, or the growth of bilateral investment treaties, or the codification of enforceability of arbitral awards, or the enforcement of property rights, serves more and more the ensconcing of private interests which are no longer subject to any public ordering. What is even worse, nobody seems to be much disturbed, although the 'unseen hand' – accountable to no one but itself, since it substitutes now for the *manus gubernatoris* of yore which kept the world going – is obviously no longer 'liberally' spreading the accumulated wealth and providing the necessary public goods. If the future is simply 'private', as one of the 'visionaries' of the new age suggests, then we'd better beware. But that is an issue that will have to be taken up another time.

---

[15] The traditional distinction of public and private international law is *ex initio* problematic since the corpus of rules binding on states is based primarily on the private law instrument of 'contract' and private international law is based on different 'national' conflict of law procedures which determine which national regulation shall prevail in cases where the contending parties are different 'nationals'.

References

Abbott, Andrew (1988) *The System of Professions: An Essay in the Division of Expert Labor* (Chicago, IL: University of Chicago Press).

Anghie, Antony (2004) *Imperialism and the Making of International Law* (Cambridge: Cambridge University Press).

Aristotle (1981) *Politics*, transl. Thomas A. Sinclair (London: Penguin).

Baldwin, David (1989) *Paradoxes of Power* (New York and Oxford: Blackwell).

Brandt, Reinhard (2009) *Die Bestimmung des Menschen bei Kant* (2nd edn) (Hamburg: Meiner).

Davis, James W. (2005) *Terms of Inquiry* (Baltimore, MD: Johns Hopkins University Press).

Dewey, John (1946) *The Public and Its Problems* (Chicago, IL: Gateway Books).

Getachev, Adom (2019) *World Making after Empire: The Rise and Fall of Self-Determination* (Princeton, NJ: Princeton University Press).

Goethe, Johann Wolfgang von (2014 [1808]) *Faust* I & II (Princeton, NJ: Princeton University Press).

Hoffman, Philip T. (2015) *Why Did Europe Conquer the World* (Princeton, NJ: Princeton University Press).

Horn, Christoph (2014) *Nichtideale Normativität: Ein neuer Blick auf Kant's politische Philosophie* (Frankfurt: Suhrkamp).

Husserl, Edmund (1929) *Cartesian Meditations: An Introduction to Phenomenology*, transl. Dorion Cairns (Amsterdam: Kluwer Academic Publisher).

Jackson, Patrick Thaddeus (2011) *The Conduct of Inquiry in International Relations: Philosophy of Science and Its Implications for the Study of World Politics* (Abingdon: Routledge).

Kant, Immanuel (1957) *Prolegomena*, ed. Karl Vorländer (Hamburg: Meiner).

Kant, Immanuel (1991 [1784]) 'Idea for a universal history with a cosmopolitan purpose', in Hans Reiss (ed), *Kant: Political Writings* (2nd edn) (Cambridge: Cambridge University Press), pp 41–53.

Kant, Immanuel (1991 [1786]) 'What is orientation in thinking', in Hans Reiss (ed), *Kant: Political Writings* (2nd ed) (Cambridge: Cambridge University Press), pp 237–49.

Kant, Immanuel (1991 [1795]) 'Perpetual peace', in Hans Reiss (ed), *Kant: Political Writings* (2nd edn) (Cambridge: Cambridge University Press), pp 93–130.

Kant, Immanuel (1991 [1798]) 'The contest of faculties', in Hans Reiss (ed), *Kant: Political Writings* (2nd edn) (Cambridge: Cambridge University Press), pp 176–90.

Kant, Immanuel (1998) *The Critique of Pure Reason*, ed. and transl. Paul Guyer and Allen W. Wood (Cambridge: Cambridge University Press).

Kennedy, David (2016) *A World of Struggle: How Power Law and Expertise Shape the Global Political Economy* (Princeton, NJ: Princeton University Press).

Kratochwil, Friedrich (2000) 'Constructing a new orthodoxy? Wendt's "Social Theory of International Politics" and the constructivist challenge', *Millennium* 29, pp 73–101.

Kratochwil, Friedrich (2019) 'Summum ius, summa injuria: critical reflections on the legal form, inter-legality and the limits of law', in Jan Klabbers and Gianluigi Palombella (eds), *The Challenge of Inter-legality* (Cambridge: Cambridge University Press), pp 42–68.

Kratochwil, Friedrich (2020) 'On engagement and distance in social analysis', *International Theory*, pp 1–15.

Kratochwil, Friedrich (2021) *After Theory, Before Big Data: Thinking about Praxis, Politics and International Affairs* (Abingdon: Routledge).

Kratochwil, Friedrich and John Gerard Ruggie (1986) 'The state of the art, or the art of the state', *International Organization* 40, pp 753–76.

Kristeva, Julia (1993) *Nations without Nationalism* (New York: Columbia University Press).

Lapid, Yosef and Friedrich Kratochwil (1986) 'Revisiting the national: toward an identity agenda in neorealism', in Yosef Lapid and Friedrich Kratochwil (eds), *The Return of Culture and Identity* (Boulder, CO: Lynne Rienner), pp 105–26.

Lindahl, Hans (2018) *Authority and the Globalization of Inclusion and Exclusion* (Cambridge: Cambridge University Press).

McNeill, William H. (1963) *The Rise of the West* (Chicago, IL: University of Chicago Press).

Morgan, George W. (1968) *The Human Predicament: Dissolution and Wholeness* (Providence, RI: Brown University Press).

O'Neill, Onora (2005) 'The dark sides of human rights', *International Affairs* 81, 2, pp 427–39.

Parker, Geoffrey (1988) *The Military Revolution: Military Innovation and the Rise of the West 1500–1800* (Cambridge: Cambridge University Press).

Perraudin, Frances and Rupert Neate (2017) 'Sackler Trust halts new philanthropic giving due to opioid lawsuits', *The Guardian*, 25 March, available at: https://www.theguardian.com/uk-news/2019/mar/25/sackler-trust-halts-new-philanthropic-giving-due-to-opioid-crisis-lawsuits, accessed 19 March 2021.

Pistor, Katharina (2019) *The Code of Capital: How the Law Creates Wealth and Inequality* (Princeton, NJ: Princeton University Press).

Plato (2008) *The Symposium*, ed. Margaret C. Howatson and Frisbee C.C. Sheffield (Cambridge: Cambridge University Press).

Rousseau, Jean-Jaques (1967) 'The social contract', in Lester G. Crocker (ed), *Rousseau: The Social Contract and the Discourse on the Origin of Inequality* (New York: Washington Square Press).

Schatzki, Theodore R., Karin Knorr Cetina and Eike von Savigny, eds (2000) *The Practice Turn in Contemporary Theory* (New York and London: Routledge).

Schmidt, Kjeld (2018) 'Practice theory: a critique', in Volker Wulf, Volkmar Pipek, David Randall, Markus Rohde, Kjeld Schmidt and Gunnar Stevens (eds), *Socio-Informatics: A Practice-based Perspective on the Design and Use of IT Artefacts* (Oxford: Oxford University Press), pp 105–37.

Seidman, Steven (1994) *The Postmodern Turn: New Perspectives on Social Theory* (Cambridge: Cambridge University Press).

Sharman, Jason Campbell (2019) *Empire of the Weak: The Real Story of European Expansion and the Creation of the New World Order* (Princeton, NJ: Princeton University Press).

Smith, Steve (2004) 'Singing our world into existence: International Relations theory and September 11', *International Studies Quarterly* 48, pp 499–515.

Steele, Brent J. (2019) *Restraint in International Politics* (Cambridge: Cambridge University Press).

Tetlock, Philip E. (2005) *Expert Political Judgment: How Good Is It? How Can We Know?* (Princeton, NJ: Princeton University Press).

Tetlock, Philip E. and Dan Gardner (2015) *Superforecasting: The Art and Science of Prediction* (New York: Crown Publishers).

Tilly, Charles (1993) *Capital, Coercion and European States, A.D. 990–1992* (Oxford: Blackwell).

Tomasello, Michael (2003) *Constructing a Language* (Cambridge, MA: Harvard University Press).

Tomasello, Michael (2009) *Why We Cooperate* (Cambridge, MA: MIT Press).

Wendt, Alexander (1999) *Social Theory of International Politics* (Cambridge, MA: Harvard University Press).

Index